Psychology, Science, and History

Psychology, Science, and History

An Introduction to Historiometry

Dean Keith Simonton

Yale University Press   New Haven and London

Designed by Sally Harris/Summer Hill Books,
Perkinsville, Vermont.
Set in Times Roman type by
The Composing Room of Michigan, Inc.
Printed in the United States of America by
Vail-Ballou Press, Binghamton, New York.

Library of Congress Cataloging-in-Publication Data

Simonton, Dean Keith.
Psychology, science, and history: an introduction to
historiometry/Dean Keith Simonton.
    p.   cm.
Includes bibliographical references and index.
ISBN 0-300-04771-1
1. Historiometry.   I. Title.
D16.13.S58   1990
901—dc20   90-35617
                                      CIP

The paper in this book meets the guidelines
for permanence and durability of the Committee
on Production Guidelines for Book Longevity
of the Council on Library Resources.

10   9   8   7   6   5   4   3   2   1

To Sabrina Dee

Contents

Figures

Tables

Acknowledgments

Because elsewhere I have narrated the peculiar path by which I came upon the research program here advocated (Simonton 1990b), let me merely name the individuals who have given me, in one form or another, the encouragement so essential to one whose personal vision propels him through often hostile territory: Robert Abelson, Robert Albert, Teresa Amabile, Paul Baltes, Frank Barron, James Birren, Donald Campbell, David Cole, Kenneth Craik, Mihaly Csikszentmihalyi, Stephanie Dudek, Alan Elms, Suitbert Ertel, David Feldman, Jeanne Ferris, Howard Gardner, John Gowan, Howard Gruber, Ravenna Helson, James M. Jones, David Kenny, Colin Martindale, William McGuire, Robert Merton, Vernon Padgett, Derek Price, Mark Runco, David Sears, Lee Sechrest, Lee Sigelman, Morris Stein, Robert Sternberg, Peter Suedfeld, William McKinley Runyan, Philip Tetlock, Eric Wanner, Hans Wendt, David Winter, Zhao Hong-Zhou, and Harriet Zuckerman. Here I have obviously taken advantage of the egalitarian properties of alphabetical order rather than try to make fine distinctions of relative worth and influence. Needless to say, to acknowledge these teachers, scholars, and editors is by no means equivalent to a statement that they all endorse my designs. On the contrary, their impact on my thought often took the form of constructive criticism.

Last but most deserving of my deepest appreciation are my wife, Melody, and my stepdaughter, Mandy, who together provided an environment conducive to the writing of this book. In contrast, my infant daughter, Bree, did everything in her power to prevent this book from happening, and it took the miracle of modern day-care to enable me to avoid this happiest of all uncontrollable distractions. To her I nonetheless dedicate this book, if only in the hope that the next time I assume such a big undertaking she will be more supportive of her daddy's struggles!

1 **Introduction**

"All generalizations are dangerous, even this one," Alexander Dumas fils reportedly said. Even so, the human mind seems to take an insatiable delight in discovering and announcing general principles, patterns, or regularities. This predilection is evident in the ease with which writers—scholars and popular authors alike—slip into notoriously insecure "historical generalizations." Although such broad statements may concern a wide range of topics, the most striking often concern the rise and fall of human civilization, especially the appearance and disappearance of exceptional creators, leaders, and miscellaneous celebrities (Norling 1970, chap. 6). For example, Macaulay, in his essay on Milton, propounded the view that "as civilization advances, poetry almost necessarily declines."

Nor has this affinity for the general waned among modern historians. Hidden within almost any article or book is an abundance of sweeping assertions. These forays into abstraction may not always be immediately obvious, for often they provide the context for some specific interpretative or narrative remark. For example, one text on Islamic civilization proclaimed, "The paradox that the foregoing survey of culture reveals is that the period of greatest creativity occurred during the period of principalities (c. 900–1200), when the caliphs were weak and the princes driven by diverse motives were fighting against each other" (Armajani 1970, 118). This paradox exists, of course, only if one implicitly holds that creative achievement is inversely proportional to political fragmentation and military conflict—as a universal regularity of human creativity. But whether the generalizations are old or new, explicit or implicit, it is all too easy to compile a massive inventory of such abstract principles in historical writings. Some historians, especially those directing their efforts to more popular audiences, have practically converted such risky speculations into a professional enterprise. Examples include Spengler's ([1926–28] 1945) *Decline of the West,* Toynbee's (1946) *A Study of History,* and Will and Ariel Durant's (1968) *The Lessons of History.*

Nor are historians the sole proliferators of these wild propositions. An econometrics text contains the claim that "art and literature flourish in a rising economy, but they wither and perish in one that declines" (H. T. Davis 1941, 572).

An anthropologist observed that "the collapse of controls during periods of social and political upheaval opens the way for innovation" (Barnett 1953, 71), and a sociologist held that "if a sweeping survey of the field of human progress were made perhaps ninety-five percent of the advance would be found uncorrelated with the great men" (Spiller 1929, 218).

One of the most common varieties of generalizations concerns the eternal question of which is more crucial in determining the flow of history, the individual genius or the spirit of the times—the classic debate between the heroic and the zeitgeist interpretations of historical change. The most extreme position of sociocultural determinism is perhaps to be found in Tolstoy's epic novel *War and Peace* ([1865–69] 1952), the epilogues of which are devoted to dethroning Napoleon as a causal agent in the Napoleonic Wars: "A king is history's slave. . . . Every act of [his], which appears . . . an act of [his] own will, is in a historical sense involuntary and is related to the whole course of history and predestined from eternity" (343–44). On the opposite pole is Thomas Carlyle's (1841) insistence in his essay *On Heroes* that "Universal History, the history of what man has accomplished in this world, is at bottom the History of the Great Men who have worked here" (1).

Historical generalizations are indeed ubiquitous; obviously, they are also not always consistent. Advocates of the extreme zeitgeist position are clearly at loggerheads with those who praise the impact of unique genius. In a sense, historical generalizations are analogous to folk sayings; it is equally easy to collate contradictory proverbs (for example, "birds of a feather flock together" versus "opposites attract"). Conceivably, however, the fault may lie not in the generalizations themselves but rather in the way that they are derived and demonstrated. Conclusions should vary greatly in their empirical validity, and we may have realistic means to decipher the true from the false.

This book proposes to examine how historical generalizations might become scientifically demonstrable. Are there objective procedures by which we may cull from the infinite intricacies and singularities of history a finite set of robust conclusions? The special focus is how historical data may be exploited to expand our scientific understanding of human behavior. History, after all, is an immense repository of individual thoughts and actions—altruism and aggression, crime and sacrifice, ambitions and procrastinations, grand successes and monumental failures. The behavioral scientist is often attracted to history because within the complex of names, dates, and places may dwell the secrets of human nature at its best and worst. Historical data have proved especially valuable to those psychologists interested in the most outstanding forms of creativity and leadership, in the supposed geniuses of culture and society. Fair or not, history is primarily an elitist register of those personalities who appear to have "made history" as creators in science, philosophy, literature, art, and music or as leaders in war, politics, religion, and business.

To indicate how solid inferences might emerge, this chapter begins by defining the discipline of *historiometry* or, alternatively, *historiometrics,* after which a brief history of this integrative approach is offered. How historiometry compares to related endeavors in other domains of psychology, science, and history is then outlined. The chapter ends with an explicit statement of what this treatise attempts to achieve.

Definition

Historiometrics is a scientific discipline in which nomothetic hypotheses about human behavior are tested by applying quantitative analyses to data concerning historical individuals. To make this jargon-riddled passage more intelligible we need to examine three key concepts: nomothetic hypotheses, quantitative analyses, and historical individuals.

Nomothetic Hypotheses

An often repeated distinction in psychology is that between the nomothetic and the idiographic. Strictly speaking, nomothetic inquiries are those that seek general laws, whereas idiographic studies are those that favor the intensive examination of the singular case. In short, the nomothetic concentrates on universals, the idiographic on particulars. Within personality psychology, for example, where this distinction is most common, nomothetic investigators typically study hundreds of individuals in order to tease out reliable correlations between generic variables, while idiographic investigators scrutinize a single human personality (Allport 1937). This distinction extends beyond psychology to all knowledge claims.

At one extreme are those statements that purport to apply universally, throughout the cosmos. In physics, the laws of gravitation, the second law of thermodynamics, and other fundamental functions boast this sort of universality. No spot in the universe is immune from these generalizations, albeit there may exist certain singularities, known as "black holes," in which some physical laws may become only approximate at best. But the crucial characteristic of truly nomothetic statements is that any restrictions on their applicability, should there be any, do not entail specific tags that identify persons and historical periods. The special theory of relativity is confined to nonaccelerating frames of reference, but not to the idiosyncratic *Weltanschauung* of Albert Einstein, at Bern, Switzerland, in 1905.

At the other extreme, we possess idiographic propositions that make no sense without specific names, dates, and places attached. Why was Napoleon defeated at Waterloo? Had well-laid plans been upset by Marshal Grouchy's lackadaisical pursuit of General Blücher's army at Ligny? Or did the strategic situation of the French empire vis-à-vis its enemies condemn the emperor to defeat? Whatever the response, any explanation is bound intimately to a special person, place, and time, even if some general law is evoked to explain the unique event. For example, nomothetic studies would suggest that Napoleon's military prowess may have been on the wane in 1815 when he was forty-six years old (Simonton 1980a). If this generalization is accepted, then we must draw upon new particulars to explain how only a year earlier he had so skillfully (even if quite hopelessly) defended France against overwhelming odds. When a question is framed with proper names and chronological markers from the very start, it is virtually impossible to compose an answer that is not equally specific.

Between the two extremes of nomothetic and idiographic comes a host of assertions at middling levels of abstraction. Biologists propound laws of life for only one planet, and some of these principles may be further confined to the animal kingdom or even just to Homo sapiens. Economists may restrict certain generalizations to industrial societies, or capitalistic economies, or maybe solely the United States since World War II. In psychology, too, some generalizations apply to all complex organisms capable of learning, whereas others are operative only for college students or, in the clinical domain, for suicides. However, as one scholar put it: "Science in general can be described as nomothetic, while history is an idiographic study. In this sense, science is more concerned with the universal, history with the individual. In science, observations are made in order to determine laws; in history, 'laws' explain observations" (Ben-Yehuda 1983, 354).

This brings us naturally to the question of where historiometry falls on the nomothetic-idiographic spectrum. By the definition given earlier, the primary intent of this approach is to make observations by which we can test generalizations about Homo sapiens. Because the object is to remove as many particulars as possible, historiometry is most strongly allied with science. That the discipline deals with historical data when analyzing hypotheses is irrelevant. For example, one can investigate the claim that "great monarchs nearly always have some uncommon qualities of intellect and personality" (Derry 1985, 393) without citing a single proper noun or date other than references to the research literature. History may contribute the input, the basic information, but science inspires the output, the conclusions of broad application. To be sure, a historiometric hypothesis is never as nomothetic as a proposition in, for instance, theoretical physics. Some boundaries are imposed on the range of generalizability. The most patent limitation is that historiometry tests only hypotheses on human beings and then only on those personalities who have left a tangible mark on history. Yet even at their most restrictive, historiometric inquiries are aimed at making statements sufficiently abstract that not a single particularistic qualifier needs to be inserted. It is in this sense that historiometrics is nomothetic, and hence scientific, in its fundamental analytical strategy.

Quantitative Analyses

One of the hallmarks of science is quantification. In historiometrics, which shares many quantitative techniques with such approaches as biometrics, psychometrics, and econometrics, there are two aspects of quantification representing successive stages in any historiometric inquiry.

First, the historiometrician must define, or *operationalize,* central theoretical concepts to achieve *variable quantification.* A variable is any attribute of a person or thing that can assume a range of values or levels. Just as natural objects vary in weight, size, and other physical characteristics, human subjects vary in intelligence, motivation, productivity, aggressiveness, and other personal qualities. In addition, frequently historiometry deals not with variation across entities, such as personalities, but rather with variations within entities—fluctuations across time. Indeed, many historical generalizations specify how certain events fluctuate from year to year or from generation to generation. We may examine variation across cases or changes within cases, but the principle of quantification persists: Somehow numbers must be assigned to the analytical entities so that the resulting quantities reasonably reflect how the units actually differ for a given attribute. Brighter-than-average individuals should receive an above-average intelligence quotient (IQ) score; historical periods with more intense creative ferment should earn a correspondingly high number to designate the level of creativity.

Second, after the variables have been operationalized numerically, the quantities are subjected to *mathematical analysis,* usually through the use of advanced statistics. For example, one rudimentary function of statistics is to establish whether two variables exhibit a positive or negative covariation. Most historical generalizations propose that one property tends to be directly (or else inversely) proportional to another across individuals or through time. Great leaders supposedly feature some special personal qualities; the expansion of empire states is presumably antithetical to the manifestation of cultural creativity. Modern statistics offers a valuable collection of techniques by which to test these nomothetic assertions once the variables have been quantified. Not only can the direction of association be determined (as positive, negative, or zero), but the correlation's magnitude can be calculated. The absolute size of the correlation serves as a gauge of how strongly the generalization permeates the historical record and in an inverse way registers the conspicuousness of any exceptions to the rule.

This last advantage is central, given that one reason why abstractions are so dangerous is that departures from expectation invariably exist. The correlation between two variables need not be perfect but must be powerful enough to hold despite exceptions. For instance, psychometric studies have repeatedly shown that the higher a person scores in intelligence, the greater the probability that the individual will display creativity or leadership (Simonton 1985a). Yet there are neglected geniuses as well as intellectually mediocre creators and leaders. By the same token, the statistical analyses exploited in historiometrics permit generalizations to be translated into statements of probability. In doing so, abstract affirmations become more realistic and consequently more resistant to conflicting evidence. Probabilistic propositions thus have a better chance of actually being true. To say that economic prosperity increases the odds that outstanding creators will emerge is far less risky than to insist that the link between economic and cultural growth is fixed and inviolate.

The emphasis on quantification is that facet of historiometrics that probably attracts the most complaints from critics. Historians, especially, often question whether anything worth knowing can be established by allotting numbers to events. For example, Arthur Schlesinger, Jr. (1962a), an illustrious American historian, maintained that "almost all important questions are important precisely because they are *not* susceptible to quantitative answers" (770). There may be some truth in remarks like these, considering the frequency of such complaints. If I stands for an issue's intrinsic importance and R represents the rigor of the analysis, such as the level of mathematical treatment, then perhaps $I \times R = k$; that is, their product may be a constant. A trade-off may operate to coerce a researcher into a choice between precise responses to trivial questions or vague responses to profound questions.

Yet for scientists, significant problems are commonly those that best lend themselves to objective, rigorous, and (preferably) mathematical analyses. Thus Galileo preferred to investigate how fast balls rolled down inclined planes, while Gibbon, a historian, sought to learn why the Roman Empire declined and fell. Gibbon's question may be more historically important, but Galileo's subject is much more amenable to quantitative discussion and thereby becomes more *scientifically* significant. Although historiometry is also confined to those issues that can be examined using quantitative analyses, many historiometric inquiries deal successfully with the "timeless problems of history" (Norling 1970). Many historical generalizations of considerable inherent merit can readily be recast as nomothetic hypotheses suitable for quantitative scrutiny.

More critically, psychologists and other scientists definitely reserve the right to formulate their own priorities regarding which questions are most worth probing, receptiveness to analytical rigor aside. Most frequently, the behavioral scientist wishes to evaluate theories of human nature that are outside the proper purview of historians.

Historical Individuals

Several scientific endeavors besides historiometrics are overtly involved in verifying nomothetic hypotheses about human behavior through quantitative analyses. A conspicuous example is psychometrics, the discipline devoted to "mental measurement." Hence, to define historiometry uniquely requires that inquiries be confined to historical individuals. Most inquiries are dedicated to discerning the "laws of genius"—the principles by which individuals can exert a phenomenal impact on human society, culture, or politics. These inquiries are often restricted not just to historical figures but also to those strictly deceased. Unless the person's name has been inscribed in some epitaph, he or she may fail to qualify for the exclusive club, the historiometric subject pool. Nonetheless, this restriction is often ignored in research practice. It is possible, if improbable, for contemporaries to earn a place in the historical record without having died. Without objection, studies have been conducted of illustrious scientists, composers, and U.S. chief executives, all of which included one or more still-living exemplars (for example, Linus Pauling, Aaron Copland, and Richard M. Nixon). After all, a living creator, leader, or celebrity may have the same pertinent information listed in standard reference works, such as an encyclopedia and a *Who's Who,* as does a deceased personality.

Still, contemporaries almost always represent a small proportion of the total subject pool, and the center of attention remains historical humanity. Furthermore, often the nomothetic hypotheses to be tested demand that all subjects should be dead. We may wish to know, for example, whether historical individuals right before death undergo a personal transformation that is revealed in their last works or correspondence (Simonton 1989d; Suedfeld 1985; Suedfeld and Piedrahita 1984). This question has no real meaning while a person still breathes.

Two final qualifications must be placed on the expression "historical individuals," lest it be taken too narrowly. First, despite the historian's preoccupation with recounting the lives of the rich and famous, the investigator can sometimes study anonymous human behavior, as disclosed in mass movements that somehow do not thrust particular names in the limelight. For instance, considerable literature exists on collective violence, such as revolution and riot (for example, Baron and Ransberger 1978; Matossian and Schafer 1977), where the historical behavior of the masses is under investigation, somewhat ameliorating the elitist emphasis of much historiometric work.

The second qualification has to do with the use of the plural—individuals— which might indicate that historiometrics deals solely with multiple cases much as does psychometrics. In truth, the norm is for the researcher to examine hundreds if not thousands of historical figures. Thus, one study scrutinized 10,160 luminaries of Chinese civilization (Simonton 1988c). Large sample sizes are advisable whenever one wants to apply sophisticated quantitative analyses, and they are strongly recommended to ensure that results can be considered truly nomothetic. Nevertheless, it is sometimes practical to use a less ambitious sample, for example, one including 36 short-story writers—18 American and 18 Hungarian (Martindale 1988); 19 Soviet politicians (Tetlock and Boettger 1989); or 5 British novelists (Porter and Suedfeld 1981). Attention may even narrow to the singular, yielding an

"$N = 1$" case study. Actual studies have focused on Shakespeare (Derks 1989), Thomas Wolfe (Rosenberg 1989), Francis Galton (Terman 1917), Richard Nixon (Winter and Carlson 1988), and Fidel Castro (Ramirez and Suedfeld 1988). Still, these single-case inquiries must rely on a special trick, modifying the unit of analysis so that one life or career is partitioned into multiple episodes, whether creative products, speeches, or decisions.

The History of Historiometry

In constructing disciplinary history we must avoid promulgating yet another origin myth in which current preoccupations are misprojected upon supposedly seminal figures (Samuelson 1974). And we must avoid confusing the mere anticipations of present events with their causes (Sarup 1978). That said, historiometry has a long past, longer than that of professional psychology. This history can be schematically divided into three overlapping phases: Phase one emphasized the study of individual genius. In phase two psychologists yielded ground to anthropologists and sociologists far more committed to demonstrating the efficacy of the zeitgeist as an agent in history and culture. Phase three, the modern period, favors a more unified perspective on the individual within society.

Phase One: Genius

Historiometry can be traced at least as far back as the 1835 *Treatise on Man* by Adolphe Quetelet, the Belgian astronomer, meteorologist, mathematician, sociologist, and poet. Quetelet is known best for his application of statistical analyses to behavioral data, thereby initiating the field of *social statistics,* or what would today be called demography. Although the bulk of his 1835 monograph concerns delineating the "average man," hidden within its pages is the first quantitative analysis of the longitudinal relation between personal age and creative achievement. This question was again given systematic treatment in an obscure 1874 work by George M. Beard, thus making this subject one of the oldest substantive issues in both historiometry and life-span developmental psychology.

Because neither of these two inquiries had any immediate progeny, the discipline had a more fruitful beginning with Francis Galton, an English scientist, explorer, and anthropologist, as well as a grandson of Erasmus Darwin and a cousin of Charles Darwin. In 1869 Galton published *Hereditary Genius,* a classic treatment of the thesis that genius-grade achievement runs in families, owing to the genetic transmission of intelligence. This work inspired contributions by other pioneers in historiometric technique. The Swiss botanist Alphonse deCandolle responded with a 1873 book that counts as a first effort in *scientometrics,* a discipline that overlaps with historiometrics. The English sexologist Havelock Ellis (1904) produced *A Study of British Genius,* which, among other things,

examined the connection between birth order and creative success. Also significant was a series of papers by James McKeen Cattell, an American psychologist
who had worked under Francis Galton. Cattell's first historiometric study was "A
Statistical Study of Eminent Men" (1903), which offered the results of an ambitious (though quixotic) attempt to rank a thousand historical figures on all-time
eminence. Similar publications followed, most narrowing the focus to scientific
achievement (for example, Cattell 1910). A more valuable contribution, however,
may have been Cattell's acquisition of *Science,* which he edited for a half century
(1894–1944), making it the premiere general science periodical in the United
States. Under his editorship, *Science* became the vehicle for the dissemination of
historiometric studies by Cattell and others, a practice lasting until the 1950s (for
example, Lehman 1958). Among these are a pair of notes by a professor at the
Massachusetts Institute of Technology, Frederick Adams Woods.

Unlike many of his predecessors, such as Quetelet and Galton, Woods
cannot be regarded as one of the great names in the behavioral sciences, nor
perhaps even within historiometry. He is notable because he explicitly gave a
hitherto nameless enterprise a label and a definition. The date of baptism is 19
November 1909, when *Science* contained the note "A New Name for a New
Science" in which historiometry is defined as comprising those investigations
where "the facts of history of a personal nature have been subjected to statistical
analysis by some more or less objective method" (703). Woods added that "historiometry bears the same relation to history that biometry does to biology" (703), a
comparison that betrays his belief, following Galton, that the discipline had much
to contribute to the then-growing "science of eugenics" (703). Appended to the
paper is a list of a dozen historiometric studies that had appeared by 1907. In a later
issue of *Science,* Woods (1911) again advertised his new field in a full-length study
entitled "Historiometry as an Exact Science." He claimed that the technique
would further develop the "psychology of genius," and even "work towards the
solution of a wide range of historical problems, such as the causes underlying the
rise and fall of nations or other fundamental questions in history" (568). He
specifically addressed two unrelated questions: one, whether Massachusetts had
been more productive than Virginia in the production of illustrious Americans;
two, whether Sophocles or Euripides was the more phenomenal dramatist.

Oddly, these two puzzles are far more idiographic than nomothetic in tone,
although Woods did thereby develop methods that would be helpful in testing
nomothetic hypotheses. Fortunately, Woods came out with two books that far
better suggest historiometry's scientific utility. The first, the 1906 *Mental and
Moral Heredity in Royalty,* is largely an extension of the thesis introduced in
Galton's 1869 treatise. Both male and female members of several European families were assessed on intellect and virtue, the goal to prove the genetic inheritance
of two primary traits. The second book, appearing in 1913, was concerned with
The Influence of Monarchs—the first historiometric study specifically dedicated

to understanding outstanding leadership. After evaluating the effectiveness of hundreds of absolute monarchs in over a dozen European nations, Woods tried to show how their personal characteristics predicted the welfare of the nation they led. The 1906 and 1913 volumes confirmed that a new nomothetic endeavor, one requiring the quantitative analysis of historical personalities, had been created deliberately.

In 1936 Evelyn Raskin subjected the biographies of 120 scientists and 123 literary figures to statistical analyses. Another 1936 publication was less remarkable as a study, but more amazing for the personality involved, Edward L. Thorndike, a psychologist far better known for his work on the law of effect and trial-and-error learning in kittens. Thorndike built upon Woods's 1906 inquiry, elaborating the methodology to show that the correlation between intelligence and morality was actually stronger than Woods had believed. Nor was Thorndike's a fleeting fascination with historiometry, for his last work, published posthumously by his son in 1950, involved personality assessments for ninety-one eminent creators and leaders.

The really monumental development during this period was driven by another central figure in American psychology, Lewis M. Terman, at Stanford University. Only a year after he had successfully adapted Alfred Binet's intelligence measure into the famous Stanford-Binet test, Terman (1917) published a paper, "The Intelligence Quotient of Francis Galton in Childhood," indicating how IQ could be estimated for historical personalities—a score close to two hundred in Galton's case. A few years later, in 1921, this preliminary study was followed up by a psychometric examination of gifted children, thus beginning one of the most ambitious longitudinal studies in the behavioral sciences. This select group of individuals with exceptional IQs was pursued into adulthood to determine the developmental consequences of intellectual giftedness. The result was the classic series of volumes that emerged under the overall title *Genetic Studies of Genius* (for example, Terman 1925; Terman and Oden 1959).

In the second volume of this set, Terman continued to apply psychology to history. In fact, he sponsored an explicitly historiometric project by a graduate student, Catherine Cox, who extended the approach of the 1917 Galton paper to a large sample of historical figures. By exploiting state-of-the-art statistics (plus a team of collaborators), IQ scores and reliability coefficients were calculated for 301 creators and leaders, scores that were also correlated with the eminence rankings provided earlier by J. M. Cattell (1903). The object was to prove the reverse of the thesis taken up by the other volumes: Just as intellectually gifted children were expected to grow up to become accomplished adults, so were the stars of cultural and political history hypothesized to have exhibited astronomical IQ scores in youth. The psychometric and historiometric inquiries were to reinforce each other, demonstrating the same nomothetic proposition from two longitudinal ends. Cox's efforts did not stop there. She also estimated personality scores for one hundred geniuses on sixty-seven traits of character to discover whether personality complements intelligence in the attainment of the highest distinction. The result of this herculean task was the 842-page classic called *The Early Mental Traits of Three Hundred Geniuses* (1926).

Cox's book was the impetus behind a large collection of follow-up studies (McCurdy 1960; Simonton 1976a; Walberg, Rasher, and Parkerson 1980; R. K. White 1931). These extensions were encouraged by the work's publication of detailed chronologies of the childhood development of all 301 geniuses. The assigned IQ scores were and are often cited in psychology textbooks and popular literature. Even so, the heyday of phase one was over. Mainstream psychology, with the advent of behaviorism, was veering away from human subjects, and the hunger for instant progress as a bona fide science made the exploitation of humanistic data even more suspect. While psychologists were losing interest in historiometric analyses and the term itself sank into oblivion, phase two was posing a threat to the theory that genius makes history.

Phase Two: Zeitgeist

Historiometric studies began appearing in sociology almost simultaneously with their disappearance from psychology. The pioneer was Pitirim A. Sorokin, Russian émigré and founder of Harvard's Department of Sociology. In 1925 and 1926 came his two-part article on monarchs and political leaders that assessed some of the individual attributes essential for attaining distinction in world affairs. A decade later Sorokin, collaborating with his student Robert K. Merton, offered a trend analysis of the fluctuations in creative activity in Islamic civilization (Sorokin and Merton 1935). Most significant was his four-volume magnum opus, *Social and Cultural Dynamics* (1937–41). Sorokin integrated a typology of human personality with a theory of social structure, hoping to explain why systems of philosophy, aesthetics, jurisprudence, economics, and politics transform in large cycles. As part of this vast project, Sorokin liberally applied quantitative analysis to historical data. For example, for each generation of European civilization, he gauged the coming and going of all of the principal philosophical positions, in effect accomplishing the first direct measurement of the intellectual zeitgeist, a concept often discussed but which had previously eluded objective assessment.

Although Sorokin's study elicited considerable commentary within sociology, in the end his influence was far less than one might have imagined. As critics attacked his theoretical predilections and rhetorical style (both leaning toward the romantic), his notable methodological contributions were often ignored. Even though later researchers have sometimes exploited his published data and have on occasion demonstrated their reliability and validity, Sorokin fell into undeserved neglect. This downward plunge in professional appreciation was severely aggravated when Sorokin lost several battles with Talcott Parsons over the future course of sociology. The new functionalist school had little sympathy for

Sorokin's quantitative aspirations, instead advocating a qualitative mode of analysis that managed to dominate sociology for several decades.

Concomitant with these happenings in sociology was a somewhat more successful series of events in anthropology. Alfred Kroeber, a prominent American anthropologist, had decided to challenge Galton's theory of genius. One cause for Kroeber's antipathy was that the eugenics school that Galton founded was associated with highly racist doctrines, beliefs that offered a "scientific" foundation for dogmas then emerging in Germany. As a student of Frank Boas—whose doctoral degree had been recently rescinded by the Nazis—Kroeber was in the forefront of those anthropologists who sought to place culture before biology in the determination of human behavior. Compatible with this goal was Kroeber's long-term desire to remove the individual as a causal agent in history, substituting the sociocultural system instead. Anthropology was to replace psychology as the behavioral science that could most successfully expound the laws of genius. So Kroeber began to collect historical data on when notable geniuses appeared in several disciplines and civilizations. His work began in 1931 and ended in 1938, about the same time that Sorokin was conducting comparable research, a fact that Kroeber did not learn until after he was almost finished writing. Kroeber was equally unaware of the relevant research by other predecessors, especially Cattell and Cox, his starting point being Galton's 1869 contribution. Nevertheless his *Configurations of Culture Growth* (1944) is a landmark in the historiometric study of genius.

Kroeber's investigation inspired subsequent researchers to pursue kindred issues. Charles E. Gray (1958, 1961, 1966) proposed an "epicyclical" model to explain the ups and downs in the appearance of historical genius. Despite certain problems with his methods (Barber 1981; Simonton 1981a), Gray's work represented an improvement over Kroeber's, progress that Kroeber (1958) himself acknowledged. A later paper by Naroll and his students attacked the problem of cultural configurations from yet another viewpoint, this time taking advantage of recent advances in cross-cultural methodology (Naroll et al. 1971). The 1944 book is not Kroeber's only entry in historiometric history. He supervised a classic inquiry into fluctuations in women's fashions that stimulated additional inquiries into fashion changes (Richardson and Kroeber 1940; compare Lowe and Lowe 1982; D. E. Robinson 1975, 1976; Simonton, 1977d). In addition, Kroeber (1917) was perhaps the first behavioral scientist to examine empirically the curious phenomenon of multiple discovery and invention—the event in which two or more individuals independently, and often simultaneously, make the same discovery or invention. Specifically, he compiled a short list to support his contention that the cultural system, not individual genius, is what propels scientific progress.

While other anthropologists enlarged this argument, sociologists expanded Kroeber's compilation of historical examples (Ogburn and Thomas 1922). Robert K. Merton (1961), Sorokin's student, eventually identified multiples as a critical

research site in the sociology of science and proceeded to subject his own augmented collation of cases to preliminary statistical analyses. A historian of science, Derek de Solla Price (1963), began fitting stochastic models to the phenomenon, thereby integrating historiometric research on multiples with the
emerging interdisciplinary field of scientometrics. Merton and Price saw their
nomothetic hypotheses subjected to ever more sophisticated statistical analyses in
both sociology (for example, Brannigan and Wanner 1983a, 1983b) and psychology (for example, Simonton 1979a, 1986d)—results belonging more precisely to
the third phase.

Phase Three: The Individual in Society

In the past few decades psychologists have taken a new interest in the
scientific analysis of theory. This change is particularly evident in those branches
that never fully succumbed to the temptations of behavioristic psychology. Increasingly more personality, developmental, educational, and social psychologists
found adequate reasons to study historical and biographical data, making the
library once more a laboratory. What emerged were quite a few separate research
programs that overlap in time. The heterogeneity of this work makes it impossible
to recount events as a single continuous development, and few of the investigators
self-consciously saw themselves as advancing the older tradition. Therefore the
best approach is to enumerate six principal lines of inquiry in approximate chronological order of onset.

    1. Work on the relation between age and outstanding achievement was
revived by Harvey C. Lehman, from the 1930s to his death in 1966. Having
received encouragement and support from James McKeen Cattell, Edward L.
Thorndike, Lewis M. Terman, and other early historiometricians, Lehman put
forward his main conclusions in the 1953 *Age and Achievement,* the preface
written by Terman. This has become a classic in life-span developmental psychology, provoking another developmental psychologist, Wayne Dennis (for example,
1966), to conduct his own studies, and reinforcing a line of work that remains
actively pursued today.

    2. From time to time, personality psychologists have resorted to historical
data to check some cherished theory or technique. Raymond B. Cattell, one of the
leading psychometricians in the evolution of factor analysis, published two explanatory studies in which he used historical data to demonstrate the virtues of p-
technique, the method of factor analyzing time-series data (R. B. Cattell 1953;
Cattell and Adelson 1951). More fruitful was his 1963 attempt to score a sample of
illustrious scientists on his sixteen personality factors. Other researchers have also
shown how standard personality variables might be assessed on historical figures
(for example, the Historical Figures Assessment Collaborative [HFAC] 1977), with
a respectable literature emerging from the problem of assessing the character of
novelists through their autobiographical works (for example, McCurdy 1939;

Rosenberg and Jones 1972; R. K. White 1947). Of all such endeavors, the most useful may be the efforts of David Winter and his colleagues to determine how political figures score in the needs for power, achievement, and affiliation (for example, Donley and Winter 1970; Winter and Stewart 1977).

3. David C. McClelland also believed that human motivation had a part in human history, particularly whether the achievement motive contributed to entrepreneurial leadership and hence to economic prosperity. In part, this hypothesis was tested by applying content analysis to cultural materials, as reported in McClelland's 1961 book *The Achieving Society* (chap. 4). Other psychologists have likewise exploited cultural indicators to discern the causes of fluctuation in a society's "modal personality." Perhaps the most successful literature concerns the association between external threat and the authoritarian personality (for example, Sales 1972, 1973).

4. Biographical data have again been subjected to rigorous analysis. In 1962 Victor and Mildred Goertzel published *Cradles of Eminence,* a systematic examination of four hundred famous individuals of the twentieth century, which was followed in 1978 by *Three Hundred Eminent Personalities* (with their son Theodore), a work that subjected a nonoverlapping sample to statistical analyses. These studies aim at generalizations about which child-rearing practices are most conducive to the emergence of highly accomplished adults. Much recent work has focused on the impact of particular developmental experiences, like birth order, orphanhood, and role models (Simonton 1987a).

5. An utterly new approach in historiometry is the sophisticated use of computers to perform content analyses of personal documents and creative products (Stone et al., 1966). So far, computerized analysis has been applied to political speeches (for example, Hart 1984), musical compositions (for example, Paisley 1964; Simonton 1980d), and literature (for example, Martindale 1984a; Simonton 1989b). The potential classic here may be Colin Martindale's 1975 *Romantic Progression,* in which English and French poetry were subjected to rich but objective analysis to determine the psychological causes of fashion changes in literature. Since 1966, when the first issues of the journal *Computers and the Humanities* appeared, these techniques have made inroads into the humanistic disciplines; inquiries into textual criticism and musicology sometimes yield significant results for the psychology of the arts (see also R. W. Bailey 1982; Hockey 1980).

6. Social psychology suffered something of a "crisis of confidence" in the 1970s (Elms 1975) as increasingly more mainstream practitioners began to deplore the discipline's excessive reliance on experimental studies of college sophomores in laboratory cubicles (McGuire 1973). Thus encouraged to go outside the lab, several social psychologists ventured into historiometrics, its techniques actually gaining advocates with impeccable credentials in mainstream methodologies (for example, Baron and Ransberger 1978; McGuire 1976; Tetlock 1983).

In the book's final chapter, we will document more fully the contributions that these and other historiometric studies have made to psychology and allied behavioral sciences. Historiometry cannot be counted as a commonplace approach, yet it has become sufficiently respected that inquiries are again being published by competent scholars in prestigious journals. Indeed, historiometric studies won Colin Martindale and Philip Tetlock each the Behavioral Science Prize from the American Association for the Advancement of Science. And David C. McClelland and William J. McGuire, two strong defenders of the psychological use of historical data, have each received the Distinguished Scientific Contribution Award of the American Psychological Association, albeit chiefly for their more mainstream efforts.

Interdisciplinary Comparisons

Historiometry closely compares with affiliated disciplines. A Venn diagram representation of the central affinities is given as figure 1.1. Where the circles intersect some characteristic enterprises of psychology, science, and history are designated. Psychometrics is in the overlap between psychology and science, marking one psychological discipline that rightly deserves the name of science. Psychohistory and psychobiography are at the convergence of psychology and

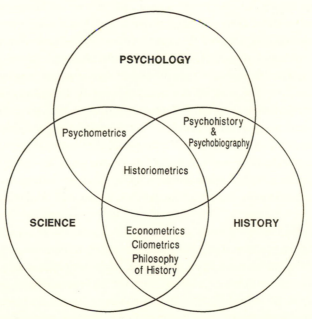

Figure 1.1 Venn diagram showing how historiometry compares with closely related subdisciplines within psychology, science, and history.

history, and econometrics, cliometrics, and the philosophy of history are at the intersection of history and science. Historiometry alone entails the confluence of all three circles. Interdisciplinary comparisons will be made as we treat the disciplines of history, science, and psychology.

History

Of the three domains in figure 1.1, history is the oldest. In the millennia since its advent, history has become one of the more finely differentiated humanities. Three subdisciplines of history now command the greatest attention in specifying how historiometrics fits in with the larger scheme of scholarly things. In historical order, these fields are historiography proper, the speculative philosophy of history, and cliometrics.

Historiography. The main business of historians has always been to write history, a task entailing two responsibilities. The first is to establish the historical facts: What happened to whom and when? Although this may seem to be the easiest part, the reality of the matter is the contrary. The most mundane fact can fuel eons of scholarly debate. Thus in the recent history of the United States, people are still willing to argue about who was responsible for the assassination of President Kennedy. Historical facts per se do not really exist; instead what historians have to deal with are historical generalizations, even theories, of a low order of abstraction.

Even the seemingly primitive datum that "George Washington was the first President of the United States" hangs on a complex web of far more rudimentary facts (Murphey 1973, chap. 1). We must have a theory that Washington existed as a breathing personality, a theory that coordinates a host of otherwise disconnected data—like the presence of Mount Vernon with its tomb and toothbrush, the references to a person with this name in various contemporary newspapers and the *Congressional Record,* portraits of a man so named by Stuart and others. Yet as in any theoretical proposition, contrary interpretations are feasible. For instance, one could advance the rival (albeit implausible) theory that Washington was the fictional creation of his contemporaries, the product of the grandest of all conspiracies to deceive the American people. What makes a fact a fact rather than a theory is not some sharp line of demarcation. Rather, facts and theories represent end points of a continuum, some facts being theories so well documented that they seem necessarily to be true. The best historical facts approach the same knowledge standing as Descartes' "I think therefore I am," which hinges on the presumed (and unprovable) continuity of the self from instant to instant.

After historians have fixed the crucial facts, the second step is to convey those facts to scholarly and lay readers. Here the historian has three major choices. First, in order of both difficulty and magnitude of generalizability, the facts, whether trivial or profound, may be arrayed on a temporal scale like a chronological table. This arrangement is common, particularly in reference works, despite the belief that chronologies are too mundane to attract the efforts of a distinguished historian. This attitude can be unfortunate, because when compiling chronologies is approached as hackwork to earn extra money, they can become riddled with errors. A recent chronology of United States history, even though under the general editorship of a noted American historian (Schlesinger 1983), evidences such grave mistakes as maintaining that Panama revolted against Nicaragua rather than Columbia in 1903 (424) or claiming that the Prohibition amendment had a "built-in seven-year time span," after which it would become inoperative (438), when the section refers only to a deadline for ratification. Chronology should not be treated as a stepchild if it is to be the true parent of all more advanced vehicles of historical information.

More honored than chronology is narrative. The historian can tell an engaging story that may rival fantasy for interest. Indeed, the line between historical narration and historical fiction is often thin, as historians frequently take some liberty with the facts to keep the reader's attention. In Herodotus and Thucydides dialogues and speeches abound despite the probable absence of verbatim transcripts. Even should such poetic license be rejected as lacking in objectivity, the historian must decide which facts to emphasize, which to suppress, and how best to array the facts more compatibly with drama and argument than with precise chronology. A claim that chronological order has no order betrays historical narrative's closer intimacy with literature than with science.

Historical distortion and omission in a narrative account become more conspicuous when a historian turns to interpretation. Frequently the scholar seeks to offer and defend a thesis, marshaling diverse facts into place. To discern history's lessons, the author may strive to convey why things happened the way they did. Historical interpretations, then, can teach us more about human nature, perhaps unearthing principles that transcend all history and should thereby make us all wiser today. Hence, interpretations of the broadest applicability turn out to be generalizations like those that opened this chapter. Abstractions from history provide the general principles from which single personalities can be understood. This facet of interpretation, of course, raises the irksome issue of how historical generalizations can be made, and a historiographic literature has been built around this subject (for example, L. Gottschalk 1963). When historians make mistakes and succumb to any of a vast collection of potential "historians' fallacies" (Fischer 1970), they are likely to fail in this class of inferences. The grander the generalization, the greater the probable error.

How do the functions of historiography relate to the goals of historiometry? One response is obvious: Historiometrics feeds on historical facts. No nomothetic hypothesis can be tested and no theoretical variable quantified without raw data about historical figures, particularly those facts made accessible in comprehensive chronologies. Ultimately, the chronological table is the foundation of virtually all historiometric inquiry. However, historiometricians have relatively little use for historical narrative. At best, narration provides a clumsy and inefficient source of basic information, whereas at worst narration may contain so few facts as to contain no useful data. Although a good narrative account may inspire a behavioral scientist to pursue a particular subject, that function is more humanistic than scientific in nature. Yet if we move one step further, the products of historical inquiry become valuable. Sufficiently speculative interpretative histories will contain many gems of historical induction. Abstract propositions, however used to explain historical details, might be elaborated into full-fledged nomothetic hypotheses amenable to quantitative inspection. Thus, the contributions of historiography to historiometry are both to establish the particulars and to suggest the universals that may be confirmed using those particulars. Despite historiography's idiographic aspirations, it is the sine qua non of historiometry's search for the nomothetic.

Philosophy of history. Philosophy joins history as one of the most ancient of all the humanities. Yet the fundamental disposition of the philosopher contrasts markedly with that of the historian. Thales is considered to be the first Western philosopher, and because science grew out of philosophy, philosophers may have much more in common with scientists than with historians. While historians preoccupy themselves with concrete particulars, philosophers prefer abstract universals. Given this stark disparity in outlook, the term "philosophy of history" seems an oxymoron. How can proper names, places, and dates have a happy marriage with The Good, The Beautiful, and The True? It turns out that there are two separate modes of combination, one modest, the other grandiose.

On one hand, we have those philosophies of history that merely discuss the nature of historical inquiry (for example, Danto 1965; Gardiner 1974): What constitutes historical knowledge or understanding? How does history compare with other disciplines in aims and methods? Even if the answers to these questions interest philosophers and historians alike, this brand of philosophical history has little direct relevance to historiometry. Historiometric inquiries seek not historical but scientific knowledge and explanation. So long as the epistemologists conclude that historical data exist, then the historiometricians can proceed without glancing back at the philosophical controversies that attend such metahistorical matters.

However, there are more speculative, and hence less reputable, philosophies of history where the goal is to describe the entire pattern of history, to propose historical generalizations that apply to all masterpieces, all geniuses, all revolutions, all empires, all civilizations. This ambitious practice is about as old as history itself and shows no sign to vanish. Illustrious Chinese annalists, especially Pan Gu, first provided a theoretical framework to explain the rise and fall of dynasties, a concern that may also be read in Ibn Khaldūn's notable *Introduction to History,* written around 1377. Among many other ventures in the last two centuries, these earlier examples were joined by Hegel's *Philosophy of History,* Marx's *Capital,* and Spengler's *Decline of the West.* The most ambitious and complete attempt in recent history is clearly Toynbee's theory of the rise and fall of all world civilizations (1946). With his grand scheme he endeavored to explicate not just the waxing and waning of political systems, but also the appearance and disappearance of creative activity. In other words, Toynbee sought one scheme to handle genius-grade achievement of all kinds—political and military leadership alongside intellectual and aesthetic creativity. In scope, *A Study of History* compares with Sorokin's (1937–41) *Social and Cultural Dynamics*.

The reactions from Toynbee's colleagues in history were certainly no more favorable than the reviews that Sorokin received from his fellow sociologists (see, for example, Geyl 1958). The historian's broad skepticism about abstractions assumes astronomical proportions when confronted with generalizations that purport to operate throughout all history and over the entire globe. Nevertheless, the speculative philosophy of history enjoys certain affinities with historiometry. Both are motivated to unearth the regularities of human behavior in the historical world, and thus both are nomothetically driven. Indeed, philosophers of history have proposed a number of historical laws that have been subjected to historiometric scrutiny (for example, Naroll et al. 1971; Simonton 1978b).

In other critical ways, however, the philosophy of history and historiometry diverge. For one thing, practitioners of the philosophy of history seem determined to prove a pet theory, summoning facts and arguments more like a lawyer than a scientist. Historiometricians, in contrast, prefer to state their theories as specific hypotheses that are then honestly put at risk of refutation before real data. Worse, many philosophers of history buttress much of their theory building on tenuous analogies. Thus Spengler employed the much-abused organic metaphor, comparing the birth, life, and death of civilizations with the life course of a single organism, two rather different phenomena to say the least. Or the analogy may bridge two otherwise distinct historical events, as when Toynbee took the rise and fall of classical Western civilization as the prototype for all world cultures. Historiometry avoids explanation that uses overarching analogies. Instead, the historical data are handled solely in terms of quantitative measures. The only postulate is that certain variables, such as creativity and leadership, have comparable meanings in various times and places—analogies of a far lower order of abstraction.

Therefore historiometry may be perceived as a hypothesis-testing, analytical, and quantitative (rather than a speculative, synthetic, and qualitative) philosophy of history, yet only after appending an additional proviso. Much philosophy of history deals with big-scale entities, like whole civilizations and political systems. While historiometry might handle such massive aggregates—as work on the rise and fall of empires attests (Taagepera 1978, 1979)—the main thrust must be toward the single human being. Civilizations and imperial states could possibly say something about behavior at the personal level, but most of the time historiometricians (and psychologists) will want to examine individuals more directly.

Cliometrics.   Recently history has seen the development of a discipline easily confused with historiometry. That field is *cliometrics,* or, more broadly, "quantitative social science history" (Kousser 1984). Given that in some versions of Greek mythology Clio was the Muse who patronized history, cliometrics and historiometrics appear as etymological synonyms. Both begin with historical data and both are characterized by quantitative analyses. Yet cliometrics is far more idiographic in tone. Cliometricians tend to be social scientists who seek quantitative answers to historical questions. An example of a typically cliometric problem is whether slavery in the antebellum South was economically profitable (Conrad and Meyer 1964; Fogel and Engerman 1974). The response is of the utmost significance in understanding American history, but it may shed little light on related issues—such as whether the latifundia of ancient Rome were profitable—and might contribute even less regarding the broader economic feasibility of slavery.

Another contrast between historiometrics and cliometrics has to do with the theoretical base on which each operates. Historiometrics has no conceptual commitments but rather comprises techniques for testing nomothetic hypotheses of diverse origins, the generalizations having to pertain only to human behavior. In cliometrics, however, the foundation of a given study is usually current economic theory. It is for this reason that cliometrics was once styled the "new economic history" or "econometric history." For the most part, the considerable nomothetic assets of macroeconomics, combined with the sophisticated quantitative tools of econometrics, are maximally exploited to explain some critical idiographic issue. Yet the nomothetic framework itself is not what is open to empirical confrontation. Economic theory is unmolested by any test of the particularistic hypothesis that slavery was a reasonably profitable enterprise in the American South before the Civil War. Admittedly, not all quantitative history is inspired by economics, for the "new social history" may use quantitative methods more as does demography (for example, Achenbaum 1978). And the "new political history" may apply statistics to the past in a manner that merges with political science proper (for example, Bogue 1968). Yet the focus remains on the description and narration of particulars rather than on the discovery and confirmation of universals.

As in the case of the philosophy of history, we need not detail the controversy that has raged over the assignment of numbers to the past. Cliometricians have made a strong case on behalf of their discipline (for example, Aydellote 1971; Benson 1972; C. Erikson 1975; Floud 1984; Fogel 1975), and several cliometric studies have some claim to being classics in historical inquiry (for example, Fogel and Engerman 1974; Fogel 1964). Numerous books discuss and illustrate the methodologies usually involved and the substantive issues best attacked (for example, Aydellote, Bogue, and Fogel 1972; Floud 1973; Lorwin and Price 1972; Rowney and Graham 1969); even a few journals have emerged that welcome the quantifier's technical spelunking (for example, *Historical Methods* and the *Journal of Interdisciplinary History*). Nevertheless, the professional opposition is both great and intense, having enlisted the critical words of many notables. For example, besides the negative opinion proffered by Arthur Schlesinger, Jr. (1962a), we also have the complaints of Jacques Barzun, as voiced in his 1974 *Clio and the Doctors: Psycho-history, Quanto-history, and History*.

This controversy warns us that historiometricians should not expect a more sympathetic ear than the cliometricians have received. Both historiometrics and cliometrics are dedicated to the quantitative analysis of history, an operation that some historians perceive as virtually sacrilegious. More unfortunate still is that historiometricians do not share the cliometrician's desire to solve problems of intrinsic interest to most historians. The subject matter of historiometrics stays within the domain of science in a well-advertised quest for behavioral laws. Hence, if cliometrics is spurned by historians, historiometrics should earn a less courteous greeting. Yet the main point is that these two quantitative disciplines have distinct functions vis-à-vis history: Cliometrics applies science to history; historiometrics exploits history to do science.

Science

Assuming that historiometry will eventually join the ranks of established sciences, it may be well to inquire about older disciplines that have already gained acceptance, considering first the natural sciences and then the social sciences.

Natural sciences.   A distant relative to historiometry is astronomy, a discipline at one time acclaimed the "queen of the sciences." This was the first natural science to introduce quantification as well as the first to take full advantage of advanced mathematics. Presumably the successful prediction of a solar eclipse by Thales on 28 May 585 B.C. was made possible by an astronomical science already well along in Babylonia. By the time of Ptolemy, astronomy had reached a level of sophistication unmatched by any other science for almost two millennia, until the advent of Newton's *Principia Mathematica*. Yet almost from its inception astronomy entailed, in effect, the testing of nomothetic hypotheses by applying quantitative analysis to historical data. The propositions were Pythagorean and Platonic notions about how mathematics permeated the universe, as ideal forms dominated the most perfect manifestations of reality, taking even concrete existence as pure, crystalline spheres. The Ptolemaic system was an affirmation that the cosmos spoke in circles, that complex but precise arrangements of circles or epicycles could explain the motions of the planets, moon, and sun across the sky. The historical data concerned not the stars of history but rather certain stars of the heavens and their innumerable companions. Given that astronomical cycles take centuries to decipher, modern astronomers have had no other recourse but to rely on primary data collected by others who lived years before—just as historiometricians must do.

Of course, those earlier data collectors were usually astronomers like themselves, so it is not a matter of one discipline exploiting data gathered laboriously by another discipline. Yet the astronomers and historians—or more properly the astrologers and annalists—often were the same in ancient civilizations. Thus the great Sima Qian, the father of Chinese historiography, was the court astrologer responsible for recording both astronomical events and historical events; noting down eclipses and incursions were all part of the same task. Hence, astronomy is a historical enterprise at once nomothetic and quantitative, only the subject matter contrasting drastically with historiometry.

In comparison to anything in historiometry, however, the mathematics of astronomy is much more sophisticated, the measurements and predictions far more accurate. No historiometric treatise may ever surpass the intimidating formal fireworks to be found in the *Treatise on Celestial Mechanics* by the Marquis de Laplace. Historiometricians must struggle to cope with far more elusive events, behaviors not so readily captured in numbers having several significant figures—and even less readily predicted. Historiometry must grapple with happenings that are the upshot of dozens, hundreds, even thousands of determinants. In these respects historiometry is more fairly compared to those earth sciences that are also historical but that must acknowledge a confusing plethora of pertinent but imprecisely assessed factors.

The nearest kin are likely to be meteorology and paleontology. Meteorology endeavors to predict the present given the past using thousands of data points, yet at best offering statements of probability for each forecast. Meteorology will also, on occasion, use historical records, this excursion being especially common in climatology, a subject that has an important bearing on the history of human civilization (Rotberg and Rabb 1981). Paleontologists seek to show how new life forms emerged over geological time, just as historiometricians seek to show how new cultural forms appeared over historical time. Like historiometry, too, the paleontological record is incomplete, with gaps that render truly decisive tests of many rival theories difficult. Nonetheless, the historical record far surpasses the paleontological record in completeness and accuracy, giving historiometric statements the potential to surpass in scientific value those promulgated by paleontologists.

Whatever the truth of this last prophecy, historiometry is not without friends in the natural sciences, for many reputable disciplines are at root historical. Curiously, the links between historiometry and the earth sciences is more than conceptual, for some important contributors to the disciplines are the same people or are at least closely connected. In the case of meteorology, a landmark book is *Weather Prediction by Numerical Process,* written by the physicist Lewis Fry Richardson in 1922. In 1939, on the eve of World War II, Richardson published the article "Generalized Foreign Policy" in the *British Journal of Psychology Monograph Supplements,* which represents his first attempt at understanding arms races and war by applying differential equation models to historical data.

The association is likewise intimate between historiometry and paleontology, which did not escape being a merely descriptive labor until Charles Darwin established in 1859 a strong case for the evolution of species by natural selection. Darwin's thinking had a profound impact on the functionalist school of psychologists. Among the illustrious members of this movement are Francis Galton, James McKeen Cattell, Edward L. Thorndike, and Lewis M. Terman—all pioneers of historiometry. This conjunction of stars cannot be dismissed as mere coincidence. The functionalists were fascinated with individual differences—the variation that supposedly serves as the engine of evolutionary change—and thus it was in character for them to investigate geniuses whom they thought represented the highest evolutionary attainments. Terman's *Genetic Studies of Genius* was specifically engaged in proving Galton's thesis that geniuses were best adapted to life and living, not only intellectually but socially, emotionally, and physically. Both functionalists and evolutionists were interested in how organisms change over time, even though for functionalists this took the guise of learning and development. The intrinsic kinship between these two disciplines is implicitly acknowledged by Darwin's own reaction upon reading the first classic of historiometry, Galton's *Hereditary Genius:* "I do not think I ever in all my life read anything more interesting and original."

Social sciences. Understandably, historiometry is far more closely related to the behavioral sciences. One of the most intimate relations is that between historiometrics and econometrics, a discipline close to cliometrics as well. Econometrics, like much cliometrics, is dedicated to comprehending human behavior having to do with economic activity. But where cliometrics has more interest in applying economic theory to specific historical events, econometrics is committed to the verification of nomothetic ideas, revealing a closer affinity with historiometrics. Unlike historiometrics, however, econometrics characteristically operates on aggregate data, such as yearly or quarterly statistics on the economy of a whole nation or industry—the domain of macroeconomic theory. Nevertheless, many of the techniques devised by econometricians have proved extremely valuable in historiometrics. On rare occasions the econometrician may even scrutinize the same phenomena as a historiometrician. For instance, the connection between individual age and exceptional achievement has been treated by both economic models of "investment in human capital" and information-processing models of human creativity (Simonton 1988b).

Another apparent contrast between the econometrician and historiometrician is that the econometrician tends to study data collected by economists, whereas the historiometrician tends to analyze data collected by scholars in another discipline, history. Indeed, one of the main achievements of econometrics is the diversity of ways to quantify central facets of economic systems, such as the gross national product. Therefore, even though econometrics and historiometrics both deal with historical data, historiometrics is one step removed from the original source, putting it at the level of recent political science research, which is often fundamentally historiometric. For example, when political scientists conduct inquiries into the factors underlying the performance of the American chief executive, the primary source of data is the historical record, whether actual histories or official government archives (for example, J. Holmes and Elder 1989; Kenney and Rice 1988). Although it may seem a disadvantage to depend on other disciplines or professions for one's data, this dependence can be an asset. The historiometrician, as much as the political scientist, can use information gathered by scholars who were totally blind to the nomothetic hypotheses to be tested. For econometricians, the definitions of key economic variables are sometimes confounded by the theoretical model used to compound them.

Behavioral and natural scientists have combined to establish a new discipline specifically devoted to the quantitative study of science and scientists—scientometrics. This emerging field has much in common with historiometrics, and any statistical analysis of historical scientists that looks for generalizations about the workings of science at the individual level counts as both scientometrics and historiometrics. In this intersecting set, for example, are the quantitative studies of multiple discovery and invention, age and scientific productivity, and role modeling in science (Simonton 1988e). However, scientometrics is both more narrow and more broad than historiometrics. Although scientometrics is by definition confined to scientific activity, historiometrics can delve into almost any human behavior of historical consequence. Even so, scientometrics is less restricted in its methodology. Any means to scrutinize science using science will do, such as surveys and interviews (for example, Zuckerman 1977). Indeed, scientometrics often takes the shape of citation analyses, as in the work of Garfield (1979), which often study who is most often referred to in the scientific literature and by whom. Even if there are times when citational analyses merge with historiometric studies (Simonton 1984i, 1985b), they are rare. While historiometrics puts more stress on historical personalities, citational analysis emphasizes contemporary stars.

Quantitative cross-cultural anthropology is the social science with the strongest resemblance to historiometry (see Naroll 1968; Rohner 1977). Ethnographers have accumulated mounds of information on virtually every facet of human cultures across the globe, data that have been consolidated in huge data bases, such as the Human Relations Area Files at Yale University (Naroll and Michik 1975). For hundreds of cultures we have assessments of child-rearing practices, religious rites, economic resources, artistic attainments, military proclivities, and so on. This information is repeatedly analyzed to extract the cross-cultural universals of human nature (for example, Textor 1967). In short, this "hologeistic" or "holocultural" research, like that in historiometry, tests nomothetic statements quantitatively (Levinson 1977). Many of the methodological problems are likewise similar to those that plague historiometry. Both must cope with gaps in the record; both strive to measure the seemingly immeasurable.

Cross-cultural methods, in fact, can often be applied to historiometric problems with only minor modifications. Raoul Naroll, a leader in quantitative cross-cultural methods, was also an innovator in historiometry, advancing the tradition laid down by Kroeber (Naroll, Bullough, and Naroll 1974; Naroll et al. 1971). David C. McClelland (1961), in determining the association between the achievement motive and economic prosperity, tested hypotheses on both historical and cross-cultural data, using much the same approach. Colin Martindale (1976) has applied his content-analytical methods to folk tales from forty-five preliterate societies, thereby extending the techniques he devised for English and French poetry. Yet one critical difference is obvious: Cross-cultural surveys do not examine historical figures, for most of the material on human cultures is anonymous. Of the hundreds of societies past and recent, only a dozen or so have attained the status of civilizations in which annalists have recorded the coming and going of indigenous creators, leaders, and celebrities. There are nonetheless circumstances where cross-cultural research can contribute to substantive issues in historiometry, including the dependence of artistic creativity on the sociocultural system (for example, Barry 1957; Lomax 1968).

Psychology

Psychology occupies a unique position among the sciences. Essentially psychologists focus on the organism. Whether the sea snail *Aplasia* or the more advanced Homo sapiens, it may be scrutinized from a host of legitimate perspectives. Some psychologists adopt a natural science viewpoint that overlaps genetics, neurology, physiology, or ecology; examples are behavioral genetics, psychophysiology, and comparative psychology. Others are more in sympathy with the social sciences, such as linguistics, anthropology, sociology, political science, and economics, as in social, political, organizational, and cross-cultural psychology. What holds all of this centrifugal activity in place around a single enterprise is a concentrated attention on individual behavior, for above all, psychology is the premier behavioral science. Of course, other social sciences use behavioral science, as when the political scientist examines voter behavior, or when the economist studies consumer behavior. Yet the centers of these kindred disciplines lie elsewhere, whether in political institutions or in economic systems. Because historiometricians hope to make contributions to behavioral science, historiometry can be compared to other practices within psychology. The endeavor connects with psychohistory and psychobiography, on the one hand, and psychometrics, on the other.

Psychohistory and psychobiography. About the same time that Woods (1909) provided a new name for a new science, Sigmund Freud was introducing an entirely different approach to the psychological analysis of history. In 1910 he published *Leonardo da Vinci and a Memory of his Childhood,* the first classic in psychobiography, or the application of psychoanalysis to biography (Elms 1988). Later he collaborated with William C. Bullitt on another psychological study, a vitriolic attack on President Woodrow Wilson (Freud and Bullitt 1967). Since Freud, the output of psychobiographies has expanded appreciably (Runyan 1988a) and includes such influential contributions as Erik Erikson's psychobiographies of Mahatma Gandhi (1969) and Martin Luther (1958) and another treatment of Woodrow Wilson by Alexander and Juliette George (1956). It would be hard to name a historical figure, famous or infamous, who has not been placed on the psychoanalyst's couch. Some political figures have been treated so many times— like Adolf Hitler and Richard M. Nixon—that psychohistory has become a conspicuous subdiscipline of political psychology (Cocks 1986).

On occasion, academic psychologists have indulged in psychobiographical studies, the most conspicuous example perhaps being Henry Murray's lifelong preoccupation with Herman Melville (for example, Murray 1951). Yet psychobiography has been better received among those historians and political scientists who view it as a more scientific approach to the analysis of the personal motives that drive political actors (Langer 1958). Psychobiography has thus become an interdisciplinary endeavor at the intersection of psychology and history, subsumed under a more comprehensive discipline known as *psychohistory,* or the broader "science of historical motivation" (deMause 1981, 179). Besides the psychoanalysis of individuals, psychohistorians can decipher the personalities of groups, nations, and periods. The expansion of psychohistory is reflected in the advent of such journals as the *Psychohistory Review* and the *Journal of Psychohistory,* as well as the publication of whole books devoted to the topic (for example, Cocks and Crosby 1987; Runyan 1988b). For psychologists proper, the primary text is *Life Histories and Psychobiography* by William McKinley Runyan (1982).

Even though psychohistory is popular with laypersons who want to understand the inner psychological workings of the rich and famous, the response from the scholarly community is mixed, at times hostile (Simonton 1983e). Some critics take aim at the psychoanalytic nature of almost all work. Given that the scientific status of psychoanalysis remains in doubt, some consider it premature to impose psychoanalysis on the facts of history (for example, Stannard 1980). Although defenders of psychohistory have argued that nonpsychoanalytic studies are feasible—taking advantage of current research in the psychological journals—the hegemony of psychoanalysis has yet to be broken. And so long as virtually all psychohistory and psychobiography is written by psychiatrists, historians, and political scientists rather than by professional psychologists, it is unlikely that such studies will enter the mainstream of scientific psychology.

Critics also maintain that this psychoanalytic perspective reduces the rich complexity of a historical personality to diagnostic labels, creating what might be more correctly styled *pathography.* Working under the motto "no childhood, no psychohistory" (deMause 1981, 181), the psychohistorian all too often must amplify seemingly trivial (and uncertain) details of an individual's early development into the cause of the adult character (Tetlock, Crosby, and Crosby 1981). In the notorious "Hitlerature," speculations may digress to the origins of Hitler's supposed kinky sexual hobbies. Such preoccupations seem to endorse the statement "psychohistory is merely gossip," to paraphrase Oscar Wilde. These complaints are explicit in the main title of David E. Stannard's (1980) critique *Shrinking History: On Freud and the Failure of Psychohistory*. In the crucible of psychoanalysis, the overwhelming richness of historical causality is confined to a simple, and often simplistic, elemental substance.

Nevertheless, defenders of the faith are not in short supply, and tremendous advances have been made in psychohistorical methodology since Freud's day (J. W. Anderson 1981; McAdams and Ochberg 1988). Consequently, psychohistory will likely persist, especially in history where Freud's influence is growing as fast as it is diminishing in psychology and science (for example, Gay 1985). Whatever the status of psychohistory and psychobiography, whether as science or as history, historiometry is distinct (Simonton 1983e).

1. Historiometry is committed to quantitative analysis, whereas numbers and mathematics are virtually nonexistent in psychohistory, where qualitative discussion reigns supreme. Freud was not particularly competent in mathematics, a deficiency that may have set the tone for all subsequent work. Psychohistorians will avoid quantitative analyses even when the question lends itself to psychometric treatment (Simonton 1989b).

2. Historiometry is nomothetic, psychohistory idiographic. Where historiometricians attempt to abstract generalizations from history and biography, psychohistorians seek to explain the details of a specific historical event or person. Historiometricians are inductive, proceeding from the particular to the general, whereas psychohistorians are deductive, going from the general to the particular. Where history clarifies only the type of measurement in historiometry, psychology specifies merely the type of history or biography being executed in psychohistory and psychobiography.

3. Historiometry prefers the analysis of multiple cases, psychohistory and especially psychobiography the scrutiny of the single case. Only by subjecting respectable samples to statistical analyses can reliable regularities be abstracted from history. Hence, historiometry has superior potential for contributing to the development of psychological theory of any kind, including even that which is psychoanalytic (see, for example, Martindale 1975; Matossian and Schafer 1977; Simonton 1989b). Psychohistory and psychobiography, in contrast, are less interested in developing new theory but rather hope to demonstrate how a given theory helps to illuminate the single historical case. In practice, this often means that "history is not of interest for its own sake; rather, it is used to popularize or confirm current psychoanalytic theories" (Kohut 1986, 343). This proclivity of psychohistory often evokes negative reactions from historians that duplicate the adverse responses of many historians to cliometrics (Barzun 1974).

Given these contrasts, historiometry's strengths and weaknesses lie apart from any praise or complaints allotted to psychohistory and psychobiography. Historiometric studies must be judged by what they contribute to science, whereas psychohistorical studies must be assessed by what they contribute to history.

Psychometrics. The pioneer in the measurement of the intellect was Galton. About a dozen years after Galton's 1869 historiometric classic came his 1883 *Inquiries into Human Faculty,* a landmark psychometric treatise. Fascinated with individual differences in basic abilities, Galton set up an "anthropometric" laboratory designed to assess individuals on physical and cognitive attributes. He also introduced into psychology the statistical conceptions of correlation and regression, ideas that his biographer, Karl Pearson, was later to develop into the product-moment correlation coefficient, the single most useful statistic in both psychometrics and historiometrics. The intimate relation between the disciplines continued to the time of Terman (1917, 1925) and Cox (1926), *Genetic Studies of Genius* incorporating both historiometric analyses of 301 historical geniuses and psychometric analyses of 1,528 children who scored at the "genius level" on standardized IQ tests.

When historiometrics came to a temporary standstill shortly after the Terman volumes, psychometrics continued growing at an accelerated pace, eventually becoming one of the most scientifically sophisticated of all subdisciplines of psychology. The persistence of psychometrics ultimately helped historiometrics, for when historiometrics experienced a renaissance, a sizable inventory of new techniques was waiting to be used, renewing the connection between the two disciplines. Just as the Stanford-Binet IQ test inspired the assessment of intelligence of historical figures (Cox 1926; Terman 1917), many other psychometric instruments have been adapted for historiometry (for example, R. B. Cattell 1963; HFAC 1977; McClelland 1961; Simonton 1986h; Suedfeld and Rank 1976; Winter 1973). In addition, much of the psychometric literature regards the development of valuable statistical techniques of great power in historiometrics. Finally, a series of provocative psychometric investigations has shown the superiority of statistical predictions over clinical assessments—of mathematics over intuition (Faust 1984; Meehl 1954). This advantage of the quantitative over the qualitative is equally historiometry's edge over both psychohistory and the philosophy of history.

The central issues behind the practice of historiometrics form the basis of this book. Chapter 2 examines the fundamental nature of the data, chapter 3 variable quantification, chapter 4 measure reliability, chapter 5 instrument validity, chapter 6 basic statistical analyses, chapter 7 procedures for causal inference, and chapter 8 certain fine points. These chapters survey the diverse methodological issues, providing concrete illustrations from published inquiries. Owing to the nature of the discipline, the biggest share of these examples concerns genius, creativity, leadership, and allied topics, like aesthetics and aggression. A wider variety of substantive issues in the behavioral sciences will be mentioned to show that the method is applicable to a surprising assortment of theoretical questions. Chapter 9 features a comprehensive evaluation of the contributions that historiometry has made, and can yet make, to psychology, science, and history.

This book is not a manual on "doing" historiometry. Statistical analyses and other techniques will be discussed in general terms only, at the conceptual level. Sufficient references are given so that an interested reader will know where to turn for more guidance. Instead of details, the aim is to discuss, given a nomothetic hypothesis of a particular form, the optimal approaches for a quantitative test on a historical population. What we should learn is that all generalizations are dangerous, especially historical generalizations, and yet a selection of such propositions can contribute to the progress of behavioral science. Hegel once complained that "what experience and history teach is this—that peoples and governments never have learned anything from history, or acted on principles deduced from it." Historiometry, at the very minimum, has the potential of rendering this particular historical generalization obsolete.

2 Data

Centuries ago Plutarch complained, in his biography of Pericles, that "so very difficult a matter is it to trace and find out the truth of anything by history." Insert "iometr" between the "r" and "y" in the last word of this quote and Plutarch's complaint remains valid. Much of the time historiometry is a laborious business. The most extensive labors usually occur at the outset, when the nature of the raw data must be determined, and then the appropriate information collected. The investigator must first decide on the appropriate unit of analysis for multiple cases: individual geniuses, generations, creative products, battles, decisions, and so forth. Second, the researcher selects the best strategy for sampling the analytical units to be studied: Who (or what) will become the subjects of measurement and analysis? Third, pertinent information must be compiled from the archives—whether histories, biographies, or anthologies—nearly without exception the most arduous part of any project.

Unit of Analysis

Investigators must always ask, What entities are we studying? For most psychologists, the answer is obvious: the individual organism, especially the human subject. Psychoneurologists may adopt single neurons as their analytical units, and social psychologists may take as their units whole groups, yet the dominance of the individual persists. Historiometricians, too, frequently have the single human being as the unit of analysis. Nevertheless, often a principle of human behavior cannot be adequately examined without resorting to some other unit, compelling the researcher to shift perspective. This necessity is apparent from the immense variety of historical generalizations in what entities are being referred to—masterpieces, geniuses, years, centuries, nations, civilizations, and so on. Despite the variation, analytical units are either cross-sectional or time-series, although a nomothetic hypothesis can sometimes be tested only by mixing analytical units in unique combinations.

Cross-Sectional Units

Many historical generalizations implicitly specify the person as the unit of analysis. Certainly when Lord Acton observed that "power tends to corrupt, and absolute power corrupts absolutely. Great men are almost always bad men," he was referring to differences across individuals. Accordingly, historiometricians must attend often to persons, different investigations varying primarily in the range of subjects considered. Ambitious researchers take on historical figures in all walks of life, even villains. This breadth is most pronounced in the classic inquiries of Galton (1869), Cattell (1903), Cox (1926), and Thorndike (1950). Although recent researchers sometimes use the same wide cross-sections of achievers (for example, Eisenstadt 1978; Goertzel, Goertzel, and Goertzel 1978; Walberg, Rasher, and Parkerson 1980), more restricted cross-sections are more common. Sometimes eminent leaders are the focus of attention, whether American presidents (Winter 1987b), prime ministers (Ballard and Suedfeld 1988), Soviet politburo members (M. G. Hermann 1980a), monarchs (Woods 1913), revolutionaries (Suedfeld and Rank 1976), or miscellaneous heads of state, politicians, legislators, and royalty (for example, Blondel 1980; Cell 1974; M. G. Hermann 1977, 1980b; Sorokin 1925, 1926; Woods 1906). Other times the nomothetic hypotheses direct the inquiry toward distinguished creators of history, among them scientists (Adams 1946), philosophers (Simonton 1976f), literary figures (Martindale 1988), classical composers (Schubert, Wagner, and Schubert 1977), and artists (Martindale 1986b). Whatever the particular achievement, the analytical unit remains the individual. Yet there are many circumstances in which the cross-sectional analyses must comprise entities either smaller or larger than the historical personality.

At one extreme, an investigator may realize that a generalization is more directly tested not on individual achievers but rather on single acts of achievement. When Voltaire cynically claimed that "God is always on the side of the big battalions," the implication was that the best analytical unit may be the battle rather than the general. And so some researchers have examined a cross-section of military engagements, such as 326 critical battles of Western history (Simonton 1980a) or the subset of battles fought by Robert E. Lee (Suedfeld, Corteen, and McCormick 1986)—the first of these studies actually showing that Voltaire's conclusion was correct regarding casualty figures but not tactical victories. Other inquiries into leadership adopt such analytical units as legislative acts (Rohde and Simon 1985) and political decisions during crisis (Tetlock 1979).

This fragmentation of the individual career into cross-sections of historical episodes is even more apparent in studies of creativity, perhaps since many generalizations have to do with the attributes of masterworks rather than masterworkers. Hence, cases for analyses have included scientific discoveries and inventions (Brannigan and Wanner 1983b; Simonton 1979a), short stories (Martindale 1988;

Simonton 1988a), plays (Potter 1980; Simonton 1986f), epics (Adamopoulos 1982), sonnets (Simonton 1989b, 1990d), musical compositions (Cerulo 1984, 1989; Simonton 1986a), and even single melodies (Martindale and Uemura 1983; Simonton 1980d). Breaking down a career into bits is often desirable in the discipline of scientific aesthetics. Psychological theories of the arts commonly yield propositions about why some aesthetic creations are more successful than others, even when created by the same artist. W. H. Auden observed that because great poets write so much, "The chances are that, in the course of his lifetime, the major poet will write more bad poems than the minor" (quoted in Bennett 1980, 15). Under these conditions, the single aesthetic product constitutes a far more natural unit of analysis than does averaging across the total corpus of an individual artist's uneven work.

But there may be special situations in which larger units are the norm. For instance, one inquiry into the vice-presidential succession effect—where "accidental" presidents perform less well than duly elected chief executives—took candidate teams as the research unit (Simonton 1985c). More inclusive aggregates are possible beyond dyads, including whole nations and civilizations, but this usually occurs only as part of time-series designs (for example, Feierabend and Feierabend 1966; Naroll et al., 1971; Simonton 1976b). One problem with employing large aggregates is that it is often extremely difficult to define their boundaries (Nisbet 1969). None would experience difficulties differentiating, say, Thomas Aquinas from al-Ghazālī, but drawing a bold line dividing medieval Christian and Islamic civilizations is a far more delicate task. In which cultural pile does one place the Jewish philosopher Moses Maimonides or the hybrid court of Emperor Frederick II in Sicily? Moreover, if the study is truly restricted to units as large as civilizations, the number of cases may be prohibitively curtailed. Toynbee (1946) counted fewer than two dozen world civilizations, ignoring those that were arrested in their development (for example, the Polynesian). Yet given historiometry's dependence on a large N for complex statistical analyses, this sample size may not prove sufficient to test anything interesting. Lastly, few historical generalizations provocative to behavioral scientists require analyses of such ponderous cross-sectional units. If historiometry concentrates on human behavior, then with only minor exceptions studies will always inspect either individuals or samples of individual behavior. But whatever the choice, the unit of analysis must be primarily dictated by the substantive issues at hand, even though other considerations will sometimes enter the discussion.

Time-Series Units

Whereas cross-sectional units are used when the hypothesis pertains to variation across separate entities, such as individual differences in intelligence or personality, time-series units are appropriate whenever one is looking at a single entity over time—at temporal fluctuations for one or more variables within the same cross-sectional unit. What makes time-series units particularly useful is that many historical generalizations have to do with how creativity, leadership, and other behavioral phenomena change over time, either alone or with other, presumably causal events (Norling 1970, chap. 6). To illustrate, one historian of psychology conjectured that "it cannot be mere chance that is responsible for the frequency with which periods of social turmoil and political reform are empirical in their philosophical complexion" (D. N. Robinson 1986, 248). This statement, if true, would mark a contribution to our knowledge of how philosophical creativity and revolutionary leadership interrelate over time. Yet an inquiry confirming this proposition did not examine a cross-section of philosophers and revolutionaries but rather a series of aggregate units moving through historical time (Simonton 1976g).

Just as cross-sectional units may come in an assortment of shapes and sizes, so too is there a diversity of time-series units. Where a cross-sectional unit is primarily defined in terms of spatial scope or level of aggregation, a time-series unit is defined by duration. At the brief end we have studies of how the day-to-day variation in ambient temperature affects collective violence and violent crime (for example, Baron and Ransberger 1978), and at the long end we have inquiries into how creative activity changes in civilizations as measured century by century (for example, Naroll et al. 1971). Most investigations select units between these extremes, whether weeks (Phillips 1980), quarters (C. A. Anderson 1987), years (Copeland 1983), Congresses (Lee 1975), half-decades (Rainoff 1929), decades (Schneider 1937), or generations (Martindale 1975). Occasionally investigators will employ variable time-series units, although this is generally not an advisable procedure. For example, to verify his epicyclical theory of ups and downs in creative achievement, Gray (1961, 1966) subjected history to a periodization (for example, "Florescent City-State Period" or "Degenerate Baroque") that produced units ranging from twenty to two hundred years. Given that the partitioning of history into periods is thoroughly arbitrary (Nisbet 1969), Gray could be accused of selecting his units so that the crests and troughs of civilization would fall in the right locations to confirm his complex model (Taagepera and Colby 1979). Nonetheless, circumstances arise when the time units may be varied, at least in a systematic and predetermined pattern that avoids the intrusion of potential bias. For instance, time-series analysis of scientific discoveries in Western civilization have sometimes combined century, half-century, and quarter-century units together to get around the scarcity of pertinent events in antiquity (Simonton 1975d; Sorokin 1937–41).

What are the appropriate criteria for choosing the length of the temporal unit? Often the answer is dictated emphatically by the hypotheses to be tested. In political psychology, inquiries into how international crises and other historical events impinge on presidential popularity perforce take the poll results as given, on a more or less monthly basis (Kernell 1978; Mueller 1973); and investigations into

how suicide rates decline during presidential election years are necessarily designed around four-year intervals (Boor 1980; Boor and Fleming 1984; Wasserman
1983). Nevertheless, matters get more complicated when there is no "natural
unit," a common perplexity when the investigator seeks to tabulate the frequency
of discrete events into consecutive periods. One obvious factor is that the unit
chosen must be longer than the longest duration of an event. A more subtle factor is
that the unit should be long enough to escape serious "floor" effects wherein a
large percentage of units have no events counted in them. The reliability of such
event tabulations is a direct function of the length of the time-series units (Allison
1977). Hence, time series that record events decade by decade will boast superior
reliability over those recording the same events year by year; or holding the unit
size constant, events more rare cannot be measured as reliably as events more
common. Counting assassinations of political figures on a yearly basis is more
hazardous than counting all homicides.

    This potent incentive to cut history into thick chunks is counterbalanced by
other considerations. First, recognizing that history does not get any longer simply
because one has opted for long units, choosing longer units means fewer total
units. Yet advanced statistical analyses require respectable sample sizes, putting
pressure on briefer units. A second consideration is more substantive: What is the
nature of the process that one wishes to study? For most psychologists, whose
natural concentration is the individual, temporal cuts a century long look pre-
posterous, however valuable such monumental units might be to anthropologists,
sociologists, or political scientists who study phenomena that take much longer to
unfold over time. Apparently, the longest time-series unit that psychologists can
contemplate without getting dizzy is the generation. But how long is a generation?
Can a generational unit really be linked with behavior happening at the individual
level?

    Often a generation is defined as a group of individuals who experienced the
same definitive life event in the same year, whether their own birth, marriage, first
job, or first child. Yet these entities are probably better styled "cohorts" and
treated with traditional cohort analyses (Ryder 1965). Therefore, we reserve the
term generation for units that are at least a dozen years long, the most common
being 15 (Ortega y Gasset [1933] 1962), 20 (Martindale 1975), 25 (Matossian and
Schafer 1977), and 30 years (Mannheim 1952). Of these four, the middle two have
the convenient asset that they are evenly divisible into whole centuries, which is an
advantage when running data quality controls. But theoretical considerations must
be brought to bear on this choice. Preferably, the generational unit should be such a
dimension that correspondences can be established between events and conditions
operating at the aggregate level and developmental experiences and changes occurring at the individual level. An excellent illustration of this correspondence is the
generational analysis put forward by Ortega y Gasset ([1933] 1962), who argued
for fifteen-year generations that could then be integrated with a five-stage partition

of a human life: childhood at 0–15 years, youth at 15–30 years, initiation at 30–45 years, dominance at 45–60 years, and old age at 60–75 years. Here the initiation phase is that of optimal creativity, whereas the dominance phase is that of maximal leadership. Having synchronized personal development with the fifteen-year periodization of the larger milieu, Ortega could discuss (albeit, in his case, qualitatively) the interplay between the two levels of individual growth and historical movement.

A similar scheme has been offered that partitions the human life into three longitudinal phases—developmental, productive, and consolidative—which are likewise interlinked with generational changes, only this time by twenty-year periods (Simonton 1984c). If historical figures are assigned to that generation in which they were forty (or would have attained forty), then individuals at generation g will average around 20 in generation $g - 1$ and around 60 in generation $g + 1$, which numbers reasonably approximate the central ages for the three longitudinal phases: The developmental period falls between 10 and 30, the productive between 30 and 50, and the consolidative between 50 and 70. Moreover, just as in Ortega's framework, this scheme can be used to assay developmental influences. Personalities who are in their productive period at generation g are in their developmental period in generation $g - 1$, so that political, cultural, and economic events and conditions in the latter generation might be found that affect the level of activity in the former generation. Besides providing a correspondence between individual and aggregate levels, this definition has the advantage that twenty-year periods are closer to what most researchers intend as a reasonable size for a generational unit.

The definition of the time-series unit is much more problematic than the definition of a cross-sectional unit, since most entities are discrete, whereas time is continuous. Only when the course of a phenomenon is subdivided by institutional—as by successive Congresses or presidential administrations—can the partitioning of history be in some sense "natural." Still, since so many propositions are expressed in longitudinal terms, there is no other choice but to confront the issues head on before dealing with empirical tests.

Mixed Units

In the abstract, cross-sectional and time-series units may be decided upon separately. The temporal course of any cross-sectional unit can be partitioned into time-series units of any duration. In concrete studies, however, the choice of the appropriate units across and within units tends to be integrated. Generally, the bigger the spatial unit, the larger the possible temporal unit. To illustrate, when studying the careers of creators, it makes no sense to use units a century long, but rather decades or half decades (for example, Dennis 1966; Lehman 1953). And even if one would normally employ large time units for large spatial units—generations for civilizations, decades for nations—there is no reason why smaller time units, like years, could not be used. The primary restriction would simply be the avoidance of floor effects from an insufficiency of pertinent events. Hence, there is great flexibility. Often different combinations of spatial and temporal units will be exploited in the same investigation in order to attack a problem from as many angles as possible. For instance, an inquiry into the vice-presidential succession effect incorporated a time-series analysis of one hundred consecutive congressional units, a cross-sectional analysis of forty-nine president-vice-president teams, and cross-sectional analysis of sixty-nine presidents and vice-presidents taken separately (Simonton 1985c). That the various kinds of units can be integrated into a single research design complicates matters. Sometimes this mixture merges individual and aggregate data in one analysis; other times cross-sectional and time-series data are married.

Individual-aggregate analyses. G. W. F. Hegel ([1821] 1952, 149) offered the following compromise in the classic debate between genius and zeitgeist theorists: "The great man of the age is the one who can put into words the will of his age, tell the age what its will is, and accomplish it. What he does is the heart and essence of his age, he actualizes his age." Voltaire, who according to one biographer was famous precisely because he was "so effectively the spokesman of his age, so characteristically its representative, so completely its embodiment" (Redman 1968, 40) is an example. These statements, both general and specific, combine two contrary levels of analysis. At the individual level, the genius towers over his or her contemporaries, commanding the ear of an entire age that seeks an articulate champion of inchoate thoughts. At the aggregate level, the giant sociocultural milieu acts on the puny individual. How can generalizations like these be accommodated by a single unit of analysis? The solution is to unify the two levels in one design.

A study of 2,012 Western philosophers demonstrates how this might be accomplished (Simonton 1976f). The basic goal was to determine why some thinkers are far more eminent than others are: Aristotle outclassed his contemporary Xenocrates, just as Descartes exerted far more influence than his contemporary Henri de Roy. So the fundamental unit of analysis must be the individual. These thinkers could then be differentiated on several individual characteristics besides fame, like the breadth and originality of their philosophical systems. Yet each thinker was also assigned to a generation in which he or she flourished to gauge the impact of the cultural and political context. More crucial were measures of how the philosopher's own beliefs matched those of his or her predecessors, contemporaries, and successors, comparing the philosophical positions of each thinker to the prevailing zeitgeist at the aggregate level of the entire intellectual community before, during, and after the thinker's adult career. Interestingly, the analysis revealed that Hegel was off the mark: The most illustrious intellects tend to be those who least conform to the dominating views of their age! It is the also-rans of intellectual history who best constitute the zeitgeist.

Individual-generational analysis has been applied to questions beyond philosophical creativity. Studies of 772 Western artists (Simonton 1984a) and 696 classical composers (Simonton 1977c) indicated how a creator's success depends on being at the right place at the right time—on being an integral part of a national cultural climax. Varying degrees of aggregation yield other possible combinations of levels.

Cross-sectional time-series. Behavioral scientists of all types often have difficulty conceiving designs that mix different units. Individual-aggregate analyses are complex enough, yet cross-sectional time-series analyses look even more imposing. Here multiple entities are examined across time, although not necessarily at the same historical points. The earliest example in historiometry is likely the "pilot cross-historical survey" of Naroll and others (1971) that investigated why creative activity climbs and descends in civilizations. They took data on four world cultures—Western, Islamic, Indian, and Chinese—and divided the history of each culture into century-sized units. They showed that the appearance of exceptional levels of creativity, as registered by the number of creators per time unit, was positively associated with the level of political fragmentation or the number of sovereign states within the civilization area (see also Schaefer, Babu, and Rao 1977; Simonton 1975e, 1976d, 1976f). This supports Kroeber's (1944, 794) induction that "it is certainly true that high achievements by suppressed nationalities are rather rare" as well as Danilevsky's "second law of the dynamics of great cultures" that "in order for the civilization of a potentially creative group to be conceived and developed, the group and its subgroups must be politically independent" (quoted in Sorokin [1947] 1969, 543). It also smiles on Toynbee's (1946) hypothesis that the rise of massive empire states rings the death knell for a civilization's creative vigor.

For psychologists another application of cross-sectional time series to history enjoys more utility. A cross-section of individual personalities can be analyzed into consecutive age-periods to study how biographical and historical events affect the course of a career. This attack was first launched on ten top classical composers whose lives were partitioned into five-year age periods in order to detect how compositional productivity was enhanced or inhibited by age, biographical stress, physical illness, and political violence, among other potential determinants (Simonton 1977a). Five-year units have also been used to analyze the careers of five British novelists (Porter and Suedfeld 1981), ten distinguished psychologists (Simonton 1985b), and twenty-five absolute monarchs (Simonton 1984f). Because cross-sectional time series slice lives into periods, the number of analytical units can be valid even when the number of cross-sectional entities is small. For example, in the inquiry into the careers of absolute monarchs, the twenty-five rulers together yielded a total of 238 five-year age periods, more than enough to measure the impact of personal age on a leader's political success (Simonton 1984f).

Cross-sectional time-series designs can also be integrated with individual-aggregate designs to construct rich research strategies. The career changes in hundreds of individual creators can be scrutinized against the aggregate backdrop of alterations in the sociocultural milieu. For example, an examination of 15,618 themes in the classical repertoire addressed the hypothesis of Hegel, showing that the dependence of genius on the zeitgeist may hold only earlier in a career (Simonton 1980d). The melodic structure of thematic material for a composer at the onset of a career closely matches the dominating melodic styles of the time. Yet as composers reach maturity, they increasingly find their own unique voice, and so intimacy with the musical milieu diminishes. This growing independence has aesthetic implications insofar as those compositions that go against the musical vogue tend to earn more appreciation by posterity; the genius who spurns the fashions of the day avoids turning unfashionable later. It becomes more excusable, then, that when a violinist griped about one of Beethoven's Razoumovsky quartets—which represent a stark break with the Haydnesque quartets of Opus 18—the composer could respond with the prophetic words "Oh, they are not for you, but for a later age!" (Knight 1973, 67).

One of the disadvantages of historiometry, then, is equally one of its major virtues. Investigators cannot take for granted what the unit of analysis will be, but rather they must always carefully tailor the research design to best fit the hypotheses to be tested. Historiometrics is not for those psychologists who like to play Procrustes by cutting and stretching every research question into an identical, preconceived analytical framework.

Sampling Strategies

Once the unit of analysis is decided, the next choice involves which units to sample. This question is sometimes automatically settled by the intrinsic limitations on the hypothesis. If the abstraction concerns, for example, all Nobel laureates in science, then the whole universe of these prize winners should come under view. This is the strategy of *universal sampling*. A drawback here is that it proves adequate solely when the problem refers to a well-defined population of historical figures. In fact, universal sampling normally works only when the historical generalization contains some built-in restriction in scope, as indicated by proper names or specific dates. When Schlesinger (1948) hypothesized that in United States history "the great Presidents were strong Presidents" (73), he moved from the abstract toward the concrete. This generalization might be extrapolated to political leaders of all kinds, yet we are under no obligation to test the hypothesis on a sample any broader than the three-dozen or so chief executives of a single country.

Where nomothetic hypotheses lack intrinsic boundaries, we must lean on other sampling criteria. To examine all scientists or politicians who ever lived on this planet is virtually impossible. Yet even when the potential subject pool is not overwhelming, we may wish to narrow the choice still more to obtain a more manageable and cost-effective sample size. Additional selection criteria are often sought, deciding most frequently according to the eminence criterion, random selection, and data adequacy.

Eminence Criterion

"What you call 'spirit of the ages' / Is after all the spirit of those sages / In which the mirrored age itself reveals," said Goethe ([1808–32] 1952, 16). Accordingly, if we wish to understand how individuals participate in the meanderings of events we call history, perhaps the best place to begin is with those individuals who have made history happen most, through their thoughts and actions. The oldest and most persistent criterion for selecting subjects has been eminence: Quetelet ([1835] 1968), when tabulating how dramatic output varies with age, said that he would confine the sample by considering only "those works truly deserving of mention which are given in the Repertory of Picard for France, and the British Theatre for England" (book 3, 75). Almost a century later, Cox (1926) was deciding who would be in her exclusive sampling of 301 geniuses, and she began with those names at the top of J. M. Cattell's (1903) ranking of historical personalities.

More recent investigators have continued this practice in a diversity of ways. When Eisenstadt (1978) examined how orphanhood contributed to the development of notables, he took those individuals who had at least one column in an encyclopedia, obtaining thereby 699 figures in all domains of attainment. When the Goertzels wanted to study the developmental factors behind achieved eminence in the twentieth-century world, they sampled only those persons who were notable enough to have biographies written about them in public libraries, or around four hundred individuals for one inquiry (Goertzel and Goertzel 1962) and around three hundred for a follow-up (Goertzel, Goertzel, and Goertzel 1978). As the sample sizes indicate, the eminence criterion does not always ensure a small number of subjects. On the contrary, when the illustrious are accompanied by their less obscure but still notable colleagues, the samples may run into the thousands. There are at least 2,012 thinkers who exerted some influence on Western intellectual history, and at least 2,026 scientists and inventors boast a permanent spot in the annals of science.

Often the investigator must reduce the sample size by making the selection criteria more stringent still: The cast must not only be eminent but call only the greatest of the illustrious. Thus, one study was limited to the fifty most famous American neurosurgeons (R. Davis 1987). Another narrowed attention to the ten most highly ranked composers (Simonton 1977a), and yet another concentrated on the ten psychologists who were most highly cited in the research literature (Simonton 1985c). Indeed, the investigator can always isolate a single creator or leader for examination. Of course, when we are dealing with sample sizes smaller than a dozen individuals, the unit of analysis is seldom the individual, but rather a creative product or leadership action. Even so, by applying the eminence criterion to the selection of individuals we automatically change the potential supply of smaller analytical units into which those individuals' careers are partitioned.

The eminence criterion is the most popular deciding factor. The more famous the historical figure, the more biographical information is available; the stars of history are literally well known. For instance, Napoleon was ranked by Cattell as one of the most renowned individuals of all time; "since the beginning of the 20th century, more than 200,000 volumes have been published on Napoleon and his times" (Godechot 1974, 838). The reliability of data abstracted from biographical sources is therefore positively correlated with the distinction of the biographees (Cox 1926; Simonton 1976a). Moreover, to understand how certain individuals manage to impose their personalities on history, we can profitably examine the supreme exemplars of the phenomenon. The first prerequisite of any theory of creativity is that it successfully handle the life of Descartes, Shakespeare, Beethoven, and Michelangelo. The first requirement for a theory of leadership is that it adequately deal with Napoleon, Lincoln, Luther, and Garibaldi. If the more illustrious figures are atypical of the also-rans, then the former are preferred over the latter. Since by some criteria, the most distinguished representatives of an achievement domain are rather typical of the whole anyway (Simonton 1986b), the eminence criterion urges the researcher to start with the crucial subjects before descending to the less secure test cases.

Admittedly, this rule for selection has its liabilities. When eminence is gauged by the amount of space a subject gets in a standard reference, biases are likely. Some contaminants are ethnocentric, given that more space may be allotted to compatriots than to foreigners (Sorokin 1937–41, vol. 1, 143). Cox (1926) included 131 citizens of Great Britain and the United States among her 301 geniuses, and Eisenstadt (1978) had 313 of the same two nationalities among his 699. Drastic disproportions may also exist in the coverage of diverse activities. It is far easier to narrate a politician's career or to give a synopsis of a writer's key works than it is to describe what happens in a musical composition or a painting, and space allocations are assigned accordingly. Cox (1926) collected 103 poets, novelists, and essayists, along with 85 political and military leaders, but only 13 artists and 11 musicians; Eisenstadt (1978) gathered 251 literary figures and 279 political and military luminaries, but merely 57 artists and 23 composers.

Fortunately, there are several ways to deal with such instances of over- and underinclusion. One route is to introduce statistical controls. Another approach imposes some stratification scheme over the eminence criterion. For example, a study of revolutionaries first identified key events—such as the American, Russian, Chinese, and Cuban revolutions—and then picked the most prominent figures in each, thus avoiding the embarrassment of obtaining a sample consisting solely of American revolutionaries (Suedfeld and Rank 1976). Another study comparing scientific and literary creativity first adjusted the standards so that creators in the two groups were almost equally represented (Raskin 1936). Therefore, the eminence criterion remains valuable even if it must be accompanied by further selection criteria to attain a desirable representation of persons in the several national and achievement areas.

Random Selection

The eminence criterion seems far removed from the strategy considered ideal in psychology—random sampling. For example, opinion surveys, such as those conducted by professional polling organizations, aspire to get a sample of respondents that is for all practical purposes a random draw from the population. Moreover, inferential statistics usually posits that each member of the total population has an equal probability of entering the restricted sample. Because historiometry prefers the eminence criterion, its orientation here is more in tune with the humanities.

The rationale for randomly selecting analytical units is to acquire a sample representative of the population to avoid a systematically biased sample. In historiometry, however, random selection does not necessarily achieve this aim. The best representatives of creativity are those who are most universally recognized as creative geniuses; the most representative leaders are those whose actions have led history along new paths. Hence, it is best to use the most typical exemplars of a phenomenon and then move to the less characteristic examples until a proper sample size is obtained. Otherwise the sample would not be representative. Suppose an inquiry into philosophical achievement randomly sampled 10 percent of the thousands of thinkers available, by chance alone including Xenocrates and de Roy but excluding Aristotle and Descartes. Certainly the consequence would be a sample far less persuasive than if an eminence criterion were imposed that places Aristotle and Descartes securely in the inquiry. The sampling strategy that ensures that the "brightest and the best" will be examined should certainly prove more convincing. The final decision is thus made not on the properties of random samples but on the requirements of scientific persuasiveness.

This argument applies to cross-sectional units, yet a random selection procedure is seldom advisable for time-series units. Most of the techniques developed for time series presume that the analyses are conducted on contiguous time units, preferably also equally spaced—a data arrangement unattainable under random sampling. Nonetheless, special situations arise where random selection is extremely helpful, for example, in the content analysis of creative products and primary documents like letters and speeches. Where there is no reason to favor one portion as more representative than another, sections of text may be randomly chosen, a strategy seen repeatedly in studies requiring complex content analyses (for example, Martindale 1975). Yet even in content analysis it is sometimes possible to select a manageable set of representative texts without random sampling—as in the work on presidential leadership that exploits highly indicative inaugural or state-of-the-union addresses (for example, Winter 1987b).

Data Adequacy

Like the paleontological record, the historical record has irksome gaps. Therefore, no matter how the previous two sampling criteria are administered, the ultimate arbitrator is whether we can obtain scientifically adequate data on the units sampled. This is most apparent in the time-series analysis of civilizations—for the farther back we go, the less we know. The history of every culture begins in the mists of legend and progresses in fits and starts toward the rich data base of contemporary times. A generational analysis based on Chinese history cannot be extended back to the Shang dynasty that ruled around four millennia ago, no more than a time series founded on European history can realistically commence with Homer. At some point the data become insufficient and too inaccurate to support even counts of basic events.

Often this inadequacy reveals itself in floor effects, wherein a large percentage of the time units take on zero values for key variables, as if nothing had happened! Also, one begins increasingly to stumble across dates of the type "somewhere between the X and Y centuries," as well as to encounter a profusion of anonymous achievements or proper names that have mythological status only. When these warning signs appear, the investigator should shorten the time series so that more adequate measures obtain. Because any truncation is perforce arbitrary, the researcher may often wish to analyze the data on time series of various lengths to demonstrate that the choice of cut-offs does not substantially affect the outcome of the hypothesis tests. For instance, a time-series analysis of creativity and leadership in Chinese civilization examined 141 generations from 840 B.C. to A.D. 1979 and 124 generations from 600 B.C. to A.D. 1879, with the same results in both cases (Simonton 1988c).

Frequently the time series may be shortened, not so much because the data become unreliable but because the phenomenon under investigation established a conspicuous presence farther along the range. For instance, studies of executive veto behavior usually examine all presidential administrations since Washington as well as the limited range of administrations beginning with Tyler or Lincoln in which the executive veto first became a frequently exploited piece of executive equipment (Copeland 1983; Simonton 1987c). One inquiry into presidential veto behavior even found it desirable to exclude all presidents before Truman, which, of course, necessitated that the unit of analysis be shifted from the Congress or year to the individual veto act (Rohde and Simon 1985). In the extreme case, the data may only be sufficiently ample for contemporaries, thereby making a strict historiometric analysis off limits.

What this last example implies is that data adequacy is contingent on something else besides how far back one looks. This sampling criterion depends equally on the nature of the data to be collected. History records some types of events earlier and better than others. It first and foremost is a record of dramatic political events that drastically affect the lives of every one in a society. Cultural events, which more often appeal to a smaller elite, get a slow start in the chronicles. In addition, no matter how detailed the annals, some events simply cannot be conspicuous until a civilization or society reaches a certain level of complexity or sophistication. While it is technically possible to analyze scientific contributions extending back to classical Greece, researchers more often begin their analyses with Copernicus, and sometimes certain disciplines fail to provide sufficient data until the last hundred years (Price 1978; Simonton 1975d). This holds for psychology, a field that has "a long past but a short history" (for example, Simonton 1985b; Suedfeld 1985; Zusne 1976). Ironically, it can also happen that events are too recent for there to be quality information on a subject. If one is tabulating the appearance of eminent achievers in each generation, the number of data sources may rapidly diminish as the present nears, requiring that the most recent generations be deleted (for example, Simonton 1975e, 1988c). Likewise, in studying how personality relates to veto usage in consecutive presidential administrations, we cannot include an incumbent president who is still entering vetoed bills into his personal diary (Simonton 1987c).

The problem of data adequacy also affects cross-sectional data. Most of the time the eminence criterion will help ensure that sufficient data, but often other criteria must also be imposed. When Cox (1926) put together her elite sample, she began by taking only those in the upper ranks of Cattell's (1903) list and by excluding those born before 1450. Yet after imposing these Draconian sampling rules, Cox was still compelled to delete a creator as illustrious as William Shakespeare for the inescapable reason that virtually nothing is known about his early years, making even the roughest estimation of his childhood IQ totally impossible. When Cox sought to assign scores on dozens of personality traits, she was obliged to cut the sample yet further, to a privileged one hundred for whom the record was sufficiently ample. Such considerations frequently compel the investigator to restrict a sample to a specific area of achievement or even to confine attention to the achievers of a single civilization or nationality.

It occasionally happens, too, that the hypotheses under investigation dictate that only certain cross-sectional cases will provide effective empirical tests. For instance, one of the difficulties in researching the relation between age and leadership is that leaders seldom serve very long in their nation's highest office, nor do they always enjoy sufficient power to exert their will over political events. The solution is to examine leaders who served long enough that an age curve can be reliably estimated and who had superior political power. Hence, one inquiry took as its sample solely absolute monarchs like Louis XIV and then further confined the sample to those twenty-five European monarchs who reigned at least thirty-six years, with an average tenure of forty-three years (Simonton 1984f). Such a narrowly selected sample exhibited developmental changes that could not be found in American presidents, whose average term in office is only a half-dozen years and only once reached a dozen years.

The drastic reduction in sample size owing to scanty data is especially problematic in content analytical studies of personal documents. Numerous measurement techniques require ample collections of speeches, letters, diaries, or other primary verbal statements. Sadly, however, many historical figures of magnitude are *not* apt to leave anything revealing about themselves. Thomas Jefferson was by all accounts tremendously in love with his wife and chose never to marry again after her tragic early death; he also opted to destroy all the letters that had been exchanged between them, denying subsequent scholars access to the more personal side of this most enigmatic man. Even when the investigator needs only to analyze the content of public statements by public figures, empty places may appear in the sample. Winter (1987b) may have devised a way to determine an incumbent's motivational profile on the basis of the inaugural address, however, five chief executives never delivered an address and therefore left nothing to analyze.

As previously noted, the researcher must display appreciable flexibility in choosing the proper analytical unit; the same openness must be seen in the sampling strategies that determine specific units for examination. In both instances, the decisions must be predicated on the quality of the historical data along with the nature of the scientific propositions studied. As a consequence, even when the same basic phenomenon is subjected to repeated scrutiny, the definitions and sampling of units may vary from study to study. This diversity is displayed by the investigations into classical music that have inspected cross-sections of 696 composers (Simonton 1977c), 80 composers (Schubert, Wagner, and Schubert 1977), or 76 composers (Hayes 1981, 212–14); cross-sections of 15,618 themes by 479 composers (Simonton 1980d), 5,046 themes by 10 composers (Simonton 1980c), 2,240 themes by 7 composers (Paisley 1964), or 252 themes by 252 composers (Martindale and Uemura 1983); and cross-sections of 1,935 compositions by 172 composers (Simonton 1986a), 105 compositions by 1 composer (Simonton 1987b), or 44 compositions by 14 composers (Cerulo 1984). The freedom of unit definitions and sample size is limited only by the raw data and the psychologist's imagination and determination.

Archival Compilation

Given a research design, the next step demands far more self-discipline and determination than intellect: The raw data must be collected in a form that can be readily quantified. This usually means going to archives and compiling a data base on the phenomenon. Occasionally the data will be ready-made, and all the researcher will have to is use it, yielding a "secondary analysis" of data previously compiled by others. Examples include the various investigations that have grown directly out of the Woods (1906) data (Simonton 1983d; Thorndike 1936), the Cox (1926) data (McCurdy 1960; Simonton 1976a; R. K. White 1931), the Thorndike (1950) data (Knapp 1962), and the Sorokin (1937–41) data (Klingemann, Mohler, and Weber 1982; Martindale 1975; Simonton 1976e).

Indeed, one of the genuine assets of historiometric research is something that can be called *unit replicability*. In most psychological studies, the sample of subjects is constantly changing, so that investigators cannot determine whether the results would have been the same had another factor been assessed. The sole option is to gather data on a new batch of volunteers or respondents with the new variable added. In historiometry, everyone has direct access to the same group of individuals, making starting all over again unnecessary. For instance, a cottage industry has developed around how economic events influence the incumbent president's standing in the polls of American citizens (Monroe 1984). Each successive investigator adds new variables or novel methodological refinements but uses the same initial data base so that discrepancies cannot result from reliance on different test cases.

If the research question is off the beaten track, nonetheless, the investigator will seldom have any other recourse than to start the data compilation from zero. On compiling raw information, a few tips may be useful (see also Floud 1973, chap. 2). Because most historiometry, like most historiography, must begin with a chronology of relevant events, it is fortunate that most libraries abound in volumes that provide exhaustive chronological tables. Some of these sources aim at presenting all key events of world civilization (for example, Grun 1975; Langer 1972; Mayer 1949; Steinberg 1964; N. Williams 1968, 1969). Others focus on a particular national heritage or achievement domain, such as almanacs, time tables, and encyclopedias of American history (for example, Carruth 1979; Kull and Kull 1952; Morris 1976; Schlesinger 1983; Urdang 1981) or chronologies, biographical dictionaries, and encyclopedias of science (for example, Darmstaedter 1908; Feldhaus 1904; Parkinson 1985; T. I. Williams 1974) or of battles (Dupuy and Dupuy 1970; Eggenberger 1967; Harbottle 1971). In select topic areas, more specialized fact books proliferate, like the data on the American presidents (for example, Kane 1974; Taylor 1972). Detailed information is even available for single individuals. For instance, every major composer in the classical repertoire has had his works catalogued and dated and his life converted into chronologies. Volumes offer the collected works, complete correspondence, and comprehensive speeches of many notable figures.

But a caveat: Data sources must be picked carefully. Whenever possible, information from more than one reference should be used, permitting cross-checks. Particularly with biographical data, different biographers will often disseminate contrary interpretations of the same historical personality, differences that are reflected in their choices of which events to mention and which to omit. For transhistorical surveys, like generational analyses of whole civilizations, care must be taken to employ only sources that cover the whole period under scrutiny. For instance, studies of Chinese civilization should exclude works that cover only a single dynasty, such as Tang or Song, rather than the whole of Chinese history (Simonton 1988c; Ting 1986). The researcher must display common sense in collating empirical materials. Historiometry differs not one iota from either history or science on this score.

Everyone who has engaged in the quantitative analysis of historical data must confess that much tiresome work is mandatory (Aydellote 1971, 8). Considerable thought must be given to research design, and hours of labor committed to the compilation of information from archives. Unfortunately, the laboriousness of data collection cannot often be lessened by research assistants. Those cognizant of essential historical facts—that more than one major composer is named Bach (J. S., C. P. E., J. C., W. F., and others); that Leonardo Vinci was an obscure musician, but Leonardo *da* Vinci an illustrious artist; that George Sand and George Eliot were both women; that Lord Kelvin is the same person as William Thomson, and Count Rumford the same as Benjamin Thompson; that Jesus of Nazareth was born a handful of years "before Christ" (B.C.) and that there exists no 0 B.C./A.D.; or that Ronald Reagan was the fortieth president but only the thirty-ninth man to be president—are not always the same individuals who are keen on scientific abstraction and mathematical precision.

More critical, historiometricians should always stay close to their data. Consistent contact with the particulars of history is essential for effective research. Complete familiarity with the facts facilitates improvements in sampling and measurement strategies and can even inspire new hypotheses. Sprinkled throughout most histories and biographies are generalizations that purport to be laws of human behavior and hence represent suggestions for further research. So investigators on any project must continue to work "at the bench" rather than rely on subordinates. No first-class historiometric study in the past century and a half has been published by a researcher who avoided on-hands contact with the raw data. Thomas Edison once said that "genius is one per cent inspiration and ninty-nine per cent perspiration." The scientific study of genius and other historical phenomena just may entail the same proportions of brain and brawn.

Early historiometry too often assumed a rather primitive guise: the compilation of lists, reminiscent of the inductive strategy recommended by Francis Bacon in his 1620 *Novum Organum*. Hence, even though Galton (1869) performed some statistical manipulations on the eminent figures that parade in his *Hereditary Genius*, much of the book's persuasiveness stems from the sheer weight of the lists showing family connections. Opponents of this genius theory merely repeated the practice, whether we look at the list of nearly 150 putative multiples in science and technology compiled by Ogburn and Thomas (1922) or the long lists of geniuses coalescing into configurations gathered by Kroeber (1944). Yet the scholar is ever in danger of committing the "Baconian fallacy" when he or she does nothing more than arrange names, dates, and places across pages of text (Fischer 1970, 4–8). The data may not "speak for themselves," but instead they may require goading and coaching, and the first step in a more developed analysis is quantification. Indeed, sometimes just assigning numbers to a phenomenon alters the overall perspective instantaneously, a possibility depicted in the following conversation that James Boswell ([1791] 1952, 507–8) recorded in his *Life of Johnson:*

> BOSWELL. Sir Alexander Dick tells me, that he remembers having a thousand people in a year to dine at his house: that is, reckoning each person as one, each time that he dined there.
> JOHNSON. That, Sir, is about three a day.
> BOSWELL. How your statement lessens the idea.
> JOHNSON. That, Sir, is the good of counting. It brings everything to a certainty, which before floated in the mind indefinitely.

Frequently a hypothesis that previously looked secure by a qualitative inspection of the data becomes obviously invalid once the same facts convert into quantitative form. Thus, the traditional zeitgeist interpretation of multiple discovery and invention was easily cast into doubt simply by counting how often multiples actually occur (Schmookler 1966, chap. 10; Simonton 1988e, chap. 6). The quantitative analyses of family pedigrees and historical contiguities for creators and leaders compelled major qualifications in the theories cherished by both Galton and his opponent Kroeber (Bramwell 1948; Simonton 1983d, 1988c). Edward L. Thorndike affirmed that "whatever exists must exist in some quantity, and therefore can be measured" (quoted in G. Murphy 1968, 14), whereas all of these instances imply that the "can" should be replaced with a "must" if we wish to avoid inferential mistakes. This chapter therefore examines (1) the various breeds of measurement scales that can be applied to historical data and (2) the chief measurement sources for these quantifications.

Measurement Scales

It has become standard in psychometrics to distinguish among four types of scales (Nunnally 1978). All scales concern how numbers are assigned to phenomena, yet they differ in the conceptual sophistication required for the quantification to take place. The scales accordingly vary in the complexity of the statistical analyses they can support. In ascending order, these are the nominal, ordinal, interval, and ratio scales.

Nominal Measures

Science begins with a nomenclature by which phenomena are described and then proceeds to the classification of events into categories. Nominal scales are part of this fundamental process by which names are assigned and class membership allotted. Such measures represent the smoothest possible transition, the tiniest quantum leap, from qualitative to quantitative analysis, accomplishing the explicit designation of whether or not a given entity possesses a particular attribute. Sometimes the resulting measure is dichotomous, that is, units can be sorted into two mutually exclusive classes, such as gender, which can be either male or female. For instance, an examination of the transfer of individual differences across generations in hereditary monarchies had to distinguish kings from queens, owing to gender contrasts in such inheritance (Simonton 1983d). Other examples include having variables that code whether eminence was achieved as a creator or as a leader (Simonton 1976a), a national anthem was a march or a hymn (Cerulo 1988), revolutionaries as either successes or failures (Suedfeld and Rank 1976), and presidents as assassinated or not (Kennedy and Rice 1988).

In such situations, a *dummy variable* should be used that equals unity (1) when a characteristic attribute is present and that equals zero (0) when the attribute is absent. The critical point here is that the assignment of numbers to cases does not have genuine numerical significance. The numbers are nominal insofar as they do no more than name or classify. Hence, to label kings with 1's and queens with 0's tells us absolutely nothing about male and female monarchs. We could just as easily reverse the numerical allotments without altering the statistical results substantively. Where applicable, however, it is less confusing to have unity represent presence and zero represent absence—a guise of Boolean algebra in which 1 = true and 0 = false. To have the variable "assassinated" equal 1 if the leader was murdered and equal 0 if otherwise, we make unity denote the presence of a distinct event that most leaders manage to avoid.

Matters become more complicated, naturally, when nominal scales contain more than two possibilities. A study of scientific creativity might have to handle differences across several disciplines, such as mathematics, astronomy, physics, chemistry, biology, medicine, and technology. Happily, the coding of such "polychotomous" nominal scales can be carried out simply by translating the multilevel distinctions into a series of dichotomous zero-one dummy variables. For example, one dummy variable might code whether or not the scientist was a mathematician, another whether or not the individual was a physicist, and so forth. Classifications of any number of categories can be converted into quantitative form for statistical analyses. This transformation normally entails the creation of zero-one dummy variables, where each dummy registers the presence or absence of some attribute or the membership or nonmembership in a single category of the classification scheme (see Cohen and Cohen 1983, chap. 5).

Nominal scales may represent the most primitive of all measures, but problems still prevent easy application to concrete historical data. The most trying difficulty is that category membership is not always readily detected. In the literature on cross-cultural surveys, there has been considerable discussion of how the appearance or absence of a characteristic can be inferred from incomplete information (Naroll 1968; Whiting 1968). Should an ethnography not mention rape at all in a particular culture, does that mean that this crime did not occur? Or is it just a matter that the ethnographer (or informant) was squeamish about noting? Likewise, if a biography fails to mention whether a historical figure lost a parent at an early age, does this signify conclusively that orphanhood was not a part of the individual's development? Or does it merely reflect the biographer's skimpy treatment of childhood experiences? Many of the criteria used to pry out an answer from cross-cultural surveys can also be applied to historiometrics. If the ethnographer provides rich details about sexual practices and crimes against persons in a given culture and still fails to observe rape, then rape may not be a prominent behavior in that society. Similarly, if the biographer provides tremendous detail about early childhood, including birth order, education, and parental backgrounds, then one can infer the absence of orphanhood with more assurance. Normally, some minimal criterion must be established about what information must be present before the absence of a trait can be inferred solely on the basis of circumstantial evidence.

The bottom line is that nominal measurement, no matter how rudimentary, cannot proceed without adequate data. In addition, nominal scales demand a clear idea of how the categories can be precisely delineated. Indeed, one of the chief virtues of defining nominal scales is that it makes investigators think long and hard about exactly what they mean by certain vague concepts. As a case in point, much of the controversy concerning the best interpretation of the multiples phenomenon depends on what counts as a multiple. For those who favor extremely generic definitions of discoveries and inventions, multiples are ubiquitous (Graber 1985; Lamb and Easton 1984), while for those who restrict the term to those contributions that are virtually identical (or at least homologous rather than analogous), multiples are so rare as to present no serious challenge to a genius theory of scientific progress (Patinkin 1983, 1985; Schmookler 1966, chap. 10). Was Newton's calculus truly identical to that of Leibniz—so interchangeable that the growth of higher mathematics would have been the same if either Newton or Leibniz had died in the crib? Are the evolutionary theories of Darwin and Wallace so equivalent that the author of the theory becomes irrelevant? The answers to questions like these can often plunge the researcher into a labyrinth of perplexing philosophical issues (Simonton 1988e, chap. 6). Yet this knotty enigma entails nothing more than a dichotomous classification of contributions into multiples and singletons. Hence, the fact that nominal scales can be quantified cannot be taken as an excuse for the researcher to circumvent the big questions about how historical events can be categorized in the first place.

Ordinal Measures

In truth, a nominal scale is frequently a higher-order scale in disguise. Take the situation where the goal is to determine why some U.S. presidents are great whereas others fall short. One option might be to define a dummy variable that equals 1 if a chief executive can boast a portrait by Gutzon Borglum on the side of Mount Rushmore but equals 0 if not. Hence, Washington, Jefferson, Lincoln, and Theodore Roosevelt would all earn a 1 on the greatness scale, the remaining nearly three dozen presidents, a 0. It should be obvious that this dummy variable has a different status than, say, one that codes gender in a zero-one fashion, where the assignment has no genuine significance but serves solely as a mathematical trick to convert names to numbers. In the instance of the dichotomous greatness measure, however, matters are to the contrary: The four honored presidents have something the omitted chief executives do not, namely the quality of greatness. Because 1 > 0 and greatness surpasses mediocrity, the variable coding is no longer completely arbitrary, given that a certain (although vague) isomorphism links the variable values with the historical phenomenon. What this Mount Rushmore scale roughly approximates is not a nominal but an ordinal scale. Variables are ordinal whenever entities can be ranked according to their possession of an attribute so that numbers can be assigned to those entities that exhibit precisely the same rankings.

In genuine ordinal scales each unit is allotted a unique number showing the unit's placement with respect to all other units for the characteristic assessed. The two-level scale provided has too many tied ranks: four presidents tied for first place and thirty-five presidents tied for last place. Nonetheless, starting with Schle-singer's polls of historians and political scientists (1948, 1962b) and continuing through the two most recent rankings published in R. Murray and Blessing (1983), American chief executives have been ranked from Franklin D. Roosevelt and Abraham Lincoln to Grant and Harding. Typical ranks are shown in table 3.1. In similar fashion, Farnsworth, after polling musicologists, ranked the one hundred most distinguished classical composers from Bach, Beethoven, and Mozart at the top to Clementi and Tartini (1969) (table 3.2).

These two rankings are typical in that the numbers assigned usually run in the reverse direction of the attribute evaluated. Thus, in the ranking of the presidents, Lincoln usually gets a 1 and Harding a number equal to the total sample size; likewise in the ranking of composers, Bach receives a 1 against Tartini's score of nearly a hundred times greater. This reversal is done simply for its intuitive appeal. The average person on the street can readily understand the concept of being "number one" versus "coming in last place," so the ranks are given numbers as if those evaluated represented ranked chess players. Nevertheless, for ordinal data to become truly useful in statistical analyses, the assigned numbers are inverted. Inversion makes the numbers correspond (roughly) to how much of a quality a unit contains.

For some variables, ordinal scales naturally correspond to the phenomenon of interest. As an example, if the object is to discover how an individual's birth order affects the development of creativity or leadership, the order that a person entered the family is clearly an ordinal characteristic. People speak of the first child, the second, and so on down to the last born (though the occasional emergence of twins indicates that tied ranks are conceivable). Nonetheless, for other variables, ordinal scales may depart considerably from an optimal mode of measurement. In rankings of presidential greatness, for instance, the placement of those at the top and the bottom of the list is often clear, whereas those in the middle range, the mediocre chief executives, are less well differentiated, as indicated by the intrusion of tied ranks and variable ordinal placements from one ranking to another. Similarly, the most illustrious composers in the classical repertoire can be readily ranked, but as the ordinal measure descends into the truly esoteric, tied ranks abound, as is apparent in table 3.2. Ordinal scales fail to capture the true separation of individuals on the attribute being assessed, which requires more sophisticated measurement.

Ordinal scales should not be spurned, however, even when applied to phenomena where this mode of quantification is approximate at best. Many scientific disciplines saw their first advances when they moved from nominal to ordinal measures, a definite form of progress. The Mohs hardness scale in mineralogy assigned numbers according to whether a test substance could be scratched by a range of materials from diamond (10) to talc (1), and the stellar magnitudes assigned by astronomers before the introduction of photometers were also ordinal.

Table 3.1 *Rankings of U.S. Presidents*

President	Schlesinger 1948	Schlesinger 1962	Bailey-Kynerd	Porter	Chicago Tribune
1. Washington	2	2	1	2	2
2. J. Adams	9	10	21	10	15c
3. Jefferson	5	5	5	4	5
4. Madison	14	12	22	13	17
5. Monroe	12	18	8	17	16c
6. J. Q. Adams	11	13	30	18	19
7. Jackson	6	6	7	7	7
8. Van Buren	15	17	11	19	18
9. W. Harrison	—	—	—	—	—
10. Tyler	22	25	18	28	28
11. Polk	10	8a	17	9	10
12. Taylor	25	24	23	27	26
13. Fillmore	24	26	19	29	31
14. Pierce	27	28	26	33	33
15. Buchanan	26	29	27	35	34
16. Lincoln	1	1	2	1	1
17. A. Johnson	19	23	31	31	30
18. Grant	28	30	24	32	32
19. Hayes	13	14	9	20	22
20. Garfield	—	—	—	—	—
21. Arthur	17	21b	14	24	24
22. Cleveland	8	11	15	15	13
23. B. Harrison	21	20	20	25	25
24. McKinley	18	15	10	16	11
25. T. Roosevelt	7	7	4	5	4
26. Taft	16	16	16	21	20
27. Wilson	4	4	6	6	6
28. Harding	29	31	29	36	36
29. Coolidge	23	27	25	30	29
30. Hoover	20	19	28	22	21
31. F. Roosevelt	3	3	3	3	3
32. Truman	—	9a	12	8	8
33. Eisenhower	—	22b	13	12	9
34. Kennedy	—	—	—	14	14
35. L. Johnson	—	—	—	11	12
36. Nixon	—	—	—	34	35
37. Ford	—	—	—	26	23
38. Carter	—	—	—	23	27

Source: Rankings taken from Schlesinger (1948), Schlesinger (1962), Kynerd's (1971) interpretation of Bailey (1966), and Murray and Blessing's (1983) presentations of the Porter (1981) and *Chicago Tribune* (1982) surveys.
aPolk and Truman actually tied.
bArthur and Eisenhower actually tied.
cJ. Adams and Monroe actually tied.

Table 3.2 *All-time Eminence Rankings of Classical Composers*

1. J. S. Bach	26. Machaut	50.5 Fauré	77. Praetorius
2. Beethoven	27. Schütz	52. Dowland	77. Borodin
3. Mozart	28. Liszt	53. C. P. E. Bach	77. Gounod
4. J. Haydn	29. Mussorsky	54. Rimsky-Korsakov	79. M. Haydn
5. Brahms	30. Corelli	55. Perotinus	80.5 Sousa
6. Handel	31. D. Scarlatti	56. Wolf	80.5 Sullivan
7. Debussy	32. Gabrielli	57. Bartók	82.5 Bellini
8. Schubert	33. Couperin	58. Grieg	82.5 Janáček
9. Wagner	34. Gluck	59. Weber	85. Donizetti
10. Chopin	35. Puccini	60. Gibbons	85. Webern
11. Monteverdi	36. Franck	61. Sweelinck	85. Willaert
12. Palestrina	37. Dvořák	62. Schoenberg	87. Offenbach
13. Verdi	38. Buxtehude	63. J. Strauss, Jr.	88.5 Ravel
14. Schumann	39. Bruckner	64. Saint-Saëns	88.5 Delius
15. des Pres	40. Sibelius	65.5 Telemann	91. Elgar
16. de Lassus	41. Rameau	65.5 Lulli	91. Hindemith
17.5 Purcell	42. Frescobaldi	67. Landino	91. Satie
17.5 Berlioz	43. Okeghem	68. MacDowell	93.5 Cherubini
19. R. Strauss	44. Stravinsky	69. J. C. Bach	93.5 Foster
20. Mendelssohn	45. A. Scarlatti	70. Leoninus	95. de Rore
21. Tchaikovsky	46. Dunstable	71. A. Gabrieli	96.5 Boccherini
22. Vivaldi	47. Bizet	72.5 Carissmi	96.5 Franco of Cologne
23. Mahler	48. Gesualdo	72.5 Pergolesi	98.5 Clementi
24. Byrd	49. Rossini	74. Marenzio	98.5 Tartini
25. Dufay	50.5 de Victoria	75. Smetana	(The next 4 are tied)

Note. Adapted from Farnsworth (1969, 228). Copyright 1966 by Music Educators National Conference. Adapted by permission.

Moreover, in many situations ordinal scales provide approximations close enough to reality that false conclusions are not a danger (but see Henry 1982). For instance, greatness correlates with the number of years the president served as a wartime commander-in-chief, no matter whether rankings are used or a superior measurement that considers the actual spacing on greatness (Simonton 1987d).

Interval Measures

When the numerical separation between any two values represents the distance between the two units on the attribute measured, we have an interval scale. A standard example is an individual's assessed IQ. When Cox (1926) held that Napoleon had an IQ as high as 145, Rembrandt 155, and Beethoven 165, she was claiming that the difference between Beethoven and Rembrandt is equal to the difference between Rembrandt and Napoleon; and to learn that Galileo may have boasted an IQ of 185 is tantamount to discovering that he was more brilliant than Beethoven as Beethoven was more brilliant than Napoleon. In an interval scale, the gaps between values carry substantive meaning, contrasting with the ordinal scale where the numbers assigned convey only how the entities might rank along the attribute, for the intervals between successive ranks are arbitrary and therefore devoid of meaning. Of course, an interval scale is always an ordinal scale, too, for one cannot represent the distances between attributes without equally representing the rankings on those attributes.

One useful way of emphasizing the disparity between the two scales is to ask what happens when a scale is subjected to a data transformation. Whereas ordinal properties are preserved by any monotonic transformation, interval properties are only invariant under the more restricted linear transformations. Hence, if we take logarithms of an ordinal scale, the relative placements of the scale are unaffected, but the log-transformation of an interval scale will necessarily squash the intervals between large scores more than those between small scores. Hence, log-transformations of the rankings in tables 3.1 and 3.2 may be made with impunity, while similarly subjecting the IQ scores given earlier would make the difference between Galileo and Beethoven *less* than that between Beethoven and Napoleon. The only permissible operation is a linear transformation, such as adding or subtracting a constant or multiplying or dividing by a constant—manipulations that maintain the relative size of the differences between scores. Because the numbers that compose interval scales possess more meaning, it is far easier to distort their representation of phenomena by interfering with data transformations.

Interval scales are about as commonplace in historiometrics as they are in psychometrics. The IQ estimates that Cox estimated for her 301 geniuses are clear examples. More crude, but still counting as interval approximations, are her assessments of a subset of one hundred geniuses on sixty-seven character traits, where she defined the steps of the trait-rating scale as follows (Cox 1926, 169):

+3   denotes the possession of a very high degree of the quality as compared to the average.

+2   denotes the possession of a degree of the quality distinctly above the average.

+1   denotes the possession of a degree of the quality slightly above the average.

0   denotes the possession of the average degree of the quality among youths in general.

−1   denotes the possession of somewhat less than the average.

−2   denotes the possession of distinctly less than the average.

−3   denotes the lowest degree of the quality as compared with the average.

This type of "rank category" scale, with various adjustments, is common in historiometric research. Woods (1906) rated 395 male and 276 female royalty on the two traits of intellect and virtue using a 10-point integer scale, and Simonton (1986h) had a team of raters assess thirty-nine U.S. presidents on three hundred traits using a seven-point integer scale. Individual creative products or leadership acts can be similarly assessed. For instance, Halsey (1976) rated 4,101 compositions in the classical repertoire on aesthetic significance and listener accessibility using a five-point scale, and work on integrative complexity rates political speeches along a seven-point scale (for example, Tetlock 1981a).

Such ratings provide only crude approximations to true interval scales. Unlike the IQ scores in which a large number of values are allowable, these 5-, 7-, and 10-point scales tend to crush reality into a restricted set of numerical values. One can always expand the number of levels to enhance the precision of the measure, but only by increasing the hardships that judges must face when applying highly differentiated instruments. Surely if Cox had forced her raters to employ a 100-point scale for all sixty-seven traits, the task of assessing the one hundred geniuses might have been insurmountable. Fortunately, the rough nature of these scales usually fails to prevent the researcher from getting the same results obtainable from more elaborate measures. Furthermore, the approximation inherent in individual scale items is frequently alleviated when they can be consolidated into larger scales. For example, the adjectives on which the thirty-nine presidents were assessed could be collapsed into just fourteen personality dimensions, each consisting of enough items that the interval properties of the composite scales are secured (Simonton 1986h). The analogy here again is the psychometric assessment of intelligence; the final composite IQ score is based on the summation of a host of single items that are dichotomously scored as either right or wrong.

Because intervals scales can undergo linear transformations without loss of information, these measures are frequently standardized to facilitate comparisons across different variables or data sets. The classic example is the IQ, which is arbitrarily assigned a mean of 100 and a standard deviation of 16 (or sometimes 15). Hence, an intellect of the caliber of a Leibniz, with an estimated IQ perhaps as high as 205, can boast an IQ about seven standard deviations above the mean IQ (Cox 1926). Another mode is to reset the mean at 50 and the standard deviation at 10, yielding scores that look a lot like percentages. For instance, in table 3.3 we see the scores that thirty-four U.S. presidents received on the three crucial motives of power, achievement, and affiliation through an analysis of inaugural addresses (Winter 1987b).

By far the most popular form of standardization requires that the mean be set at zero and the standard deviation at unity, producing what are often called "z scores." This alteration is accomplished by first subtracting from each score for a case the mean score across all cases and then dividing this difference by the standard deviation across all cases. When a z score is zero, the individual is thus average on a given characteristic; if negative, below average; and if positive, above average. This manner of data presentation is thus fairly intuitive. In fact, Cox's rating scale is an attempt to obtain rough z scores directly from the data rather than through data transformations, for standard scores higher than +3 or less than −3 are extremely rare. To illustrate, we see in table 3.4 some interval ratings of American presidents that have been placed in this standard form (Mar-

Table 3.3   *Motive Imagery Scores for Inaugural Addresses of U.S. Presidents, 1789–1981*

President		Motive scores					
		Standardized			Raw		
	Date	Ach	Aff	Pow	Ach	Aff	Pow
1. Washington	1789	39	54	41	3.85	3.85	4.62
2. J. Adams	1797	39	49	42	3.89	3.03	4.76
3. Jefferson	1801	49	51	51	5.65	3.30	6.59
4. Madison	1809	55	51	57	6.84	3.42	7.69
5. Monroe	1817	57	46	51	7.22	2.41	6.62
6. J. Q. Adams	1825	48	51	37	5.43	3.40	3.74
7. Jackson	1829	43	47	45	4.48	2.69	5.38
8. Van Buren	1837	42	48	40	4.38	2.83	4.38
9. W. Harrison	1841	32	41	40	2.56	1.52	4.31
10. Tyler	—	—	—	—	—	—	—
11. Polk	1845	33	41	50	2.65	1.43	6.32
12. Taylor	1849	53	53	41	6.39	3.65	4.56
13. Fillmore	—	—	—	—	—	—	—
14. Pierce	1853	49	44	50	5.72	2.11	6.33
15. Buchanan	1857	46	47	42	5.05	2.53	4.69
16. Lincoln	1861	36	45	53	3.34	2.23	6.97
17. A. Johnson	—	—	—	—	—	—	—
18. Grant	1869	56	47	36	7.02	2.63	3.51
19. Hayes	1877	51	48	48	6.07	2.83	6.07
20. Garfield	1881	46	35	49	5.09	0.34	6.10
21. Arthur	—	—	—	—	—	—	—
22. Cleveland	1885	53	46	63	6.52	2.37	8.89
23. B. Harrison	1889	37	45	45	3.49	2.18	5.45
24. McKinley	1897	47	41	46	5.30	1.51	5.55
25. T. Roosevelt	1905	62	38	38	8.14	1.02	4.07
26. Taft	1909	44	38	58	4.79	0.92	7.93
27. Wilson	1913	66	49	53	8.83	2.94	7.06
28. Harding	1921	48	57	42	5.41	4.51	4.81
29. Coolidge	1925	44	46	45	4.69	2.47	5.43
30. Hoover	1929	68	45	48	9.18	2.16	5.94
31. F. Roosevelt	1933	53	44	61	6.37	2.12	8.50
32. Truman	1949	56	65	78	6.91	5.99	11.98
33. Eisenhower	1953	43	57	49	4.50	4.50	6.14
34. Kennedy	1961	50	85	77	5.9	9.59	11.81
35. L. Johnson	1965	55	59	49	6.77	4.74	6.09
36. Nixon	1969	66	76	53	8.94	8.00	7.06
37. Ford	—	—	—	—	—	—	—
38. Carter	1977	75	59	59	10.60	4.89	8.16
39. Reagan	1981	60	51	63	7.78	3.28	9.01

Source: Winter (1987b, 198). Copyright 1987 by the American Psychological Association. Adapted by permission.
Note. Ach = achievement, Aff = affiliation, Pow = power. Standardized scores have mean of 50 and standard deviation of 10, whereas the raw scores are expressed in terms of motive images per 1,000 words.

Table 3.4 *Evaluations of U.S. Presidents*

President	\ Standardized Scores						
	1	*2*	*3*	*4*	*5*	*6*	*7*
1. Washington	1.78	0.89	0.44	1.72	0.86	−0.41	0.57
2. J. Adams	0.61	0.41	0.34	0.37	0.26	−0.02	−0.85
3. Jefferson	1.47	1.18	0.91	1.31	1.11	0.81	1.35
4. Madison	0.23	0.05	0.03	0.10	0.02	0.55	0.58
5. Monroe	0.17	−0.02	−0.06	0.13	−0.31	0.40	1.03
6. J. Q. Adams	0.16	−0.22	0.01	−0.24	−0.14	1.18	−1.15
7. Jackson	0.87	1.37	1.51	0.83	1.08	−0.74	−1.40
8. Van Buren	−0.37	−0.34	−0.24	−0.46	−0.56	−0.47	0.19
9. W. Harrison	—	—	—	—	—	—	—
10. Tyler	−0.78	−0.72	−0.56	−0.80	−1.29	0.09	−1.09
11. Polk	0.30	0.55	0.59	0.50	−0.26	−1.44	−0.19
12. Taylor	−0.96	−0.72	−0.86	−0.99	−1.38	−0.76	0.12
13. Fillmore	−1.19	−1.22	−1.22	−1.14	−1.72	0.36	0.27
14. Pierce	−1.29	−1.33	−1.29	−1.25	−1.73	−0.17	0.16
15. Buchanan	−1.28	−1.19	−1.26	−1.14	−0.98	−0.02	0.01
16. Lincoln	2.10	1.74	0.93	2.07	1.42	−0.61	1.50
17. A. Johnson	−0.30	−0.40	0.12	−0.40	0.03	0.66	−2.18
18. Grant	−1.50	−1.36	−1.37	−1.38	−0.05	−0.55	0.59
19. Hayes	0.59	−0.69	−0.74	−0.64	−1.06	−0.29	0.14
20. Garfield	—	—	—	—	—	—	—
21. Arthur	−0.52	−0.68	−0.69	−0.52	−1.32	−0.45	0.18
22. Cleveland	0.25	0.18	0.20	0.11	−0.29	0.08	−0.88
23. B. Harrison	−0.89	−0.97	−0.95	−0.86	−1.52	−0.33	0.19
24. McKinley	−0.39	−0.30	−0.34	−0.21	−0.33	−0.25	0.49
25. T. Roosevelt	1.18	1.36	1.61	1.26	1.20	−0.57	0.19
26. Taft	−0.05	−0.17	−0.16	−0.01	0.09	−0.04	0.01
27. Wilson	1.01	1.35	1.05	1.11	1.42	4.23	−2.23
28. Harding	−1.84	−1.66	−1.66	−1.61	−0.15	−0.81	1.17
29. Coolidge	−0.99	−1.17	−1.37	−1.20	−0.37	−1.41	−0.83
30. Hoover	−0.09	−0.23	−0.14	−0.29	0.24	1.00	−1.01
31. F. Roosevelt	1.57	1.98	2.06	1.91	1.52	−0.62	1.31
32. Truman	0.94	1.06	1.25	1.12	1.08	−0.44	0.31
33. Eisenhower	−0.29	−0.43	−0.59	−0.32	0.82	0.13	1.21
34. Kennedy	0.63	0.68	1.06	0.36	1.18	1.14	1.61
35. L. Johnson	0.06	1.00	1.39	0.53	1.12	−1.01	−0.47

Source: Table reconstructed from data reported in tables 2–8 of Maranell (1970). Based on a survey of 571 members of the Organization of American Historians.
Note. Evaluations run as follows: 1 = general prestige, 2 = strength of action, 3 = presidential activeness, 4 = accomplishments of their administrations, 5 = amount of respondents' information, 6 = idealism (versus practicality), and 7 = flexibility.

anell 1970). If these scores are compared with those in table 3.1, it should be clear that presidential ranking tends to correspond to a chief executive's score on general prestige, strength of action, presidential activeness, and accomplishments of his administration (but not idealism or flexibility). Low-ranked presidents tend to earn negative *z* scores on these four assessments, high-ranked presidents positive *z* scores, whereas presidents in the middle ranks are prone to get scores near zero. Moreover, scores above $+3$ or below -3 are rare.

The justification for standardization scales is to make scales easier to interpret, especially when comparing how individuals differ on two or more variables. In table 3.4, for instance, we can directly compare a president's relative standing on attributes as diverse as strength and idealism without any mental gymnastics. Moreover, because standardization usually requires only linear transformations of the original data, the interval qualities of the scores are unchanged. However, this invariance does not hold for the final measurement level, that of the ratio scale.

Ratio Measures

Moles ([1958] 1968) published an assessment of classical composers adopting a line of attack different than Farnsworth's (1969). Instead of having musicologists rank the contestants according to posterity's praise, he counted the number of times each composer appeared on concert programs and from these frequencies calculated the percentage of times that each was represented in the active repertoire (see table 3.5).

Although some reshuffling occurs in comparison with the rankings—Tchaikovsky is manifestly more popular with bourgeois audiences than with cognoscenti—the overall pattern betrays a conspicuous consensus. The top seven on Mole's list are in the top ten of Farnsworth's, for instance, and both put Tartini near the bottom. Nonetheless, the percentages feature implications not found in the rankings. In the first place, it is evident that these proportions represent an interval scale. The difference between Mozart and Brahms in performance frequency is equivalent to that between Brahms and Chopin, in both cases a difference of 2 percent. Yet it should also be apparent that the numbers harbor meaning beyond that obtainable from an interval measure: Not just the distances between two scores correspond to some underlying reality, but the ratio of two scores carry significance besides. Thus, we can declare with confidence that Wagner is performed exactly twice as often as either Schumann or Chopin. The ratio of two scores has substantive meaning because there exists in this measure a definite zero point; a composer might be performed not once in any concert program anywhere. Only 250 musicians had a minimum of one work heard by audiences, when the number of eligible composers is at least a few times larger. The fact that the ratio of any two scale values has empirical implications, marks the assessments in table 3.5 as a ratio scale.

Ratio measures form the bedrock of the physical sciences. Distance, time, and mass are critical variables in these disciplines, and all three are ratio scales par excellence. Progress in science has usually been synonymous with movement up from nominal and ordinal scales through the higher-order interval and ratio scales. From the qualities of "hot" and "cold" of Greek natural philosophy evolved an

Table 3.5   *Relative Performance Frequencies of Works by 250 Classical Composers*

6.1	Mozart	1.0	Purcell	0.45	Milhaud	0.25	Glinka
5.9	Beethoven	1.0	Puccini	0.4	Bartók	0.25	Granados
5.9	J. S. Bach	0.95	Grieg	0.4	Borodin	0.25	Gretchaninoff
4.2	Wagner	0.95	Weber	0.4	Bruckner	0.25	Khatchaturian
4.1	Brahms	0.95	Prokofiev	0.4	Vivaldi	0.25	Hindemith
3.6	Schubert	0.95	Berlioz	0.4	Elgar	0.25	Lalo
2.8	Handel	0.95	Rossini	0.4	Mascagni	0.25	Leoncavallo
2.8	Tchaikovsky	0.95	Ravel	0.35	Offenbach	0.25	des Pres
2.5	Verdi	0.85	Rimsky-Korsakov	0.35	Palestrina	0.25	Poulenc
2.3	Haydn	0.85	D. Scarlatti	0.35	Monteverdi	0.25	de Lassus
2.1	Schumann	0.7	Franck	0.35	Shostakovich	0.25	Boccherini
2.1	Chopin	0.7	Gounod	0.35	Schoenberg	0.25	Bellini
1.75	Liszt	0.7	Vaughan-Williams	0.35	Walton	0.2	Telemann
1.75	Mendelssohn	0.65	Bizet	0.35	Honegger	0.2	Pergolesi
1.7	Debussy	0.65	Couperin	0.3	Albéniz	0.2	Enesco
1.65	Wolf	0.6	Mahler	0.3	Buxtehude	0.2	J. C. Bach
1.6	Sibelius	0.6	Rameau	0.3	Chabrier	0.2	C. P. E. Bach
1.4	R. Strauss	0.6	Saint-Saëns	0.3	Delius	0.2	Berg
1.3	Mussorsky	0.6	Massenet	0.3	Gershwin	0.2	Bruch
1.3	Dvořák	0.55	Donizetti	0.3	Lully	0.2	Britten
1.3	Stravinsky	0.45	Falla	0.3	Suppé	0.2	Corelli
1.2	Fauré	0.45	Scriabin	0.3	A. Thomas	0.2	Busoni
1.2	J. Strauss	0.45	Meyerbeer	0.25	Bloch	0.2	Dukas
1.1	Smetana	0.45	Gluck	0.25	Delibes	0.2	Ponchielli
1.0	Rachmaninoff	0.45	Paganini	0.25	Glazunov	0.2	Tartini
						6.0	150 others (1 each)

Note. Adapted from Moles ([1958] 1968, 28–29. Copyright 1968 by University of Illinois Press. Used by permission.

ordinal scale that recognized that "hotter" and "colder" could be arranged along a single dimension. With the emergence of actual thermometers, beginning with Galileo and continuing with Fahrenheit, Réaumer, and Celsius, temperature acquired interval properties. Finally, with the advent of the Kelvin scale, temperature obtained a zero point (-272 C°) and hence ratio characteristics.

Because this progression has been seen so many times in the physical sciences, critics have decried the dearth of ratio scales in the behavioral sciences. Take the assessment of IQ, which surely represents one of the most notable achievements in either psychometrics or historiometrics. To say that Copernicus may have had an IQ as large as 160 is not tantamount to observing that he was three times more intelligent than a moron—a ridiculous remark because intelligence is not sufficiently refined as a concept to support the specification of a zero point. What kind of intellect would a human being have to descend to before earning a 0 IQ—the brains of a monkey, rat, cockroach, or paramecium? Does a single tropism deserve at least 1 IQ? Clearly intelligence measures have some catching up to do before they can be compared with temperature gauged on an absolute scale.

Cognitive theories of human information processing will probably have to attain the sophistication of thermodynamic theory, which is what inserted the zero in the thermometer.

Even so, ratio scales are actually fairly common in historiometry. Sometimes this is simply because physical properties provide desirable variables. The most patent case in point is time, which often takes the guise of an individual's age. Historical figures orphaned at age twenty are beyond doubt twice the age of those orphaned at ten, for the accumulation of years necessarily begins at birth, when age equals zero. That Newton was a posthumous child, his father having died before Newton's birth, is irrelevant to this fundamental reality, given that we can always assume that an individual must be born before parental loss can exert a developmental influence. Less common are studies that incorporate distance measures, such as physical height (Holmes and Elder 1989), and temperature, which has from time to time found a place in empirical work (for example, Baron and Ransberger 1978). In instances like these, the unit of measure is identical to that in the physical sciences, and thus the ratio attributes can be taken for granted.

Yet another variety of ratio scale is far more prominent in the literature—the event frequency count. Here the investigator simply tabulates how often certain well-defined events occur for each cross-sectional or time-series unit. The scores in table 3.5 are of this nature, except that the raw data have been converted into percentages (rendering them "ipsative"). Other examples include counting the number of legislative acts signed by each president (Simonton 1986g) or the number of vetoes of each consecutive Congress (Lee 1975), and counting the contributions made by creative individuals (Dennis 1954a) or the number of contributions created during each age period over the course of a career (Dennis 1966; Lehman 1953). At a more aggregate level we can even tabulate the frequency of creators, discoveries, battles, coups d'état, assassinations, homicides, or suicides each year, decade, or generation (for example, Rainoff 1929; Simonton 1975e; Sorokin 1937–41). The zero point of all such counts is apparent to anyone, for a zero score defines the circumstance when the event being tabulated did not occur even once; since it is self-evident that an event cannot happen less than not at all, negative values are impossible. It is equally clear that two tabulated events are twice one, and forty events four times ten. Hence, we can readily maintain that Franklin D. Roosevelt vetoed 106 times as many bills as did Abraham Lincoln (635 versus 6), and that Mozart composed 4.6 times as many symphonies as Beethoven (41 versus 9). Event frequency counts represent the most secure ratio scales in historiometry.

Needless to say, those with a more humanistic turn of mind may feel that the events counted are not always equivalent, apples and oranges being lumped together. Investigators have a route around this potential objection, namely weighted rather than unweighted tabulations. For instance, many generational time-series analyses have counted the number of achievers in each time period, weighting each individual according to the eminence or influence attained (for example, Gray 1958, 1966; Simonton 1975e, 1976g; Sorokin 1937–41). In this way, a figure like Immanual Kant will contribute more tallies to the overall count than a lesser figure like Franz Aepinus, his contemporary. In a similar vein, presidential veto behavior has been weighted according to how the two houses of Congress responded to a particular veto (Simonton 1987c), and creative products have been weighted according to their social impact or magnitude of achievement (Simonton 1977a). See, for example, in table 3.6 the weighting scheme for musical compositions in the classical repertoire.

Table 3.6 *Weighting Scheme for Works in the Classical Repertoire*

I. *One* point for the following minor activities:
   A. Musical sketches, fragments, revisions, etc.
   B. Harmonizations, arrangements, transcriptions, orchestrations, pasticcios, reductions, etc.
   C. Canons, musical clocks, cadenzas, exercises, solfeggien, vocalises, variations contributed to set of variations by various composers, etc.
II. *Three* points for dance or march movements for solo through orchestra (i.e., *any* cotillons, galops, German dances ["deutsche"], landler, ecossaise, allemandes, minuets [with trios], waltzes, Hungarian dances, marches, sarabandes, courants, polonaises, mazurkas, gigues, tarantellas, bourees, boleros, musettes, gavottes, hornpipes, quadrilles, contredances, military marches, etc.)
III. *Five* points for the following single-movement works:
   A. Instrumental solos (e.g., fugues, passacaglias, rondos, fughettas, arias, contrapunti, chaconnes; barcarolles, berceuses; preludes, capriccios, toccatas, fantasies, rhapsodies, romances, intermezzi, nocturnes, impromptus, ballades, scherzos, albumblatten, divertisements, bagatelles, inventions, moments musicaux, arabesques, etudes, fantasias, concerti, pastorales, canzonas; allergri, andanti, largi, cantabiles, allabrevi)
   B. Vocal music for solo voice through chorus with chamber accompaniment or less (e.g., keyboard): e.g., art songs or lieder for voice and piano, arias or ariettas for voice and piano, motets, one-movement cantatas
IV. *Ten* points for the following single-movement works:
   A. Orchestral works (e.g., overtures, symphonic or tone poems, symphonic sketches, variations, preludes (N.B.: for dance music see II)
   B. Instrumental solo(s) with orchestra (e.g., single movements of concerti, church sonatas for organ and orchestra)
   C. Vocal music for solo voice through chorus with orchestral accompaniment (e.g., arias, airs, ariettas, scenas, songs or cantatas, vocal duets, trios, quartets)
      N.B.: includes miscellaneous church works unless known otherwise (viz., kyries, salve reginas, psalms, santi, offertoria, te deums, anthems, hymns, miserere, graduals, jubilates, etc., but for motet see III-B)
V. *Fifteen* points for the following multimovement works:
   A. Instrumental solos (e.g., any sonata, suite, partita)
      N.B.: if single-movement of same, then 5 or 3 points according to rules II and III-A above
   B. Duo sonata or other instrumental duet (e.g., any violin or cello sonata, suite or sonata for piano four hands or dual piano)
      N.B.: single-movements of above counted same as solos (see II or III-A)
VI. *Twenty* points for the following multi-movement works:
   A. Instrumental chamber works (viz., any trio, quartet, quintet, sextet, septet, octet, nonet, etc.); if single-movement of same, then 5 points
   B. Divertimenti, serenades, cassations, or similar works called by some other name (e.g., nocturn, feldpartita, concertante)

(continued)

Table 3.6 *Continued*

VII. *Twenty-five* points for the following theater music:
    A. Dramatic serenades, puppet operas, burletta, intermezzi, interludes, etc.
    B. Ballet and masques
    C. Incidental music
VIII. *Thirty* points for the following multimovement works:
    A. Concerti, symphony concertanti, concerti grossi, etc. (if single movement, see IV-B)
    B. Church or secular cantatas (for one-movement cantatas, see III-B or IV-C) and magnificats
    C. Light opera *per act* (assumed = 2 if unknown): e.g., any singspiel or operetta
IX. *Thirty-five* points for the following multimovement vocal works:
    A. Medium opera *per act* (assumed = 3 if unknown): e.g., opera buffa, drama giocoso
    B. Oratorio or passion *per part* (assumed = 3 if unknown)
X. *Forty* points for the following large forms:
    A. Symphonies and orchestral suites (if single movements of same, see IV-A)
    B. Heavy opera *per act* (assumed = 3 if unknown): e.g., opera seria
XI. *Fifty* points for the following large forms:
    A. Masses (except Bach's "Lutherin" which equal 20 according to IV-C)
    B. Music drama *per act* (viz., both Wagner and Debussy)
XII. *Special considerations:*
    A. If work written for nonconcert instrument, divide score by two and round up; nonconcert instruments include baryton, mechanical organ, glass harmonica, lire organizzate, mandoline, guitar, argeggioe, etc.
    B. If any doubts about the proper number of points, give *lowest* classification

Note. Weighting scheme devised for Bach, Handel, Haydn, Mozart, Beethoven, Schubert, Chopin, Wagner, Brahms, and Debussy from Simonton (1977a, 1980c). Adjustments are probably necessary if applied to other composers, especially those earlier or later in music history.

Even if weighted tabulations do not enjoy the same direct meaning as straightforward unweighted counts, the ratio character of the scales remains. The zero point stays at the same place in both unweighted and weighted measures; only the movement away from the baseline differs. The situation is analogous to determining the center of gravity of a nonhomogeneous body, which demands that each finite section of that body be weighted according to mean density. Admittedly, deciding on what weighting scheme to employ is not as easy as in the physical case, and often the weights allotted to separate events will have arbitrary elements. How much more is a decisive battle worth than a minor skirmish? To what extent is an opera valued more than a cantata? As difficult as these issues are, inquiries have repeatedly shown that most weighted measures are "robust" under reasonable modifications of any weighting schemes (for example, Simonton 1977a, 1989b). Indeed, weighted measures very often are so strongly correlated with utterly unweighted measures that much the same results obtain under both sets of measures (Simonton 1988c, 1989b; Sorokin and Merton 1935). This near-identity is yet another instance of the classic psychometric principle of "it don't make no never mind": Composite indices are robust under alternative weighting schemes. Thus such measurement is less onerous than it would seem.

At the close of the previous section we noted that ratio scales, unlike interval scales, cannot undergo standardization without being degraded to a lower level of measurement. Just as a logarithmic transformation destroys an interval but not an ordinal scale, standardization obliterates a ratio but not an interval scale. This is because conversion to z scores or other standard form usually involves the addition or subtraction of a constant, namely the mean value for the variable. Adding or subtracting the same quantity from both the numerator and the denominator of any ratio alters the value of the quotient. To standardize is thus to undermine the substantive interpretability of a ratio assessment. Career age in z-score form has less punch than plain career age. Nonetheless, when we subject measures to statistical analyses, data transformations are often executed without respecting the high-class features of the ratio scales. Since almost all analytical techniques assume nothing better than interval scales, one should not become overly protective of those variables that happen to be blessed with the ratio stigmata.

Measurement Sources

The preceding discussion focused on the nature of the measures rather than where such measures come from, even though the latter question deals with the fascinating problem of how historical materials can be converted into a scientifically serviceable form. There are three main sources from which such quantifications may emerge: content analytical, biographical, and transhistorical data. Actually, the examples of measurement scales show that these three sources by no means exhaust all possibilities. Many inquiries incorporate the results of surveying the experts on a particular question. Thus, Farnsworth (1969) obtained his rankings of the classical composers by sending questionnaires to musciologists, and Maranell (1970) surveyed historians for his ratings of the American presidents (see also Ballard and Suedfeld 1988; McCann and Stewin 1987). Other investigators have naive observers apply rating scales to historical stimuli to discern the subjective impressions of masterworks. This tactic has been used, for example, to establish the psychological validity of cross-media artistic styles (Hasenfus, Martindale, and Birnbaum 1983). But in the three sources discussed below, the measurements ensue directly from the archives.

Content Analytical Data

Most historical figures of any consequence have left behind a supply of primary materials from which we may cull key variables through content analyses. For creators, these personal artifacts include the original creative products on which their reputations must rest—paintings, musical compositions, poems, philosophical treatises, and the like. For leaders, there are speeches, diplomatic exchanges, proclamations, judicial opinions, and communiqués. Both creators and leaders, as well as celebrities, may also leave behind volumes of correspondence, personal letters that can reveal the more intimate details of a historical personality. Moreover, sometimes the aim of a content analysis is to extract the modal mood or personality of an entire culture, in which case almost any artifact of popular culture may become the vehicle for inferring psychological attributes—comic books, newspapers, television shows, movies, posters, personal names, architecture, furnishings, and so on. Because the literature on content analysis is old and vast (for example, Holsti 1969; R. P. Weber 1985), we can do no more than provide an overview of the principal ways that primary documents can be converted into meaningful numbers. In general, these approaches can be subdivided into two broad categories, the subjective and the objective.

Subjective indicators.   A content analytical measure is styled "subjective" whenever it relies heavily on the intuitive judgments of human raters. This designation recognizes that there are some psychological constructs that do not lend themselves to mindless computations. At any rate, most historiometric examples of subjective measures entail the extension of psychometric assessment schemes to historical materials. The earliest such applications involved the Thematic Apperception Test (TAT) advanced by Henry Murray (1938). The fundamental assumption of this projective measure is that human beings, when confronted with ambiguous stimuli, tend to project their own implicit or latent motives onto each stimulus. The original TAT contained a series of pictures portraying scenes with one or more individuals engaged in some unclear activity or thought, the subject then being instructed to write a story about what was going on. These stories, or "protocols," can be scored for the presence of certain motives, as evidenced by the appearance of telltale images. With a little ingenuity, these scoring methods can be adapted for use with historical documents and artifacts.

The innovative research on the relation between the achievement motive, or *n*Ach, and economic prosperity first demonstrated this possibility. In McClelland's work (1961, chap. 4), the connection between these two variables is explored in the histories of ancient Greece, pre-Incan Peru, Spain in the late Middle Ages, England between the Renaissance and the Industrial Revolution, and the United States (see also Bradburn and Berlew 1961; Cortés 1960; deCharms and Moeller 1962). With immense finesse, achievement needs were assessed for whole peoples across time by the content analysis of cultural materials. Most commonly, the TAT scoring schemes were applied directly to written documents, like the popular literature of the era or children's readers designed to socialize a nation's youth. Less frequent but more remarkable are studies that extracted motive scores from graphic materials, such as the decorations on ancient Greek vases or Peruvian funeral urns. This extension of the TAT technique followed findings that the visual features of spontaneous doodles are associated with the achievement motives of those who draw them (Aronson 1958).

The achievement motive is not the only human desire that can be tapped through content analysis, for the power motive has received considerable attention as well, especially in Winter's *Power Motive* (1973). Here Winter shows how the power motive can be assessed on single historical figures, namely American chief executives. Given that TAT was originally designed for use on individual verbal behavior, it is an easy step to subject inaugural addresses to content analyses. In a long series of investigations, Winter and his colleagues scrutinized most of the U.S. presidents, obtaining motive scores not just on the power motive, but also the needs for achievement and affiliation (Donley and Winter 1970; Wendt and Light 1976; Winter and Stewart 1977). An example was shown in table 3.3, which gives both a raw count of motive images per one thousand words and the scores transformed into a mean of 50 and a standard deviation of 10. The resulting motive profiles have been shown to predict important facets of presidential performance, such as the odds of military interventions, arms limitation treaties, assassination attempts, scandals, and even ultimate historical reputation. And motive scores of presidents at the individual level have been compared with those of the United States as a whole to demonstrate that the margin of victory on election day hinges on the match between leader and follower profiles on power, achievement, and affiliation needs (Winter 1987b). Political leaders of other stripes have also become the object of these measures, among them southern African leaders (Winter 1980) and 1988 presidential candidates (Winter 1988), and so this methodology can easily spread to personages of any kind.

TAT-inspired inquiries look at human motivation, yet subjective content analysis can certainly divulge cognitive characteristics as well, such as attitudes and styles of thought. The most productive research program in this domain is that on integrative complexity. This research, too, involved the conversion of an established psychometric device into a content analytical coding scheme, this time the source measure was the Paragraph Completion Test (PCT) (Schroder, Driver, and Streufert 1967). PCT assesses individual differences in human information processing by gauging how many perspectives a person can simultaneously consider and how well those diverse points of view are unified into a single position. This measure lends itself naturally to the content analysis of verbal materials. As will be documented later, research on integrative complexity has shown that how leaders score on this cognitive ability relates to their decision-making effectiveness, ideology and policy orientations, electoral victory, revolutionary success, and military prowess (for example, Suedfeld and Rank 1976; Tetlock and Boettger 1989). Integrative complexity has also been applied to the lives of creative individuals (Porter and Suedfeld 1981; Suedfeld 1985; Suedfeld and Piedrahita 1984).

The above studies by no means represent all subjective indicators. Besides other analytical strategies devised specifically for personal documents—like evaluation assertion analysis (Tetlock 1979)—virtually any psychometric measure can be transformed into a content analytical instrument of some type (for example, L. A. Gottschalk, Uliana, and Gilbert 1988; McCurdy 1947; Zullow, Oettingen, Peterson, and Seligman 1988). However, subjective content analysis often must confront two serious drawbacks. First, these techniques require the intuitive assessments of judges, and therefore the measures are not always reliable. The chief solution to this problem is to impose rigorous training procedures and to employ multiple assessors. Moreover, whenever possible the judges should be blind to the hypotheses being tested and should even be kept ignorant of the identity of the historical figures under examination. Sometimes these desiderata may be obtained by taking full advantage of previously published ratings. Thus, the *Great Books of the Western World* anthology (Hutchins 1952) contains a *Syntopicon* that identifies specific sections of scientific, philosophical, and literary masterpieces that deal with thousands of discrete subjects. These scholarly and informed assessments have been used as content analytical measures (for example, Simonton 1976f, 1983a, 1986f, 1989b). To reveal the range of topics in even a limited domain, the themes treated by at least two of the 154 sonnets by Shakespeare are listed in table 3.7 (Simonton 1989b).

The second difficulty is more severe: When humans are asked to make precise judgments on complex materials, the amount of data that can be processed in a given time is necessarily curtailed. Therefore the subjective content analysis usually demands that the researcher sample only a small fraction of the entire collection of available documents. The alternative is to devise a highly objective measure that can be applied more quickly and easily. Ideally, if the coding scheme is truly objective, the human raters can be dispensed with altogether, fast digital computers serving as research assistants instead.

Objective indicators. When the goal is to analyze the content of large quantities of printed text in the quickest and most error-free manner possible, the optimal procedure usually involves reducing the coding scheme to straightforward word counts. Assuming that the desired constructs can be operationally defined in terms of the expected frequencies of certain key words, computers can work far more rapidly than any human being can, enabling mounds of raw text to be processed painlessly but precisely. Requisite computer programs consist mainly of a large dictionary and an inventory of conceptual categories into which the word frequencies can be credited. The programs deliver the frequencies for each category for each unit of text. At first these programs were available only for mainframe computers, but now content analyses can be performed on a researcher's desk-top computer (for example, Mohler and Zuell 1986).

The first general-purpose content analytical program was the General Inquirer system (Stone et al. 1966). This has been used to tap the ideological and motivational preoccupations of presidential candidates as revealed in their nomination acceptance speeches (Smith, Stone, and Glenn 1966). With a more specialized goal in mind, Hart (1984) conceived a computerized content analysis that could be usefully applied to addresses of U.S. presidents. This scheme identifies words that register an executive's rhetorical manifestations of activity, realism, certainty, optimism, complexity, variety, self-reference, familiarity, human interest, embellishment, and symbolism. Yet from a purely historiometric perspec-

Table 3.7 *Themes in Shakespeare's Sonnets According to the Syntopicon*

Topic	Description[a]
1. Art 3	Art as imitation: 67–68
2. Art 5	The sources of art in experience, imagination, and inspiration: 32, 78–85, 100–6
3. Beauty 1b	Beauty and truth: the beautiful as an object of contemplation: 14, 54
4. Beauty 3	Beauty in relation to desire and love, as object or cause: 20, 24, 54, 130
5. Beauty 7d	Beauty in the moral order: 93–96
6. Chance 6a	Chance and fortune in the life of the individual: 25, 111
7. Chance 12b	The love and hatred of change: 15, 25, 49, 60, 64–65, 116, 123
8. Family 6a	The desire for offspring: 1–17
9. Honor 1	The relation of honor and fame: praise and reputation: 69–70, 121
10. Honor 2d	Honor or fame as a mode of immortality: 55, 65, 81
11. Immortality 6a	Immortality through offspring: the perpetuation of the species: 1–17
12. Immortality 6b	Enduring fame: survival in the memory: 55, 65, 81
13. Language 9	The language of poetry: 21, 76, 78–79, 130
14. Love 1e	The intensity and power of love; its increase or decrease; its constructive or destructive force: 14–116
15. Love 2b	Friendly, tender, or altruistic love: fraternal love: 1–116
16. Love 3a	Friendship and love in relation to virtue and happiness: 25, 137–52
17. Love 3d	The heroism of friendship and the sacrifices of love: 87–90
18. Poetry 3	The inspiration or genius of the poet: the influence of the poetic tradition: 100–8
19. Poetry 6a	The expression of emotion in poetry: 76, 78–79, 82–85
20. Poetry 8b	Critical standards and artistic rules with respect to the language of poetry: the distinction between prose and verse; the measure of excellence in style: 21, 76, 82, 130
21. Rhetoric 2b	The canon of excellence in style: 21, 76, 82, 130
22. Sense 6	The role of sense in the perception of beauty: the beautiful and the pleasing to sense; sensible and intelligible beauty: 54, 69, 93–95
23. Time 7	The temporal course of the passions: emotional attitudes toward time and mutability: 1–19, 25, 49, 55, 59–60, 63–65, 115–16, 123
24. Truth 8c	Truth in relation to love and friendship: the pleasant and the unpleasant truth: 137–52

Note. Adapted from Simonton (1989b, table 1). Copyright 1989 by Duke University Press. Adapted by permission.

[a]The numbers given after the colon identify the sonnets in which that theme is represented.

tive, perhaps the most remarkable example is Martindale's Regressive Imagery Dictionary (1975) that can tap primary and secondary process thinking in written documents of all kinds, whether prose or poetry. A brief description of this program will give the flavor of this line of attack.

In Martindale's system, certain words create "tags" which make up categories that then compose more general summary categories (see also Martindale 1984a). Thus, the summary category primary process is defined by the categories drives, sensation, defensive symbolization, regressive cognition, and icarian imagery, whereas a secondary process is indicated by the categories abstraction, social behavior, instrumental behavior, restraint, order, temporal references, and moral imperatives. The categories for, say, regressive cognition are unknown, timeless, consciousness alteration, brink-passage, narcissism, and concreteness, whereas the words that tag, say, consciousness alteration include "dream," "sleep," and "wake." Examples of words for all categories are shown in table 3.8. Martindale has validated his dictionary in a series of investigations on both contemporary subjects (for example, in drug states) and historical figures (for example, poets suffering psychopathologies), so this measure effectively captures the two alternative thinking modes (Martindale 1986a). More important, Martindale (1975, 1984b, 1986a), by subjecting hundreds of lines of poetry to computerized analysis, has shown how literary styles change over time, thereby learning many facts of profound relevance to any theory of the creative process. Furthermore, objective scores on primary and secondary processes are demonstrably predictive of aesthetic success (Simonton 1989b).

Linguistic expression is not the sole documented behavior amenable to objective content analysis. Virtually any medium of communication can be so treated, albeit sometimes only with considerable awkwardness. The nonverbal communication that most welcomes rigorous frequency counts is music, the most mathematical of all artistic endeavors. Hence, it is not surprising that several investigators have devised coding schemes for the objective analysis of musical expression. Brook (1969) proposed a "Plaine and Easie Code" by which the chief characteristics of a melody can be translated into machine-readable form, and Cerulo (1984, 1988, 1989) has developed methods by which more elaborate attributes can be directly assessed. One of the most amazing discoveries in this research is that relatively simplistic analyses of melodic structure can reveal a tremendous amount about the creative process and personality. Paisley (1964) was the first to indicate that the two-note transition probabilities for the first four notes of a melody usually suffice to reveal the style unique to a composer. Each composer has a favored means of constructing a melody, a predilection that can be picked up by a computer. For instance, "Mozart liked to repeat a tone in consecutive notes while Bach preferred to move up or down a semitone" (p. 236). Indeed, when errors are made in stylistic identifications, the computer's mistakes are those that a music listener would make. Thus some of Beethoven's thematic material can pass for the musical thoughts of Haydn, Beethoven's teacher in his early Vienna years.

In a long series of inquiries, Paisley's analytical approach has been extended to the first six notes of the 15,618 themes that are most often heard in the concert hall, opera house, or recording studio (Simonton 1980c, 1980d, 1984h, 1986h, 1986a, 1987b, 1989c). Both two- and three-note transition probabilities were used to gauge each theme's melodic originality and to assess compositions on how melodic structure varies as a musical work unfolds during performance. The main two-note transition percentages from which these measures derive are given in table 3.9. Needless to say, it would be virtually impossible to obtain the same

Table 3.8 *Regressive Imagery Dictionary Categories and Sample Words*

Summary category	Sample words
Primary Process	
Drives	
Oral	breast, drink, lip
Anal	sweat, rot, dirty
Sex	lover, kiss, naked
Sensation	
General sensation	fair, charm, beauty
Touch	touch, thick, stroke
Taste	sweet, taste, bitter
Odor	breath, perfume, scent
Sound	hear, voice, sound
Vision	see, light, look
Cold	cold, winter, snow
Hard	rock, stone, hard
Soft	soft, gentle, tender
Defensive symbolization	
Passivity	die, lie, bed
Voyage	wander, desert, beyond
Random movement	wave, roll, spread
Diffusion	shade, shadow, cloud
Chaos	wild, crowd, ruin
Regressive cognition	
Unknown	secret, strange, unknown
Timelessness	eternal, forever, immortal
Consciousness alteration	dream, sleep, wake
Brink-passage	road, wall, door
Narcissism	eye, heart, hand
Concreteness	at, where, over
Icarian imagery	
Ascend	rise, fly, throw
Height	up, sky, high
Descend	fall, drop, sink
Depth	down, deep, beneath
Fire	sun, fire, flame
Water	sea, water, stream
Secondary process	
Abstraction	know, may, thought
Social behavior	say, tell, call
Instrumental behavior	make, find, work
Restraint	must, stop, bind
Order	simple, measure, array
Temporal references	when, now, then
Moral imperatives	should, right, virtue

Source: Martindale (1984a, 10). Copyright 1984 by Kluwer Academic Publishers. Used by permission.

Table 3.9 *Two-Note Transition Percentages for 15,618 Classical Themes*

%	1	2	3	4	5	Average
			Transitions			
11	G G (11.2)					
10	G C (10.6)					
	C C (7.5)					
7		G G (7.0)				
						G G (6.7)[d]
	C D (6.4)					
		C C (6.2)				
6						
			G G (5.7)			
						C C (5.3)[d]
	C G (5.2)					
5						
				G G (5.1)		
			C C (4.9)			G C (4.9)[c]
	G E (4.6)				G G (4.6)	
		C D (4.4)		D C (4.4)		C D (4.4)[a]
	G A (4.3)			C C (4.3)		
	E E (4.2)					
4	C B (4.0)					
	E F (3.9)			C D (3.9)	C D (3.9)	
					D C (3.9)	
		G C (3.8)				
				G F (3.7)	C C (3.7)	
		D E (3.6)	G C (3.6)			
			C D (3.5)			
	C E (3.4)		B C (3.4)		E D (3.4)	
		D C (3.3)	D C (3.3)		G F (3.3)	
		F G (3.3)	E D (3.3)			
	G F (3.2)				G C (3.2)	C B (3.2)[a]
						C G (3.2)[c]
		E E (3.1)	E E (3.1)	G C (3.1)	C B (3.1)	G F (3.1)[b]
3		C B (3.0)	C B (3.0)		D E (3.0)	E E (3.0)[d]
						E D (3.0)[b]
						D C (3.0)[b]
	E D (2.9)		C G (2.9)	A G (2.9)	F E (2.9)	G E (2.9)[c]
			G F (2.9)	C G (2.9)	F G (2.9)	G A (2.9)[a]
			E D (2.9)			
			F E (2.9)			
		C B (2.8)	D E (2.8)		B C (2.8)	E F (2.8)[a]
		E G (2.8)	E F (2.8)		G A (2.8)	
			G A (2.8)			
		G E (2.7)		B C (2.7)	A G (2.7)	
				E G (2.7)		
	E G (2.6)		A G (2.6)	D E (2.6)	E F (2.6)	E G (2.6)[c]
			E G (2.6)	E E (2.6)		
			F G (2.6)			
		B C (2.5)	G E (2.5)	G A (2.5)	C G (2.5)	
		C G (2.5)				
		E D (2.5)				
		F E (2.5)				

(*continued*)

Table 3.9 *Continued*

%	1	2	3	4	5	Average
		D E♭(2.4)		E F (2.4)	G E (2.4)	D E (2.4)[a]
		E F (2.4)				
						B C (2.3)[a]
		G A (2.2)	E♭D (2.2)	G E (2.2)	E E (2.2)	C E (2.2)[c]
		G F (2.2)				
		C E (2.1)	F G (2.1)		E♭D (2.1)	F G (2.1)[a]
					E G (2.1)	F E (2.1)[b]
						G A (2.1)[a]
2		A B (2.0)	F E (2.0)			A G (2.0)[b]
		A G (2.0)				
			D E♭(1.9)	E C (1.9)		
				E G (1.9)		
				F G (1.9)		
			C E (1.8)	C E (1.8)		E♭D (1.8)[b]
				E♭D (1.8)		
	G A♭(1.7)	E C (1.7)	E C (1.7)		C E (1.7)	
					E C (1.7)	
	C E♭ (1.6)					E C (1.6)[c]
	G E♭ (1.6)					
		E♭D (1.5)			A♭G (1.5)	
		B A (1.4)	A♭G (1.4)	A B (1.4)	A B (1.4)	D E♭(1.4)[a]
		A♭G (1.4)		A♭G (1.4)	B A (1.4)	
					D E♭(1.4)	
		C E♭ (1.3)		B A (1.3)		
				D D (1.3)		
				D E♭(1.3)		
				F E♭(1.3)		
	E♭D (1.2)		B A (1.2)		D D (1.2)	A B (1.2)[a]
	E C (1.2)		D D (1.2)		D G (1.2)	
	G F♯ (1.2)		E♭F (1.2)		F E♭(1.2)	
			G A♭(1.2)			
		D D (1.1)	A B (1.1)		F D (1.1)	B A (1.1)[b]
						A♭G (1.1)[b]
						D D (1.1)[d]
1		F♯ G (1.0)	E♭C (1.0)	E♭F (1.0)	F F (1.0)	
					G A♭(1.0)	
N ≥ 1%	20	29	31	30	32	28
Total N	157	184	190	200	204	204
%Total	82	78	78	75	76	76

Note. Adapted from Simonton (1984h, table 1). Percentage of times transition appears given in parentheses.
[a]Scale ascent [b]Scale descent [c]Triad [d]Repeat

assessments using raters to evaluate thousands of themes by hundreds of composers. Moreover, these content analytical measures have been shown to relate to the form and medium of expression, to current conditions in the composer's personal life, and to the larger musical and sociocultural milieu.

Despite the apparent successes of objective, and especially computerized content analyses, these instruments remain rather crude. Speed and efficiency are often purchased with conceptual imprecision. The recent advances in computer technology notwithstanding, computers remain stupid information processors, their sole asset being the quickness at which they can make simple-minded decisions. So-called artificial intelligence is far more artificial than intelligent. Because a digital computer is extremely literal, it cannot search for complex shades of meaning, nor can it gauge a construct in a more comprehensive context. Objective counts and frequency tabulations will not, therefore, replace subjective coding schemes. Only when computers can intelligently read text, purview art, or listen to music with genuine comprehension and appreciation can objective techniques totally replace the subjective.

Biographical Data

The distinction between cross-sectional and time-series units returns when psychologists exploit material on historical lives. Investigators can either assess individual differences on a characteristic trait or measure longitudinal fluctuations in a target behavior.

Cross-sectional variation.　　Sometimes the researcher is fortunate to have data already in a form amenable to quantification. The only need is to count appropriate occurrences directly from the archival source, which occurs in studies of cross-sectional variation in lifetime creative productivity. When Dennis (1954a) wanted to examine individual differences in total output across scientists, he began by consulting the *Catalog of Scientific Literature, 1800–1900,* put out by the Royal Society of London, and then merely counted the number of entries for sampled case. Likewise, when Lee (1975) determined contrasts among the U.S. presidents in the use of the veto power, he could easily exploit published lists of all vetoes for each president. In short, if the historical activity under scrutiny is sufficiently well defined and manifestly important to become the object of an archival compilation, the behavioral scientist need not fret much about how to quantify the data. This convenience holds not just for adult performance data but also for childhood experiences, for which pertinent data are often readily available.

For more subtle human attributes assessment of cross-sectional variation is not so easy. One option is to take advantage of the content analytical strategies already discussed (for example, McCurdy 1947; Rosenberg 1989; R. K. White 1947), yet investigators do not always have recourse to this approach, owing to a dearth of workable documents or to an absence of suitable coding schemes. The desired variables may then have to be tapped directly from biographical data. Woods (1906) and Thorndike (1936) long ago showed how two important personality traits—intelligence and morality—might be culled from biographies of royal family members, and both Cox (1926) and Thorndike (1950) examined about a hundred eminent creators and leaders on several dozen characteristics. Recent researchers have also modified regular psychometric measures and constructs for use on biographical materials. In 1963, R. B. Cattell suggested how the 16 Personality Factor Inventory might differentiate the dispositions of scientific luminaries, and Etheredge (1978) demonstrated how American chief executives and their foreign policy advisers could be evaluated on extroversion and dominance proclivities (see also M. G. Hermann 1980a; HFAC 1977; Hoffer 1978). For a better idea of how this mysterious translation process actually comes about, let us examine the inquiry that discriminated thirty-nine U.S. presidents on numerous character attributes (Simonton 1986h).

Biographical accounts of American chief executives are rich in qualitative personality descriptions. Character sketches are sometimes provided by the biographer as a thumbnail summary of the life-history data, yet often included are the more personal accounts of contemporaries. For instance, William H. Herndon described his law partner, Abraham Lincoln, as follows (Armbruster 1982, 172–73):

> He was morally and physically courageous, even-tempered and conservative, secretive and sagacious, skeptical and cautious, truthful and honest, firm in his own convictions and tolerant of those of others, reflective and cool, ambitious and somewhat selfish, kind to all and good-natured, sympathetic in the presence of suffering or under an imaginative description of it, lived in his reason and reasoned in his life. Easy of approach and perfectly democratic in nature, [he] had a broad charity for his fellow-men and had an excuse for unreflective acts of his kind, and in short he loved justice and lived out in thought and act the eternal right. . . . I do not say that he never deviated from his own nature and his own rules. His nature, the tendency of it, is as I state. . . . Lincoln struggled to live the best life possible. This I know.

As is apparent in this passage, it is a simple matter to transcribe the data with all identifying material removed, so that raters would not know whom they were evaluating. This was in fact accomplished for all thirty-nine American presidents using many biographical sources so as to smooth over the idiosyncracies of any one source (Simonton 1986h). A team of nine independent judges then rated the subjects on the descriptors of the Gough Adjective Check List (ACL; Gough and Heilbrun 1965). These adjectives are listed in alphabetical order from "absent minded" to "zany," with many useful descriptors between. Out of the original three hundred adjectives, the raters reached consensus on one hundred and ten.

These ratings were then subjected to a factor analysis (a technique treated in chapters 4 and 6) that collapsed the one hundred and ten traits into distinct groupings of fourteen general personality dimensions. These factors are as follows (with characteristic ACL items in parentheses): moderation (moderate and modest versus temperamental and hasty), friendliness (friendly and outgoing versus unfriendly and cold), intellectual brilliance (having wide and artistic interests),

Machiavellianism (sly and deceitful versus sincere and honest), poise and polish (poised and polished versus simple and informal), achievement drive (industrious and persistent), forcefulness (energetic and active), wit (humorous and witty), physical attractiveness (handsome and good-looking), pettiness (greedy and self-pitying), tidiness (methodical and organized), conservatism (conservative and conventional), inflexibility (stubborn and persistent), and pacifism (peaceable versus courageous). The resulting assessments are presented in table 3.10. Because these are z scores, presidents with scores near zero are average on the trait, negative scores signifying presidents below average, and positive scores representing presidents who are above average.

We will have more to say about these scores when we use them to illustrate diverse statistical techniques. For now it should be clear that the conversion process is quite feasible. Moreover, one's confidence in this approach is increased when one learns that independent investigators converge on the same differentiations of character and that these biographical scores are compatible with results obtained from content analysis (see Simonton 1986h). At the same time, it is obvious that the technique is extremely laborious. To collect suitable data and then translate them into scores on specific personal attributes requires considerable time and many independent raters. A trade-off consequently emerges between the number of historical figures assessed and the number of traits on which those individuals can be differentiated. Hundreds of royalty could be discriminated on the two traits of intellect and virtue (Simonton 1983d; Thorndike 1936; Woods 1906), but Cox (1926) and Thorndike (1950) could examine only about a hundred creators and leaders on several dozen aspects of character. And in the foregoing study, a mere thirty-nine personalities were the subject of three hundred descriptive ratings (Simonton 1986h). Given this drawback, assessments like these are rare, especially in comparison to direct counts of overt behaviors.

Longitudinal variation.　In assessing activities within, rather than across, individual careers, matters can still be relatively easy. Given the time-series unit, nothing more may be required than the ability to count events recorded in chronological life histories—an endeavor tedious but certainly not conceptually complicated. Illustrations of this direct procedure are in the extensive literature on the relation between age and outstanding achievement (Dennis 1966; Lehman 1953; Quetelet [1835] 1968). After dividing a human life into consecutive age periods—usually either decade or half-decade intervals—all one needs is an ample list of achievements and the tabulations can begin unhindered. The accomplishments may range from creative products, like musical compositions, to successful acts of leadership, like legislation or battle victories. Nor are personal attainments the only happenings that may be registered in this analytical format. To test hypotheses about how specified external events affect performance as a creator or leader over time, the events can equally undergo tabulation in parallel time series. The scores also will require nothing more than immediate countings from readily available chronological data on the pertinent historical events. In this way, Beethoven's creativity over his career has been examined as a function of concurrent warfare (Simonton 1987b), just as the generalship of Beethoven's contemporary and one-time idol, Napoleon, has been linked with the broader efficacy of the French military machine over the same historical periods (Simonton 1979b).

Yet as in the case of assessing individual differences, occasionally a researcher seeks to gauge longitudinal changes in more elusive variables. Again, content analyses may help (for example, Sears, Lapidus, and Cozzens 1978). Thus, longitudinal fluctuations in the integrative complexity of five British novelists have been assessed by subjecting their correspondence to content analysis (Porter and Suedfeld 1981), just as shifts in melodic originality over the career of ten top classical composers have been documented by using the two-note transition probabilities given in table 3.9 (Simonton 1980c). Nevertheless, sometimes a crucial variable can be evaluated only by devising a coding scheme for use with raw biographical data, a difficult task again often eased by modifying psychometric measures already validated on contemporary populations. For instance, both the Global Assessment Scale (Spitzer, Gibbon, and Endicott 1975), which gauges changes in psychiatric health, and the Social Readjustment Rating Scale (T. S. Holmes and Rahe 1967), which determines occurrences of potential life stressors, have been adapted to biographical information, including the five novelists and ten composers just mentioned (Porter and Suedfeld 1981; Simonton 1980c). To give a more concrete notion of how these applications come about, a list of life-change events and their corresponding scores that was used in the examination of ten classical composers (Simonton 1977a) is presented in table 3.11. Given this scale, along with a chronology of personal events in the life of a historical figure, the total level of biographical stress occurring in each age period can be tabulated. The final score is a weighted count of life-change events, tragic occasions like the death of a spouse carrying more force than mere inconveniences, like a change in residence.

So the creation of biographical time series looks like a one-way, two-step process: We first select the time-series unit, or age period, into which a life history can be subdivided; then and only then will we insert the required variable scores for each consecutive unit according to some quantification procedure. Nevertheless, as suggested earlier, the second step can be confounded with the first. The size of the analytical unit should not be so small that most of the variable entries assume zero values. Hence, it makes no sense to tabulate creative output day by day, even if products could be so dated accurately; nor would one wish to count battles on a daily basis, given how rare these events are and how battles may last longer than a single day. At the same time, the age periods should not be too large, for fear of jeopardizing the levels of freedom requisite for worthwhile statistical tests. Consequently, the investigator must select biographical units in light of available data on which the measurements must be founded.

When Cox (1926) examined developmental changes in the intellectual

Table 3.10 *Standardized Scores on Personality Dimensions for U.S. Presidents*

President	Factor													
	1	2	3	4	5	6	7	8	9	10	11	12	13	14
1. Washington	0.5	-0.4	0.3	-0.3	1.1	1.1	-0.0	1.1	0.0	-0.4	1.2	-0.3	0.1	0.1
2. J. Adams	-1.6	-1.5	0.6	-0.7	-0.1	0.9	0.0	-0.8	-0.9	0.6	-0.6	-0.1	0.9	-1.2
3. Jefferson	0.5	0.4	3.1	-0.3	0.2	0.6	-0.1	-0.2	0.3	-1.3	2.1	-2.0	-0.6	1.4
4. Madison	1.0	-0.4	0.6	-0.2	0.6	-0.1	-0.9	-0.3	-0.9	-0.8	0.6	-0.0	-0.6	1.4
5. Monroe	1.0	0.1	-1.4	-1.2	0.1	-0.1	-1.3	-0.7	-0.2	-1.1	-0.3	0.2	-0.4	0.5
6. J. Q. Adams	-0.4	-1.5	1.2	-0.6	0.3	0.2	-0.0	-0.9	-0.9	-0.6	-0.4	-0.3	0.5	-0.6
7. Jackson	-2.0	-0.7	-0.6	-0.2	-1.1	-0.0	1.7	-0.8	-0.6	1.1	-1.7	-1.3	1.4	-1.4
8. Van Buren	1.2	0.7	-0.3	2.3	1.9	-1.0	-1.1	1.3	-0.6	-0.1	-0.1	0.2	-1.0	1.0
9. W. Harrison	-0.2	-0.4	-0.1	0.4	0.1	0.2	-0.4	-0.2	-0.1	0.7	-0.6	0.6	0.3	-0.9
10. Tyler	-1.0	-0.8	0.2	0.0	0.5	0.6	-0.1	-0.7	-0.3	-0.1	-0.7	-0.8	2.3	-0.9
11. Polk	-0.9	-2.1	-0.6	2.2	0.6	1.4	0.9	-1.5	-1.1	1.1	1.4	-0.5	1.8	-0.6
12. Taylor	0.4	0.8	-1.2	-0.9	-2.0	-0.4	-1.0	-0.3	-0.7	-0.1	-0.9	-0.8	-0.7	-1.0
13. Fillmore	1.1	1.0	-0.7	-0.4	0.8	-0.5	-0.8	0.3	2.0	-0.3	-0.1	-0.4	-1.1	0.9
14. Pierce	0.3	1.3	-0.3	-0.3	0.1	-1.0	0.3	0.0	2.2	0.4	0.0	-0.4	-0.7	0.8
15. Buchanan	0.8	0.2	-0.8	-0.2	1.2	-1.5	-0.8	-0.3	0.2	0.9	2.4	1.1	-1.0	0.4
16. Lincoln	1.0	1.0	08	-0.5	-1.2	-0.0	-0.7	2.0	-0.7	-1.3	-1.2	0.1	-0.8	0.6
17. A. Johnson	-1.8	-0.7	-1.2	-1.0	-1.9	1.8	0.6	-1.0	-0.7	0.6	-1.0	-0.3	2.0	-1.8
18. Grant	0.2	-0.5	-1.4	-0.6	-1.7	-4.2	-0.4	-0.6	-0.4	0.4	-1.4	-0.1	0.9	-0.3
19. Hayes	0.2	-0.7	-0.1	-0.4	0.6	-0.4	-0.5	-0.6	-0.5	0.2	0.5	1.4	-0.0	0.1

	1	2	3	4	5	6	7	8	9	10	11	12	13	14
20. Garfield	0.2	-0.1	0.9	-0.0	0.2	0.6	0.2	-0.1	-0.6	-0.1	0.2	-0.1	-0.4	-0.6
21. Arthur	0.8	1.1	0.9	-0.6	1.6	-1.4	-0.6	-0.3	-0.1	1.4	-0.7	-0.1	-1.0	0.4
22. Cleveland	0.8	-0.4	-0.5	-0.9	-0.6	0.6	0.0	0.2	-1.1	-0.7	0.1	1.1	1.2	-0.8
23. B. Harrison	0.3	-1.2	-0.7	-0.6	0.7	-0.6	-0.7	-1.1	-0.4	-0.7	-0.1	-0.1	-0.3	-0.6
24. McKinley	1.0	0.5	-0.6	0.0	1.1	-0.7	-0.2	-1.0	-0.8	-0.3	-0.9	1.9	-0.9	0.6
25. T. Roosevelt	-2.3	-0.4	0.9	0.6	-0.5	0.6	2.7	-0.3	1.7	-0.9	-1.4	-1.9	0.7	-1.8
26. Taft	1.1	0.8	0.0	-1.0	-1.0	-0.4	-1.9	0.5	-0.1	-0.5	0.6	1.1	-1.0	1.5
27. Wilson	-1.3	-1.2	1.3	-0.4	0.8	0.4	0.8	1.0	0.2	-0.2	-0.0	-0.3	2.2	1.0
28. Harding	1.1	1.5	-2.0	-0.1	-0.2	-1.0	-1.3	-0.7	-0.1	2.0	-0.5	0.2	-1.3	1.6
29. Coolidge	0.6	-1.2	-1.5	0.6	-0.8	0.6	-1.7	1.7	0.4	-0.6	1.3	1.6	0.0	0.8
30. Hoover	0.4	-0.9	0.5	-0.1	-0.2	0.6	0.2	-0.8	-0.6	-0.6	1.8	0.4	0.1	1.3
31. F. Roosevelt	-0.1	1.4	0.9	1.7	0.9	0.1	1.3	1.0	-1.1	1.9	-0.9	-1.1	-0.6	-0.3
32. Truman	-1.5	-0.1	0.2	0.3	-1.9	0.6	0.2	-0.4	-0.6	-0.7	-0.8	-0.8	0.7	-1.3
33. Eisenhower	0.8	1.2	-0.7	-0.9	0.0	0.1	-0.5	-0.2	-0.6	0.5	1.3	1.1	-1.0	0.4
34. Kennedy	0.3	1.1	1.8	0.5	1.3	0.8	0.7	2.6	-0.8	2.0	-0.7	-0.6	-0.7	-1.0
35. L. Johnson	-1.6	0.4	-0.2	2.4	-1.5	0.7	2.2	1.0	0.7	1.0	0.3	-0.3	0.2	0.0
36. Nixon	-0.8	-1.6	0.4	2.9	0.3	1.0	0.7	-1.0	4.3	-0.9	0.2	-0.5	0.7	-0.8
37. Ford	0.6	1.3	-0.6	-0.8	-0.3	-0.0	0.5	0.3	-0.1	-0.7	-0.0	1.0	-0.6	0.2
38. Carter	0.7	0.7	-0.0	-0.5	-0.5	-0.2	1.1	-0.8	0.4	0.0	0.3	1.0	-0.9	1.8
39. Reagan	0.2	1.4	0.4	-0.2	0.4	0.4	0.6	2.4	-0.6	1.7	-0.1	2.2	0.0	-0.6

Note. Adapted from Simonton (1986e, table 3). Copyright 1986 by the American Psychological Association. Used by permission. Factors are defined as follows: 1 = moderation, 2 = friendliness, 3 = intellectual brilliance, 4 = Machiavellianism, 5 = poise and polish, 6 = achievement drive, 7 = forcefulness, 8 = wit, 9 = physical attractiveness, 10 = pettiness, 11 = tidiness, 12 = conservatism, 13 = inflexibility, and 14 = pacifism

Table 3.11 *Biographical Stress Events and Their Weights for Ten Classical Composers*

I. *Legal difficulties*
   A. Litigations and lawsuits: 30
   B. Detention in jail or exile to avoid arrest: 63
II. *Economic problems*
   A. Major loan: 20
   B. Troubles with creditors: 30
   C. Aversive change in financial state (or business readjustment): 30
III. *Educational changes*
   A. Change in schools: 20
   B. Beginning or ceasing formal schooling: 26
IV. *Vocational changes or problems*
   A. Job change: 20
   B. Trouble with boss or superiors: 23
   C. Change in responsibilities at work: 29
   D. Begin or end work (not fired or retired): 36
   E. Retirement: 45
   F. Being fired from work: 47
V. *Mobility*
   A. Change in permanent residence—city or town (per move):30
   B. Change in permanent residence—nation (per move): 40
VI. *Interpersonal problems*
   A. Duels, fights, and other physical confrontations: 10
   B. Argument with friend: 10
   C. Disappointed or unreciprocated love: 15
   D. Beginning and/or end of a reciprocated love affair: 40
   E. Death of a close friend: 37
VII. *Family problems*
   A. Gain of a new family member (including adoption): 39
   B. Change in health or behavior of family member: 44
   C. Death of close family member (excluding infants): 63
VIII. *Marital difficulties*
   A. Marital reconciliation: 45
   B. Marriage: 50
   C. Marital separation: 65
   D. Divorce: 73
   E. Death of spouse (unless separated): 100

Note. The events were drawn from the lives of ten classical composers studied in Simonton (1977a); the weights were adapted from T. Holmes and Rahe (1967).

power of 301 geniuses, she could not possibly assess the IQ for each in annual units, however common this practice may be in psychometric studies of contemporary subjects. Not enough quality information exists on which to calculate reliable IQ estimates over intervals so short (not even considering the labor involved). So her strategy was to generate IQ scores for only two bulky chunks of early development, namely 0 to 16 years of age and 17 to 26 years. Taking such big slices, Cox obtained adequate IQ scores and was still able to prove the longitudinal stability of intelligence scores across the first quarter century of cognitive growth (Simonton 1976a). The choice of unit and of measure entails an iterative process that eventually converges on an optimal compromise.

Transhistorical Data

When we speak of transhistorical data, we mean information about changes in whole sociocultural and political systems over historical time. We have already discussed how the investigator may take advantage of the full reservoir of detailed chronologies, biographical dictionaries, and anthologies from which a host of transhistorical counts can be readily generated. Anthologies can also supply primary documents that can be subjected to content analyses, just as this technique can supplement regular biographical data. In addition, there are previously published data that may be employed immediately, thereby eluding laborious tabulations of raw data. Quincy Wright's *A Study of War* (1965), for instance, contains comprehensive tables of mass violence, with detailed information about the nations involved, the nature of each conflict, and other valued facts that have been incorporated with little change in other inquiries (Simonton 1980b, 1986a). Likewise, Sorokin's (1937–41) masterwork includes tabular information on an incredible range of topics, such as war duration and battle casualties, internal disturbances (weighted by duration, extent, and intensity factors), philosophical belief systems (weighted by the distinction of each philosopher), scientific discoveries and technological inventions, and stylistic and content changes in the visual arts (see, for example, Klingemann, Mohler, and Weber, 1982; Martindale 1975). Finally, some research institutions are committed to the compilation and maintenance of data bases on a particular transhistorical subject. The Correlates of War Project at the University of Michigan is a case in point (Singer 1981).

As the last citation hints, Voltaire exaggerated only slightly when he cynically claimed that "history is little else than a picture of human crimes and misfortunes." Even the annals of the earliest civilizations take care to list battles and conquests, assassinations and revolts—cultural events in the arts and sciences receiving detailed registration only later. Hence, it should come as no surprise that many transhistorical inquiries concern how political, artistic, and intellectual events change and covary (Simonton 1984d). The preoccupation with the rise and fall of civilization is, of course, characteristic of speculative philosophies of history as well. On the other hand, should the inquiry venture outside these emphases of the historical record, the researcher must frequently exhibit extraordinary ingenuity to obtain manageable measures of the desired constructs.

Numerous examples are witnessed in work on the connection between the achievement motive and economic prosperity (McClelland 1961, chap. 4). We observed earlier that motivational variables could be tapped through TAT-inspired content analyses, but how does one go about gauging the national well-being of an entire country over time? Certainly none of the transhistorical studies reviewed in McClelland's book concerned periods recent enough that the researchers could expropriate the more obvious measures, such as the gross national product (GNP), unemployment, inflation, or balance-of-trade statistics. Instead, the investigators relied on such proxy indicators of economic expansion as the geographic distribution of the Greek pottery jars that transported wine and olive oil, the amount of public building in the Virú valley of Peru, the number of ships cleared from Spain for the New World, the rates of gain in London coal imports, and the number of patents per capita issued by the United States Patent Office (Cortés 1960; Bradburn and Berlew 1961; deCharms and Moeller 1962). We may no doubt quibble with this or that operational definition, yet as a group the various studies seemed to converge on the same conclusion, therein reinforcing these imaginative solutions to an otherwise nasty problem.

By narrowing attention to current history, many hardships at once disappear. The sizable literature on presidential popularity concentrates on post–World War II chief executives, giving investigators access to approval ratings that must be the envy of historians fascinated with the popularity changes in, say, Louis XIV or Shi Huangdi of Qin China (for example, Kernell 1978; Mueller 1973; compare Benson 1967). Researchers equally obtain the full range of historic events along with direct economic indicators. Likewise, research on the connection between twentieth-century collective violence and environmental conditions incorporates measures of the prevailing ambient temperature, a variable truly unavailable in prior centuries (C. A. Anderson 1989). Bastile Day took place on 14 July, and Independence Day occurred on 4 July, but we can only speculate about whether these rebellious events fit the modern pattern.

Even so, restriction to recent history does not circumvent all obstacles, for the human mind can always conceive ever more subtle variables that challenge the inventiveness of the ingenious investigator. Take the research on the link between authoritarianism and external threat as a case in point (Simonton 1990e). The nomothetic hypothesis is that the cluster of traits belonging to the authoritarian personality is given a boost whenever a people must face highly threatening conditions. The latter independent variable is most often assessed by some readily available economic measure, but how can one assess the modal level of authoritarianism in a whole nation? The solution is to exploit cultural indicators of one or more symptoms of this broad syndrome. Hence, economic depression has been linked with conversion rates to authoritarian rather than to nonauthoritarian churches (Sales 1972); the prominence of power and toughness in comic strip characters and the harsh punishment of sex crimes (Sales 1973); the preference for highly authoritarian television programs (Jorgenson 1975); the frequency of parapsychological research in the professional journals (McCann and Stewin 1984); sales statistics for books on astrology and the occult (Padgett and Jorgenson 1982); and the electoral success of power-oriented presidential candidates (McCann and

Stewin 1987). In like fashion, when Winter (1973) wanted to evaluate the need for power in diverse national histories, he chose to exploit cultural indicators rather than depend on exhaustive content analyses: The ups and downs were tied to the appearances of Don Juan as a character in the national literatures; the infusion of this soldier of fortune and master of sexual conquests could then be linked with the occurrence of imperialistic wars. Consequently, with a little resourcefulness, transhistorical data can provide virtually endless sources for all sorts of variables revealing crucial facets of human nature.

This chapter has conveyed both the opportunities and the complexities attached to historiometric quantification. Often the difficulty is not so much to isolate a suitable measure but rather to choose among myriad alternatives. Whenever researchers experience this embarrassment of riches, they always have the option of assessing the psychological construct two or more ways so as to detect whether the results are robust under alternative operational definitions. Another reasonable choice is to pull off the shelf of tricks one of the statistical techniques that permit one to collapse several rival indicators into a single index—methods revealed in the next chapter. All in all, the picture for quantification looks most bright: Plunging into the historical record to test scientific conjectures does not require that a psychologist don a methodological straitjacket.

Admittedly, we can carry quantification too far, and sometimes historiometry has earned a bad name when operational definitions have been pushed to the outer reaches of tenuousness. Galton himself was a frequent transgressor. According to his biographer, Karl Pearson, Galton's motto was "Whenever you can, count." And so, Galton once used numbers to test once and for all the efficacy of prayer (1883). Arguing that the British monarch benefits every evening from the benevolent thoughts of millions of devoted subjects ("God save the queen"), Galton determined whether the royal heads of state indeed enjoyed a higher life expectancy than that allotted to the poor blokes who count themselves lucky if their names are honorably mentioned in their children's prayers. That kings and queens boasted no special privileges on this score was considered proof enough that the deity failed to respond to human supplications. Ridiculous abuses like these are what make historiometrics appear like a hysterical quantomania. Hence, in some way or another it is incumbent upon any investigator to establish that a quantification actually evaluates the construct dictated by theory—a prime concern of the following two chapters.

4 Reliability

"Anything but history, for history must be false." So replied Sir Robert Walpole when his son offered to read something to him. If historiometry is founded on history, how can the resulting structure be more secure than its foundation? This question is especially delicate insofar as historiometry, unlike history, purports to be a scientific activity. Should history and science have divergent standards of truth and falsehood, surely scientific standards must be more stringent. All the unit definition niceties and quantification procedures would be worthless if the outcome were riddled with error and misrepresentations. Between quantification and analysis the scientist must make a convincing case for the quality of the measures.

Happily, there is a rich and long-evolving literature on how to deal with error in science. These developments began in the physical sciences, the hard disciplines (which were once quite soft). The more dependably soft disciplines in the behavioral sciences have also developed an impressive armory against the ever-present influx of error in precious data. Of these weapons, the most valuable may be the techniques invented by psychometricians. Because psychological concepts are so elusive, psychometrics has adopted divide-and-conquer tactics, measures of psychological attributes differing along two separate evaluative criteria, namely reliability and validity.

To be reliable an instrument must be precise, assessing a construct with optimal accuracy; to be valid, however, the instrument must measure what it claims to measure, precision be what it may. This psychometric distinction is important because a test might be extremely accurate but assess the wrong attribute—a common criticism of standard IQ tests. Naturally, these two criteria cannot be totally independent, for a measure that has zero reliability cannot be valid either. Even so, these judgmental touchstones are sufficiently distinct that we may examine separately the reliability and validity of the most frequently used instruments. Reliability will be the concern of this chapter, validity the topic of the following chapter.

A persistent issue in psychometric theory has been how to determine the amount of error permeating a set of measurements. Therefore, it seems natural that this concern entered early in the development of historiometrics. In Woods's evaluation of the comparative creativity of Sophocles and Euripides (1911), the sources of error were a major point of discussion; in Cox's IQ estimates (1926), great pains were taken to calculate their reliability as well; and Thorndike's (1936) improvements upon Woods's (1906) study of the intelligence-morality correlation considered more completely possible measurement errors. Most early applications of psychometric methods to historical data rested on the valuable statistic known as the *reliability coefficient*, and so it is this omnibus tool that we examine first. Yet with more recent advances in multivariate analyses, another device, *factor analysis*, became better known, first in psychometrics and then in historiometrics. After we look at factor analytic responses to the reliability problem, we turn to other potential ways of gauging error—miscellaneous statistical tests and logical criteria.

Reliability Coefficients

When psychometricians pass judgment on a measure's reliability, they may assign a number that ranges from zero to unity. A reliability exactly zero signifies that the instrument is merely a cumbersome and expensive random-number generator; the measure yields no signal, only pure noise, and therefore is scientifically impotent as a gauge of anything other than how down-feather soft a field of inquiry remains. By comparison, a reliability coefficient of 1 represents perfection or diamond hardness as a science. Only physical measurements, such as time, height, and weight so closely approximate unity reliability that we may safely dispense altogether with having to compute these coefficients. In contrast, the majority of psychological instruments fall in a range from the .60s to the .90s. In the roughest terms, intelligence tests tend to feature reliabilities around .80, attitude questionnaires around .70, and personality inventories as low as .60, although appreciable variation exists among measures of the same type. It is also not rare for an investigator to waste considerable time developing a measure of some psychological construct only to discover that the reliability is .50 or lower. Needless to say, if a psychologist submits for publication a research result based on measurements with so much error, it is likely to be rejected. Yet ironically, the reliabilities for separate reviewer opinions in refereed journals in the behavioral sciences range only between .20 and .30 (Lindsey 1988). Obviously psychologists must tolerate an immense intrusion of error in their professional lives, especially when we contrast the figures with the low rejection rates and high consensus in the natural sciences.

Psychometric theory features a lengthy list of means by which reliability coefficients can be estimated. The three that have the most relevance for historiometry are alternative-measures, test-retest, and internal-consistency coefficients (Nunnally 1978, chap. 7).

Alternative Measures

Say we obtain two independent assessments of the same variable across a collection of analytical units. If the two measures tap the same dimension in much the same manner, the instruments may be viewed as at least approximately "parallel." The most common approach to gauging reliability here is to calculate the Pearson product-moment correlation between the two alternatives. This workhorse statistic ranges from -1 to $+1$, with 0 marking the absence of any relation whatsoever. Because a negative reliability coefficient is meaningless—if such a number emerges then the investigator may have inadvertently inverted one of the two scales—this statistic in practice yields a coefficient between 0 and 1, as required. For instance, Kynerd (1971) evaluated the reliability of presidential greatness ratings by calculating the correlations between alternative rankings; thus the two nearly contemporaneous ratings by Schlesinger (1962b) and Sokolsky (1964) correlated .95. Similarly, when two alternative counts of lifetime productivity were estimated for 789 scientists, one measure using biographical and the other historical sources, the correlation between the two assessments was .79 (Simonton 1979a).

In these instances, the unit of analysis is the individual historical figure. Yet reliabilities can be estimated for measurements on other kinds of units as well. In a study of the differential popularity of compositions in the classical repertoire, the correlations between two independent indicators yielded coefficients of .67, .74, and .60 for Beethoven, Bach, and Mozart, respectively (Simonton 1983b). On a gross scale, generational time series that record the number of philosophers for each twenty-year period across the course of Western intellectual history produce a reliability coefficient of .75, again by computing a product-moment correlation between distinct tabulations (Simonton 1976f). Because these reliabilities fall in the ranges typical of psychometric tests, alternative historiometric measures do an excellent job measuring what they set out to measure.

Just like regular psychological instruments, reliabilities can vary appreciably from measure to measure, but certain principles tell us whether we should raise or lower expectations for specific coefficients. One criterion is how much variation the units display for the trait being assessed. Intelligence tests cannot adequately differentiate a group of subjects confined to stratospheric grades of intellect, and so historiometric measures cannot be more accurate. Accordingly, the reliabilities of the IQ scores assigned to Cox's 301 geniuses (1926) are only around .50. Likewise, the reliabilities given in the previous paragraph for the audience appeal of musical compositions by the three top composers are lower than holds for the larger collection of composers (Simonton 1986a). Besides, the three coefficients were computed over only those compositions that have an established position on concert programs, deleting the lesser known works by this triumvirate. If the comparisons had included *all* of Beethoven's songs, Bach's cantatas, and Mozart's Masonic music, the reliability coefficients would no doubt be much higher. So when criticizing the reliability of any historiometric assessment, one must always fairly weigh whether the variance on the attributes has been so truncated that really high coefficients are absolutely inconceivable.

A second criterion is the nature of the construct being assessed. In psychometrics, measures of cognitive skills, like IQ tests, feature higher reliabilities than indicators of motivational states or dispositions, a disparity that repeats itself in the historiometric literature. When Cox (1926) assessed her geniuses on sixty-seven character traits, she deliberately narrowed her sample to the one hundred personalities with the most adequate biographical data. Yet doing so only prevented a potential disaster: The reliabilities for these personality assessments were no higher than those for the IQ scores. Despite taking solely those who resided in the top one-third on data richness, in only 27 percent of the cases did the reliability increase from the IQ to the trait estimates. The data may have been more refined, but the constructs measured were equally more nebulous.

Content analytical studies display the same tendency. Integrative complexity is a cognitive characteristic that can be coded from text with a great precision, independent assessments of the same text accordingly hovering in the upper .80s and .90s (for example, Tetlock, Hannum, and Micheletti 1984). In contrast, human motivation is far less precisely defined and even less definitively quantified. Projective tests such as TAT and the Rorschach test seldom boast impressive reliabilities, and their historiometric counterparts follow suit. For instance, two separate assessments of the power, achievement, and affiliation motives in the same batch of American presidents—although conducted under the direction of a single expert investigator—correlate .39, .52, and .88, respectively (Simonton 1988d; compare Winter and Stewart 1977; Winter 1987b).

Even transhistorical inquiries, which benefit from far more public data, the anticipated size of the coefficient varies with the nature of the construct measured. For example, data on war duration can feature a reliability coefficient of .82, whereas battle casualty data for the same conflicts may have a reliability that descends to .46 (Simonton 1976e). And the consensus on scientific discoveries and musical composition is such as to ensure reliabilities for generational time series of around .90, while comparable aggregate measures for the visual arts and the humanities may sink to the .70s (Simonton 1975e, 1976f, 1977c). The dependence of reliability on the measure's content can frustrate the perfectionist scientist who is granted little latitude for quantifying variables so that they all meet uniformly high standards.

Finally, alternative-measure reliabilities will usually differ from historical period to historical period and from one nation or discipline to another. Again looking at the 1926 Cox study, the correlation between the reliability of her IQ estimates and the year that the genius was born is a bit over .40, certainly a magnitude of association that cannot be ignored (Simonton 1976a). Thus, despite her restricting the sample to luminaries born since 1450, the recent figures still have biographies that contain more detailed data about early development. To show what may happen in cross-national data, the correlations between Sorokin's (1937–41) tabulations of scientific creativity, which are based on Darmstaedter's (1908) monumental chronology, and two alternative measures, one gathered by a Japanese scholar and the other from an American reference book (Yuasa 1974) are given in table 4.1. The counts were tabulated in fifty-year periods across the histories of four separate European nations. Even if these pairwise correlations are basically honorable, a peculiar exception intrudes in the Italian data, Darmstaedter and Heibonsha differing on the fluctuations in the contributions of Italian scientists.

If two independent measures of the same construct are truly parallel, then the correlation between them has a convenient interpretation: The square root of the reliability estimates the association between each measure's scores and the real values of the variable under perfect assessment. In psychometric terms, this square root is the correlation between fallible and true scores (Nunnally 1978). Therefore, to hold that integrative complexity can be assessed with a reliability of .97 is to maintain that the correlation between observed and actual scores on this construct can be .98. On the other hand, given that the power motive may be scaled with a reliability of only .39, the correlation between fallible and true scores may be merely .62. However, a warning is appropriate when two measures are not exactly parallel. Often one assessment is superior to the other, either because the data are better, one rater is more thoroughly trained, or some other cause. In this situation, the square root of the reliability coefficient will not fairly represent how well the best instrument corresponds to reality. In the extreme case, should one measure be pure noise and the other capture the true scores infallibly, the correlation between the two measures will still be zero, making us careful in judging reliabilities. The

Table 4.1 *Product-Moment Correlations: Sorokin's Science Measures and Two by Yuasa*

Source	Nation			
	England	*France*	*Germany*	*Italy*
Heibonsha ($N = 8$)	.98**	.88**	.98**	.22
Webster ($N = 7$)	.96**	.995**	.99**	.82*

Note. Adapted from Simonton (1976b, table 1, 138); based on Sorokin (1937) and Yuasa (1974).

Yuasa's two sets of measures were tabulated by fifty-year periods from a Japanese and an American reference work, whereas Sorokin's were originally tabulated into twenty-five-year periods (here collapsed into fifty-year periods) from a German reference work; *$p < .05$ **$p < .001$.

unacceptably low coefficient in table 4.1 probably betrays a lack of attention to Italian science by Heibonsha, an inference underlined when we learn that the correlation between Heibonsha and Webster for Italy is −.24 (Simonton 1976b).

Test-Retest

From time to time reliabilities result from testing the same persons on two separate occasions with the same instrument. An intelligence test might be administered to the same subjects a year apart, and the correlation coefficient between the two performances taken as the reliability coefficient. This route is particularly favored when other reliability estimates are unavailable. Yet for the test-retest method to work well, there cannot be any carryover effects that exaggerate the correlation between the original exam and its sequel. The subjects might remember a large proportion of the items and how they responded to them. At the same time, the investigator must posit that the assessed characteristic is relatively constant over the time interval so that the resulting reliability coefficient is not underestimated either. These two considerations obviously function in opposition so that it is most difficult to ensure proper balance. Expanding the time lapse between first and second administrations lessens the intrusion of practice effects, but also renders less likely the assumption that the attribute has been invariant over the interim. No wonder, then, that this approach is not popular among psychometricians.

Nor is the test-retest technique a favorite tool of historiometricians, Cox providing a rare instance. When she calculated IQ scores across two separate age groups (0–16 and 17–26), the strong congruence between them could be specified by the correlation of .82 (Simonton 1976a). Nevertheless, something akin to test-retest reliabilities emerge when one investigator deliberately strives to replicate the ratings of a predecessor on the same units. One illustration is Thorndike's (1936) independent assessment of royal family members on intelligence and morality to discern the adequacy of Woods's (1906) prior quantifications. Using raters blind to the earlier scores, Thorndike was able to show that the test-retest reliabilities for intellect ranged from .77 to .81, whereas those for virtue were .64 to .69—again the reliabilities of the more cognitive concept surpass those for the dispositional concept. In these particular test-retest coefficients, the stability of the subjects on the traits are not at issue, nor need we concern ourselves with carryover effects, given that the targets of inquiry were all deceased. What these reassessments tell us is that the way psychologists perceive intelligence or morality is sufficiently stable over three decades that the terms mean the same thing when assigned to the same people.

This last demonstration may seem mundane when scrutinizing perceptions of personality traits, yet this question acquires urgency when we look at perhaps the single most prominent concept in all historiometry—the notion of greatness, eminence, fame, or reputation. Besides its use as a sampling strategy, this notion provides one of the field's most popular dependent variables (Simonton 1984d). Galton (1869) first put this idea in the spotlight by defining genius in terms of achieved distinction, or reputation, which he took to mean "the opinion of contemporaries, revised by posterity . . . the reputation of a leader of opinion, of an originator, of a man to whɯ n the world deliberately acknowledges itself largely indebted" (33). This solution to the definition problem is nonetheless overturned at once should it be easily shown that the attainment of recognition is too fickle and mean to provide a stable index of personal disposition. If genius is a property of individuals, but our measures of this attribute depend on the judgments of contemporaries and posterity, then a diminutive test-retest reliability would necessarily destroy Galton's position. Especially for geniuses no longer living, we cannot expect personal qualities to vary according to the whims of later judges. True geniuses should transcend fashion's caprice. What Ben Jonson said of Shakespeare should be valid for all luminaries: "He was not of an age, but for all time."

Investigators often resort to Galton's operational definition, so it is understandable that much time has been relegated to proving the test-retest reliability of eminence assessments. A whole chapter of Farnsworth's *Social Psychology of Music* (1969) carries the responsibility of proving that aesthetic taste is lawful and stable rather than arbitrary and transient. Over (1982) demonstrated that "in the case of psychology there was no individual who was markedly out of favor in 1903 but markedly in favor in 1966–70, or vice versa" (60), the correlation across nearly three fourths of a century hitting .72. Rosengren (1985) indicated that the reputations of literary figures are similarly durable, with a reliability around .61. These findings run counter to the beliefs of some who find fame unreliable. Gregor Mendel, the founder of quantitative genetics, is far more famous now than he was back in 1865; J. S. Bach in his own day enjoyed less renown than did the now more obscure Telemann. However, such cases are too rare to negate a valid regularity. More important, these perturbations become trivial when contrasted with the full spread in fame. One day Beethoven stands above Mozart on the charts, another day he must yield the limelight to his younger contemporary, yet at no time in the history of music appreciation has either had to compete for attention with the likes of Gebel, Reicha, or Türk, rivals of the same era and musical tradition. In the same vein, despite the virulent anti-Semitic efforts of Lenard (1933) to place Hasenöhrl above Einstein in the pantheon of scientific notables, it is the latter name that now exclusively earns the accolades.

The exquisite test-retest reliability is perhaps best appreciated in the various determinations of the differential greatness of U.S. presidents. In table 3.1 some rankings were offered and interval scalings were presented in table 3.4. Let us integrate these and other scorings into a single table, converting all the numbers to z scores to facilitate comparisons across successive attempts. Table 4.2 offers a series of nine "greatness tests" intermittently scattered over a thirty-five-year period. Although the scores are not all measured on the same scale, and some scores represent one-person estimates while others show the results of surveying hundreds of experts, the ratings suffice to get the point across.

A quick scan across the rows convincingly shows that the ratings are not identical, and so a scholar inclined to specialize in the bark patterns on single tree trunks would maintain that the discrepancies discredit the enterprise. This was the position adopted by the historian Thomas Bailey in his 1966 book *Presidential Greatness* (this despite his willingness to put in his own two bits on the rating game). Nevertheless, an expert in the worldwide distribution of forests would spot a striking regularity. Presidents with scores near zero on one rating tend to have similarly mediocre assessments on other ratings, and chief executives conspicuously above or below the mean level in one column are prone to persist in their high or low status throughout. The only genuine instability in the table concerns Kennedy, but this is because the early ratings were momentarily deflected by the well-established "tragedy effect" (Lehman 1943; Mills 1942; Simonton 1976a). At any rate, the test-retest reliability from the first to the last rating is an impressive .95. Presidential greatness is not bestowed with levity.

To be sure, one could argue that any reputational consensus is merely an artifact of nonindependent judgments, the historiometric counterpart of psychometric carryover effects. It has been specifically argued, for instance, that persistence in literary fame reflects solely the dependency of one generation of critics on those preceding (Rosengren 1985). Although not utterly erroneous, it is not the whole story either. The influence of one scholar upon a successor can just as well operate to *reduce* the test-retest reliability of an eminence assessment. Scholars, especially critics, frequently establish their own reputations by attacking the opinions passed down by those before them, so that the torch is not so much passed on as blown out. A specific example of explicit dissent is found in table 4.2. Bailey's (1966) ratings were put forward as a pointed antidote to the Schlesinger (1948, 1962b) polls, which were found objectionable on several counts. Ironically, even if the rival ratings harbor certain idiosyncrasies (to be discussed later in this chapter), Bailey failed to overthrow the overall consensus. The correlation between his and Schlesinger's first and second rankings are .73 and .75, respectively, reliabilities a safe distance from zero and far from negative.

Nor is cantankerousness or iconoclasm the only detriment. Often the transhistorical stability of distinction is weakened by the continual insertion of new names to the list of contenders for posterity's acclaim. Each time a candidate is added to the roster, some reshuffling of the previous rankings must occur. In the Farnsworth (1969) ratings given in table 3.2, it is evident that when Debussy won the tenth-place spot on the ordinal scale, predecessors from Monteverdi to Verdi had to be bumped downward. This demotion to make room for more recent inductees may entirely explain why Farnsworth found that reputational test-retest reliabilities tend to be slightly higher the more closely spaced the separate measures are in time, just as is frequently discovered in psychometric studies (see

Table 4.2 *Standardized Greatness Scores for U.S. Presidents*

President	Schlesinger		Rossiter	Bailey-Kynerd	Sokolsky	Maranell-Simonton	Porter	Chicago Tribune	Murray-Blessing
	1948	1962							
1. Washington	1.5	1.5	1.2	1.6	0.6	1.2	1.6	1.6	1.9
2. J. Adams	0.7	0.7	0.5	-0.6	0.6	0.4	0.8	0.3	0.6
3. Jefferson	1.2	1.2	1.2	1.2	1.4	1.2	1.4	1.3	1.5
4. Madison	0.1	0.4	-0.9	-0.7	-0.2	0.1	0.5	0.1	0.2
5. Monroe	0.4	-0.2	-0.9	0.9	-0.2	-0.0	0.1	0.2	0.2
6. J. Q. Adams	0.5	0.3	-0.2	-1.5	-0.2	-0.1	0.0	-0.0	0.1
7. Jackson	1.1	1.1	1.2	1.0	1.4	1.2	1.1	1.1	1.0
8. Van Buren	0.0	-0.1	-0.2	0.6	-0.2	-0.4	-0.0	0.0	-0.3
9. W. Harrison	—	—	—	—	—	—	—	—	—
10. Tyler	-0.8	-1.0	-0.2	-0.2	-0.2	-0.9	-0.9	-0.9	-0.8
11. Polk	0.6	0.9	0.5	-0.1	0.6	0.4	0.9	0.8	0.4
12. Taylor	-1.2	-0.9	—	-0.8	-1.1	-1.0	-0.8	-0.7	-0.7
13. Fillmore	-1.1	-1.1	-0.9	-0.3	-1.1	-1.4	-1.0	-1.2	-0.9
14. Pierce	-1.4	-1.3	-1.6	-1.1	-1.1	-1.4	-1.4	-1.4	-1.1
15. Buchanan	-1.3	-1.4	-1.6	-1.2	-1.1	-1.2	-1.6	-1.5	-1.3
16. Lincoln	1.6	1.6	1.2	1.5	1.4	1.7	1.7	1.7	2.0
17. A. Johnson	-0.5	-0.8	0.5	-1.6	-0.2	-0.2	-1.2	-1.1	-1.2

	C1	C2	C3	C4	C5	C6	C7	C8	C9
18. Grant	−1.5	−1.5	−1.6	−0.9	−1.9	−1.2	−1.3	−1.3	−1.4
19. Hayes	0.2	0.2	0.5	0.8	−0.2	−0.8	−0.1	−0.3	−0.4
20. Garfield	—	—	—	—	—	—	—	—	—
21. Arthur	−0.2	−0.6	0.2	0.2	−0.2	−0.8	−0.5	−0.5	−0.5
22. Cleveland	0.8	0.6	0.5	0.1	0.6	0.1	0.3	0.5	0.1
23. B. Harrison	−0.7	−0.4	−0.9	−0.4	−1.1	−1.1	−0.6	−0.6	−0.7
24. McKinley	−0.4	0.1	−0.2	0.7	−0.2	−0.3	0.2	0.7	−0.2
25. T. Roosevelt	0.9	1.0	1.2	1.3	1.4	1.4	1.3	1.4	1.3
26. Taft	−0.1	0.0	−0.2	0.0	−0.2	−0.1	−0.2	−0.1	−0.2
27. Wilson	1.3	1.3	1.2	1.1	1.4	1.2	1.2	1.2	1.2
28. Harding	−1.6	−1.6	−1.6	−1.4	−1.9	−1.4	−1.7	−1.7	−1.6
29. Coolidge	−0.9	−1.2	−0.9	−1.0	−1.1	−1.1	−1.1	−1.0	−0.9
30. Hoover	−0.6	−0.3	−0.2	−1.3	−0.2	−0.1	−0.3	−0.2	−0.4
31. F. Roosevelt	1.4	1.4	1.2	1.4	1.4	1.9	1.5	1.5	1.9
32. Truman	—	0.8	1.2	0.4	0.6	1.1	1.0	1.0	0.9
33. Eisenhower	—	−0.7	0.5	0.3	−0.2	−0.2	0.6	0.9	0.5
34. Kennedy	—	—	—	—	1.4	0.8	0.4	0.4	0.4
35. L. Johnson	—	—	—	—	—	0.8	0.7	0.6	0.6
36. Nixon	—	—	—	—	—	—	−1.5	−1.6	−1.3
37. Ford	—	—	—	—	—	—	−0.7	−0.4	−0.6
38. Carter	—	—	—	—	—	—	−0.4	−0.8	−0.6

Note. Adapted from Simonton (1981b, table 1) and Simonton (1986c, table A1).

Simonton 1990c). The correlation matrix for space allocations in three different types of reference books taken from the 1900s to the 1960s by decade intervals is given in table 4.3. The farther apart the assessments, the lower the test-retest correlations, yet even when the two gauges are divorced by over a half century, the coefficients remain between .82 and .88. The line allotments for the separate entries do not shift capriciously, the addition of new entries notwithstanding.

One last factor that can vitiate the genuine continuity in distinction concerns the variance truncation problem mentioned as a culprit in alternative-measures reliabilities. Those scholars who like to rate the presidents of the United States experience a luxury denied most others—the feasibility of evaluating a whole population. With the exception of William Harrison and Garfield (both of whom died too early in their first terms to be attractive to raters), all past chief executives (as of 1983) are to be found carefully pegged in tables 3.1, 3.4, and 4.2. But in other contexts such an exhaustive endeavor would be practically impossible. *Who's Who in Science* (Debus 1968) contains over thirty thousand entries, but the most exhaustive eminence ratings to date managed to handle just 2,026 scientists and inventors (Simonton 1990a). Farnsworth's (1969) rankings concentrated on ninety-two classical composers when the total number of also-rans was at least 1134 (Illing 1963). So when one admits to the hall of fame only the most illustrious figures from history, the test-retest stabilities must suffer attenuation. Accordingly, the correlation between the eminence scores of Cox's 301 geniuses and a more

Table 4.3   *Intercorrelations in Space Allocations for Classical Composers*

Histories	1920s	1930s	1940s	1950s	1960s
1900s	.90	.88	.78	.86	.82
1920s		.90	.88	.91	.89
1930s			.90	.94	.92
1940s				.94	.94
1950s					.96
Music encyclopedias					
1900s	.77	.74	.72	.75	.82
1920s		.91	.89	.88	.87
1930s			.95	.94	.94
1940s				.94	.96
1950s					.97
General encyclopedias					
1900s	.90	.88	.88	.92	.88
1920s		.94	.91	.95	.91
1930s			.93	.96	.93
1940s				.96	.93
1950s					.97

Note. Adapted from Farnsworth (1969, 119). Reprinted, by permission, from *The Social Psychology of Music,* 2d ed., by P. R. Farnsworth, copyright 1969 by Iowa State University Press, Ames, Iowa   50010.

recent rating is merely .43 (Simonton 1976a). Given that the Cox scores were taken directly from Cattell (1903), who exploited reference works written in the nineteenth century, we have here a continuity spanning almost a century. Still, the coefficient would certainly have been larger if Cox had taken all of the one thousand historical figures on the Cattell list, and it would be more impressive still were all historical personalities assessed, however inconceivable the task.

Internal Consistency

Whenever a latent trait is measured more than twice, a certain inelegance emerges in calculating reliability coefficients using bivariate correlations. If k is the number of separate indicators of a construct, then $k(k - 1)/2$ is the number of distinct coefficients derived from all possible pairings, a number that gets large fast as k grows. Therefore, if we possess multiple indices of the same attribute, we are most likely to compute coefficient alpha, the internal-consistency reliability, using the formula

$$\alpha = \frac{k}{k - 1} \left(1 - \frac{\Sigma \sigma_i^2}{\sigma_c^2} \right),$$

where k is the number of measures, σ_c^2 is the variance of the total composite obtained by summing the scores, and σ_i^2 represents the variances of the separate measures that go into that sum ($i = 1, 2, 3 \ldots k$). Just like the other reliability coefficients, alpha ranges from 0 to 1 and features the same interpretative significance.

Coefficient alpha has proved valuable in specifying the reliability of the omnipresent eminence measures. To obtain a truly effective index of the differential distinction attained by a sample of creators or leaders, the investigator should not rely exclusively on a single indicator. A cardinal principle of psychometric theory is that the errors inherent in any one measure tend to cancel out when many such measures are added to form a single overall score. In intelligence testing, which offers the best illustration, the IQ is not determined by performance on a single question—whether an arithmetic or vocabulary problem—but rather on the summary performance on a multitude of items. The reliability of the whole, then, exceeds the individual reliabilities of the parts. In this way numerous fallible scores can in concert inch toward the Holy Grail of the true score.

So when the goal was to differentiate 2,026 scientists on distinction, dependence on a single criterion, such as receipt of a Nobel Prize, would have been ill-advised. Accordingly, multiple indicators were generated by looking at space allocations in encyclopedias and biographical dictionaries, citations in histories and chronologies, independent ratings by several experts, and so forth, obtaining fifteen different measures altogether (Simonton 1990a). The composite score produced by summing these assessments then could claim a coefficient alpha of .94.

By the same technique, the differential acclaim of 772 artists was gauged by a twenty-seven-item composite with an alpha reliability of .86 (Simonton 1984a); the comparative fame of 2,012 philosophers was determined by a ten-measure total score with a reliability of .94 (Simonton 1976f); the relative fame (or infamy) of 342 monarchs was defined by a thirteen-component measure having a coefficient of .90 (Simonton 1983d); and the variation in greatness of thirty-three presidents was assessed by a five-item composite with an alpha reliability of .98 (Simonton 1981b).

Computation of internal consistency coefficients is valuable beyond the eminence ratings of historical figures, for this technique is equally useful in empirical aesthetics when the desire is to differentiate a sample of artistic creations on comparative merit. Thus, the relative success of the thirty-seven plays by Shakespeare was evaluated by first defining nineteen indicators of the frequency of performance, quotation, citation, and the like, and then merging these assessments into a composite index of dramatic popularity boasting a coefficient alpha of .88 (Simonton 1986f). The resulting scores for the Shakespeare canon are given in table 4.4, together with the estimated dates. These estimates were themselves composites of thirteen separate datings with an alpha reliability of .999, a remarkable coefficient not just because it is a hair's breadth from perfection, but also because *only* dates that conflicted with each other were included in the list of indicators. Scholarly controversies over rival datings must be mere tempests in teapots if the disagreements are so minuscule that they feature no genuine consequences for questions of measurement (see also McCurdy 1953, 48).

The last example shows that internal consistency reliabilities can be calculated for concepts other than differential distinction or success. Any construct that can be tapped several ways can be measured using a linear composite, that is, a simple summation of the several indicators, and then coefficient alpha estimated. For instance, earlier we mentioned how the presidents were evaluated on fourteen distinct personality dimensions, each of these being a composite of several adjectives from the Gough ACL (Simonton 1986h). These composite scores can thus be assigned corresponding alpha reliabilities, namely, moderation .98, friendliness .96, intellectual brilliance .90, Machiavellianism .92, poise and polish .89, achievement drive .82, forcefulness .89, wit .71, physical attractiveness .98, pettiness .33, tidiness .70, conservatism .85, inflexibility .92, and pacifism .79. So the applicability of this psychometric device is universal; composite measures of all sorts of constructs assessed at any level of analysis may be tagged with an internal-consistency reliability coefficient. But why was there so much variation in reliability across the fourteen personality dimensions? One cause is that these factors tap latent variables that vary in the ease of assessment; it is easier to achieve consensus on a president's physical attractiveness than on his pettiness. Yet another reason is more general, namely that the composites differ in the number of items that compose them. Thus moderation consists of fifty-eight adjectives, whereas pettiness contains only two (greedy and self-pitying). In general, holding

Table 4.4 *Popularity Ratings and Estimated Composition Dates for Thirty-seven Shakespearean Plays*

Play	Popularity	Date
1. *Henry VI*, part 1	16	1591 (1592)
2. *Henry VI*, part 2	17	1591 (1592)
3. *Henry VI*, part 3	15	1591 (1592)
4. *Comedy of Errors*	31	1592 (1592)
5. *Richard III*	44	1593 (1593)
6. *Titus Andronicus*	20	1593 (1592)
7. *Two Gentlemen of Verona*	20	1593 (1593)
8. *Love's Labours Lost*	24	1593 (1595)
9. *The Taming of the Shrew*	54	1594 (1593)
10. *Romeo and Juliet*	84	1595 (1596)
11. *Richard II*	38	1595 (1594)
12. *Midsummer Night's Dream*	69	1595 (1596)
13. *The Merchant of Venice*	68	1596 (1598)
14. *King John*	20	1596 (1595)
15. *Henry IV*, part 1	45	1597 (1596)
16. *Henry IV*, part 2	33	1598 (1597)
17. *Much Ado About Nothing*	46	1598 (1599)
18. *Henry V*	51	1599 (1597)
19. *Julius Caesar*	53	1599 (1598)
20. *As You Like It*	62	1599 (1598)
21. *Merry Wives of Windsor*	37	1600 (1600)
22. *Twelfth Night*	65	1601 (1602)
23. *Hamlet*	138	1601 (1603)
24. *Troilus and Cressida*	25	1602 (1600)
25. *All's Well That Ends Well*	26	1602 (1604)
26. *Measure for Measure*	47	1604 (1604)
27. *Othello*	77	1604 (1602)
28. *King Lear*	85	1605 (1604)
29. *Macbeth*	94	1606 (1606)
30. *Anthony and Cleopatra*	46	1607 (1609)
31. *Timon of Athens*	16	1607 (1605)
32. *Coriolanus*	24	1608 (1609)
33. *Pericles*	18	1608 (1608)
34. *Cymbeline*	35	1610 (1610)
35. *Winter's Tale*	43	1610 (1609)
36. *The Tempest*	69	1611 (1609)
37. *Henry VIII*	27	1613 (1613)

Source: Simonton (1986f, table 1). Copyright 1986 by Elsevier Science Publisher. Used by permission.
Note. Parenthetical dates are those indicated on stylistic evidence alone (i.e., verse tests).

other influences constant, internal consistency reliability increases with the number of variables forming the sum (Nunnally 1978). Hence, it is advisable to accumulate as many alternative indicators as possible, especially when the underlying concept strongly resists error-free measurement. The more elusive the variable, the more items must go into the pot before a passable reliability emerges.

These are not the only things that affect alpha reliability. Truncated variation can undermine coefficient alpha just as it can for the simpler reliability coefficients. Internal consistency reliabilities can vary according to other circumstances as well. Thus, when over two thousand scientists were distinguished on fame, the reliability of a twenty-three-item composite was found to differ across historical period, nationality, and discipline (Simonton 1984i). The reliabilities range from .68 for the twentieth century to .85 for the sixteenth century, from .76 for the United States to .91 for the Netherlands, and from .73 for the earth sciences to .90 for physics. Every single one of these coefficients is worthy of attention, yet the variation is substantial. Consensus on scientific greatness is easier to achieve in some conditions than in others. As a case in point, the consensus on scientific distinction is higher in the mathematical and physical sciences than in the behavioral and applied sciences.

Factor Analysis

When the internal consistency for a set of items is high, the summary indicator can be said to assess a single latent dimension. But should the measures entering into the linear composite be heterogeneous, more than one dimension may underlie the collection of items, a condition that undermines reliability. Hence, piling measure upon measure may not enhance internal consistency if those items tap distinct factors. The common method for detecting a motley mixture is to *factor analyze* the variable pool, which accomplishes two related tasks. First, the true dimensionality of the measures can be determined so that the k measures can be assigned to a smaller set of m factors. Because these factors represent rather disparate dimensions, they will not correlate highly, and the internal consistency of the items defining each factor will be respectable. Second, the analysis provides estimates of the amount of variance in the total array of variables that can be accounted for by each factor. The variance explicated by a latent construct is actually associated with the internal consistency of the corresponding factor composite. Again, because statistical niceties are best left to texts (for example, Gorsuch 1983), the goal here is to show how the method enables us to address two issues germane to reliability evaluations.

Dimensionality

Under the assumption that multiple indicators all pertain to the same concept, factor analysis should produce one unified dimension. There are many approaches to testing for this hypothesized unidimensionality, yet perhaps the simplest is to conduct a *principal components* analysis. This technique directly determines how many factors exceed the minimum criterion for component variance, namely unity. This threshold is based on the fact that factor analysis is almost always done on z scores, and therefore the variance of any one item is one.

Because the variance of a principal component represents the amount of variance in the total variable pool explicated by the component, a factor with less than a unity variance explains less variance than does a single variable (but see Zwick and Velicer 1986). On the other hand, the maximum variance that can be dispatched by any factor is equal to the total variance available in the multiple indicators, which, for variables standardized to a unit deviation, equals k, the number of variables factored. The more initial variance taken up by any one factor, the less that can be left to be absorbed by the remaining factors; the sum of the variance of each factor extracted cannot exceed the total variance in the variables. From this we obtain the ideal unidimensional solution under principal components: One factor has a variance close to k, whereas all other potential factors have variances < 1.0, and preferably close to 0.

To demonstrate, when the thirteen contradictory datings of Shakespeare's thirty-seven plays were subjected to a principal components analysis, only one factor had a variance surpassing unity, and that single dimension exhibited a variance just shy of thirteen (12.9), leaving the remaining "factors" with variances uniformly near zero (Simonton 1986f). Therefore, all datings, whatever their putative discrepancies, tap but one homogeneous construct, thereby justifying their merger into the dates provided in table 4.4. Needless to say, not all tests for the presence of a single factor are this clear-cut, but strong unidimensional scales pass by this touchstone. Thus, when the differential eminence of classical composers was assessed by six indicators (including the scores in tables 3.2 and 3.5), a single dimension emerged even though that one factor had a variance equivalent to about four items (Simonton 1977c). Similarly, when the comparative influence of absolute monarchs was gauged by thirteen indicators, a unidimensional solution resulted despite the fact that the one factor had a variance equal to only half of the items. What makes these two analyses yield single-factor conclusions is merely that no rival factors displayed variances above the minimum criterion of unity, the variance of a single standardized item.

Matters can be less certain than even this, naturally. Perhaps only one underlying construct may be evident in the items, but one or more of those items turns out to be a poor indicator of that latent variable. The best hint that an inferior item lurks in the collection is the item's factor loading, which is essentially the correlation between the item and the factor (a kind of item-composite correlation). Like any correlation coefficient, the factor loading varies from -1 to $+1$, where a negative loading reveals an inverse indicator and a positive loading a direct indicator. Should the absolute value of a loading near zero, or at least fall well below .40 or .30, reliability may be improved by deleting that item from the total score. For instance, when the popularity of eighty-one plays was assessed using several alternative indicators, a single principal component had a variance exceeding unity, with all factor loadings but one ranging from .71 to .81 (Simonton 1983a). The delinquent indicator, which claimed a loading of only .26, was a measure of how often the play has been successfully converted into an opera. Evidently, what makes for dramatic success is not close to what makes for an operatic success, a fact proved by how Shakespeare's plays have faired when set to music. *King Lear* and *Hamlet* have yet to stimulate the creation of operas as popular as those inspired by *Romeo and Juliet* and the *Merry Wives of Windsor*. If the goal is to devise a coherent measure of dramatic popularity, successful conversions to operatic format are best ignored.

There remain a few more difficulties with dimensionality tests that should instill caution in any investigator. One problem is that factor analysis can reveal only the dimensionality of the multiple measures when the set of indicators is truly multiple. With only two or three indicators, a single-factor solution is almost guaranteed, unless the indicators fail to intercorrelate in the first place, a situation that would automatically cancel any need for factor analysis. On the other hand, if the supply of alternative measures becomes truly impressive, then it becomes even more likely that more than one factor will meet the minimum criterion. As the number of variables grows, the chances increase that at least two variables will have something in common besides what they share with the general factor. As one example, when twenty-three ratings of scientists were subjected to a principal components analysis, fully six factors had variances above one (Simonton 1984i). This result is fairly typical, for the number of factors satisfying the minimum test tends to be between one-fifth and one-fourth the number of initial variables (that is, $k/5 \leq m \leq k/4$). This outcome does not necessarily threaten the inference of unidimensionality as long as the main factor dominates the others. Increasing the number of variables not only enlarges the number of nontrivial factors that may appear but also enhances the potential explanatory power of the single best factor, so that the relative status of the latter with respect to rivals may remain undiminished. For instance, although twenty-seven indicators of artistic distinction yielded four factors by the unit variance rule, one factor monopolized most of the variation, accounting for over ten times as much variance as the next most prominent factor (Simonton 1984a). Given that the three also-ran factors could claim variances only slightly above unity, the result remained unidimensional.

In these examples, single-factor results are highly probable because the investigator has taken pains to gather a set of indicators that bear a prima facie connection with the same latent attribute. If aberrant items are allowed to creep in to create a more heterogeneous array of variables, the unidimensionality of the whole is no longer a sure thing. The intrusion of irrelevant or digressive indicators will become obvious when the factor analytic results are carefully surveyed. To show how logic is applied in this circumstance, we can go back to the ratings of the American chief executive (Simonton 1986g). Here the data taken from tables 3.4 and 4.2 were factor analyzed along with some additional ratings—sixteen indicators all told. Actually, because the assessments were not done on all presidents from Washington through Reagan, the analysis was performed on two different correlation matrices, one using pairwise deletion (each correlation calculated for all presidents scored) and the other listwise deletion (all correlations computed for only those presidents who have no missing values on any rating). The outcomes for both analyses are given in table 4.5. The results are so similar in the two situations that we can concentrate attention on the listwise results.

Two principal components had variances above unity, but the variance of the first was about six times larger than that of the second. Furthermore, the two factors contrast immensely in substantive interpretation. Factor I is a self-evident "greatness" dimension, given that all explicit ratings of presidential performance have rather high loadings on this first factor. Yet the Maranell (1970) assessments of idealism and inflexibility, as well as the Murray-Blessing (1983) measure of a president's controversiality, have loadings far too low to be considered part of this factor. These three indicators do load strongly on factor II, however, along with the Bailey-Kynerd greatness rating (T. A. Bailey 1966; Kynerd 1971). What this second factor measures, therefore, is a bipolar dimension where at one pole are chief executives who are idealistic, inflexible, highly controversial, and poorly regarded by Bailey, and at the opposite pole are those who are more pragmatic, flexible, noncontroversial, and highly regarded by Bailey. These results pinpoint

Table 4.5   *Factor Analysis of the Assessments of U.S. Presidents*

Rating	Deletion Strategy					
	Listwise			Pairwise		
	I	II	h^2	I	II	h^2
Schlesinger, 1948 poll	0.97	0.03	0.95	0.98	0.02	0.96
Schlesinger, 1962 poll	0.98	0.02	0.99	0.97	0.03	0.93
Rossiter (1956)	0.91	0.16	0.96	0.90	0.16	0.84
Sokolsky (1964)	0.96	0.15	0.98	0.95	0.15	0.93
Bailey (1966) through Kynerd (1971)	0.79	−0.37	0.92	0.80	−0.40	0.80
Maranell (1970)						
Prestige	0.97	−0.03	0.97	0.96	−0.02	0.93
Strength	0.98	0.06	0.99+	0.98	0.11	0.97
Activeness	0.94	0.17	0.98	0.93	0.23	0.91
Idealism	0.16	0.50	0.54	0.14	0.39	0.17
Flexibility	0.08	−0.85	0.81	0.12	−0.65	0.44
Accomplishments	0.98	−0.06	0.99	0.98	−0.03	0.96
Information	0.80	0.12	0.92	0.80	0.15	0.67
Porter (1981)	0.98	−0.05	0.99	0.97	−0.08	0.96
Chicago Tribune (1982)	0.98	−0.06	0.99	0.96	−0.11	0.94
Murray-Blessing (1983)						
Greatness	0.98	−0.11	0.98	0.98	−0.14	0.97
Controversiality	−0.08	0.86	0.84	−0.00	0.87	0.76
Eigenvalue (λ)	11.6	2.0		11.5	1.7	
Percentage of common variance	85	15		87	13	
Percentage of total variance	72	12		72	11	

Note. Modified from Simonton (1986g, table 1).

the basis for Bailey's hedged dissent from the other assessments of presidential greatness: This historian of the presidency had little patience for idealistic, inflexible, and controversial chief executives, preferring the more melba-toast politicians of American history. In any case, this two-factor analysis proves that the sixteen measures do not form a unified dimension, although a subset of variables that exclude the three items with the lowest loadings should have an impressive coefficient alpha, for the correlations range from .79 to .98. So restricted, the composite measure would be clearly unidimensional.

Variance Explained

Conceivably a set of indicators might be unidimensional, yet the amount of variance explained by that single factor could be too small to lend the dimension much endorsement. Or, a factor that explains much variance might appear but only with one or more conspicuous rivals in explanatory power. Consequently, the full utility of factor analysis does not materialize until it specifies the relative importance of the dimension in handling the full array of indicators. Because the factor loadings are correlations, the square of any coefficient gives the proportion of variance shared between item and factor. In table 4.5, for example, the loading of the first Schlesinger poll on factor I is .97, which when squared, yields .94, meaning that 94 percent of the variation in this one indicator overlaps that in the linear composite that defines the dimension. In contrast, the idealism measure, with a loading of .16 on factor I, has a squared loading of .02, signifying that only 2 percent shared variance; successful presidents are neither more nor less idealistic than the White House failures.

But we can do more with these squared loadings than simply interpret the item-factor overlap, for by adding up all the squared loadings down the column of coefficients for the entire factor, we obtain the absolute variance claimed by that factor. This sum of squared loadings is most often styled the *eigenvalue* or *latent root* (λ). In table 4.5 the eigenvalue of factor I is 11.6 and that for factor II 2.0. Given that the total variance in the set of sixteen variables is equal to 16, the number of variables factored, the proportion of total variance can be computed as the ratio of the eigenvalue to the number of variables (that is, for any factor j, the proportion is λ_j/k). Therefore, factor I handles 72 percent ($100 \times 11.6/16$) and factor II handles 12 percent ($100 \times 2.0/16$), showing that the greatness dimension is the most critical for comprehending the set of sixteen variables. By estimating the total variance accommodated by a given factor, one can gauge how well multiple indicators assess a unified dimension. If only one factor satisfies the variance criterion, it is hoped that all factor loadings are high and accordingly that the proportion of total variation is impressive.

The dating of Shakespeare's plays offers the ideal outcome, for the factor loadings of the thirteen alternative datings are without exception near unity and the single-dating factor claims almost 100 percent of the total variance available

(Simonton 1986f). More typical is what happened in estimating the differential success of 696 classical composers using six measures: The factor loadings ranged from .68 to .86 and the one factor accounted for 60 percent of the total variance (Simonton 1977c). Even when more than one dimension emerges, as often happens with a large number of indicators, the expectation remains that the most important factor will command between 50 and 80 percent of the total variance. Thus, when the relative reputation of artists was gauged using twenty-seven indicators, the first factor took 60 percent of the whole variation, with item-factor correlations ranging from .57 to .89, and with the remaining three factors each left with 5 percent or less, confirming the expected cohesion of the multiple indices (Simonton 1984a).

One final application indicates an additional feature of this approach to discerning measurement error. Weitman, Shapiro, and Markoff (1986) wanted accurate estimates of the population of France before the onset of the French Revolution, where they had access to twenty separate and seemingly inconsistent "precensal" estimates. Yet as in the Shakespeare datings, these discrepancies turned out to be rather superficial relative to the total variation in the data. A principal-components analysis yielded an eigenvalue of 17.6 for the first factor of three, indicating that a single population dimension handled 88 percent of the total variation. The factor loadings of the separate indicators on this "birth count" component ranged from .54 to .99, with the seventeen best measures ranging between .92 and .99. Also calculated was a statistic not yet discussed, namely the *communality* for each variable (h^2). If instead of summing the squared-factor loadings down the columns, we add them across the rows, we obtain an estimate of the total amount of variance that the given variable shares with all the extracted factors. If a variable's communality is low, it cannot be measuring the same thing as the other variables. In table 4.5 we see that the indicators of presidential greatness all enjoy extremely high communalities. Weitman and his collaborators also obtained communalities almost as respectable, ranging from .81 to .99, with an average of .95. The conclusion from this factor-analytic recycling of historical statistics is that however discordant the twenty population figures may appear to the naked eye, the consensus in the measures is actually impressive. One must always be wary of judging the distributions of whole forests by the microscopic examination of the bark of a single tree.

Other Gauges of Error

The several approaches to obtaining reliabilities by no means represent rival techniques; alternative-measure, test-retest, and internal-consistency reliability coefficients often can be combined with factor analysis to implement a comprehensive search for measurement error (see, for example, Simonton 1989b). We have, moreover, touched only the top items in the psychometrician's tool kit; no mention has been made of the multitrait-multimethod technique, confirmatory factor analysis, and other readily available methods (for example, Campbell and Fiske 1959; Long 1983a). Instead of treating these more specialized devices, which seldom see historiometric applications, we should touch upon two additional options for verifying the reliability of measures. These roughly split into further statistical tests and various logical tests.

Statistical Probes

Researchers must always be sensitive to workable mathematical approaches to the evaluation of data adequacy, but once we move beyond standard reliability assessments, the alternatives become highly idiosyncratic to the needs of a particular research problem. To hint at the diversity of this quantitative miscellany, we will inspect projects that are varied in means and ends. What most of these have in common is the use of multiple regression rather than correlation to check for measurement error. Multiple regression permits the researcher to predict a criterion variable given two or more predictor variables, creating a multivariate prediction equation.

Considering again the rudimentary question of how well we can date the Shakespeare canon (Simonton 1986f) let us refer to table 4.4. The dates emerge from consolidating thirteen discrepant datings of the thirty-seven plays, yet these dates merely compile separate educated guesses into a single chronological index, which is thus less subjective. Admittedly, these datings are not totally arbitrary, given that Shakespearean scholars use pertinent facts as guides, including scattered records of performance and publication. Nevertheless, the archives are so flimsy that conclusive dates cannot be inferred objectively. This tenuousness remains for the "internal evidence" that is based on stylistic changes in the poet's writing over the course of his dramatic career. Scholars have identified several indicators that can be reduced to objective counts that exhibit shifts over time. These include the proportion of speech endings, double endings, light or weak endings, and, most simply, prose as distinguished from verse. These content analytical attributes offer clues to dating under the reasonable assumption that Shakespeare's expressive growth was consistent and progressive.

Because literary critics normally apply these diagnostic criteria qualitatively, they cannot guide dating with any precision. The accuracy of the counts notwithstanding, the scientist must step in to make some advance on the problem (see, also, Brainerd 1980). By exploiting multiple regression, subjectively determined dates can be predicted using objectively determined stylistic measures, a solution that yields the parenthetical dates given in table 4.4. The correlation between the two columns of dates is around .97, but we do not need this number to convince us that a strong concordance exists between subjective and objective datings. Here we have a statistical check on the datings that depends on a criterion other than the dates themselves, namely Shakespeare's literary maturation. Significantly, longitudinal changes in his stylistic development contradict traditional scholarly claims, constituting a statistical contradiction of intuition that we will witness again in this treatise.

Moving from the level of the product to that of the individual, we can provide a different example of how multiple regression may contribute to the verification of measure reliability (Simonton 1983d). An inquiry into the personality of 342 monarchs took advantage of the scores already provided by Woods (1906, 1913) on intelligence, morality, and leadership. Thorndike (1936) previously demonstrated the reliability of the intelligence and morality assessments, yet a double-check was implemented that adopted an altogether distinct strategy. After gathering ample biographical data, the kings, queens, regents, and sultans of Europe were all rated on seventy-six descriptors using a nine-point scale. The three global measures were each regressed on these more narrow adjective ratings to discern whether intelligence, morality, and leadership could be partitioned into several components. The outcome was confirmatory: The most intelligent monarchs were more often described as able, intelligent, shrewd, and educated; the more moral royal leaders were seen to be moral, prudent, well meaning, and popular, but definitely not licentious, tyrannical, or treacherous; and rulers scoring higher on leadership were characterized as able, intelligent, shrewd, brave, just, vigorous, ambitious, moral, practical, and accomplished, but not influenced by others or bigoted. The correlations between the predicted scores based on the adjective assessments and the three evaluations from Woods were .75, .70, and .75 for intelligence, morality, and leadership, respectively.

For our final illustrations, the analytical unit is altered to yet a higher level of aggregation, namely transhistorical data. Voltaire once said that "all our ancient history, as one of our wits remarked, is no more than accepted fiction," and one of those fictions has to do with when events occurred. Shakespeare's plays may be datable with minimal error, but certainly much older chronologies will suffer from more serious imprecisions, a potential intrusion of error that can be revealed a number of ways. One route is to look for *heteroscedasticity* in the errors of prediction as the time-series units recede into antiquity. That is, do the errors become more extreme as we move far back in time? For instance, one time-series analysis scrutinized the sociocultural and political determinants of creative activity for 127 consecutive twenty-year generations, from 700 B.C. to A.D. 1839 (Simonton 1975e). As expected, the variance of the residuals, or prediction errors, grew slightly larger as the units descended into the distant past ($r = -.26$ between the date and the absolute value of the error), a tendency that may reflect inferior data reliability for chronologies constructed for antiquity. In contrast, the multiple regression equations designed to predict presidential greatness found no such enlargement of predictive error as the data retreated from Carter back to Washington, suggesting that heteroscedasticity of this kind is less problematic over more recent historical intervals (Simonton 1986h).

For an investigator suspicious of dating inaccuracies, the option is also available of defining *dating bias dummy variables*. As an example, one study determined the impact of war and civil violence on the annual count of scientific discoveries from A.D. 1500 to 1903 (Simonton 1980b). A nominal scale was encoded by dummy variables registering whether the date for a particular year ended in 5, 0, or 50 (for example, 1505, 1520, or 1550). If the historian has a hidden proclivity for providing dates with round numbers, favoritism toward the half-decade, decade, or half-century marks would trigger bigger counts in these years relative to those years with less facile chronological assignments (for example, 1506, 1519, or 1551). Just such an inclination was identified, the biases accounting for 15 percent of the variance in the annual fluctuations. In contrast, this prejudice, ignorance, or laziness on behalf of round-number dates lessens considerably when the time-series units enlarge from yearly to generational data (Simonton 1975e), revealing that it is far easier to place an event or person into a twenty-year time slot than into a one-year unit without injecting dating biases.

Apropos of this last point, Allison (1977) has recommended a reliability check that does *not* involve multiple regression but that *is* directly applicable to time-series counts of event frequencies. Like the internal-consistency reliability coefficient, this statistical test entails the ratio of variances and is derived under the postulate that the tabulations exhibit a Poisson distribution, a common enough experience in real data. The resulting number generally looks and acts like a regular reliability coefficient, and so it deserves more attention than it has so far received in empirical work. An investigation into generational changes in creativity and leadership in Chinese civilization used this statistic to show that the reliabilities ranged from .52 to .97, with a mean of .81 (Simonton 1988c). These results are compatible with what happened when data reliability was calculated by more traditional means. One important implication of this test is that, given the same raw chronology of events, the reliability of their tabulation becomes higher as the time-series units get wider. Generational data would therefore prove more reliable than annual data—precisely what happens when we inspect dating bias dummy variables in time-series regression equations.

Logical Probes

Apart from all of these advanced statistical gauges of error, no substitute exists for the introduction of a little common sense. For one thing, if history is reliable enough to support a science, independent investigators should converge on the same historical generalizations from the same data base. When Thorndike (1936), by gathering his own data and ratings, confirmed a correlation between intelligence and morality across 305 historical royalty, Woods's (1906) preliminary venture on this subject was reinforced. Sometimes it is one and the same researcher who endeavors to provide the desired replications, with much the same effect. For example, Sales (1972, 1973) hoped to prove that threatening conditions, especially economic downturns, oblige an increase in a nation's authoritarianism. Now the assessment of the authoritarian personality in an entire population is no easy task, and the business must perforce rely on cultural indicators of questionable reliability. Nonetheless, by operationally defining an impressive array of alternative measures and confirming the hypothesis on each, the reliability of the separate assessments emerges as less precarious. To replicate the nomothetic statement on diverse indices (for example, the popularity of books on astrology, the harshness of punishments for sex crimes, the power exhibited by comic strip characters, interest in psychology and psychoanalysis, and the rates of conversion to dogmatic churches) only strengthens our beliefs in both hypothesis and measurement. The logical criterion that finds application here is commonplace in the natural sciences. Physicists, chemists, or biologists seldom provide reliability checks for published data, but when separate laboratories publish almost identical conclusions about a phenomenon, the independent measures endorse each other as a side benefit of establishing the principles that motivated the several investigations to begin with.

One further logical criterion is valuable in finding the reliability of psychological instruments. Historians should be advised, and scientists perhaps reminded, that data reliability is never an absolute characteristic; it must be determined relative to a study's specific substantive needs. What may be problematic in one inquiry may prove impertinent in another, even when both resort to the same raw data, a point illustrated by another example taken from research on Shakespeare. One of the oldest controversies in Shakespearean scholarship concerns the true authorship of the plays. Some dissenting scholars have argued that some less obscure Elizabethan personality wrote the plays, either Francis Bacon, Edward de Vere, William Stanley, or Christopher Marlowe. Even those scholars who accept the traditional attribution to Shakespeare may debate endlessly about how much of each play is his rather than the less inspired creation of some collaborator—often getting down to the nitty-gritty task of allotting this or that line to one or another hack. One might infer from all this that to employ data on Shakespeare's dramatic output is risky.

The last inference, however, depends on the specific hypotheses addressed by any inquiry. If these data are used to study how creative productivity changes with age, some worrying might be in order, and so a superior measurement might instead be a count of the number of lines that are safely attributed to Shakespeare. Precedent for this procedure is a study of composers that counted the number of themes created for each longitudinal unit, deleting all quotations of other composers' melodies (for example, the numerous variations on Paganini's 24th Caprice) or in the "public domain" (for example, the innumerable expropriations of the *Dies Irae*) (Simonton 1977a). By comparison, say that the study is inspired by questions in psychological aesthetics, so that the goal is to discern (1) why some of the plays are more successful on the stage while others are granted at best occasional and ill-received revivals or (2) how political or social events influence the thematic content of a drama. Then it is utterly irrelevant who composed each drama. Thus, the conclusion that the more popular plays feature "madness or frenzy due to emotional excess" or that plays written when the playwright's nation was under attack by a foreign power are more prone to treat the theme of "conquest, empire, political expansion as ends of war" depend not at all on any presumption of authorship (Simonton 1986f). The former finding depends solely on a reliable differentiation of which plays are frequently performed, and the latter finding presumes only that the plays have been reliably dated so that they may be properly linked with current events.

In this example, reliability is contingent on the hypothesis being addressed. Closely related is the situation where an apparent absence of data consistency turns out to be a less problematic matter of selecting the most suitable variable definition. In the histories of Chinese civilization, one can find tremendous discrepancies regarding the beginning date of the Mongol (Yuan) dynasty: 1234, 1259, 1260, 1264, 1279, and 1280—a range exceeding two generations! If our conjectures concern how dynastic disruptions affect intellectual or aesthetic creativity, are the Chinese chronicles too riddled with error to support a scientific test? No, because these consecutive dates actually apply to distinct political events: In 1234 the Mongols conquered the Jin Empire in northern China, and thus for the first time governed a large population of Chinese people; in 1259 Mangu died leaving Mongol leadership to Kublai, who was to become the first Yuan emperor of China; in 1260 Kublai was proclaimed grand khan over the Mongolian hordes; in 1264 Kublai obtained the submission of his rebellious brother Arikbugha, thus becoming the uncontested ruler of the vast empire, and in the same year he set up his capital at Beijing, thereby making China the center of imperial government; in 1279 the last pretender to the throne of the Southern Song dynasty drowned during a climactic battle; and in 1280 Kublai Khan became master of all China. Because no disagreement exists on the six dates, the seeming contradictions are only superficial, discrepancies resulting from differences over which event best symbolizes dynastic transition. The task left to the researcher, therefore, is to decide which operational definition optimally complies with the theory underlying the hypothesis.

"Common sense is not so common," to quote Voltaire again, and such is the historiometrician's frequent experience. Historians too quickly criticize quantitative studies according to blanket judgments of data reliability that often prove totally irrelevant to the substantive issue at hand. Complaints about reliability must always recognize that the error permeating the historical record may or may not obstruct the scientist's designs. Indeed, in some instances, the data from the past are more supportive of quantitative analyses than they are of the qualitative disquisitions favored in historiography. Historians typically examine extremely specific questions where reliable data are few and far between, whereas historiometricians usually study hypotheses at such high levels of abstraction that conclusions may be robust despite the presence of error. For idiographic research, a single missing detail may be critical to an interpretation, while in nomothetic research any one datum has no impact whatsoever on the conclusions drawn from the entire investigation.

This robustness of scientific measurement in the face of historical error is bolstered by the dependence on multiple indicators and large-N samples. Statistical inquiry developed for some time before it was realized that the errors inherent in any single measure on any single case can become impertinent when aggregated across measures and across cases (Stigler 1986). It may prove no consolation to the historian whose enthusiasms extend more to each part than to the whole, yet for historiometricians it is comforting to know that the whole can indeed surpass the quality of its parts.

5 Validity

At times, the reliability of historiometric assessments cannot be at issue. Whenever content analyses are executed by computer, the resulting scores are, in a sense, error free. Calculate the test-retest reliability for assessing primary process imagery in literary text (Martindale 1975) or melodic originality in musical compositions (Simonton 1980c), and the outcome is 1.0. Nevertheless, the most precise instrument may prove useless if it cannot boast another feature as well—validity. Here the issue is not so much how accurate a measurement is as whether the measure measures what it should. If random errors were removed from the assignment of numbers to units so that reliability is absolute, the indicators may still not gauge the underlying constructs.

A notorious case in psychometric history is Galton's (1883) anthropometric laboratory. Wanting to assess individual differences in intellectual ability, Galton gauged such capacities as visual acuity and reaction time. As a disciple of the British empiricist school, he believed that all knowledge came through the senses, and consequently the intellect could only be as powerful as the perceptual apparatus that supplies raw data; and reaction time bears an apparent link with the speed of information processing and thereby captures a notion akin to a person's being "quick witted." Besides the seeming relevance, these attributes could be measured with impressive accuracy by taking full advantage of many fine instruments borrowed directly from the prestigious field of psychophysics. All the logic and precision notwithstanding, Galton's endeavors were misdirected, as subsequent researchers learned how performance on his tests did not correspond to behaviors that would otherwise be considered intelligent. Eventually, Binet had to develop a rather different measure of intellectual capacity, the instrument that Terman transformed into the Stanford-Binet IQ test. More directly gauging cognitive skills, this test sacrificed some reliability in order to acquire superior validity.

The validity of historiometric quantifications will be examined from two distinct perspectives. We begin by discussing how psychometricians go about validating measures to see whether these approaches can be expropriated by historiometricians. We then will treat the principal sources of systematic bias in historical data. Concluding this chapter is an evaluation of the validity of a single variable that plays a star role in historiometric work—eminence, fame, or greatness.

Types of Validity

The psychometric literature mentions three main routes to measure validation (Nunnally 1978, chap. 3). These are content, predictive, and construct validity. Although the relative utility of the three types of validity is not the same in historiometrics as in psychometrics, all three can have a place in the overall determination.

Content Validity

An instrument enjoys content validity when it is composed of items that adequately sample the domain under assessment. Thus, an intelligence test features content validity to the extent that it consists of questions or problems that address the full range of cognitive abilities—verbal, mathematical, spatial, analytical, and so on—that are thought to lie behind intelligent behavior. When a historiometric instrument is adapted from a standard psychometric instrument, the content validity of the former is often transferred from that of the latter. For example, under the assumption that the three hundred descriptors of the Gough ACL (Gough and Heilbrun 1965) capture the full array of traits germane to the assessment of contemporary subjects, it seems defensible to extend this instrument to historical figures (HFAC 1977; Simonton 1986h). Similarly, once the imagery that betrays an individual's power, achievement, or affiliation needs has been established in psychometric studies, it is a minimal step to carry these over to political, literary, and artistic materials handled in historiometrics (McClelland 1961; Winter 1973).

As justifiable as these adaptations appear, the investigator must remain wary. The content validity of a historiometric assessment is by no means equivalent to the content validity of the psychometric instrument that inspired its creation. For instance, when the three hundred ACL adjectives are applied to thirty-nine U.S. chief executives, many descriptors prove to be irrelevant, owing to either ceiling or floor effects. A ceiling effect occurs for a descriptor like "ambitious," because almost all politicians must have this quality, and a floor effect intrudes on a descriptor like "zany," given how inconceivable it is for zaniness to sit in the Oval Office (Simonton 1986h). This inclusion of impertinent items, naturally, can be easily fixed by deleting those that fail to differentiate the presidents properly. More problematic, however, is the possible omission of items that are representative of the domain. Hence, when the personality traits of 342 monarchs were evaluated, it was found necessary to add new descriptors, such as "tyrannical," "treacherous," "cruel," and "licentious" (Simonton 1983d). These terms seldom apply to everyday populations or even to American presidents, but they are mandatory if realistic personality profiles are sought for kings, queens, sultans, and regents. Some hereditary rulers dove into gruesome political and personal depravities that would otherwise be missed (Woods 1906).

Even when the historiometrician cannot benefit from the labors of the psychometrician, the content validity of a variable quantification can often be readily certified. The best illustrations perhaps come from those studies that attempt to gauge the comparative aesthetic success of creative products. Thus, the "dramatic popularity" of the thirty-seven Shakespearean plays was differentiated using a multitude of distinct indicators, such as inclusion in anthologies, frequency of live performance in Shakespearean festivals, representation in books of popular quotations, and so on (Simonton 1986f). Likewise, when the "compositional popularity" of hundreds of works in the classical repertoire was assessed, the multiple-indicator index included the frequency of separate recordings and selection for recording anthologies, citation in record-buying guides, music appreciation texts, and histories of music, inclusion in music score anthologies, and so forth (Simonton 1980d). Analogous measures have been constructed to assess creators, leaders, and other historical celebrities on eminence, fame, infamy, or greatness (Simonton 1984d, 1987d). If one wishes to record an individual's impact, what better gauge can there be than to measure the personal influence on the broadly conceived historical record? Measures that depart from these specific preoccupations can still boast considerable validity. This holds for gauging military success by tactical victory or defeat on the battlefield (Simonton 1980a; Suedfeld, Corteen, and McCormick 1986); legislative accomplishments by the number of administration-sponsored bills passed (Bond and Fleisher 1984; Rivers and Rose 1985) or reliance on the executive veto (Copeland 1983; Lee 1975; Simonton 1987c); lifetime productivity by counts of actual contributions (Dennis 1954c; Simonton 1977c); and so forth. In these instances, the content validity is manifest.

Admittedly, there are other domains in which content validity may be at risk. This problem is most prone to arise when the phenomenon cannot be tapped directly but must be probed indirectly through "proxy" indicators. When Matossian and Schafer (1977) tested their theory of how population pressure causes political violence, they had to assess transhistorical fluctuations in hypothesized intervening variables that concerned family relationships. Lacking data on the intensity and emotional valence of mother-son, father-son, and sibling-sibling interactions in the general population, the investigators had no other choice but to examine the family circumstances of famous writers over the same periods. Yet the assumption behind this substitution was that changes in family tensions for writers would parallel changes in family tensions for the populace as a whole. The mean level may be distinguishable, but the ups and downs must be synchronous.

Oblique assessments like these are commonplace not just in historiometry, but in the behavioral sciences generally. A "measurement gap" almost always intrudes between abstract theory and concrete empirical data, necessitating the formulation of "auxiliary theories" that link concepts to observations (Blalock 1968). Nonetheless, the problem is often particularly acute for the psychologist who exploits history. The facts of the past are often more friendly to the plans of the sociologist, economist, political scientist, or demographer than to the more particularistic fascinations of the psychologist. Annals are often more a repository of collective behavior than individual behavior, and whenever the historian treats the single personality, that individual invariably is among the elite few. Even so, the psychologist has no other choice than to do the utmost with what is available, even when this necessitates some compromise with content validity. Besides, any apparent liabilities on this score can often be mitigated if the measures do well by the two other validation criteria.

Predictive Validity

Many psychometric instruments hold implications for how an individual would be expected to score on other closely related variables, and violated predictions therefore undermine the credibility of a measure. Hence, a severe criticism often leveled against creativity tests is that, whatever their supposed content validity (as manifest measures of divergent thinking or associational remoteness), their predictive success, when weighed against actual acts of creativity, is often dismal. Predictive validity, unlike content validity, can be expressed in numerical form. Just as we may have a reliability coefficient, so we may have a validity coefficient, both statistics having a range from 0 to 1. The validity coefficient, like the reliability coefficient, is commonly nothing more than the correlation between two variables. Whereas for reliability the correlation is often calculated between two alternative measures of the same concept, for predictive validity the correlation is estimated between the instrument and some external criterion of its validity. Occasionally, however, the validity coefficient is a multiple correlation between a battery of tests and some criterion—something especially likely in measures employed in personnel selection. In addition, validity is sometimes established in terms of a discrete prediction. An example can be found in research on using the *Science Citation Index* for determining the quality of a scientist's work, a practice vindicated when it supported the prediction of a Nobel laureate in chemistry (Ashton and Oppenheim 1978).

To offer a more bona fide historiometric illustration, the dramatic popularity scores assigned to Shakespeare's plays were validated by asking two professors of English literature to rate all thirty-seven works according to whatever criteria satisfied their fancy but without any knowledge of the then unpublished scores given in table 4.4. The archival measure correlated .38 with social realism, .52 with characterization, .55 with personal expression, .56 with "achievement" (how successful the play was in attaining its ambitions), .58 with "amplitude" (how ambitious a play was in what it set out to accomplish), .64 with judged landmark creations, and .72 with overall aesthetic quality (Simonton 1986f). The broader the scope of the experts' subjective rating, the closer is its correspondence with the objective citation score. Predictive validity always depends on whether the criterion matches the purposes of the instrument being evaluated.

Strict tests for predictive validity are uncommon in historiometrics, for it is more in the nature of such inquiries to deal with "postdictions." Because history advances perpetually backward in time, most often a measure can be validated only by "backcasts," not forecasts. An example of postdictive validity may come from the research on how historical events deflect the approval ratings that an incumbent president receives in the polls. When Mueller conducted his pioneer investigations (1973), one predictor was war, which he defined by a dummy variable marking whether the nation was in a state of war or peace when the respondents were surveyed. Because Mueller could consider only presidents from Truman to Johnson, he was essentially determining the impact of the Korean and Vietnam wars on the popularity of these two presidents, as distinguished from the pair between them, Eisenhower and Kennedy. He came to the surprising conclusion that the Korean War may have depressed Truman's standing with the American people—by around 18 percentage points—but that the Vietnam War had no detrimental impact on Johnson's approval rating. In a critique partly entitled "How . . . Insufficient Care in Measuring One's Variables Refuted Common Sense and Led Conventional Wisdom Down the Path of Anomalies," Kernell (1978) demonstrated that a discrete war-versus-peace measure will not do. A more valid indicator for both wars is casualty figures just before each poll; for the Vietnam War we can exploit the number of bombing missions over North Vietnam. Given these refinements, LBJ's popularity was considerably damaged, the net effect of this controversial war being about 3 percentage points per month. Considering that everyone at the time, including Johnson himself, thought the Vietnam War had cost him considerable support, Kernell's alternative measures yield results more compatible with expectation. Statistics on casualties and bombings boast superior postdictive validity, even though neither indicator necessarily has more content validity than a basic state-of-war dummy variable.

Construct Validity

In the early evolution of psychometric theory, content and predictive validity carried full responsibility for measure validation. If an IQ test contains items representative of the domain of relevant information-processing abilities, and if scores on that test successfully predict performance on tasks that presumably require cognitive skills (such as doing well in schoolwork), the psychometrician could rest satisfied that the instrument's quality had been defended. Eventually, however, psychologists came to realize that validity, like beauty, is more than skin deep.

Because the ultimate aim of any assessment is to assign scores that correspond precisely to some underlying construct, it is incumbent on the investigator to establish that the measurement and the construct are truly isomorphic with respect to the variety of variables that define human behavior. More briefly, the test must behave just as the elusive construct would be expected to behave were it possible to gain access to the genuine scores. Consequently, unlike content and predictive validity, the determination of construct validity demands more than a single homogeneous demonstration. Indeed, usually the expectation is a lifetime of psychometric scrutiny until the properties of a measure are completely delineated.

Probably the best point of departure now is to provide a concrete example from the historiometric literature. Earlier we came across an objective scheme by which a computer calculated the melodic originality of 15,618 themes that virtually define the substance of classical music (Simonton 1980d, 1984h), and we have noted that the reliability of this measurement cannot be moot. Consequently, the real matter that must concern any user of this measure is whether it is valid. This issue is especially urgent given that the validity of this indicator is less than obvious. After all, melodic originality is estimated only by examining two-note transition probabilities for the first six notes only (or first five transitions) of each theme, this estimation being performed after first transposing all melodies to a C tonic (namely, C major and C minor for all major and minor keys). Hence, after ignoring the theme's key, rhythm, tempo, instrumentation, and any harmonic accompaniment or counterpoint, all that remains is unadulterated melodic structure (compare Cerulo 1989). Given the abstraction that this measure demands, in combination with the fragment of raw data on which it is based, can we have any assurance that "melodic originality" is the appropriate label to assign the resulting scores?

A proper response to this query necessitates the enumeration of a range of results all of which converge on an affirmative, albeit continually tentative, conclusion. Let us begin by recalling Paisley's (1964) demonstration that the distinctive style of a classical composer is given away by the two-note transition probabilities for just the first four notes, a finding later replicated for 479 musicians using the first six notes (Simonton 1980d). In Paisley's terms, the stylistic secrets of creators are contained in "minor encoding habits" so trivial that the creators themselves are seldom aware of their mannerisms. This surprising result suggests that the two-note transition probabilities in table 3.8 are richly packed with information, enough so that a Mozart can be objectively discerned from a Beethoven. In addition, the two-note transition probabilities carry the same information to be found in three-note transition probabilities for the same 15,618 themes. The correlation between melodic originality based on two- and three-note combinations is .81, a sizable congruence, especially in view of the downward bias in the correlation owing to floor effects on the three-note indicator (Simonton 1984h). This is not all, for the following four points reinforce our faith that a computer can grapple with a construct seemingly so intangible as melodic originality.

1. The originality of the themes making up a composition varies in an understandable manner with other properties of the piece. To begin with, melodic originality is generally higher in purely instrumental music than in vocal works, a contrast reflecting both the inherent limitations on the vocal apparatus and the tendency for the text to carry more weight in stimulating the emotions of listeners (Simonton 1980d). Likewise, no matter what the instrumentation, chamber works, such as sonatas and quartets, harbor more original thematic material than can be found in theatrical works, such as operas and ballets, the themes comprising concert compositions, such as overtures, tone poems, concerti, and symphonies, falling midway between these two extremes (Simonton 1980d). Surely the more impressive the resources available to the composer for exciting the audience, the less crucial becomes melodic originality for attaining the artistic goal. In a chamber piece, with only a handful of instruments at most, heavy reliance must be placed on the melodic content; in theatrical productions, by comparison, not only is a fully equipped orchestra standing ever ready, but sets, costumes, plot, characterization, and stage business carry much of the burden in maintaining audience attention. Compositions headed for the concert hall rather than the recital room or the theater would naturally come between these two extremes in the need to enlist the stimulative powers of melodic originality.

The measure has also been validated against more fine-grained aspects of music. Themes in minor keys rate higher in originality than those in major keys: Transitions containing E-flat, A-flat, and B-flat, although perfectly legitimate for themes in C minor, are less probable than those containing E, A, and B, the proper notes of the C-major scale (see table 3.9). This finding fits the commonplace observation that melodies in minor keys sound more unusual, plaintive, sad, or exotic than those in major keys—a tendency also reflected in the "blue note" (minor third) in classic jazz (Simonton 1987b). The variation in melodic originality as a piece progresses is also correlated with metric variation, or the utilization of variable and unusual time signatures throughout a composition (Simonton 1987b). Melodic originality is exploited in much the same manner as metric originality to keep the interest of music appreciators from flagging.

2. The melodic originality found in compositions changes across time, in a comprehensible way, at three distinct levels of analysis. Starting at the level of a single work, originality in large compositions is a curvilinear, backward-J function of the order of the movement in which the theme appears (Simonton 1987b). The first movement contains the most original material, the last movement the second most original, while the least original themes are located in the middle movement(s), on average. This empirical tendency, naturally, parallels the structure so often witnessed in the larger instrumental forms, especially symphonies, quartets, trios, and sonatas. A dramatic and rousing first movement, often in sonata-allegro

form, is traditionally succeeded by one (or two) middle movement(s) in *aba* song (and minuet or scherzo and trio) form(s), after which there bursts out an exciting finale, commonly in sonata-allegro or rondo form.

Shifting from the creative product to the creative individual, as composers get older, the melodic originality that fills their compositions tends to increase progressively, a developmental trend only slightly qualified by a modest dip sometime after one's fifty-sixth year (Simonton 1980d). In addition, as pointed out in chapter 2, the zeitgeist originality of a composer's work, which regards whether melodic structure departs from the prevailing styles of the day, grows linearly with age (Simonton 1980d). These age curves, which were estimated across 479 composers, comply with theories of artistic motivation that postulate that creative artists are driven by an urge to produce ever more original works, surpassing what has been contributed by others and themselves (for example, Martindale 1986a).

Switching finally to the aggregate level of a whole musical tradition, if mean melodic originality is plotted as a function of the date that the themes were conceived, the secular trend depicted in figure 5.1 obtains. Melodic originality began low in the Renaissance, climbed to a peak in the early Baroque (as represented by Monteverdi and especially Gesualdo), and then declined to a trough a bit higher than the starting point around 1500. From that secondary low point, which

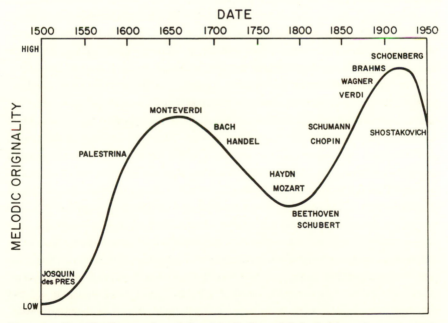

Figure 5.1. Trend line for repertoire melodic originality for 15,618 classical themes by 479 composers active from 1500 to 1950 according to the fit of a fifth-order polynomial in historical time. (Taken from Simonton 1980d, figure 1. Copyright 1980 by American Psychological Association. Adapted by permission.)

is illuminated by the themes of the classical period proper (when melodies are often constructed around triads and chords), melodic originality began a new ascent during the romantic period, attaining an even higher crest in the rich chromaticism of the late and postromantics, such as Wagner and Mahler, and ultimately in the atonal and serial note permutations of Arnold Schoenberg and his school in Vienna; but after around 1917, diatonic music again became more in vogue, as composers like Prokofiev, Copeland, and Shostakovich backed off from the more daring music of their earlier years. Even Schoenberg resigned himself to writing music more accessible than his 1912 *Pierrot Lunaire,* such as his 1942 Piano Concerto. The broad picture is that of a cyclic pattern superimposed over an underlying upward trend, another temporal trend, this time one transhistorical, that is consistent with theories of aesthetic evolution (Martindale 1986a). Further, the movement presented in figure 5.1 is virtually identical to the trend that musicologists say holds for melodic chromaticism, an intimately related concept. Increasing the prominence of notes outside the key signature automatically increases the melody's score on originality, for chromatic notes tend to form original two-note transitions; the only real exception to this rule is F-sharp to G, a favorite route by which composers slide into the dominant (see table 3.9).

3. Apart from any general temporal trends within compositions, within creative careers, or within the musical zeitgeist, melodic originality responds to the circumstances in which a work is composed. For one thing, biographical stress in a composer's life, as assessed by adapting the Holmes and Rahe (1967) scale to longitudinal data (see table 3.11), tends to raise the level of originality in concurrent compositions (Simonton 1980c, 1987b). If "music sounds the way emotions feel," and if these stressful events can be supposed to have induced emotional responses in the composers, this reaction exemplifies the personal expressiveness of much music. In a like vein, melodic originality may increase when a composer suffers bouts of physical illness (Simonton 1987b). Originality also goes up when the composer's nation is at war, especially when the hapless creator finds himself in a war zone (Simonton 1987b; compare Cerulo 1984). And the originality of melodies composed by "provincials" has a greater likelihood of being less conspicuous than the originality of themes created by "cosmopolitans" operating near or at the center of musical activity for their generation (Simonton 1986a). There is even some tendency for originality to drop in those periods in which a composer is most prolific in melodic ideas, an inverse relation that suggests a trade-off between quantitative output and creative imagination (Simonton 1986a). But perhaps the most provocative result concerns the swan-song phenomenon, or last-works effect (Simonton 1989c). As composers near death, no matter what their age, a rapid change takes place in their compositional style. One such shift regards melodic originality, which declines in the final years, a "terminal drop" in line with other findings (Porter and Suedfeld 1981; Suedfeld 1985; Suedfeld and Piedrahita 1984).

4. Lastly, computer-generated scores on melodic originality are congruent with how compositions are subjectively perceived by others, whether naive listeners or musicological experts. For example, when the melody is actually performed on a violin, ratings on "arousal potential" correlate positively with objective determination of originality (Martindale and Uemura 1983). Readers may convince themselves of this consistency by looking at the melodies shown in table 5.1. These vary greatly in originality, as shown in the mean percentages of times the five transitions occur (gauged by either the consecutive percentages or the summarized percentages in table 3.9). The theme by Haydn sounds like the nursery song "Twinkle, Twinkle Little Star," whereas the theme by Mozart is so (uncharacteristically) odd that the quartet it introduces has been forever called the "Dissonant." "If Mozart composed it, he must have had a reason," said Haydn on hearing the opening!

Equally important are studies showing how melodic originality affects the aesthetic impact of a piece. Works that score high in originality are likely to receive higher ratings in aesthetic significance but lower ratings in listener accessibility, and a similar effect holds for compositions that feature high scores on the variability of melodic originality (Simonton 1986a, 1989c). Furthermore, by plotting "thematic fame" or "compositional popularity" according to the level of originality, we get the curvilinear inverted-backward J function seen in figure 5.2; the most successful themes are those that exhibit medium levels of unpredictability. Yet if forced to state a preference between trite tunes and chaotic pitch sequences, the typical aficionado of classical music opts for easy listening. This curve replicates laboratory studies in experimental aesthetics that show how appreciation is

Table 5.1 *Sample Themes and Average Transition Percentages by Two Methods*

Composer	Composition	First Six Notes						Average Transition Percentage General	Average Transition Percentage Specific
Haydn	Symphony no. 84, 2nd movement	C	C	E	E	G	G	4.0	4.0
Beethoven	"Waldstein" Sonata, 3d movement	G	G	E	D	G	C	3.5	4.1
Diabelli	Beethoven's 33 Variations on a theme	C	B	C	G	G	G	4.4	3.8
Brahms	Symphony no. 1, 4th movement	G	C	B	C	A	G	2.5	3.9
Menotti	The Medium "Mother, Mother"	C	C	B	B	A♯	C♯	1.9	2.1
Liszt	Grand Galop Chromatique	G	G♯	A	A♯	B	C	0.5	0.6
Mozart	"Dissonant" Quartet (Introduction)	A	G	F♯	G	A	B♭	1.0	0.5
Liszt	Faust Symphony, 1st movement	A♭	G	B	E♭	F♯	B♭	0.2	0.0
Gesualdo	"Moro lasso"	G♯	G	F♯	F	F	B	0.0	0.0

Note. Adapted from Simonton (1984h, table 3, 13).
For average transition percentages, the general method uses the frequencies across all five two-note transitions, whereas the specific method uses the frequencies calculated separately for each two-note transition before averaging them across all transitions. Melodic originality scores for these themes require that these percentages be inverted (by making them negative).

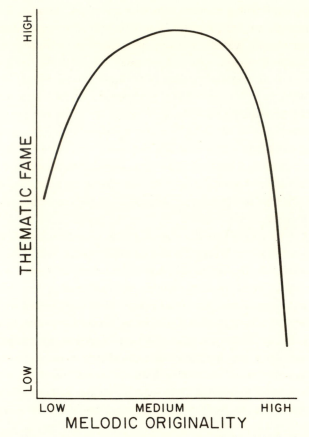

Figure 5.2. Curvilinear relation between thematic fame and melodic originality for 15,618 classical themes by 479 composers. (Taken from Simonton 1983b, figure 1.)

governed by an "optimal arousal model" (Berlyne 1971). Aesthetic preference entails a compromise between the understandable but boring and the stimulating but anxiety-inducing, a modest amount of chromaticism and angular melodic lines striking the right balance. On the other hand, again as noted in chapter 2, a U-curve connects popularity with zeitgeist originality, meaning that the most successful pieces are those that buck the stylistic conventions dominant at the time of composition, such as those traced by the trend in figure 5.1 (Simonton 1980d).

The above results were detailed to illustrate how construct validity can be fixed by embedding a measure in a complex network of relations. It should be obvious that computer-calculated melodic originality yields scores that function the way we would expect them to function were we to have direct access to the hypothesized construct. Other examples include Martindale (1975, 1986a), who validated his Regressive Imagery Dictionary or McClelland (1961) and Winter (1973), who validated their extensions of TAT into the historical universe. Whenever we must grapple with measures of difficult constructs, we should validate our instruments by proving that the scores interlock with other variables in a pattern compatible with the way that the construct would be expected to operate according to theory and common sense.

Sources of Bias

Because the most reliable measures get us nowhere if they yield scores that are invalid, we must examine the chief routes by which measures can become systematically biased—errors of aggregation, indeterminant baselines, retrospective assessments, and structural contrasts.

Aggregation Errors

There is a widespread belief that outstanding accomplishments are the prerogative of youth. Machiavelli ([1516] 1952, 36) observed that Fortune is "always . . . a lover of young men, because they are less cautious, more violent, and with more audacity command her." And Einstein held that "a person who has not made his [or her] great contribution to science before the age of thirty will never do so" (quoted in Brodestsky 1942, 699). But what is the scientific standing of this nomothetic claim that older persons make less history than do geniuses in their prime? One response would be to compile lists of achievements of individuals in advanced old age, thus noting how Humboldt wrote his masterpiece *Cosmos* from age 76 to 89, how Goethe finished the second part of *Faust* while he was in his seventies and eighties, and how Verdi completed *Otello* at 74 and *Falstaff* at 85 (see Lehman 1953, chap. 14). It would be taken as a critical datum that the French chemist Chevreul not only contributed his last scientific paper at 102, but when he was in his nineties began research in an utterly new field, studying the psychological effects of old age and thereby becoming a pioneer in gerontology. But these testimonials get us nowhere: Advocates of youth can always cite counterexamples in such abundance that the original question remains (see Lehman 1953, chap. 13). Newton's *annus mirabilis,* in which he originated most of the ideas that were eventually to make him famous, occurred when he was about twenty-three. Think of how many great poets, composers, and mathematicians managed to make lasting contributions to civilization without living beyond their twenties or thirties (for example, Keats and Shelley, Schubert and Mozart, Galois and Abel).

It is clear, then, that something more systematic is required. The investigator must first gather a comprehensive list of all landmark accomplishments in a given domain of achievement and then tabulate these events into consecutive age periods, such as five-year or ten-year intervals, according to the individual's age when the contribution was made—exactly the procedure followed by Quetelet ([1835] 1968), Beard (1874), Lehman (1953), and more recent authors. When this plan is applied, the summary age curve is predictable: Achievement increases rapidly to a definite peak, after which a decline sets in (Simonton 1988b). In figure 5.3 we find the typical result for three separate creative domains (compare Dennis 1966).

From the standpoint of reliability, considerable beauty dwells in this analytical strategy. The career of any one individual is plagued with all vagaries of extraneous inputs, such as physical illness, parental responsibilities, administrative chores, and even war and civil disturbances (Simonton 1988b). Thus, the age curve for a single achiever would be riddled with noise, as this or that event deflected the trajectory up and down whimsically. Only by adding across a large sample of historical figures do we obtain summary statistics for each age period in which the random shocks to a single career can cancel each other out. This aggregation procedure is a well-accepted approach to improving the picture in an initially fuzzy image.

It is not immediately obvious, but to ensure reliability, precious validity may have been sacrificed. The age curve that results from aggregation may be systematically biased against appreciating how much senior colleagues add to culture and politics. Suppose that for any individual the actual age curve is strictly positive monotonic, so that at no point in a career can we speak of an age decrement in the late years of life. Let us also make the defensible assumption that people vary tremendously in expected life span. What happens when we count the number of contributions made each age interval over a respectable sample of contributors? Clearly, in the age periods after, say, forty, there will be fewer and fewer survivors from the Grim Reaper's restless work, and consequently the aggregate counts will

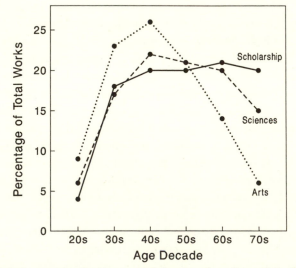

Figure 5.3. Typical age curves for three general domains of creative activity. Source: Based on tabulations in Dennis (1966, table 1).

decline proportionately. The upshot would be an age curve that exhibits a dramatic drop in the totals despite the utter lack of a negative slope in any of the individual careers that figure into the overall tallies. The presumed age decrement may represent more artifact than fact (Dennis 1956a, 1958; compare Lehman 1956).

This aggregation bias may operate just as well at the beginning end of the age curve, although in a different manner. One information-processing model of the creative process predicts an age curve such as that shown in figure 5.4. Notice that the career onset is expected to show a concave-downward productivity curve, yet what happens when we test this prediction against data aggregated across enough individuals to remove random unit-to-unit fluctuations? If creators vary according to when they launch their professional careers (Simonton 1990a), then the initial part of the aggregated tabulations will be in all likelihood concave-*upward* even though the curve for each separate case matches the theoretical hypothesis (Simonton 1989a). In addition, because individuals will not always begin output at the start of the same age period, the aggregate tabulations will be depressed for the initial time-series unit (Simonton 1988b, 1989a). Those who commenced output at twenty-nine cannot add too many tallies to the unit 25–29 or 20–29 years of age. Only by redefining the units in terms of career rather than chronological age can this aggregation error be avoided (Simonton 1984b).

This source of invalidity is sometimes referred to as the "compositional fallacy" because the inferential failure ensues from combining into a summary

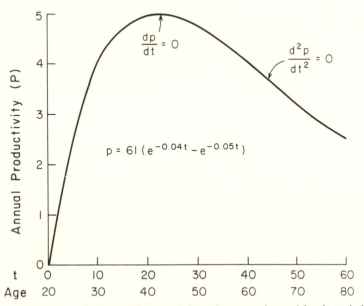

$$\frac{dp}{dt} = 0$$

$$\frac{d^2p}{dt^2} = 0$$

$$p = 61 \left(e^{-0.04t} - e^{-0.05t} \right)$$

Figure 5.4. Age curve predicted according to an information-processing model under typical parameters. (Taken from Simonton, 1984b, figure 1.)

tabulation sets of measurements that are not homogeneous concerning certain characteristics (Simonton 1988b). If everyone began their careers at the same age, died at the same age, and had the same composition with respect to other potential contaminants (for example, discipline, gender), then we need not fear the aggregation process. This statement at once suggests a route around the difficulty, namely decomposing the heterogeneous sample into subsamples more uniform regarding potential confounding factors. For instance, when Dennis (1966) tried to show that the age decrement was not nearly so intimidating as Lehman's data (1953) implied, he restricted his sample to individuals who lived to be octogenarians, and then safely tabulated the creative products into consecutive decades from the twenties through the seventies, but no further than the seventy-ninth year. Although this did not remove the aggregation bias attending the first one or two decades, Dennis did manage to obviate any worries about whether the declines in the final decades were spurious. Other solutions exist as well, including the calculation of the aggregate output for each longitudinal unit on a per capita basis and the analysis via a cross-sectional time-series design (Simonton 1988b). Whatever the specific procedures adopted, this aggregation error is serious enough that it cannot be ignored with impunity.

The compositional fallacy is not the sole example that may be given of aggregation bias. In the above illustration, the investigator possesses data at the individual level yet prefers to aggregate across units to obtain a smoother, more stable curve. Therefore, the option is always open of disaggregating the data so that they may be reassembled so that biases vanish. Occasionally, however, a social scientist must deal with facts irrevocably compiled in aggregate form, as in the demographer's exploitation of census data. In such instances, there may emerge an "ecological fallacy" (Hannan 1971; W. S. Robinson 1950), an error that also has been recognized as a potential irritant in the scientific analysis of history (Murphey 1973, 156–69). This occurs when individual characteristics are inferred from attributes discerned solely at the aggregate level. To provide a classic example, a close look at the United States in some portions of its history can turn up a peculiar paradox: Those states with the most impressive economic prosperity often feature the most damnable illiteracy rates. Are we to conclude that learning to read and write is antithetical to occupational advancement and material success? Obviously these two statistics are not talking about the same people in each geographic unit. Those states with superior economic opportunities—owing to the fruitful labors of an educated populace—may attract a bigger share of immigrants from abroad who have been denied the educational opportunities of native born citizens. If we could somehow disassemble the data more carefully—breaking them down by county, neighborhood, or block—the match between individual and aggregate characteristics would be tighter. Few of the well-heeled are unlettered, and hardly any of the illiterate can afford new heels.

A similar phenomenon can take place across history. For example, at one time the modal age for tuberculosis mortality was increasing, an odd result given that there was no particular reason to believe that persons were becoming more susceptible to the disease at later ages (Frost 1939). However, this secular trend was an artifact of the tendency for enhanced public hygiene to lower the incidence of new cases among the younger generations, so that most deaths come to the older generations that were exposed more seriously to the bacterium. At the individual level, tuberculosis was still just as likely to find a youthful victim, but at the aggregate level older persons were more liable to have been at risk for most of their lives. This explanation was only possible by breaking down the population into successive cohorts consisting of people of the same age, and then establishing the invariance of tuberculosis onset within each cohort.

Fortunately, even when historiometricians deal with aggregates, they usually do so in such a way that aggregation error is seldom a serious concern. Nevertheless, one must be eternally careful when drawing inferences from group means and percentages, for these may say nothing whatsoever about the individual proclivities of historical personalities.

Indefinite Baselines

A respectable bibliography could be compiled of inquiries that purport to show that orphanhood, or parental loss early in life, makes a considerable impression on the development of achieving individuals (for example, Albert 1971; Eisenstadt 1978; Martindale 1972; Silverman 1974). It is easy enough to cite concrete examples from the historical record: Lenin was a teen-ager when he lost his father; Napoleon was about fifteen when his father died; and Beethoven's mother died when he was sixteen, his father when he was eighteen (for a representative list, see Illingworth and Illingworth 1969, 34–35). But are these cases representative of the bigger picture? Perhaps the most systematic demonstration that the response may be affirmative is to be found in a paper by Eisenstadt (1978) that attempted to answer the query "Is parental loss a primary pathway to creativity and eminence?" (220). By examining 573 creators and leaders in virtually every domain of human achievement, he showed that almost half lost a parent before age 21, and one-quarter lost a parent in the first decade of life. As impressive as these statistics look at first, we must ask two questions before we can entertain belief in a real effect.

First, what is the expected rate of parental loss in the noneminent population, which should serve as the basis for comparison? Given that 75 percent of the eminent in the Eisenstadt sample lived in previous centuries, might not his statistics reflect merely higher orphanhood rates for all individuals in medically less auspicious eras? If so, and a proper comparative baseline could be fixed, the supposed effect would disappear (see Woodward 1974). The use of baselines drawn from contemporary populations, the most common tactic, will obviously not do.

Second, can we offer a convincing argument that the orphanhood rates in the samples have not been shifted upward owing to sampling biases? Maybe biographers are more prone to report the death dates of parents when they die at relatively young ages, these being more dramatic events. Parents who have more normal life spans may pass away unnoticed, because the historical figure by then is a mature adult no longer under direct parental influence. What is mandated is some way of estimating a baseline for any such reporting bias, a difficult though not impossible task. But if no elaborate procedures are implemented, one could never be sure that the orphanhood effect actually exists. In fairness to Eisenstadt, out of an initial sample of 699 historical figures, complete information was available on 82 percent or 573 figures, indicating little latitude for sampling bias—yet the first issue remains.

The baseline problem exists not just for orphanhood effects, but for any search for biographical effects. Once in a while sufficient data are available to establish a perfectly adequate comparison group. For instance, when Hudson (1958) wished to show that academic prowess may not necessarily contribute to success as a scientist, he hunted down the undergraduate records of Fellows of the Royal Society of London and a matched group of controls that failed to earn that distinction. In circumstances where data on obscure personalities are inaccessible, historical figures may be contrasted against each other by dividing them into achievement domains. Thus, in one study of 314 eminent leaders, creators, and celebrities of the present century, it was shown that literary figures tend to come from unhappy home environments, whereas better home conditions favor scientists, religious leaders, and philosophers (Simonton 1986b). Contrasts in biographical experience may accordingly determine the area in which an individual achieves even if we cannot compare these individuals against a "normal" population of valid controls.

From time to time, the problem is not so much the absence of any plausible baseline as a superfluity of alternatives. Take the question of how to evaluate properly the legislative leadership of U.S. presidents. There are available for modern chief executives independent estimates of success rates, as gauged by the proportion of administration-sponsored bills that saw passage in Congress. Still, it does not take an acute observer of the political scene to recognize that these "legislative box scores" cannot be taken on face value. One of the eternal truths of American politics is that presidents attain more of their legislative goals when their own party controls the House and Senate. Therefore, a valid assessment of a lawmaker's effectiveness demands that each president be contrasted against some proper baseline that adjusts for the number of allies on Capitol Hill. Yet, this baseline has more than one definition.

Hammond and Fraser (1984), for instance, proposed three separate "chance" baselines for judging the chief executive's success pushing bills through. The first posits that each member of Congress in effect decides to vote for or against a bill by flipping a coin; the second inserts the stipulation that these coin-tossers be split into two party factions (one represented by the sitting president); and the third permits the intrusion of loose coalitions that can cut across nominal party divisions. These diverse reference points for comparison often lead to different assessments. Only the first baseline implies that practically all presidents do better than expected. On the other hand, some consistency in a few rankings do rise above the three separate baselines, enough at least so that generalizations are possible. For example, Eisenhower, Kennedy, Nixon, and Carter frequently outperform expectation, thus belying their historical reputations. In contrast, Lyndon Johnson may have a somewhat exaggerated image as a phenomenal legislator, because by all three baselines, Carter's effectiveness in the Senate throughout his four years ranks above Johnson's in the Senate of the Ninetieth Congress. Perhaps the best lesson to abstract from this demonstration is that all reasonable reference points should be scrutinized and then the final assessments founded on findings that hold across all. Whatever the decision, the necessity of devising explicit baselines must now be manifest.

Retrospective Assessments

A serious complaint registered in historiography concerns the "fallacy of presentism," a subtle form of anachronism "in which the antecedent in a narrative series is falsified by being defined or interpreted in terms of the consequent" (Fischer 1970, 135). In this nunc pro tunc fallacy, the past is viewed only through glasses deeply colored by the obsessions of the present, as presented in Herbert Butterfield's *Whig Interpretation of History* (1931). "Whig history" is defined in the preface as the "tendency in many historians to write on the side of Protestants and Whigs, to praise revolutions provided they have been successful, to emphasize certain principles of progress in the past and to produce a story which is the ratification if not the glorification of the present." Speaking in more general terms, the past may undergo incessant revision by uncautious or unscrupulous historians in the present—scholars with an axe to grind, a perspective to advertise, or an ideology to promulgate.

A parallel problem confronts those engaged in the posthumous evaluation of historical personalities. For instance, when Cox gauged her 301 creators and leaders on IQ and sixty-seven personality traits, she had no choice but to quantify her measures from biographical data compiled by historians. Yet these latter scholars could rely on posterity's hindsight to tailor the factual presentation to be consistent with modern images of the essential qualities of "genius." Needless to say, should this distortion happen, history cannot provide the foundation for testing scientific hypotheses, for the data have been surreptitiously rewritten to comply with theoretical expectation. So how can we reject the hypothesis that the past embodies no more than the myths and mores of the present?

First, the boundaries of the potential invalidating bias must be recognized. This issue cannot be obliterated simply by ensuring that the assessors are blind to the identity of the historical figures. For example, when thirty-nine presidents of the United States were assessed on three hundred ACL adjectives, the biographical descriptions were abstracted with all identifying references removed, thereby preserving the anonymity of those assessed (Simonton 1986h). While this procedure effectively guards against retrospective impositions at the hands of the raters, we still must contend with the opportunity for bias in the original historical materials from which the biographical sketches were extracted. That the biographers themselves were obviously ignorant of the hypotheses under investigation does not preclude concern insofar as those hypotheses may have been themselves surmised from conceptions widely held in the intellectual community. For instance, historians know which chief executives were great and which were not, and at the same time these historians share notions about the roots of this cross-sectional variation—ideas that may then govern the selection of data to present in narrative accounts of individual figures. The naive researcher endeavoring to test these historical generalizations will consequently succeed only in confirming that the reshaping of the record has proved efficient.

On the other hand, this problem plagues only measures that provide considerable latitude for the injection of post hoc appraisals. Certainly objective behavioral measures, such as tabulations of total creative output or counts of legislative acts, are immune from this contaminant. In addition, even subjective evaluations are safe so long as the subjectivity dwells in the raters rather than in the raw data. For instance, the content analysis of systematically sampled primary documents, if care is taken to extirpate identifying material, need not suffer from retrospective bias. This independence holds for the numerous inquiries into the antecedents, correlates, and consequences of integrative complexity. Thus, because Suedfeld and Rank (1976) did not know which revolutionaries produced which documents when the latter were scored on this construct, the assessments could not have been twisted by the knowledge of which revolutionaries counted as successes and which as failures. The more objective the content analytical coding scheme, the less we have to worry about retrospective biases even when the source of the materials is known. To cite an incontrovertible case, the assessment of melodic originality in classical compositions cannot be tainted by posterity's evaluations given that the scores resulted entirely from a computer analysis of two-note transition probabilities.

But what do we do when the circumstances favor the pernicious slant of historical hindsight? Essentially the problem becomes one of establishing construct validity. The task is twofold.

First, the investigator should show that the assessment, however retrospective, relates with other variables and is compatible with theoretical expectation. Returning to the presidential example, the scores the chief executives received on intellectual brilliance in table 3.10 correlate with other performance variables in a substantively understandable fashion (Simonton 1986h). For instance, intellectual brilliance is negatively associated with the margin of victory in the general election, an inverse association that is consistent with theory and research regarding the link between intelligence and popular leadership (Simonton 1985a). Admittedly, the biographers may have guided their compilations with the scientific research in mind, but even this objection can be overruled if we can establish relations with factors unknown and perhaps even unknowable to any historian. The power and achievement motives of the chief executives, as assessed by the content analysis of inaugural addresses, fall into this category, and therefore it is significant that retrospective assessments of forcefulness and achievement drive (see table 3.10) correlate, respectively, with power and achievement drives (Simonton 1986h). Given the subtle nature of the latter, content analytical measures—scorings of leader motivation can correlate with objective behaviors without correlating with public images of a leader (Winter 1980)—it is unlikely that historians were able to modify their personality descriptions in favor of these two hidden motivational attributes. This inference is reinforced by the fact that almost all biographical sketches were compiled *before* these ratings were published, and no biographer exhibited any awareness whatsoever that such techniques existed.

Second, the researcher should demonstrate that the retrospective assessment does *not* behave as it would were the historians merely projecting present values onto past realities. One diagnostic has to do with the way individuals, scholars and laypersons alike, form impressions of others. When engaged in person perception, observers act as "cognitive misers" who process information by simplistic rules: (1) the items that inform the subjective judgments tend to be few in number, usually only a half dozen accounting for the lion's share of the variation; (2) the input concentrates on highly salient, even obvious facts that conform to schematic stereotypes; and (3) the information tends to be combined by simple linear and additive functions rather than complex (and probably more realistic) curvilinear and interactive relations (Faust 1984). As an example, we will later detail how presidential greatness is almost totally explicated by the linear and additive functions of only six conspicuous facts.

By comparison, inflexibility, the thirteenth column of scores in table 3.10, is far less likely to be a product of undifferentiated projections. As will be seen subsequently, this variable has rather complex relations with other variables, functions too numerous, intricate, and subtle to be handled by the impoverished information-processing capacity of the most experienced clinicians (Simonton 1983c, 1986h, 1987e). Given the demonstrated inability of individuals, even experts, to generate such intricate configurational assessments, it is improbable that scores on inflexibility represent mere editing of the historical record to accommodate modern prejudices. Considering the inability of observers to perceive covariance between two variables except when the relation is close, any contamination by a priori expectations is most likely to generate unrealistically impressive correlations, in stark contrast to the more modest associations actually found between inflexibility and its rather numerous correlates (Simonton 1986h, 1988d; Wendt and Light 1976).

These comments should not be interpreted as a dogmatic claim that retrospective measurements are invariably unbiased. On the contrary, the construct validity of such assessments must be carefully documented just like any other evaluation. Still, historians are normally so enthralled by the idiosyncrasies characterizing a chosen subject that they are oblivious to the larger picture. This fascination makes understandable the tendency of historians to report curious anecdotes and contemporary descriptions that can only embarrass the received tradition. For instance, biographies of President Lincoln seldom resist quoting the personality sketch provided by his colleague Herndon, a depiction containing several items, such as "skeptical" and "somewhat selfish," far removed from the legend rehearsed every 12 February in the United States.

This myopic attention to particulars allows humanistic scholars to "see" generalizations demonstrably not in their data. At the same time, this inundation of the rare abstraction by the cornucopia of concrete trivia makes the narration of historical personalities far more valid than might be surmised from untested speculations on the faults of historical reporting. For example, despite the historian's belief that great presidents are strong leaders, the assessment of forcefulness, which of all fourteen factors in table 3.10 most closely captures the strength dimension, shows no evidence of being confounded with historical appraisals of greatness. This trait fails to correlate with the ratings in table 4.2. Indeed, every personality factor that some historian or political scientist has identified as contributing to presidential success has turned out to be irrelevant when that personality attribute is gauged directly from the biographical archives (Simonton 1987d, 1988d, 1990f). This ubiquitous null effect suggests that no feedback process connects post hoc judgments of executive performance with the procedures by which historians collate the raw biographical descriptions. Whether this dissociation holds for all retrospective assessments cannot be assumed without a reasonable attempt to fix the construct validity of the instruments. Even so, it is illegitimate to presume that such posthumous evaluations are guilty until proved innocent.

Structural Differences and Change

A recurrent question in cross-cultural research is whether a given construct can have the same meaning as one moves from one society to another (Przeworski and Teune 1970, chap. 6). The fundamental assumption of science is that universals exist, whereas the equally basic truth in any attentive survey of the ethnographic record is that cultures display almost infinite variety. And so, what may be a valid index of an underlying construct in one culture may be invalid in the next. For comparative inquiries to succeed, investigators must somehow devise an indicator sufficiently generic that it transcends all cultural heterogeneity. Should the invented measures work according to theoretical expectation, they receive endorsement by the criterion of construct validity. However, if paradoxical results emerge from data analyses, the operational definition is in deep trouble, suggesting that the time has come to search for a new measure with improved cross-cultural invariance.

Historiometricians enjoy one advantage over cross-cultural researchers in that the societies they study are far more homogeneous. Because historiometry focuses on human behavior in civilized cultures that have developed enough complexity to have produced a history, the investigator is clearly dealing with a select subset of all possible worlds. The raw data are largely about individuals who have left a mark on the annals of literate cultures with urban concentrations. These historical figures come from societies that form an elite exception relative to the attainments of the overwhelming majority of human cultures (Carneiro 1970). Consequently, it is much easier to go back and forth between distinct nations without paralyzing anxieties about whether the measures are systematically changing substantive meaning. Thus, Tetlock could examine the link between integrative complexity and political ideology in both United States senators (Tetlock 1981a, 1983; Tetlock, Hannum, and Miceletti 1984) and British members of Parliament (Tetlock 1984) without worry that the operational definitions had lost contact as they leaped across the Atlantic (compare Tetlock and Boettger 1989). In parallel fashion, L. H. Stewart (1977) could inspect the interaction of birth order and the political zeitgeist in the leadership of both U.S. presidents and British prime ministers with little fear that his variables were not valid in both nations. That both sets of inquiries obtained the same substantive conclusions in both national systems further strengthens our belief that these measures transcend structural contrasts between the two nations.

The most severe obstacle, admittedly, is not structural differences across spatial units but structural change over historical time. The key reality of history is alteration. The historian records wars, conquest, revolutions, laws, reforms, movements, and innovations in religion, science, and art. Each successive generation springs from a new context that never before existed. This holds even after holocausts like Genghis Khan's Mongolian hordes or the Black Plague of the middle fourteenth century, for then history becomes no less than a phoenix arising from its own ashes.

The one-way arrow of historical change means that later historical figures are not directly comparable to their predecessors. How can we lump Napoleon with earlier generals to study military genius? Can the mass conscript armies of revolutionary and Napoleonic France be compared with the professional soldiers of the Roman legions, or the firing of muskets and bayonet charges matched with hurling spears and closing in with sword and shield? Does it not make a difference that Napoleon could see himself as the heir of Charlemagne, Julius Caesar, and Alexander the Great, whereas these earlier commanders had fewer (and less varied) paragons and precedents? Is it feasible to define variables that maintain their validity across such a diversity of circumstances? Reliability concerns aside, an operational definition that is on target in one period may hit wide of the mark in another stage of human existence.

Those sciences that lean heavily on historical data have come up with several responses to enigmas like these. Economists may confine their dynamic models to the post–World War II period to avoid the complications introduced by the military conflict, economic depression, and political disruption. Political scientists who study the correlates of war and military success will often test their notions separately for modern and premodern warfare, the divisional point often taken as 1815, the year of Napoleon's defeat at Waterloo (for example, Diehl 1985; Houweling and Siccama 1985). A couple of other devices are also available. For one thing, if the investigator is testing hypotheses using a time-series regression analysis, the residuals can be examined for heteroscedasticity. Should a construct have changed its meaning so that a variable's measurement becomes increasingly oblique as the analytical units recede into the past, the validity loss should show up as augmented prediction errors in more ancient times (Simonton 1975e). Because this check is the same as that for verifying reliability, the existence of heteroscedasticity does not discriminate between the two threats to measure quality.

A more powerful technique is to introduce interaction terms that statistically test for the transhistorical stability of the proposed causal structure. If the relations between dependent and independent variables systematically vary across time, then one explanation may be that our measurements are not transhistorically invariant. In several inquiries into the determinants of presidential greatness, the transhistorical persistence of the derived prediction equations was routinely tested by inserting the appropriate terms for interaction effects (Simonton 1986g, 1986h, 1988d). War, assassination, scandal, and other events may be different now than in the preceding century, but so far as we are concerned only with how these events affect reputation, those differences mean nothing. The antecedents of greatness have the same predictive power whether we are looking at the Virginia dynasty or the imperial presidency, and the regression slopes for the predictor variables transcend any dissimilarities between the two Johnsons. This generality would be impossible without variable definitions sufficiently generic to transcend the peculiarities of each era of American history. Assassination must be defined so that it does not matter that the pistol that killed Lincoln was far less advanced than the rifle that murdered Kennedy.

The Infamy of Fame

A defense of the scientific worth of historiometric instruments is not tantamount to a blanket claim that these measures are near perfect. On the contrary, historiometricians have repeatedly documented the sources of error in their assessments and tabulations. No doubt an ethnocentric bias appears in who earns entries in standard reference works, and an analogue of this prejudice is conspicuous in all data having any historical depth, namely the "epochcentric" (Simonton 1984g) bias, or what has also been styled the "discount" effect (Taagepera and Colby 1979). Because current and recent events tend to be more intrinsically interesting than events further back in the remote past, historians have an inclination to record more recent happenings disproportionately. Transhistorical counts of almost any class of events invariably display an overall exponential decay curve as one moves backward in time (Simonton 1981a; Taagepera and Colby 1979). As the eternal present goes inexorably forward, the decay curve is dragged behind like a comet's tail in the solar wind.

Admittedly, a portion of this curve may be ascribed to a substantial increase in the quantity of available events, an increase that probably parallels growth in the human population—accordingly that should be approximately exponential. Nevertheless, this material change cannot entirely account for the discrepancy in event counts between ancient and modern times. Open up any history of China and it is immediately apparent that military conflicts and domestic transformations of the current century are allotted ample space, whereas nearly a millennium of history under the Zhou dynasty is often assigned about the same number of pages. It would be all too easy to surmise that this disproportion reflects a contrast in our knowledge, but that inference would be wrong. The annals of early China are replete with details: About 90 B.C. Sima Qian was able to compile a classic history that alone fills many volumes. A historian writing for a modern readership will suppose, with justice, that most contemporaries are not very curious about the trials and tribulations of the obscure emperors and petty princes in that feudal age. Hence, the discounting of events circumvents potential ennui. If historiography were written backwards, from the present to earlier times—then this altering of the past might not be as urgent. A person could simply read about the most pertinent period and then stop.

The epochcentric bias, though troublesome, can normally be accommodated by methodological means, mostly through statistical controls. Still, this bias does suggest a broader debate that must involve any treatise on historiometry—the historical and scientific status of fame. Because so many studies measure differential eminence, greatness, or popularity of achievers or achievements, we must know what these assessments signify. Even in those investigations where the dependent variable is objective performance, such as battlefield victory or legislative success, differential eminence often supports the sampling strategy. After looking at the objections to this dependence on fame, we shall provide historiometry's rejoinder.

The Caprice of History

Fortune is often fickle, approbation and opprobrium dispensed frequently without reference to an individual's intrinsic attainments. Machiavelli ([1516]

1952, 135) warned that "a prince may be seen happy to-day and ruined to-marrow without having shown any change of disposition or character." This whimsy of contemporaries is magnified in posterity, confounding a person's historical reputation without regard to genuine merits and demerits. In the lines "Some are born great, some achieve greatness, and some have greatness thrust upon them" (*Twelfth Night,* act 2, scene 5), Shakespeare captures three possibilities, only the second seeming friendly to the just correspondence between personality and acclaim. Yet even this supposedly relevant factor hides a twisted story: Individuals may choose to achieve fame through infamy. A tale is told of a certain Herostratus who, on the exact day that Alexander the Great was born, sought an equal fame by burning down the Temple of Diana at Ephesus. True examples abound of personages who reserved a spot in the annals solely by an inordinate destructiveness. The names of Genghis Khan, Tamerlane, and Hitler leap at once to mind—all leaders whose genius was of the evil kind.

On a smaller scale, there are those otherwise insignificant individuals who enter historians' records simply because they pulled off assassinations of noted figures, were captured as spies or conspirators, or engaged in some other act of negative achievement (Goertzel, Goertzel, and Goertzel 1978). Hence, it is more than eminence not reflecting merit, for it may do so in an inverse relation to inherent goodness. Indeed, one with no conspicuous virtues but no outstanding vices can be swept into the dustpan of historical nonentities. In the *Decline and Fall of the Rome Empire,* one finds this faint praise of Titus Antoninus Pius, one of the less noticed emperors of the late empire: "His reign is marked by the rare advantage of furnishing very few materials of history; which is, indeed, little more than the register of the crimes, follies and misfortunes of mankind" (Gibbon [1776–88] 1952, vol. 1, 32). This cipher in the annals of political history would have done his historical conspicuousness far better if he had emulated Nero or Caligula!

The most fundamental difficulty with history, is that it is in no small part the creation of historians. Historians are people, with all the prejudices and instabilities of the species. Certainly they can have religious or ideological predilections that obstruct an objective view of a person's real worth in world civilization. Aspirants may merit exceptional kudos in the historians' eyes if they actively pursue the right by sacrificing their lives for The Great Cause. "He lives in fame that died in virtue's cause," noted Shakespeare in *Titus Andronicus* (act 1, scene 2), or as George Bernard Shaw cynically quipped, "Martyrdom is the only way in which a man can become famous without ability."

The partial dependence of posthumous fame on the values of each successive generation of historians implies some instability in posterity's praise. "Worldly renown is naught but a breath of wind, which now comes this way and now comes that, and changes name because it changes quarter," complained Dante (c. [1307] 1952, 69). Luminaries in one decade may suffer their lights to be blown out in the next, only to be rekindled yet later. Even worse, if a historical figure happens to find a champion or an accuser in a scholar with an eloquent pen, reputation may be resuscitated or tarnished for reasons unrelated to the individual's proper place in the record of accomplishments. As Lord Byron ([1818–23] 1949, 156) said,

> And glory long has made the sages smile,
>   'Tis something, nothing, words, illusion, wind—
> Depending more upon the historian's style
>   Than on the name a person leaves behind.

Bailey (1966) specifically argued for the operation of this effect as a principal reason why certain chief executives moved up or down between two polls of the experts conducted over a dozen years apart (Schlesinger 1948, 1962b). More recently, an excellent piece, *The Hidden-Hand Presidency*, has provoked reassessments of Eisenhower, budging him up slightly from his previously mediocre status (Greenstein 1982), whereas the reputation of Kennedy has been eroded by a number of idol-bashing exposés (for example, Wills 1981).

Because historians are still human beings, they have the same information-processing limitations. The only solution is to take shortcuts when ambling through the data. One clear manifestation of this behavior is the assignment of eponyms to historical events. When Emerson echoed Carlyle by holding that "there is properly no history; only biography," the Transcendentalist may have only been expressing a matter of cognitive convenience. It is easier to master a handful of biographies than to digest the richness of the history of millions, illustrious and obscure. Annals are accordingly reduced to bite-sized pieces, and each period is granted a name that symbolizes the era. Typical is the massive *Story of Civilization* by the popular historians Will and Ariel Durant, four consecutive volumes of which are entitled *The Age of Louis XIV, The Age of Voltaire, Rousseau and Revolution,* and *The Age of Napoleon.* Tolstoy ([1865–69] 1952, 343–44) said in his attempt to debunk Napoleon's place in world affairs: "In historical events, the so-called great men are labels giving names to events, and like labels they have but the smallest connection with the event itself." The stingy distribution of eponyms among the myriad personalities occurs in creativity as well as leadership, and with frequently bizarre effects, as is clear in an example from the history of science.

When two or more scientists working independently, sometimes simultaneously, offer the same discovery or invention to the world, the problem often arises of whom to name the discovery after. With merely two claimants a simple hyphen will do the trick, and so when William James and Carl Lange independently proposed nearly identical explanations about the self-perception of emotional states, the James-Lange theory justly emerged. Yet often there will be so many claimants that this discreet solution will consume patience faster than hyphens.

Deciding among several rivals who gets the crown may then depend on intellectual efficiency more than outright justice. Perhaps the most famous of the candidates will usurp the acclaim, reducing the number of eponymic tags; this does happen (Simonton 1979a). Nonetheless, circumstances may arise that make for an assignment that verges on historical absurdity.

Campbell and Tauscher (1966) described how the discovery "relating the apparent size of an afterimage to the distance of the surface upon which it is projected" (58) came to be known as Emmert's law of 1881 despite the existence of several, and often far more notable, rival claimants (Séguin, Lubinoff, Zehender, and perhaps even Schopenhauer). The rationale for honoring Emmert, notwithstanding that his discovery came at least a quarter-century after the first claim, includes the seemingly irrelevant consideration that he "contributed nothing else to the field" (61). Giving Emmert eponymic status avoided the confusion that might have otherwise emerged from adopting a name linked with many more distinct contributions; "the names of one-time contributors are more efficient that the names of the great who contribute many principles to science" (62). The function connecting greatness and eponymy could even be curvilinear. "The total nonentities would be omitted, the multiply great rarely represented, while the bulk of instances would come from that intermediate echelon of one-shot contributors to science" (62).

The physicist John Tyndall (1897, 17) justified the opinions of posterity by suggesting that "to look at his picture as a whole, a painter requires distance; and to judge of the total scientific achievement of any age, the standpoint of a succeeding age is desirable." Yet the illustration just given implies the contrary—that already myopic historians may stand so far back as to lose sight of what actually happened in the past. Eponymic laurels in creative endeavors, like the plaudits handed out in leadership domains, may be passed around with a sad disregard for true merit. To the extent that this invalidity infuses the historical record, fame and its family would seem to have no home in a science of human behavior. At best, historiometry could test only propositions about how historians behave.

The Science of Genius

The historiometrician denies little of what has just been said. History *is* capricious. Indeed, historiometry's main methodological task, second only to the substantive goal of verifying nomothetic propositions, is to document with as much scientific rigor as possible all of the odd turns in posterity's perspective on the past. Researchers have studied the processes by which epochcentric biases intrude on the determination of eminence. For example, an inquiry into the differential fame of Western thinkers found strong evidence that philosophers benefit if they happen to have espoused beliefs that are consistent with the twentieth-century zeitgeist, a potent "modernity bias" (Simonton 1976f). Every so often, naturally, the bias can work in the opposite direction, favoring the older over the more current achievers (Simonton 1988c). A study of 696 composers unearthed a clear "classicist bias," the grand masters taking precedence over the insecure position of the contemporary "serious" composer (Simonton 1977c). Regardless of who wins this battle between the moderns and the ancients, epochcentric biases can adversely compromise scientific validity.

Investigators have also gathered evidence for the whimsical influence of events that have almost nothing to do with actual achievement. Plotting the eminence rankings of the geniuses in the Cox (1926) sample as a function of life span, we get the graph in figure 5.5, with the curves given separately for leaders and creators (Simonton 1976a). Whatever the contrasts in the two functions, for both achievement areas a U-type curve indicates that those historical figures who live out a more normal term of life are likely to see their reputations suffer for it. The optimal outcomes are either to die tragically young or survive to become a much-respected patriarch or matriarch. The tragic effect of dying young is especially prominent for leaders; we are likely to have martyrs who sacrificed their lives for some noble end. For creators, to leave the living at about sixty is most inopportune, whereas for leaders the nadir occurs in the seventies. Significantly, these curves have been roughly replicated using the *New York Times* obituary columns; the number of lines devoted to the memory of a deceased celebrity may be expressed as a U-shaped function of the individual's age at time of death (Lehman 1943; Mills 1942).

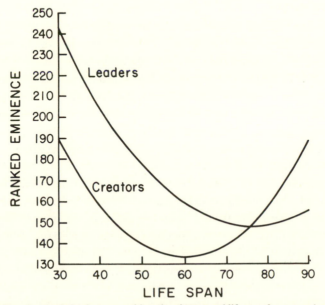

Figure 5.5. Functional relation between achieved eminence and life span for 301 geniuses of the Cox (1926) sample. (Taken from Simonton 1984d, figure 3.)

The benefits of tragic early death have been documented more directly in the work on presidential greatness (Simonton 1986g, 1986h, 1988d). Those chief executives struck down by an assassin's bullet, from Lincoln through Kennedy, receive a permanent boost in the ratings of subsequent historians and political scientists, despite the absence of evidence that those assassinated differ substantially from those not assassinated in biographical background, political experience, personality, leadership style, or political performance. Although assassinated presidents seem to be judged more virtuous, this judgment is purely subjective (Simonton 1986c). The leading factor seems to be that assassination is a dramatic event that attracts attention, historians acting on the assumption that something so eye-catching must be pertinent. Bailey (1966) enumerated forty-two criteria behind his rankings, *not one* having anything to do with whether the chief executive was murdered. Even so, Bailey rated those killed during their term of office higher than those who did not.

Other predictors of presidential greatness cluster into the same pattern. If a politician wants to go down in history as a notable chief executive, he should avoid administration scandals, serve as many years as possible as a wartime commander-in-chief, and have a long tenure in the White House. These antecedents certainly indicate the relevance of salient or conspicuous events. In contrast, more subtle indices of performance, such as popularity with the American people, success in getting administration-sponsored bills through Congress, effective negotiation of treaties with foreign powers, the quality of appointments to the Supreme Court and the Cabinet—prove absolutely irrelevant (compare Holmes and Elder 1989; Kenney and Rice 1988).

Only two predictors involve personal attributes (Simonton 1987d, chap. 5). First, on average great presidents have been war heroes before entering the nation's highest office. Given the role of political drama in swaying historians' perceptions, this finding may prove compatible with the rest, owing to the absence of concrete evidence that former war heroes perform any better as president. Second, great presidents tend to score higher on subjective assessments of intellectual brilliance. Because intelligence has been repeatedly shown to correlate positively with leadership in almost all domains (Simonton 1985a), this predictor alone fits in well with the notion that presidential greatness has some root in the personal capacities. If so, it must be counted as one of the sadder aspects of American politics that intelligent presidents are likely to be less popular with the American people (Simonton 1986h). When Victor Hugo maintained "Popularity? It's glory's small change," he was guilty of understatement; popularity and glory are in currencies of wildly divergent exchange rates! At any rate, of six predictors, only one has a direct connection to a president's individual worth: intellectual genius counts toward greatness yet is largely overwhelmed by the mostly superfluous input of more dramatic data. These last five predictors account for 78 percent of the variation in presidential greatness (Simonton 1986g), whereas intellectual brilliance accounts for only an additional 4 percent (Simonton 1986h).

Is there a non sequitur in this argument? Why not conclude that presidents with longer stays in office are truly superior political leaders? After all, in a democracy an incumbent who does well in his first term has a better chance of being reelected than one who does a lousy job. However, the odds that a president will be elected to a second term have little to do with what he accomplishes in the first term. The primary factors concern the political zeitgeist, such as whether there is an international crisis or war going on. "Don't swap horses while crossing the stream" was Lincoln's campaign slogan during the Civil War. The one element of reelection chances that would reflect the incumbent's first-term performance, namely the total number of bills signed, turns out to relate more to circumstances than to the individual (Simonton 1986g). Additionally, reelection in itself has no independent relation with greatness, even though greatness correlates with years in office if we should scrutinize one- and two-term administrations separately (Simonton 1986g). Given two presidents who served only one term, the one who spent the full four years in office will get a higher rating than the one who devoted fewer years, whether owing to death or vice-presidential succession; the same function holds for those presidents elected to a second term. By comparison, should the total tenure be statistically controlled, whether or not the president had been reelected, becomes useless as a predictor. Hence, the assessments contain something beyond the rubber stamping by posterity of the decision of voters.

Perhaps the longer a president governs in Washington, the more events that will be credited to his administration—more laws, Supreme Court appointments, battles, and other history-making events, including many not particularly under the executive purview. It is this historical activity, not demonstrated leadership, that so impresses the historians when they sit down to play the rating game. Under this interpretation, years in office do not indicate how much a president deserves the applause of the experts. Uncontrollable happenings determine a leader's historical reputation, an asset beyond the scope of the politician's personal volition.

While this hypothesis seems extremely speculative, it has received factual endorsement from an investigation concerning the comparative fame of 342 absolute monarchs (Simonton 1984g). The inquiry was partly inspired by a casual observation made by Sorokin (1925, 1926) that the most illustrious rulers tend to be the longest lived. If eminence is founded on a profusion of historical episodes, we may advance the following causal chain: The longer that hereditary monarchs live, the longer their reigns are likely to be, on average; the longer rulers reign, the more impressive the intrusion of historical events; this last variable contributes directly to the final score on distinction. To test this conjecture, we need assess the four variables in the sequence, historical activity being no more than a composite count of sundry political events (battles, conquests, laws, reforms, revolts, and so forth) (see figure 5.6).

The arrows indicate supposed causal influences, and the percentages attached to each arrow represent the proportion of variance in the effect that can be attributed to a particular cause. The hypothesized chain of causes monopolizes the

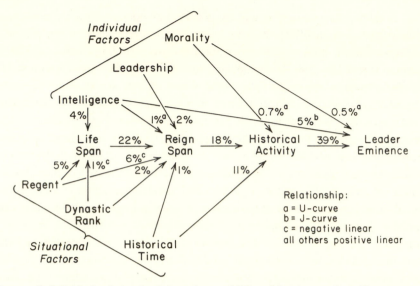

Figure 5.6. Individual and situational determinants of differential eminence of 342 European monarchs, showing both direct and indirect effects and indicating both the form of the function and the percentage of variance explained. (Taken from Simonton 1984g, figure 1. Copyright 1984 by Duke University Press. Used by permission.)

manifold relations. The central predictor of leader eminence is indeed historical activity, which is determined chiefly by reign span (plus an epochcentric bias), whereas reign span is primarily affected by life span. Because hereditary monarchs did not have to be reelected and usually served until their death, this analysis provides a purified test of the hypothesis that a long tenure in itself contributes to prominence as a leader. Long-lived, long-tenured rulers, indeed, make better eponyms.

This last conclusion is reinforced when we examine other results. The composite index of historical activity consists of many events, both good and bad, yet when the indicator is broken down into its components, the same outcome emerges. Those monarchs whose reigns were damned with more battlefield defeats, territorial losses, economic difficulties, famines, massacres, and executions, earn eponymic credit as much as those monarchs whose reins were blessed with more battlefield victories, territorial gains, economic improvements, treaties, and laws (Simonton 1984g). Furthermore, for some events it is feasible to determine whether what happened was under the ruler's direct personal control. It makes no difference, for example, whether the monarch personally led his armies into battle rather than let subordinates do it. Events over which the leader had direct control exerted as much influence in the eminence assessment as did events for which the leader assumed no immediate responsibility—a finding with parallels in the determinants of presidential popularity (Brody and Page 1975). Historians evidently do not care where the action originates so long as something fascinating is going on.

In addition, at the top of figure 5.6 are shown the consequences of three germane personality traits—intelligence, leadership, and morality—as modified and extended from earlier ratings by Woods (1906, 1913). The attributes basically explain only a few percent of the variation in any core variable in that eponymic sequence, and sometimes the explanatory power dips beneath 1 percent. The situational factors in the lower left corner of the figure boast more impressive predictive utility, and these compose only a subset of the whole collection of situational predictors. A case in point is that the more eminent rulers, like the greater presidents, are more prone to have suffered a violent death. Hence, greatness as a leader seems to be less a matter of being the right person and more a matter of being at the right place at the right time.

One last implication from figure 5.6: Character may impinge upon the eponymic chain reaction through curvilinear functions. Most intriguing is the U-curve that ties leader morality with both historical activity and leader eminence. Those who fall between virtue and vice, claim neither much action during their reigns nor much hold on posterity's attention. That this is no fluke of hereditary monarchies is proved by an analogous function regarding presidential leadership. American chief executives have been rated on *dogmatism,* a bipolar dimension that at one pole sees those politicians who are idealistic but inflexible, and at the other, those who are pragmatic and flexible (Maranell 1970; Simonton 1986g; Wendt and Light 1976). This dimension, though not identical, can be partially mapped on the morality assessments of the monarchs (a mapping bolstered by the negative association between idealism and Machiavellianism; Simonton 1986h). Presidential greatness overlaps in meaning with eminence, a congruence that has been empirically demonstrated (Simonton 1987d, chap. 5). Consequently it complies perfectly with the expectation that presidential greatness is a U-shaped function of dogmatism. The most highly praised chief executives are those who are either inflexibly idealistic or flexibly practical (Simonton 1986g). Once more, historians seem to appreciate best those personalities who depart from the norm, regardless of which direction that departure veers.

Now that historiometricians have built up an exhaustive inventory of confounding factors in the attainment of fame, why should they still show respect for this measure, as a sampling criterion and as a dependent variable? The response is that individual differences in eminence have psychological significance. In the first place, many impurities appear in such low concentrations that we need not bother about them. As an example, Maranell and Dodder (1970) wanted to know whether conservative and liberal historians disagreed on how to rate American presidents. It turns out that politically opposed scholars had divergent views of F. D. Roosevelt, "that man in the White House" according to conservatives during the Great Depression. Where liberals placed FDR second only to Lincoln, the conservatives put him fifth, only a bit higher than Wilson. Even so, that still makes him one of the nation's top executives no matter what the historian's ideological commitments. Indeed, the correlations between the two sets of ratings is .95—hardly a drastic discrepancy. Further, liberals and conservatives showed consensus on the most crucial qualities underlying greatness, including administration accomplishments and strength of action. A more recent examination of presidential greatness ratings considered a wide range of conceivable contaminants—such as the historian's age, sex, geographical region, specialty area, academic affiliation, and professional status—and found that around over 90 percent of the variance in the assessments is immune from such impurities (Murray and Blessing 1983). All in all, historians may quibble but history marches on unimpaired.

When the fickleness of history becomes more substantial, we can always introduce controls into our statistics to render these complications impotent. Thus, ethnocentric prejudices in the assessment of European monarchs could be directly dispatched simply by incorporating dummy variables that, in effect, reset the mean eminence for each nationality (Simonton 1984g). Indeed, the reason why we know so much about how extraneous factors affect eminence is because these controls were routinely implemented from the start. Besides correcting for any bias, these techniques permit direct assessments of precisely how much bias may have permeated any ratings. Error is present in all sciences, even the hardest and most exact, so science advances not by throwing up its hands in despair the moment it encounters a difficult measurement problem. Similarly, the psychologist must confront the technical issues by dividing fame into its separate components, some involving random noise (unreliability), others various systematic biases (invalidity), and (the most important) defining the core segment of the ratings that correspond to true achievement (genius). The result of this variance partitioning is a scientific affirmation of Carlyle's words: "Fame, we may understand, is no sure test of merit, but only a probability of such."

We have addressed at length the set of issues that must be resolved before scientific research can begin. Those critical of historiometrics voice one complaint above all others, namely that historical data are not adequate to the task. The architecture of science cannot build on shoddy measurements. Therefore, aspiring historiometricians should know that their indicators need not be riddled with more error than what has long proved tolerable in the behavioral sciences. Although the reliability of the instruments is uneven, the same holds true for quantifications in any scientific domain, inside or outside psychology. Ever since Michelson, the velocity of light in a vacuum has been determined to the umpteenth significant figure, whereas even the most rudimentary properties of the neutrino still escape precise determination. Moreover, we have also seen how the measures devised by historiometricians are more than reliable; they are valid. Although validity is a nebulous concept, the standard criteria show that the historiometrician cannot be faulted on this basis. Even those factors that can undermine the validity of a historiometric assessment may usually be preempted by activating the appropriate technical precautions. Respectable reliability and validity hold for even the much-abused notion of fame and infamy, ideas central to historiometry notwithstanding the critiques of opponents in psychology, science, and history. Ironically, eminence has been validated as an index of achievement in part by quantifying the sources of invalidity in the assessment of historical distinction. By objectively assessing the bias in a measurement, it is far easier to correct for that bias.

6 **Statistics**

Quantification, even reliable and valid quantification, seldom suffices. In fact, everything discussed in the last four chapters would constitute the method section of a typical article in a scientific journal. What follows are techniques that are likely be seen in the results segment where investigators use all the statistical devices that facilitate a rigorous test of the nomothetic hypotheses driving an inquiry. A major reason why older studies have sometimes failed is that they neglected to do more than survey the numbers, assuming the patterns would stand out. The information-processing discipline that only statistics affords was considered irrelevant. Therefore, pioneers like Sorokin and Kroeber would descend into inferences that could be easily contradicted by the simplest statistical manipulations of their own data (Simonton 1976c, 1977d). The fact is that people cannot adequately intuit probabilistic associations. Anyone not convinced of this inescapable cognitive law might wish to conduct the following experiment: Show naive observers the scores on presidential greatness (table 4.2) and personality (table 3.10) with instructions that they are to determine which character traits correlate most strongly with the several performance assessments—a difficult task notwithstanding that the inductive process is eased by the uniform standardization of the scores.

Because the nomothetic hypotheses to be tested are so diversified, the statistical analyses are diverse as well. Consequently, we can do no more than skim the vast surface of the available techniques. Even then, a cursory examination will require three chapters, the present chapter merely surveying univariate statistics and measures of association. For someone already expert in the statistics to be discussed, the principal knowledge to be gained is that the techniques have corresponding substantive questions on the psychology of historical behavior. For others, more curious about the nomothetic statements than competent in the analyses, the point is that some of the statistics may be worth studying in more depth. For all readers, there should grow an appreciation for the theoretical edifaces that may be built using these analytical tools.

Univariate Characteristics

Probably the simplest statistics concern univariate problems: Investigators may have measurements pertaining to a single variable, yet this is enough data to test a theory that predicts how that variable must behave. In line with the two main types of analytical units, one set of univariate statistics is suited for assessing cross-sectional variations, such as individual differences, whereas the other is appropriate for examining time-series fluctuations.

Cross-Sectional Variations

On occasion, all the researcher wishes to show is that the frequency of different values on a variable has a specific distribution. Usually the expected frequencies are predicted by a probabilistic model or theory. The most common stochastic processes are those that yield the Gaussian, Poisson, negative binomial, and beta distributions. To show that the data fit the predicted distribution constitutes a direct test of the theory. Distributional examinations of cross-sectional variation will be examined first. Less often the investigator will be engaged in what superficially seems a more modest activity, namely the demonstration that a set of discrete attributes, which might otherwise be considered independent variables, can be ordered to form a single dimension or Guttman scale.

Frequency distributions. The oldest procedure in historiometry entailed nothing more than showing that the frequency distribution of a variable across a sample of analytical units assumes an identifiable form. Quetelet ([1835] 1968) was fond of establishing the ubiquity of the normal, or Gaussian curve, a distribution approximated by the symmetrical binomial ($p = q = .5$). For Quetelet, this bell-shaped curve had incredible theoretical meaning as part of his preoccupation with outlining the properties of the "average man" (Stigler 1986, chap. 5). By a turn of fate, however, asymmetrical distributions, not those symmetrical, have proven to have greater significance. Historiometricians deal with relatively rare events, a circumstance that invariably compels the making of skewed frequency distributions. Two examples should prove this point; both are taken from that portion of the discipline that overlaps with scientometrics.

A long-standing issue in science studies is the place that an elite group may occupy in scientific advance. J. M. Cattell (1910, 634) put it this way: "We do not know whether progress is in the main due to a large number of faithful workers or to the genius of a few." Some agree with Cesare Lombroso (1891, 120) that "the appearance of a single great genius is more than equivalent to the birth of a hundred mediocrities." Others have advocated the contrary thesis, endorsing what has come to be known as the Ortega hypothesis (Cole and Cole 1972), namely that "it is necessary to insist upon this extraordinary but undeniable fact: experimental science has progressed thanks to the work of men astoundingly mediocre, and even less than mediocre. That is to say, modern science, the root and symbol of our actual civilization, finds a place for the intellectually commonplace man and allows him to work therein with success" (Ortega y Gasset [1932] 1957, 110–11). Which generalization is empirically justified, Lombroso's or Ortega's?

One clue is to inspect the frequency distribution of lifetime contributions for large samples of scientists to see whether most of the work is done by a relative handful of creative workers. Thus, Dennis (1955) looked at disciplines as diverse as linguistics, infantile paralysis, gerontology and geriatrics, geology, and chemistry, uniformly finding that the top 10 percent most prolific contributors were responsible for about half of the total work, whereas the bottom 50 percent least productive can be credited with only about 15 percent of the contributions. Indeed, typically around half of those active contribute only one work each, meaning that the most prolific contributor is several times more productive than are the least productive contributors. In psychology, for instance, the most prolific scientist claims more titles than eighty colleagues in the lowest part of the distribution, a contrast not too far from Lombroso's claim (Dennis 1954c).

So robust is this skewed distribution that it has inspired the induction of two behavioral laws. According to the Price law, if k represents the total number of contributors to a discipline, then $\sqrt{k}$ will be the predicted number of contributors who generate half of all contributions (Price 1963, chap. 3). That this principle applies as well to the arts as to the sciences is evident by a careful inspection of table 3.5: If 250 composers are credited for all that is heard in the classical repertoire, then the top $16 \approx \sqrt{250}$ should account for half of the music listening, a figure close enough to the 51 percent calculated by Moles ([1956] 1968). Lotka's law, in contrast, strives to define more precisely the actual shape of the frequency distribution: If n is the number of contributions and $f(n)$ is the number of scientists who make n contributions, then $f(n)$ will be inversely proportional to n^2, where the proportionality constant varies across disciplines (Lotka 1926). Researchers have offered theories that explicate the observed data, obtaining stochastic models for the lognormal, beta, and other distributions (Price 1976; Shockley 1957; Simon 1955). Despite the lack of consensus on the most appropriate theoretical account, all interpretations concur in rejecting the notion that the distribution is in any way normal, nor can there be any justification for concluding that the distribution is highly egalitarian (compare Dennis 1954c; Simon 1954a). When we examine actual influence as divorced from mere productivity, the distribution becomes even more elitist (Simonton 1988e, chap. 4).

The second example deals with the theoretically related topic of why multiples occur in science and technology. Earlier we noted that this phenomenon counted as an article of evidence that social determinists have advanced against the genius theory of history: Two or more scientists come up with the same idea independently, perhaps simultaneously, because at a certain point in the evolution of a discipline that contribution becomes inevitable. Hence, Kroeber (1917, 199) could emphatically assert with respect to the simultaneous and independent re-discovery of Mendel's laws by De Vries, Correns, and Tschermak that "it was discovered in 1900 because it could have been discovered only then, and because it infallibly must have been discovered then." The most favored "proof" of this interpretation is to compile long lists of multiples in the hope that sheer mass will crush all doubts. Hence, Ogburn and Thomas (1922), in an essay entitled "Are Inventions Inevitable? A Note on Social Evolution," enumerated nearly 150 multi-ples. And Merton (1961) said that he had collected 264 examples, becoming thereby so impressed with their frequency that he could hazard that "it is the singletons—discoveries made only once in the history of science—that are the residual cases, requiring special explanation" and that "all scientific discoveries are in principle multiples, including those that on the surface appear to be sin-gletons" (477).

One empirical oddity throws a monkey wrench in this traditional zeitgeist account: The frequency distribution of the multiple grades exhibits a distinctive signature. A multiple's *grade* is the number of independent workers who were honored with the discovery. Thus, the calculus was a grade 2 doublet (Newton and Leibniz), whereas the self-exciting dynamo might be considered a grade 6 sex-tuplet (Hjorth, Varley, Siemens, Wheatstone, Ladd, and Wilde). Tabulations of the number of times each grade appeared in the history of science without exception generate extremely skewed curves, the expected frequencies declining monoton-ically with the magnitude of the grade. Table 6.1 shows the resulting frequency distributions for three data sets. The same characteristic pattern merges should we break the multiples down to separate disciplines as well (Simonton 1978a), and hence the frequency distribution is robust. These results are remarkable because they fit with what we would anticipate if the generation of multiples were governed

Table 6.1 *Observed Multiple Grades and Predicted Poisson Values for Three Data Sets*

Grade	Ogburn-Thomas		Merton		Simonton	
	Observed	Predicted	Observed	Predicted	Observed	Predicted
0	—	(132)	—	(159)	—	(1361)
1	—	(158)	—	(223)	—	(1088)
2	90	95	179	156	449	435
3	36	38	51	73	104	116
4	9	11	17	26	18	23
5	7	3	6	7	7	4
6	2	1	8	2	0	0
7	2	0	1	0	0	0
8	1	0	0	0	1	0
9	1	0	2	0	0	0
μ		1.2		1.4		0.82

Note. Adapted from Simonton (1986i, table 1).

by the Poisson process, a stochastic mechanism that tends to describe not inevitable but rather rare events (Price 1963, chap. 3). This correspondence is also depicted in the table, where Poisson predicted values are compared against the observed frequencies for each grade. Chi-square tests of goodness-of-fit demonstrate that we cannot reject the inference that all discrepancies between observed and predicted frequencies are due to mere random error (Simonton 1978b, 1979a).

The theoretical implication of this analysis becomes more obvious when we notice that the Poisson parameter μ, which is the mean (and variance) of the distribution, always hovers around unity. Given that the Poisson distribution can be considered the exponential limit of the binomial distribution when event probabilities (p) are low and the number of trials (n) are high, we obtain $\mu = pn$. Hence, we are dealing with a phenomenon where the number of attempted discoveries may be quite large (for example, $n = 100$) but where the likelihood of success on any single trial is quite small (for example, $p = .01$)—hardly consistent with the idea of an inevitable event! This inherent indeterminancy receives more documentation when the Poisson formula is used to reconstruct the "multiples" of grades 1 (singletons) and 0 (nulltons). For all data sets, singletons and nulltons outnumber any grade of multiple, and for the most extensive data set of 579 multiples (Simonton 1979a), the nulltons and singletons each surpass all the multiple frequencies totalled together. Nor can one dismiss this result as an artifact of the underreporting of multiples in history, for the Poisson model actually predicts that, given the number of discoveries listed in the most comprehensive chronological sources, any published compilation underestimates the number of multiples by at least *six thousand* (Simonton 1978b).

Of course, we may not be justified in extrapolating predicted frequencies back to unobserved grades. More sophisticated stochastic models have been devised that remove all nulltons, for example (Simonton 1986d). Even so, probability models that accurately describe the data do so only by making multiples the distinctive events and singletons the more typical happenings. The telltale frequency distribution of multiple grades cannot be ignored. Furthermore, analyses of additional aspects of the phenomenon lead to the same conclusion: Rather than endorsing the zeitgeist or social-deterministic interpretation, multiples lend strong support to the notion that chance plays a predominant role in scientific discovery and technological invention. This inference has stimulated the development of a theoretical model of scientific genius, a theory that, interestingly enough, can also explain the skewed distribution of lifetime productivity that so firmly contradicts the Ortega hypothesis (Simonton 1988e).

Univariate distributional tests have proved their worth in domains besides the science of science. The Poisson distribution, in particular, is almost omnipresent, there being few human activities that do not presume this stochastic process in some sphere. In the political world, as an example, the opportunities that U.S. presidents have for filling vacancies on the Supreme Court are adequately described by a Poisson model (Ulmer 1982). There has also been some debate about whether the outbreak of international violence can be explicated in terms of a Poisson process (Houweling and Kune 1984). However basic these statistical analyses may be, their utility in historiometric studies is substantial.

Guttman scales. The opinion is hard to resist that history unfolds in stages, a notion common among the philosophers of history. Ibn Khaldūn specified five stages in the rise and fall of Moslem dynasties, and Auguste Comte felt that human progress arrived in three grand steps, the theological, metaphysical, and positive, the last marking the phase of modern science. Whenever the hypothesized sequences are relatively few, as in these two examples, analysis is rather trivial. Yet if an evolutionary progression is thought to contain dozens of separate steps, verification becomes far more burdensome. One solution is to perform a Guttman scale analysis (A. L. Edwards 1957, chaps. 7 and 8). Suppose that analytical entities may possess a set of characteristics that we may label $A, B, C,$ and so on to Z. Assume, too, that no entity may exhibit B without first showing $A,$ just as B is prerequisite for $C,$ and so forth, forming an ordinal sequence in time. In practice, naturally, the scale may not be absolutely perfect, scattered exceptions to the broad order intruding, owing to measurement errors or some unspecified disruption of the ranks. Guttman scale analysis permits one to determine whether the overall ordinal pattern persists despite the intrusion of this noise. Two concrete illustrations will show how this works with real data.

From the psychologist's perspective, the more immediately pertinent applications of Guttman scale analysis operate at the individual level of analysis. An example of considerable interest to students of leadership is an attempt by Cell (1974) to devise a measure of charisma. Concentrating on male heads of state, Cell proposed an ascending scale of objective indicators of this elusive concept, arriving at the Guttman *scalogram* in table 6.2. Hitler, Kenyatta, Mussolini, and Ataturk earn top places in charisma, in the middle fall figures such as Magsaysay, F. D. Roosevelt, and DeGaulle, and at the bottom rest the bland Ben Gurion, Frei, and Adenauer. Cell went beyond mere scaling, indicating how charisma was also associated with certain national characteristics, but discussion of these fascinating findings would take us too far beyond our present needs.

The second example requires that we change gears, and cruise through whole systems rather than individuals. Carneiro (1970) was intrigued with the possibility of scaling human cultures according to some evolutionary sequence of advancement. Societies seem to vary tremendously in their complexity, and this variation may betray an underlying scale of sociocultural change. He consequently examined one hundred cultures from all over the globe on 354 traits, these concerning subsistence, settlements, architecture, economics, social organization and stratification, political organization, law and judicial process, warfare, religion, ceramics and art, tools, utensils, and textiles, metalworking, watercraft and navigation, and special knowledge and practices. Carneiro demonstrated that ninety of

Table 6.2 *Guttman Scalogram of Charisma for Twentieth-Century Political Leaders*

Leader	Rating	Indicators										
		1	*2*	*3*	*4*	*5*	*6*	*7*	*8*	*9*	*10*	*11*
Hitler	10	1	1	1	1	1	1	1	1	1	1	1
Kenyatta	10	1	1	1	1	0	1	1	1	1	1	1
Mussolini	10	1	1	1	1	1	1	1	1	1	1	1
Ataturk	10	1	1	1	1	1	1	1	0	1	1	1
Sukarno	9	1	1	1	1	1	1	1	1	0	1	0
Nkrumah	9	1	1	1	1	1	0	1	0	1	1	0
Peron	9	1	1	1	1	1	0	1	1	1	1	0
Bourguiba	8	1	1	1	1	1	0	1	1	1	1	0
Ho	8	1	1	1	1	1	1	1	0	1	0	0
Mao	8	1	1	1	1	1	1	1	1	1	0	0
Rhee	8	1	1	1	0	1	1	1	1	1	0	0
Tito	8	1	1	1	1	1	1	0	1	1	0	0
Ben Bella	7	1	1	0	1	1	1	1	1	0	0	0
Castro	7	1	1	1	1	1	1	0	1	0	0	0
Tojo	7	1	1	1	1	1	0	1	1	0	0	0
Nu	7	1	1	1	1	0	0	1	1	0	0	0
Magsaysay	6	1	1	1	1	0	1	1	0	0	0	0
Roosevelt	6	1	1	1	1	1	1	1	0	0	0	0
DeGaulle	5	0	1	1	1	0	1	0	0	0	0	0
Jinnah	4	1	1	1	1	1	0	0	0	0	0	0
Kennedy	4	1	1	1	1	1	0	0	0	0	0	0
Nehru	4	1	1	1	1	1	0	0	0	0	0	0
Selassie	4	1	1	1	1	1	0	0	0	1	0	0
Cardenas	4	1	1	0	1	1	0	0	0	0	0	0
Lenin	4	1	1	1	0	1	0	0	—	0	0	0
Nyerere	3	1	1	1	1	0	0	0	0	0	0	0
Churchill	2	1	1	1	0	0	1	0	0	—	0	0
Nasser	2	1	1	1	0	0	0	0	1	0	0	0
Hirohito	2	1	1	1	0	0	0	1	0	0	0	0
Khrushchev	1	1	0	0	0	1	0	0	1	0	0	0
Hussein	1	1	0	0	0	0	0	0	0	0	0	0
Ben Gurion	0	0	0	0	0	0	1	0	—	0	0	0
Frei	0	0	0	0	0	1	0	0	0	0	0	0
Adenauer	0	0	0	0	0	0	0	0	0	0	0	0

Source: Adapted from Cell (1974, 272–73). Copyright 1974 by Human Relations Area Files. Used by permission.
Note. Indicators are defined as follows: 1 = picture posted in public or homes, 2 = seen as uniting the country, 3 = leader's principles followed, 4 = people make sacrifices for leader, 5 = people asked to follow new paradigm, 6 = led country to military victory, 7 = lack of interest/understanding of economics, 8 = leader gives long speeches, 9 = statue of leader in capital during tenure, 10 = sexual prowess, and 11 = females make sacrifices for leader. Scores on indicators are defined as 0 = absent and 1 = present, with a dash for no data available.

these traits formed a workable Guttman scale. Presumably, the more of these traits a sociocultural system can boast, the more it can be said to have progressed along a scale from "primitive" culture (gemeinschaft) to "civilized" society (gesellschaft). At the bottom of the scale were cultures like the Tasmanians, Bambuti, and Amahuaca, which could not even claim special religious practitioners, trade between communities, formal political leadership, or social segments above family; in the middle range come societies like the Kayan, Lango, Pokot, and Iroquois, which had these traits plus several more but lacked such things as a political leader who appoints officials, taxation in kind, military conscription, and markets; finally arrive the full-fledged civilizations like the Aztecs, Han China, the Roman Empire, Assyria, and New Kingdom Egypt, that lay claim to all of the preceding besides possessing two or more cities, an empire, a city of one hundred thousand or more, sedentary merchants, full-time architects or engineers, full-time painters or sculptors, a code of laws, monumental stone architecture, a calendrical system, and census taking.

Needless to say, details get more complicated. The evolution of sociocultural systems involves a number of semi-independent subsystems, each with their own set of traits. The traits within any subsystem may invariably develop in a fixed order, and those in another system will have their own order, but the scaling of the traits with respect to each other may adopt a wide range of possibilities. Even so, when the scale analysis is performed on the subsets of traits separately, a strong correspondence still emerged among the separate Guttman scales. The ranking according to economics, for example, correlated .79 with the political organization ranking and .81 with the social organization and stratification ranking. Although one may think that these scalings say nothing about transhistorical changes, Carneiro proved otherwise. By looking at when the same culture traits materialized in Anglo-Saxon England, their historical emergence was essentially the same as that inferred from cross-cultural data.

Even if the foregoing investigation, unlike the Cell (1974) charisma scale, provides no direct information about individual behavior, the existence of evolutionary scales, by specifying sociocultural prerequisites behind any activity, imposes some constraints on individual creativity and leadership (Simonton 1988e, chap. 6). There are certain stages in the development of any society in which formal political leaders emerge, artisans are employed by the church or state, monumental stone architecture appears, full-time painters or sculptors become conspicuous, and political empires are established. Potential geniuses born before their time can accomplish no more than the sociocultural substratum allows.

Time-Series Fluctuations

Often the investigator has captured scores on a variable for a single case analyzed over time. The substantive hypothesis for these univariate data may then involve nothing more than determining how the observations change. Do the scores tend to increase or decrease in linear fashion, or do they shift according to a more complex function of time? Answers usually require the execution of some variety of trend analysis where fluctuations in a given variable are shown to depend predictably on the time that each measurement was made on the consecutive units (Floud 1973, chap. 6). In a sense, this approach is no longer univariate, because the dependent variable, the substantive assessment, is correlated with an independent variable, the temporal sequencing, but the latter has the quality of a given, for the time measure ensues out of the methodological design rather than any measurement per se (for example, Martindale 1975). Although trends may be determined in any level of analysis, the most common applications are biographical and transhistorical time series (compare Simonton 1978c).

Instances of biographical trend analysis entail gauging how some personal characteristic or behavior varies over the individual life span. For example, the thematic content of Shakespeare's plays has been shown to change as the Bard matured (Simonton 1986f). Nevertheless, for the optimal estimation of age trends, it is often advisable to employ a cross-sectional time-series analysis that permits the calculation of the typical agewise trajectory of change across a sizable sample of cases. Thus, in one study of twenty-five absolute monarchs, criteria of political effectiveness were examined as a function of the ruler's age (Simonton 1984f). In an inquiry into the integrative complexity revealed in the correspondence of five British novelists, age-trend determinations were made in that cognitive variable (Porter and Suedfeld 1981). In any event, biographical trend analyses are of immense value in advancing our understanding of life-span developmental psychology. An important principle is that human life is far from static; rather, maturation consists in progressive and sometimes regressive change the detection of which mandates an age-trend analysis.

Transhistorical trend analyses are more prevalent in the historiometric literature. Here the secular trend is gauged over larger aggregate time series, most likely cultural traditions or political institutions in nations or civilizations. As in the biographical examples, the goal of transhistorical inquiries is to decipher how some cultural, political, or economic variable changes as a continuous function of chronological time. Trend analyses have examined the temporal shifts in the geographical expansion of empires throughout the world (Taagepera 1978, 1979), the number of discoveries in Europe since the scientific revolution (Price 1963, chap. 1, 1978), the level of primary process content in Italian painting (Martindale 1986b), and the amount of inner-directedness revealed by American movies (Frey, Piernot, and Elhardt 1981). Possibilities are consequently endless. Despite the more grandiose aims, transhistorical trend analyses operate with the same statistical equipment as their biographical counterparts. The only contrast is the obvious one: Transhistorical trends are followed over a far longer time span, owing to the superior longevity of cultures, traditions, or institutions relative to the individual—with the exception of Hitler's "thousand-year Reich."

Trend analyses may take numerous forms, depending on the specific nature of the anticipated historical change. The simplest possibility is a literally straightforward linear trend, whether positive or negative. For instance, a content analysis of eighty-one classic plays indicated a tendency for dramatists to change their favorite topics with age: As a playwright gets older, he becomes more inclined to treat questions of divine government, the value of wealth, and mystical or religious experiences, but less prone to discuss prudence (Simonton 1983a). Other times an exponential trend is expected, which implies that a linear trend will result once the data are subjected to a logarithmic transformation. In more mathematical terms, the value of a variable at t is directly proportional to e^{ct}, where e is Euler's constant ($2.718 \ldots$) and c is a positive or negative constant; taking the logarithm of the variable makes the transformed scores directly proportional to t, with c serving as the slope of the linear fit. Such trends are especially plentiful in transhistorical time series where exponential increases ($c > 0$) are often the norm (Lehman 1947; Price 1963, chap. 1). As noted in the previous chapter, these curves may result from two tendencies, one the exponential growth in population, another the exponential decay in the perception of contemporary relevance (Simonton 1981a; Taagepera and Colby 1979). Less commonly, but conceivable nonetheless, exponential trends may emerge in biographical time series as well, though almost always in the form of a decay curve (that is, with a negative exponent). An example is the swan-song phenomenon in which the last-works effect often declines rapidly with increased distance from the year of death (Simonton 1989c). Related to the exponential trend is the logistic function, which describes growth when an upper bound limits the amount of expansion that can take place. The logistic curve has been fitted to the growth of political empires (Taagepera 1978, 1979), as well as to diverse sociocultural phenomena, including invention and innovation (Mansfield 1961; Marchetti 1980; Price 1963).

Linear, exponential, and logistic trends are all described by formulas that represent general solutions to differential equations, and accordingly a theoretical process can underlie the trend lines. Even though other expected trends may ensue from an underlying model—the age curve for creative productivity graphed in figure 5.4 offering one modest example—most often theory or mathematics is not adequate to the task. In these cases the analysis may reduce to fitting polynomial functions of time, exploiting the well-known principle of mathematics ("Taylor's theorem") that any continuous function, no matter how complex, can be closely approximated by an equation in increasing powers of the independent variable. That is, we can always fit a function of the form

$$x(t) = b_0 + b_1 t + b_2 t^2 + b_3 t^3 + b_4 t^4 + b_5 t^5 + \ldots \tag{6.1}$$

Fortunately, second-order polynomials, with just the first three terms on the right of equation 6.1, will frequently suffice. In words, the dependent variable will be adequately predicted using linear and quadratic time functions. Thus, in an analysis of Shakespeare's plays, certain stylistic traits and thematic preoccupations exhibit either U-shaped or inverted-U curves (Simonton 1986f). Specifically, the proportion of blank verse first decreases and then increases to form a U-shaped function, whereas the frequency that Shakespeare discussed or exemplified conflict in human life is described by an inverted-U curve, the most prominent illustrations appearing in the great tragedies of his midcareer. Seldom must researchers go beyond these quadratic curves, although this elaboration is not unheard of. Martindale (1984a) found that third-order (cubic) polynomial time functions described trends in certain stylistic attributes in English metaphysical poetry, and the transhistorical trend line depicted in figure 5.1 was obtained by fitting a fifth-order polynomial to the melodic originality scores (Simonton 1980d). It still behooves the serious researcher to steer clear of complex polynomials as much as possible mode of analysis for univariate data assessed over time is to execute a regular time-series analysis. Two distinct time-series strategies are available, one concerned with the *frequency domain* and the other with the *time domain* (McCleary and Hay 1980, 17).

Frequency domain. That "History repeats itself" is a common enough conjecture. Putative repetitions may assume many shapes, yet the most provocative may be cycles, as in Byron's ([1812–21] 1898, 170) encapsulation:

> There is the moral of all human tales;
> 'Tis but the same rehearsal of the past,
> First Freedom, and then Glory—when that fails,
> Wealth, vice, corruption,—barbarism at last.
> And History, with all her volumes vast,
> Hath but *one* page.

Somewhat less poetically and succinctly, speculative philosophers of history may favor cyclical theories even more than ideas of progressive movement (Sorokin 1927). As far back as Pan Piao, the Chinese historians could hypothesize a recurrent pattern in the rise and fall of dynasties, a regularity that has certain parallels with the dynastic theory propounded by Ibn Khaldūn. Giambattista Vico, in his 1744 magnum opus *New Science,* advanced a theory of sociocultural development that bears some resemblance to Auguste Comte's three stages—the ages of the gods, of heroes, and men—only Vico cast these in cyclical rather than progressive terms. In the early part of this century Spengler portrayed the rise and fall of civilizations in terms of an organismic metaphor, all cultures advancing through a cycle of birth, maturity, and death, a conception having echoes in Toynbee's (1946) grand theory. Still more recently, in the influential book *The Structure of Scientific Revolutions,* Thomas Kuhn (1970), a historian of science, proposed a theory of scientific change where linear progress is replaced by an interminable sequence of normal science → anomaly → revolution → normal science. Whether wise or not, the human intellect seems incapable of looking at the long unfolding of historical events without spotting repeating patterns. Cyclical theories of history are perhaps the most popular of all historical generalizations.

The popularity of cycles notwithstanding, vigorous demonstrations that periodicities actually exist are more rare. To date, a number of investigators claim to have discerned cycles in music both popular and classical (Martindale 1984b;

Peterson and Berger 1975; Simonton 1980d), painting (Martindale 1986b); fashions both male and female (Lowe and Lowe 1982; Richardson and Kroeber 1940; D. E. Robinson 1975, 1976), scientific discoveries and philosophical beliefs (Klingemann, Mohler, and Weber 1982; Marchetti 1980; Rainoff 1929; Sheldon 1979, 1980); and even entire cultural, political, and economic systems (Gray 1958, 1961, 1966; Kroeber 1944; Sorokin 1937–41). Sometimes the period, or "wave length," of these cycles are of the order of a half decade or so (for example, Rainoff 1929), while other times the supposed cycles will span a century or more (for example, Klingeman, Mohler, and Weber 1982). Books have been written on cycles in history, providing inventories of the diverse periodicities those cycles display (for example, Dewey 1970). What makes these findings so exciting is that cycles are a prominent part of the physical world, whether we are examining the circadian rhythms of biological organisms, the oscillations of a pendulum or tuning fork, or the periodicities of the sunspot cycle or pulsars. Historical cycles put human events in the big league with phenomena of the hard sciences. According to some instinctive epistemology, if a phenomenon replicates, it must be real. More important, perhaps, is the cognitive gain acquired by reducing history to a few simple patterns. If history really does recur in a cyclical pattern, history has become less convoluted.

Nonetheless, it may be wise to maintain skepticism about the presence of regular cycles in historical data. Sociocultural indicators of various kinds will fluctuate, to be sure, yet whether these fluctuations are periodic rather than aperiodic is moot (Sorokin 1927). All too often the data have to be stretched and trimmed to make pretty wave forms come forth. For instance, Gray (1958, 1961, 1966) could confirm his epicyclical model of civilization only by varying the time units in which the creators were tabulated. While it may be possible that the time scale of historical change has altered, it seems unlikely that the natural periodization would be so arbitrary—shrinking and ballooning whimsically—as Gray found necessary to obtain nice rhythms. Sorokin (1937–41), by comparison, tested his own cyclical theory on equally spaced time units, but introduced a misleading data transformation (namely, making the generational series ipsative) that produced the appearance of a bipolar cycle between Sensate and Ideational systems that was just not there (Simonton 1976c).

More critical is the dearth of theoretical processes that would dependably generate rhythmical curves. In those sciences where cyclical phenomena are permanent residents, a simple mechanism can usually be specified that implies a differential equation whose solution yields an equation in trigonometric functions. Thus, the oscillation of a pendulum is described by a second-order differential equation $d^2s/dt^2 = -q^2s$, whose solution is $s = r \sin(qt + k)$, a recurring function. In contrast, theories that might inspire cycles in historiometric time series are far too qualitative to support construction of an appropriate mathematical model. The classic Hegelian notion of thesis-antithesis-synthesis may be typical: This process certainly hints at some cyclical development, yet it is not easy to translate such qualitative ideas into a precise quantitative version. The same intractability attends Sorokin's (1937–41) doctrine of "immanent change," Kroeber's (1944) "pattern exhaustion," and other proposed processes that are presumed to motivate cyclical behavior.

Moreover, were a theory to exist that satisfied the mathematical requirements, it would have to meet two additional demands before periodic phenomena could be anticipated. First, the cyclical process would have to dominate the sociocultural world sufficiently that all other determinants claim an influence so negligible as to be safely dismissed. Just as a pendulum exhibits merely chaotic behavior when tossed about in the wind, so will any cyclical proclivities in creativity or leadership dissipate with the onslaught of extraneous causes. Second, the data must be up to the task. Not only should measurement error be reduced to a minimum, but the time series must be long enough that expected cyclical patterns may undergo numerous realizations. The fluctuations in melodic originality between 1500 and 1950 that are graphed in figure 5.1 may seem almost cyclical, yet such an inference would be most insecure without a series a few millennia long, a prohibitive prerequisite. The more intrusive the error, or the longer the cycles, or both, the more severe the sample size requirements. Additionally, as the anticipated cycles get more intricate, the need for long and reliable time series becomes urgent. In Gray's theory (1958, 1961, 1966), waves are piled upon waves, producing both fundamentals and higher harmonics. Under the assumption that no natural or human disaster terminates the experiment, civilization would have to endure for several more millennia before the supply of data points were adequate.

If any real rhythms intrude on the historical record, most likely they result from more basic phenomena that are understandably and predictably cyclic. Perhaps the regular coming and going of the sunspots, through its impact on the climate, obliges some periodicities in the economic prosperity and hence to leadership and creativity. But if so, the optimal line of attack would be to take measurements on the supposed exogenous source of regularity and then show that this correlates with measurements on the endogenous variable. For instance, Rainoff (1929) suggested that the cycles he observed in scientific contributions resulted from underlying economic changes. To test this post hoc explanation, we must demonstrate that (1) the pertinent economic variables are indeed periodic (and, ideally, get an economist to provide a theoretical dynamic) and (2) the cyclical economic factor accounts for any temporal regularities discerned in the appearance of discoveries and inventions. Thus far, evidence does endorse the idea that the economy may influence scientific output, but this finding is not enough to support Rainoff's conjecture (Schmookler 1966).

Owing to such possibilities, the curious should not be dissuaded from rummaging for cycles, all worries and reservations aside. Yet these endeavors should at least exploit more sophisticated statistical techniques than has hitherto been the norm. Whether or not history repeats itself, historiometry definitely does. Cycles are most commonly isolated through simple inspection, an approach less than satisfactory from a scientific perspective. Yet ever since Fourier first introduced the analytical apparatus for which he provides the eponym, something better is available (Mayer and Arnez 1974). Even if the techniques are complex, computer programs that will perform these "spectral" or "harmonic" analyses abound, so that the labors are considerably eased. There have even been a few researchers who have drawn upon these statistics, perhaps even with some success (for example, Klingemann, Mohler, and Weber 1982; Lowe and Lowe 1982; Martindale 1984b). But both measurement and theory may have to experience advances before the search for periodicities in history can command unqualified respect.

Time domain. Whenever observations are made on equally spaced units, it is easy to set up mathematical models that predict repeating patterns in historical time. By hypothesizing that a variable's value at any one time is a function of the variable's value at one or more previous times, we can create a *difference equation,* the discrete analogue of the differential equation applicable to continuous variables. For example, if the variable at time t is a linear function (positive or negative) of the same variable at time $t - 1$, or the immediately preceding unit, we obtain a first difference equation; and if the variable at t is a function of the variable at both $t - 1$ and $t - 2$, we get a second-order difference equation. The general difference equation in a single variable is given by

$$y_t = c_0 + c_1 y_{t-1} + c_2 y_{t-2} + c_3 y_{t-3} + c_4 y_{t-4} + c_5 y_{t-5} + \ldots \quad (6.2)$$

where the parameters are either given by theory or estimated from the data. Depending on the coefficients' actual values, a wide range of temporal trends may be realized, including cycles with or without exponential expansion or dampening. Excellent illustrations of this analysis may be found in most texts on economic dynamics (for example, Baumol 1970).

Even if difference equations provide a vehicle for imbuing cyclical movement with substantive justification, this mode of analysis has demonstrated minimal utility in historiometric work. The closest application is a theory of "hierarchical cybernets" that shows how scientific activity might oscillate in complex but recurrent patterns (Sheldon 1979, 1980). The gist of this rather intricate model is that scientists of one generation leave an impression on those of their own and succeeding generations, an impact that may be either positive or negative, according to professional status and career stage. Although the predicted temporal signature roughly corresponds with generational fluctuations in normal and revolutionary science from A.D. 1000 to 1870, the underlying model necessitated arbitrary assumptions in order to obtain stable but persistent regularities. This is a typical drawback of difference equation models, which often obtain plausible predictions only by making implausible assumptions. The usual postulate is that the coefficients of the linear function are neither more nor less than *exactly* equal unity! With parameters less than one, the time-series fluctuations will normally dampen to a constant, whereas with parameters greater than one, the movement will become ever more crazy, soon reaching astronomical limits.

Another analytical approach shares some features with difference equations, yielding quasi-cyclic univariate time series, and yet avoids having to insert unrealistic suppositions to force everything to come out right. The technique is that of time-series analysis in the time domain, a method largely associated with the magnum opus of Box and Jenkins (1976). While originally designed for problems concerning physical systems, the methodology has been recently championed by behavioral scientists (for example, McCleary and Hay 1980). This perspective succeeds where difference equations fail by introducing a stochastic component into the models. Having added a random shock or disturbance term, the parameters of the dynamic equation can adopt numerous permissible values without worrying about the time series becoming unruly. At the same time, the stochastic models produce fluctuations that move up and down in a fashion that bears some resemblance to cycles, except that this "cyclical" behavior is aperiodic and therefore unpredictable, owing to the dirty business done by the influx of chance (see, for example, Martindale 1984b). In light of what was said earlier about the likelihood of true cycles emerging from historical data, this orientation seems prima facie more workable. Consequently, time-series analysis in the time domain probably has far more usefulness than time-series analysis in the frequency domain. Ups and downs in historical trends are more prone to be stochastic than deterministic.

The details of the Box-Jenkins method are rather complicated, but fortunately more accessible discussions have been published to meet the more practical needs of the empirical investigator (McCleary and Hay 1980). However, because these time-series techniques were initially devised for rather distinct substantive problems, some adjustments must often be made when transporting the techniques to historiometric data (Simonton 1988c). The Box-Jenkins approach is committed to post hoc, utterly empirical data fitting with an eye toward forecasting, whereas an investigator may be more motivated by the need to test a proposition based on a theoretical explanation. One manifestation of this discrepancy between blind empiricism and insightful theory concerns the handling of secular trends in the data, or what is termed *nonstationarity* in the time series. In the received tradition, the best procedure is to *difference* the data; for each observation we subtract the previous observation (that is, $y_t^* = y_t - y_{t-1}$, where y_t^* is the transformed score). For nonlinear trends, second and higher-order differencing must be implemented to get the data stationary (the first differencing removes a linear trend, the second differencing a quadratic trend, and so forth, exactly analogous to what happens when we take first, second, and higher-order derivatives of continuous functions).

Although Box and Jenkins disfavor obtaining stationary series through the deletion of deterministic trends, as represented by polynomial functions like equation 6.2, there may be a sound theoretical justification for presuming a nonstochastic source of the observed trend. Thus, if transhistorical data often follow an exponential trend on account of such factors as population growth, the proper route to stationarity is to expose the data to a logarithmic transformation and then subtract the linear trend that survives (for example, by fitting a linear time function and employing the residuals). This solution has the advantage that it does not distort the stochastic process to be estimated. For example, white noise with a linear trend added becomes, after first differencing, a stationary but moving-average process (Judd and Kenny 1981, 146–47). Furthermore, only by actually fitting a trend line do we obtain an estimate of the trend's magnitude and form, whereas the differencing strategy merely obliterates the trend without enlightening us as to its course.

The concrete operation of this revised strategy is illustrated by a study of creativity and leadership in Chinese civilization (Simonton 1988c). The expressed aim of this analysis was to verify a hypothesis that Kroeber (1944) advanced against Galton's theory of genius (1869). Galton had argued that geniuses were born, not made, whereas Kroeber maintained that only by building on the achievements of their immediate predecessors can individuals themselves achieve. Kroeber quoted the obscure Roman historian, Velleius Paterculus, who had offered the generalization that "genius is fostered by emulation, and it is now envy, now admiration, which enkindles imitation, and, in the nature of things, that which is cultivated with the highest zeal advances to the highest perfection" (Kroeber 1944, 18). This sociopsychological process might be styled the on-the-shoulders-of-giants effect, after Newton's demonstration of modesty that "if I have seen further, it is by standing on the shoulders of giants."

Kroeber's interpretation may be cast in the more formal language of generational time-series analysis. We begin by subdividing the history of a civilization into consecutive twenty-year periods, or generations, which we may number 1, 2, 3, . . . N. After collecting a sufficient sample of historical figures, we tabulate in any given generation g the number of individuals who attained forty (or would have done so) in that interval. To enhance the validity of these counts, we may wish to weight each personality according to eminence or influence. We then check against these univariate data the following stochastic model:

$$y_g = \phi_1 y_{g-1} + \phi_2 y_{g-2} + a_g \qquad (6.3)$$

Here y_g, y_{g-1}, and y_{g-2} are the scores at three consecutive generations, and a_g is a random disturbance, or shock. The two parameters ϕ_1 and ϕ_2 are estimated from the data and record the impact of the two previous generations on the indexed generation. Because individuals in generation g average twenty years old in generation $g - 1$ (and thus are in their developmental period), they are susceptible to predecessors who themselves average either forty (those at generation $g - 1$ who are in their productive period) or sixty (those at generation $g - 2$ who are in their consolidative period). If emulation has a beneficial effect, as Kroeber held, then both ϕ_1 and ϕ_2 should be nonzero and positive, although less than unity to avoid instability. On the other hand, it would make no sense to include a third parameter for generation $g - 3$ and beyond, for those persons would most likely be deceased and thus cannot serve as live models for emulation. Of course, it may very well be that those figures in generation $g - 2$, though alive, are too far past their prime to inspire a big following in generation g, in which case ϕ_2 would be zero. Yet if the data obliged omission of this second parameter, Kroeber's explanation would not be compromised.

The stochastic model defined by equation 6.3 is a second-order autoregressive process. It is autoregressive because the value of a variable in one time unit is a direct linear function of its previous values. It is second order because the previous pair of observations determine the current observation at any time. The addition of a_g is what renders this model stochastic in lieu of a deterministic, second-order difference equation. To test the model, 10,160 creators, leaders, and celebrities were drawn from fifty-six histories of Chinese civilization and tabulated into 141 generations from 840 B.C. to A.D. 1979 (Simonton 1988c). Owing to the intrusion of exponential trends in the form of $y_g = ke^{bg}$, a logarithmic transformation converts the trend into a linear function, $\log y_g = k + bg$. Once b, the slope of the line, is estimated by least-squares regression, we can use the residuals, which are now stationary or "detrended," to estimate the two autoregressive parameters in equation 6.3. Some of the findings for the seventeen areas of creative activity are given in table 6.3.

The autoregressive parameters were roughly the same for both unweighted and weighted time series across most of the seventeen categories of creative achievement. The prevailing stochastic model is that of first-order autoregression, although occasionally second-order autoregression emerges, as in the activities of invention and architecture. In the main, this prevalence suggests that individuals of about forty years old make more effective role models for emulation than do individuals around sixty, a differential consistent with the empirical results on the connection between age and creative achievement. Creative contributions tend to peak around the fortieth year, and creative individuals at their productive prime may make the best role models.

Significantly, in leadership endeavors a rather contrary result appears, a second-order autoregressive model holding, with the second parameter proving the most potent. In the Chinese data, for example, the weighted time series of rulers has $\phi_1 = .00$ and $\phi_2 = .30$, showing that it is the older leaders who provide superior objects of respect. A parallel finding, operating at the individual level,

Table 6.3   *Trends and Autoregressive Coefficients for Chinese Creators at Generation* g

Category	Unweighted			Weighted		
	Trend	g − 1	g − 2	Trend	g − 1	g − 2
Inventors	.43	.24	.25	.31	.26	.23
Mathematicians	.50	.51	—	.40	.34	—
Physical scientists	.28	.38	—	.21	.38	—
Biological scientists	.65	.29	—	.49	.23	—
Other scientists	.63	.28	.27	.56	—	—
Native religionists	.22	.31	—	*.13*	.26	.22
Alien religionists	.60	.75	—	.51	.69	—
Philosophers	.37	.50	—	*.08*	.30	—
Nonfiction authors	.87	.44	—	.62	.31	—
Fiction authors	.61	.37	—	.56	.31	—
Poets	.58	.37	*.20*	.36	.26	.30
Calligraphers	.29	.16	—	.25	.22	—
Painters	.86	.22	—	.79	.31	.11
Sculptors	*.03*	.77	—	*−.16*	.44	.44
Architects	.24	*.08*	.30	.24	.22	.22
Artisans	.32	.80	—	.27	.80	—
Musicians	*.16*	—	—	.07	.17	—

Note. Simonton (1988c, table 3). Copyright 1988 by American Psychological Association. Used by permission.
Nonsignificant coefficients are in italics (when estimated).

has been found in the leadership ratings of 342 European monarchs (Simonton 1983d). The leadership manifested by a hereditary monarch was more dependent on the leadership shown by the grandparental predecessor than that displayed by the parental predecessor. This skipping over the middle generation is compatible with research indicating that leadership often peaks at later ages than creativity (Simonton 1988b). And in Ortega's ([1933] 1962) scheme, the stage of initiation (creativity) occurs between 30 and 45 years, whereas the stage of dominance (leadership) occurs between 45 and 60 years.

As already noted, one special repercussion of autoregression is that it generally introduces quasi-cyclical patterns into time series. In the present case, if the supply of historical creators at generation *g* is a positive function of the number of generation *g* − 1 (and sometimes even generation *g* − 2), creative notables will have a tendency to cluster together in contiguous historical periods. Without this stochastic continuity, creators would be randomly distributed across time, forming a white-noise generational time series (once the exponential trend is extracted). This contiguity of creators is precisely the historical generalization that Kroeber (1944) thought invalidated Galton's (1869) heroic ideas about genius. Isolated geniuses, who supposedly emerge in the absence of cultural substrata, are relatively rare. In line with Kroeber's belief that these golden ages do not succumb to silver and dark ages in a rigidly cyclical pattern, the insertion of the random shock term guarantees that the apparent cycles will be unpredictable rather than periodic.

The foregoing illustrates only one class of time-series model, first- and second-order autoregression with positive parameters. Although this situation is probably the most universal in historiometric research, it is not the only possibility by any means. We need not say anything about moving-average models, for these have yet to show up in the data examined by the historiometrician, however common these models may be in other domains (compare Box and Jenkins 1976). From time to time, however, the investigator will chance upon first-order auto-regressive process with a negative parameter, a contingency revealed by a negative *autocorrelation*. For example, the level of dogmatism in an American chief executive correlates $-.32$ with the level seen in his immediate successor in the White House, a negative autocorrelation that ensues from two sources (Simonton 1987d, 156). First, presidents and their running mates are inclined to be complementary rather than similar on dogmatism ($r = -.27$), spelling a flip-flop should the death of the incumbent compel vice-presidential succession. Second, and more importantly, after dealing with a president who is highly idealistic but inflexible, the American people tend to react by electing a replacement who is pragmatic and flexible; and conversely, Machiavellian wheeler-and-dealer types are supplanted with more principled statesmen ($r = -.38$). Other instances of negative auto-regression have been observed for generational time series as divergent as battle casualties (Simonton 1976e) and primary process material in music (Martindale and Uemura 1983).

What makes negative autoregression fascinating is that it produces fluctuations that are more clearly cyclic. Under a first-order autoregressive model with $\phi_1 < 0$, a high score in one unit will be followed by a low score in the next, and vice versa, the clarity of the oscillations depending on the magnitude of the negative parameter. In the instance of battle casualties, if one generation suffered a devastating period of political bloodshed, its children grow up to appreciate the advantages of peace. Yet that very act of recuperation, coupled as it is with population growth and the decay of the national memory, nurtures a new generation more favorably disposed toward using military power to attain political and economic ends. The result is a negative autocorrelation of $-.30$ (Simonton 1976e). Thus was the war of the Austrian Succession and the Seven Years' War, in which a youthful Frederick the Great nearly bled Prussia white in the name of real estate acquisitions, was followed a generation later by the War of the Bavarian Succession, in which an older king managed to avoid even a single bloody encounter.

Measures of Association

In the techniques reviewed thus far, the focus was on describing the properties of a single variable. Even trend analysis, which expresses a single variable's movement as a function of historical or biographical time, can be framed as a univariate matter. A temporal trend may be granted substantive meaning by stating the time function as a solution to a differential equation specifying how the variable changes each instant. This legerdemain reduces time to a Newtonian infinitesimal that has no genuine existence. For example, the exponential trend so frequently encountered in historiometric data is defined by a time function that is the solution to the simple differential equation $dy/dt = by$ (that is, the rate of change in the variable in any instant is directly proportional to the magnitude of that variable, where the "instant" dt approaches zero in the limit). Historiometry's future would be confined were it to be imprisoned by univariate approaches like these. The majority of historical generalizations about human behavior speculate that a nexus exists between two variables. Typical is the frequently claimed cohabitation of intellectual brilliance and emotional pathology in a single mind (Prentky 1980). "There is no great genius without some touch of madness," said Seneca, which Drydn seconded centuries later with "great wits are sure to madness near allied,/ And thin partitions do their bounds divide." Because a science unequipped to test nomothetic hypotheses like these would be a pathetic enterprise indeed, the present section discusses statistics that gauge associations between two variables and among several variables.

Correlation Coefficients

Quetelet introduced univariate statistics to historical data, in the guise of the normal curve, but it was Galton who really advanced the concept of bivariate analysis (Stigler 1986, chap. 9). We owe to Galton the key ideas of correlation and regression. Galton may have had an IQ close to two hundred, as Terman (1917) estimated, yet unfortunately he lacked the mathematical sophistication to go beyond rather intuitive and concrete treatments. It took Karl Pearson to develop Galton's rudimentary hunches into a full-fledged technique that tied a measure of statistical association to the bivariate normal distribution. The result was the Pearson product-moment correlation coefficient, of all measures of statistical relations the clear favorite. However, because Pearson's derivation of the coefficient somewhat restricted its applicability, the step taken by G. Udny Yule is valuable. As someone who had studied physics under Hertz and before learning statistics under Pearson, Yule was in an ideal position to link the product-moment coefficient with the principle of least squares, a technique that had already proved its mettle in the physical and mathematical sciences beginning with the work of Legendre, Gauss, and Laplace. This connection between correlation and least squares is important because it establishes that correlational statistics need not be confined to the relatively rare circumstance where two variables just so happen to form a bivariate normal distribution.

The *Pearson product-moment correlation* between two variables, as noted before, can assume values between -1 for a perfect negative relation, through 0 for the utter absence of any association (orthogonal or independent), to $+1$ for a perfect positive correlation. Usually this coefficient is symbolized by r. Unfortunately, proliferating throughout the literature are other names and symbols for coefficients that may or may not be equivalent to Pearson's statistic (Cohen and Cohen 1983, chap. 2). Three measures of association, in particular, represent nothing more than r traveling incognito, namely the phi (ϕ) coefficient between two dichotomous variables, Spearman's rho (ρ) between two ordinal variables, and the point biserial (r_{pb}) between a dichotomous category and a continuous (interval) variable. These alternative versions of r made excellent sense in the days when all correlations had to be calculated by hand. The computation of phi, rho, and the point-biserial is simpler than computing r on the same data, but the numbers that result are identical.

On the other hand, some coefficients may masquerade as the product-moment correlation, when these are actually fraudulent. In lieu of the phi coefficient one may calculate the tetrachoric, just as the point-biserial may be replaced by the biserial. Neither replacement is a legitimate Pearsonian coefficient. Rather each of these statistics is more properly considered an estimate of what the product-moment correlation would have been had the circumstances been different. If the two variables were intervally scaled and normally distributed in the Kantian "thing-in-itself" (*Ding an sich*), then the tetrachoric gives what would have been obtained had the researcher gone beyond the mere appearances of the two dichotomous measures. This extrapolation from phenomena to noumena is suspect, given that major assumptions have to be made to justify application of these statistics (and distributional normality is not among Kant's essential categories of thought). These surrogate statistics have the specious asset that they typically yield correlation coefficients noticeably larger than what comes out of a Pearsonian r. As a consequence, sometimes quite implausible correlations may emerge, correlations that can incredibly confound multivariate analyses such as will be discussed later.

More intellectually honest are those measures of association that fall into the catchall designation of "nonparametrics." Among the many possibilities are Kendall's tau (τ) for ranked data and diverse contingency coefficients for categorized data. Despite the fact that these coefficients make fewer assumptions when testing for the statistical significance of a bivariate association, the Pearsonian r is so robust under major departures from distributional assumptions that the potential value of nonparametrics is lessened considerably (Havlicek and Peterson 1976). Moreover, as with the tetrachoric and biserial measures, nonparametric coefficients cannot enter multivariate analyses without some danger. It should be understandable, then, that these distribution-free indices of association are rarely seen in the empirical literature.

Besides, the Pearsonian coefficient has a substantive interpretability unmatched by any rival statistic. For one thing, the square of r gives the proportion of variance that is shared between the two variables, an evaluative figure ranging from 0 to 1. Thus, when an inquiry into 326 land battles discovered that a general's advantage in battle experience correlates .39 with the winning-streak advantage that he carries against his opponent, we can infer that 15 percent of the variation in the two measures is common (Simonton 1980a). Furthermore, the product-moment correlation is a regression coefficient (hence the abbreviation r) for a bivariate equation in which both dependent and independent variables are given as z scores (with means of 0 and standard deviations of 1). Hence, when we learn that the aesthetic significance of a classical composition correlates .21 with how near the composer has come to the year of death, z scores on the first variable may be directly predicted from z scores on the second by the linear equation $\hat{z}_1 = r_{12}z_2$ (Simonton 1989d). For every unit increase (or decrease) in z_2, $\hat{z}_1$ will increase (or decrease) .21 standard units (that is, over one-fifth of a standard deviation). A negative r has the same implications, only with the bivariate relation in inverse form. Accordingly, given that the assessed charisma of an American chief executive correlates $-.39$ with how old a president's father was when he died (Simonton 1988d) we can surmise that for each unit decrease (or increase) in the age at which the father dies, the perceived charisma of the president will increase (or decrease) by .39 standard units (that is, nearly two-fifths of a standard deviation).

These prediction equations, moreover, are the best possible by the classic criterion of least squares. No other coefficient will reduce the squared errors of prediction more than r. Another way of saying the same thing is that using r as the slope for the line that summarizes the scatterplot minimizes the variance of the residuals, where the latter are obtained by subtracting predicted from observed values on the dependent variable. Given these and other virtues, the Pearson product-moment correlation has become the most sturdy foundation of quantitative analysis. But if this coefficient is central, the researcher must watch out for conditions that affect the correlation's magnitude. We would like to feel that the sole determinant of r's size is the intimacy of the association between two variables. Nonetheless, certain additional factors may intervene so as to produce correlation coefficients somewhat contrary to expectation. There are five common contaminating influences, namely, measurement errors, univariate distributions, curvilinear relations, variance truncation, and extreme scores (compare Cohen and Cohen 1983, chap. 2).

Measurement error.   If one or both variables have reliabilities less than perfect, the correlation between them will be attenuated. That is, the influx of random error into the measurements causes the correlation to be closer to zero than would have been the case were perfectly reliable measures available. Should precise reliability coefficients be obtained, it is possible to estimate what the true correlation would have been under error-free measurement. The observed correlation must be divided only by the square roots of the two reliabilities. In mathematical terms,

$$\hat{r}_{12} = r_{12}/r_{11}^{1/2}r_{22}^{1/2} \tag{6.4}$$

where r_{12} is the original correlation coefficient between the two variables, r_{11} and

r_{22} are their respective reliabilities, and $\hat{r}_{12}$ is the new correlation now "corrected for attenuation." To illustrate, thirty-nine U.S. presidents have been rated on the personality trait of forcefulness (Simonton 1986h) and the leadership style of charisma (Simonton 1988d), with alpha reliabilities of .89 and .90, respectively. Their empirical correlation of .66 can therefore be upgraded to the more substantial correlation of .74, the probable degree of association between the two scores in the absence of error.

Equation 6.3 must be used with considerable caution, however. If the researcher has access to only inferior reliability estimates, the application of this formula can lead to extremely misleading results. Especially problematic is the case where one or both reliability coefficients that go into the denominator are underestimated, a situation that will overestimate $\hat{r}_{12}$—occasionally to the point of surpassing the upper bound of 1.0. When correlations are thus corrected for attenuation, they may no longer be consistent with other correlations not so transformed. The consequence can be a correlation matrix among several variables that is ill-suited for complex multivariate analyses. These warnings notwithstanding, equation 6.4 can provide an instructive gauge of how much inadequate reliability vitiates the association between two variables.

Divergent univariate distributions.   When we say that the correlation coefficient may range from -1 to $+1$, we should really add the qualification *if* the two variables have the same univariate distributions. If both are normally distributed, or both are rank-ordered measures with rectilinear distributions, or both are dichotomous scales with equal splits, then the maximum absolute value will be unity. Otherwise the largest possible correlation will fall short of that upper bound. For instance, a point biserial correlation between a dichotomous and an interval variable usually does not get much larger than around .80. Likewise, the range of r is diminished when one interval variable is highly skewed or when both are skewed in contrary directions. And a phi coefficient can only arrive at unity if the two variables are split the same amount in the same direction (for example, percentages of 30/70 and 30/70 but not 30/70 and 70/30). Nor should we be amazed that the product-moment coefficient is sensitive to the univariate distributions of the two measures being correlated. By logic alone we should demand as much. Two variables can correspond perfectly with one another only if their distributions are identical anyway. Thus, if creative productivity is a highly skewed lognormal distribution, we should not expect it to correlate 1.0 with a supposed cause, say IQ, that has a symmetric normal distribution. Some other factor besides intelligence must operate to stretch out the tail.

As this last example suggests, historiometricians face this difficulty often, given how frequently they are fascinated with distinctive phenomena with skewed frequency distributions. If we are seeking single causes of rare effects, those causes may be as rare as the effects. Fortunately, most dependent variables have multiple determinants so that we do not have to search forever for the one variable with an equivalent univariate distribution that is equally congruent score-to-score. Furthermore, because we seldom expect two variables to exhibit a one-to-one correspondence in scores, the intrusion of divergent distributions may not affect the correlation much, if at all. Even so, it is a consideration that should be in the back of every investigator's mind, especially when the correlations enter into more advanced statistical analyses. In factor analysis, which shall be discussed shortly, the occurrence of discrepant distributions cause the emergence of factors that merely represent variables with congruent univariate distributions (for example, difficulty factors in tests of mental abilities).

Curvilinear relations. Because the coefficient r is the slope of a line fitted to the points of a bivariate scatterplot, the Pearsonian correlation assesses only the prominence of a *linear* relation in a pair of measures. Yet historical generalizations are often clothed in a curvilinear form, as in this conjecture regarding the sociocultural factors most conducive to intellectual and artistic creativity: "At least moderate economic prosperity seems essential, though vast wealth does not. Allegiance to a certain set of religious or philosophical doctrines is sometimes an aid, but an excess seems clearly to stifle" (Norling 1970, 278). We have already witnessed numerous instances of variables connected by some curvilinear function, especially U and inverted-U forms. Whenever the bivariate correlation is described by a curvilinear function, and especially whenever that function is nonmonotonic, the correlation coefficient may seriously underestimate how intimately related two variables in fact are, were the restrictions to linear fit relinquished. In figure 5.5, for example, we saw that the ranked eminence of Cox's 301 geniuses was a U-function of life span, the most famous creators and leaders dying at ages either older or younger than average (Simonton 1976a). Still, the linear correlation between eminence and life span is $-.03$. Even if the minus sign picks up the fact that young martyrs have a special advantage in leadership activities, the conclusion remains that this coefficient is practically zero. In chapter 8 we will treat some of the means by which we can determine more directly the existence of these nonlinear associations. In the absence of such direct tests, we must avoid proclamations that two variables are unrelated merely because the correlation between them is zero.

Variance truncation. As mentioned in our treatment of reliability and validity coefficients, it may happen that the real correlation between two measures may be vitiated by a restriction of the variation in one or both. The same problem arises when calculating r between substantively distinct variables, should their variances be artificially truncated. For example, the correlation of .25 that Cox found between ranked eminence and IQ for her creators and leaders certainly must be an underestimate. Almost by definition, none of her geniuses was an absolute nonentity, nor were any estimated to have subnormal intellects. Surely the correlation would have been far higher were we to throw in a proper amount of totally obscure morons and imbeciles. Happily, if the investigator possesses estimates of the true variance of a variable under more inclusive conditions, a formula exists for estimating what the actual correlation should be, in much the same style as the correction for attenuation (Cohen and Cohen 1983, 70). This adjustment for variance truncation has yet to be encountered in historiometry, probably because the true variance is rarely known, but a correction may be ventured for the Cox correlation just cited. Assuming that the standard deviation of IQ in the general population is at least double that in her exclusive group, the correlation between IQ and eminence almost doubles, to .48. And because this figure still fails to consider the truncated scores on eminence, we have here another underestimate.

Extreme scores.   Given that the product-moment correlation is a function of the product of first moments about the mean for each variable, scores that depart significantly from the average carry far more weight in determining the final r than do scores that lie near or on the means of the variables. In other words, having derived r from the principle of least squares, analytical units with exceptional values on the two variables will influence the estimated slope much more than those units near the center of the bivariate scatterplot. Now this property at times invites criticism from those who view it as rather undemocratic (for example, Berk, Hennessy and McCleary 1976). This complaint, while perhaps justified when scrutinizing, say, the effectiveness of various teaching methods in elementary school, loses force when applied to historiometric questions. Historiometry, after all, is very much dedicated to the examination of those individuals who most stand out from the crowd. We therefore should desire statistics that stress the extraordinary over the run-of-the-mill. For instance, if the aim is to discover why some thinkers in Western intellectual history have so monopolized philosophical discourse, it seems not unreasonable to focus on why Aristotle surpassed Xenocrates or Descartes outbid de Roy than to split hairs by asking why (or whether) William James was more influential than John Dewey. This substantive emphasis is only endorsed by the elitist distortions of covariance-based statistics.

Admittedly, difficulties may still arise if certain historical figures receive variable scores so extreme—in the sense of being well outside the probability distribution—that the cases count as statistical *outliers*. An illustration of such a phenomenon may be seen in table 3.9, where Nixon's z score on the pettiness factor is over four standard units above the mean. What can be done with freaks of this magnitude? One common solution is unacceptable, namely the omission of all outliers. Such data trimming sometimes may be reasonable when all cases are equal in import, but in historiometry the outliers are likely to be the most consequential personages under scrutiny. What credence would we give a study of philosophical distinction that reported correlations that left out Aristotle, Lucretius, Aquinas, Descartes, and Kant because these thinkers were excessively exceptional on one or more variables? A happier solution is to transform the scores so that the offending cases are rendered less salient.

For instance, in table 4.4 we saw that Shakespeare's *Hamlet* stands head and shoulders above its closest rivals on the boards. Therefore, in many correlations between dramatic popularity and some other variable, *Hamlet*'s score will impose constraints on any line of least-squares fit, thereby distorting the coefficient that emerges. Still, it would be inexcusable to delete this play as an outlier, for to do so would invalidate the whole inquiry. Any theory of aesthetic success that works only by overlooking Shakespeare's most popular play is in deep trouble. A more workable solution is to subject the popularity assessments to a logarithmic transformation, which would bring the Danish prince down to earth. Thus, in a search for the correlates of the differential dramatic merit of the entries in the Shakespearean canon, the correlations were calculated for both raw and log-transformed popularity (Simonton 1986f). Because the same general results materialized in either case, *Hamlet* was shown not to have an intrusive impact on the substantive conclusions, outlier or not.

Multivariate Relations

Even if a weighty number of historical generalizations may be tested using mere correlation coefficients, all too often the investigator must enlist more advanced techniques by which whole batches of variables can be funneled through an integrated *multivariate* analysis. The necessity of considering bivariate relations is not bypassed when employing these methods, but only extended. For the most part, multivariate statistics provide a vehicle for extracting the underlying pattern in that rich constellation of information known as the *correlation matrix*. Because this inherent structure may adopt several distinct forms, multivariate methods are multiple rather than unitary. In the present chapter we concentrate on only one sister set of statistics, leaving for chapter 7 a discussion of other multivariate techniques that have enhanced the psychologist's scientific exploitation of historical data. We begin by discussing factor analysis, and then turn briefly to cluster analysis.

Factor analysis. We previously examined the role that factor analysis can play in fixing the reliability of multiple-item measures. It is not uncommon, however, for the investigator's purpose to be more substantive than methodological. A respectable number of measures are in the investigator's hands, and factor analysis is asked to consolidate the unwieldy collection into a smaller number of composite dimensions. If there are k variables, the quest is for m factors, where $m \ll k$. If $m = 1$, naturally, the analysis has succeeded only in showing that all measurements tap the same underlying concept, a less than enlightening outcome in the present context. A more instructive result, therefore, occurs when $m \geq 2$, implying that two or more latent variables are behind the observed bivariate associations in the correlation matrix. Assuming that at least two factors have been isolated, the next item of business is to interpret the factors, to decide which latent variables are actually being assessed. Factor interpretation is guided by the factor loadings, the correlations between each variable and a given factor. The common rule of thumb is that a variable contributes to the substantive interpretation of a factor only when its loading is *salient,* which is usually taken to mean a correlation at least .30 or .40 in absolute value. Under ideal conditions, all the variables that have salient loadings on the same factor should meaningfully cohere in a clear substantive interpretation.

An example from work on presidential leadership will demonstrate how this works in practice. The thirty-nine American chief executives, it will be remembered, have been reliably assessed on 110 of 300 descriptors from the Gough ACL (Simonton 1986g). A factor analysis generated fourteen orthogonal personality dimensions. One factor had eight adjectives with loadings of .40 or better, six of them positive and two negative. With the item-factor correlations given parenthetically, these are sly (.96), deceitful (.87), unscrupulous (.86), evasive (.85), shrewd (.72), and greedy (.48), all with positive loadings, and sincere (−.63) and honest (−.63), with negative loadings. For anyone familiar with Machiavelli's *Prince,* or who has come across the empirical literature on the "Mach scale" in personality and social psychology (Christie and Geis 1970), this particular configuration of descriptors might suggest Machiavellianism, and the dimension was so named. Needless to say, there is nothing sacred about this assignment. Other terms might serve just as well so long as they incorporate all the variables making up the factor. For example, this dimension might be called the "wheeler-dealer factor," the "Richard III syndrome," the "legalism orientation," after a school of political philosophy once the rage in ancient China, or the "Kautilya complex," after the Sanskrit author of the *Artha Sastra.*

Factor analysis has been applied to an honorable array of substantive questions. Wendt and Muncy (1979) used this technique to examine a set of biographical assessments on twenty-four American vice-presidents, obtaining thereby the dimensions of "activity-charisma," "likeability, nonthreat," and "shrewd persistence, complexity." Hoffer (1978) examined the personality characteristics of loyalists and revolutionaries during the American Revolution, using factor analysis to derive three dimensions—conservatism of temperament, cognitive rigidity, and the need for interpersonal order—that anticipated which side was taken by each figure in the political conflict. Knapp (1962) performed a secondary data analysis of the forty-eight assessments that Thorndike (1950) made on ninety-one historical individuals, arriving at the four personality factors of sanguineness, industriousness, aggressiveness, and intellectual sensitivity.

These applications are all to cross-sectional data, a practice known as R-type factor analysis as opposed to P-type factor analysis (R. B. Cattell 1953; Cattell and Adelson 1951; Simonton 1975c, 1975d, 1976c). In the last a single case, usually a nation or civilization, is evaluated on numerous variables in consecutive time-series units. The factor analysis then reveals how variation in certain variables tends to fluctuate together over time. For instance, when the discoveries and inventions tabulated by Sorokin (1937–41) are factor analyzed, three main dimensions appear, the abstract sciences (astronomy and mathematics), the applied sciences (technology, geography, and geology), and the concrete sciences (chemistry, physics, and biology), with medicine more or less on its own (Simonton 1975d). In other words, advances in chemistry, physics, and biology tend to ebb and flow together, whereas activity in these disciplines fluctuates largely without reference to concurrent movements in astronomy, mathematics, technology, geography, geology, or medicine.

We have glossed over a vast batch of details about how to perform a competent factor analysis on a set of data. The novice certainly must master the specifics of the technique before rushing into print with factor-analytic findings (see Gorsuch 1983). The psychometric literature is replete with abuses of this methodology, and there is no reason why historiometry should provide its own bad examples if it can help it. The most critical problem with factor analysis, however, is not how it is done but rather what it is done on. To offer meaningful results, the technique should not be imposed on a mishmash of miscellaneous variables, which encourages the emergence of complicated factors that defy interpretation.

Cluster analysis. Another brand of factor analysis exists besides R- and P-type, namely the Q technique, which is essentially an inversion of the R technique (Brown 1986). Where the latter sees how variables group together across individual cases, Q-type factor analysis scrutinizes how cases cluster together across variables. In other words, in R-type cross-sectional variation provides clues regarding which variables cluster together into factors, whereas in Q-type contrasts in variable profiles offer suggestions concerning which cases belong to the same class. Although Q technique per se has never seen application in historiometrics, a related method known as *cluster analysis* has displayed some utility. This starts with the scores that various cases received on a set of variables and groups those cases together that have the most similar profiles on the discriminating variables (Aldenderfer and Blashfield 1984). Development of computerized classification algorithms was greatly spurred by publication of *Principles of Numerical Taxonomy* by two biologists, Robert Sokal and Peter Sneath (1963), founders of the pheneticist school of systematics.

To continue the previous factor-analytical illustration, if we have thirty-nine U.S. presidents scored on fourteen personality dimensions, we can certainly ask which chief executives have the most similar profiles. Looking back at table 3.10 we notice immediately that some presidents tend to be high and low on the same personality traits and thus have nearly identical profiles. For example, John Adams and his son John Quincy Adams are both much higher on inflexibility than they are on friendliness, physical attractiveness, and wit—two rather unpleasant fellows it seems. Other presidents, by comparison, exhibit a personality pattern quite discrepant from their predecessors and successors, Grant providing a stark example. In judging the similarities of two profiles, the absolute elevation of the scores on the fourteen measures is not nearly so important as how scores on one variable compare relatively with those on another. Given the inherent complexity of profile comparisons, therefore, it would be extremely awkward to perform all possible pairings of the thirty-nine presidents. Cluster analysis allows us to determine mathematically and objectively which presidents form the same type and which are loners. The final product is the *dendrogram* (figure 6.1) (Simonton 1986h).

Those presidents who are tied together on the left of the figure are similar, whereas those who fail to join the others until we reach the right-hand portion of the figure display profiles at odds with the rest. As expected, the sole father and son pair linked quickly, while Grant waited for the very last minute to join his

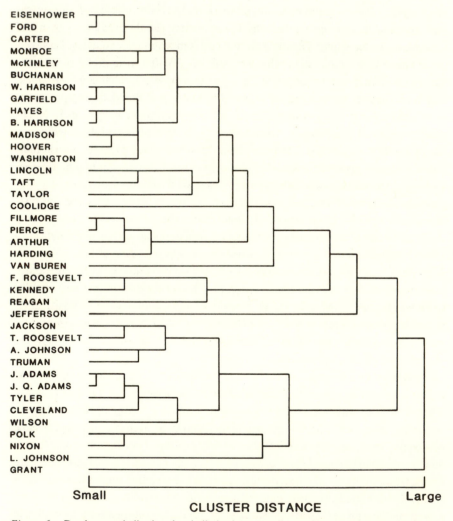

Figure 6.1 Dendrogram indicating the similarity in personality profiles for thirty-nine presidents. Most similar presidents grouped together on the left, least similar on the right. (Taken from Simonton 1986e, figure 1. Copyright 1986 by American Psychological Association. Used by permission.)

colleagues. Other presidents enter the dendrogram somewhere between, forming a hierarchical tree structure—hence the term dendrogram. The clusters that result can then be interpreted much like factors, the distances between the cases functioning in the same way as factor loadings. Hence, the two Adams's share much with Tyler, Cleveland, and Wilson, these five forming a cluster of highly idealistic, even self-righteous, and eminently stubborn presidents. Closely affiliated is another group that begins by joining Jackson and T. Roosevelt, advancing to include A. Johnson and Truman, thereby composing a larger cluster of executives far more pugnacious in their determination. Higher up the hierarchy, these two clusters connect with another formed by Polk, Nixon, and L. Johnson, this latter club containing presidents more anal-compulsive about the office, who believed in hard work, and who were obsessed with how they would ultimately stand with posterity.

Cluster analysis has thus unearthed the basic profile affinities of the thirty-nine White House occupants. However, when we induce a typology of historical figures within a domain, it should be manifest that the findings are restricted to the assessments that defined the profiles. Obtain different measurements and contrary clusters will normally emerge. For instance, a cluster analysis of the same thirty-nine presidents according to their profiles on five leadership styles yields rather distinct groupings, notwithstanding some overlap (Simonton 1988d). Furthermore, cluster analysis becomes an extremely awkward tool whenever the number of analytical units becomes large. Dendrograms used to integrate hundreds of historical figures will probably add more confusion than clarity to the psychological analysis of history. Still, the technique's usefulness has yet to be fully realized. There are several domains of historical activity where the subject pool is limited— Nobel laureates, Pulitzer Prize recipients, Supreme Court justices, Roman Emperors, Catholic pontiffs, and so forth. In such restricted populations, cluster analyses may isolate the chief routes to acclaim, as well as those who pursued less well travelled paths to societal or disciplinary kudos.

Our exposition of introductory statistics has covered much. We began by discussing various kinds of univariate approaches, the analyses of cross-sectional probability distributions and time-series fluctuations probably being relevant to the widest range of historical generalizations. We then reviewed bivariate statistics so that a researcher can be more fully apprised of the interpretive complexities involved. We concluded with a brief overview of multivariate perspectives that accommodate thick bundles of bivariate correlations. Factor analysis, in particular, enjoys an applicability that can make it a workhorse in historiometrics, just as it has already become in psychometrics.

In spite of the richness of statistical perspective, something is lacking. Many historical generalizations about human behavior are couched in causal terms. That is, one variable is supposed to be causally antecedent to another variable. From a psychological standpoint, the most intriguing of these are those propositions affirming that the individual serves as a causal agent in history. For example, when Machiavelli ([1516] 1952, 35) advised that "he will be successful who directs his actions according to the spirit of the times," an affirmative statement was being put forward about how a single individual may affect the aggregate despite the overwhelming disproportion in inherent strength. So it is imperative for us to examine how the behavioral scientist may discern causality in history.

7 Causality

Causality has long been the bugaboo of epistemologists. David Hume argued from his skeptical vantage point that causal inference may entail reading more into the data than is actually there. All we can directly experience is that one event appears to follow another. Yet somehow we manage to transmute this crude datum into the elaborate conclusion that the first event is a cause and the second is an effect, the causal event enjoying some mandated relation to the effect, a rather metaphysical notion. Immanuel Kant explained the discrepancy between world and mind by proposing that causation was an essential category of thought. Stated in modern terms, human information processing is programmed to organize experience automatically according to the concept of cause and effect. This inherent mode of cognition converts probabilistic contingencies into necessary and sufficient relations, which is accomplished by top-down (mind to world) rather than bottom-up (world to mind) processes. The tabula rasa of John Locke may indeed be blank, but our experience is etched on that slate with a writing utensil designed to add flourishes not found in phenomena.

Causality is commonly assumed to reside in people through an unfortunate logical superstition. An awareness of our own volition emerges from the first moment of infancy when we reached for an object and experienced its touch with our fingertips. By analogy, we eventually infer from our goal-directed thoughts the intentionality of other human beings, beginning with our family and moving to humanity at large. We also soon extrapolate this intentionality to the nonhuman world and thereby usher in beginning anthropomorphic fallacies. When intentions are projected to higher organisms (the family dog wants to be let outside quickly), the metaphoric extension may not be far off, but the projection becomes hazardous when it moves to creatures lower on the phylogenetic scale and absurd when applied to the inanimate world. There, anthropomorphizing means thinking that a cause somehow *wills* its effect, that the consequence ensues directly from the antecedent by some essential intentional link. Thus is the existential truth of volition, goals, and plans preposterously imposed upon a succession of events. By making a reality of a simile, a subjective continuity is placed over an objectively disconnected sequence of experiences. Causality is what glues sensory fragments into a coherent picture of the experiential world.

Causal inference becomes more precarious in the historical realm. To decipher the cause and effect of ongoing events, we can resort to experimentation, manipulating independent variables to see what happens to the dependent variable. But this effective procedure is closed to the historiometrician. To discern whether World War II would *not* have broken out had the Versailles Treaty been written differently, one cannot revise the document and then look at the vast political ramifications. One may speculate, and "counterfactual" arguments are sometimes elaborated with laudable plausibility in cliometrics (Fogel 1964). But no matter how logical, speculation cannot match experimentation. Therefore historiometricians who deal with causal judgments may be plunging into a black hole. Yet given the aspiration to test nomothetic hypotheses about human action on the stage of history, some variety of causal inference must be engaged in. Otherwise, historiometry would be prohibitively restricted. In the next two sections we examine how causality may be gained with the least intellectual cost, beginning with a definition of terms.

A more practical than metaphysical conception of causality has two components. First, X is a cause of Y if variation in (or the occurrence of) the former *directly covaries* with variation in (or the occurrence of) the latter. Second, X is a cause of Y if changes in the former are *temporally prior* to changes in the latter.

Direct Covariance

A critical qualifier is imposed on the first criterion of causality: Not just any covariance will do; the correspondence must be *direct,* not *spurious* (Simon 1954b). Experimental psychologists who frown on correlational analyses often use the derisive maxim "correlation does not prove causation." Certainly, when variable X is found to correlate with variable Y, there is no way to discern, without additional information, whether X causes Y, Y causes X, or both cause each other. This causal ambiguity is tolerable, since the absence of a correlation might mean the absence of causation. Here the proposition that X causes Y implies a correlation between measures of the two variables. No bivariate correlation, no causation. The correlation coefficient may thus falsify a causal hypothesis, when the capacity for falsifiability may be an essential requirement of science (Popper 1959).

Yet there is a more fundamental issue: the *third-variable* problem. Two variables may correlate, even very highly, without any direct causal connection. Instead, another variable may causally determine both, producing a totally spurious correlation: Z may cause both X and Y without X causing Y or, conversely, inducing a correlation between X and Y that has no causal significance at the bivariate level. The possible intrusion of spuriousness constitutes the biggest threat to inferring causality from correlations. Furthermore, it can intrude in a more subtle fashion: Rather than inflate an observed bivariate correlation, Z might actually obscure the real magnitude of statistical association between X and Y. When this happens, the correlation r_{XY} is spuriously low and controlling for Z is needed to establish the genuine strength of the causal dependence of Y upon X. The enhancement of a correlation by removing the obscuring effects of a third variable is called *statistical suppression*.

In any case, the investigator's charge is to show that the covariation between two variables is direct. A direct correlation does not mandate a positive causal connection, as when we say that Y is directly proportional to X. If increases in X cause decreases in Y, the inverse association that results is still considered direct, for here it means causal consequence. More important, to say that X directly covaries with Y does not necessitate claiming that X is the most immediate or proximate cause of Y. X may indeed cause Y, but only through the intervening variable of Z. An example of this causal chain is the theory of political violence proposed by Matossian and Schafer (1977) in which population pressures X induce hostile family interactions Z, which a generation later may take the form of revolts against authority Y. The correlation between X and Y in this causal model is not spurious, for Z elaborates the causal picture without qualifying it. It does not matter if Z is measured if our primary preoccupation is establishing the causal nexus between X and Y. When Z serves as a source of spuriousness, in contrast, we cannot dependably gauge the causal impact of X on Y without first correcting for the contaminating influence of Z, a correction that mandates assessing the analytical units on all three variables.

Let us now survey the techniques that demonstrate direct covariance by adjusting for potential sources of spuriousness. In order of complexity, these are partial correlations, multiple regression analysis, path analysis, and covariance structure modeling.

Partial Correlations

Let us refer to the three variables X, Y, and Z by z_1, z_2, and z_3, respectively, where the latter are standardized to a zero mean and a standard deviation of unity. We seek a mathematical answer to the question: Is the correlation r_{12} between z_1 and z_2 the spurious consequence of the third variable z_3? We take advantage of the two correlations r_{13} and r_{23}, which gauge the potential influence of the third variable on the two variables going into the bivariate relationship. Because these coefficients represent regression slopes, we readily obtain two bivariate equations $\hat{z}_1 = r_{13}z_3$ and $\hat{z}_2 = r_{23}z_3$. These two prediction equations provide the basis for computing the residual scores for z_1 and z_2, that is, scores with the variance these variables share with z_3 removed. In particular, we can compute $z_{1.3} = z_1 - r_{13}z_3$ and $z_{2.3} = z_2 - r_{23}z_3$, where the dot notation $z_{1.3}$ means that the variable z_1 has had its variance attributable to z_3 extracted.

The Pearson product-moment coefficient between these two residual scores gauges the direct correlation between z_1 and z_2 under the assumption that the only possible contaminating influence is z_3. If the correlation is spurious, the new correlation will be zero. This *partial* correlation, symbolized by $r_{12.3}$, is "first order," because only one variable is "partialled out" or controlled for. Of course, this test for spuriousness seems a bit awkward, requiring as it does the residuals of two bivariate regression equations. Fortunately, the partial correlation can be calculated directly from the zero-order coefficients using the formula

$$r_{12.3} = \frac{r_{12} - r_{13}r_{23}}{(1 - r_{13}^2)^{1/2}(1 - r_{23}^2)^{1/2}} \tag{7.1}$$

In the numerator hides the test for spuriousness: If the product $r_{13}r_{23}$ is identical to r_{12}, *all* of the covariation between z_1 and z_2 can be dismissed as the result of their common reliance on z_3. The denominator's sole responsibility is to standardize this difference so that it represents a Pearson product-moment coefficient. Hence, the square of the partial can still be interpreted as the proportion of variance shared between two variables, with only the added proviso that the part that a third variable may have contributed to that common variance has been surgically removed.

The earliest historiometric application of equation 7.1 occurred in 1926, as part of Cox's monumental inquiry. Cox wished to prove that her IQ estimates correlated positively with the ranked eminence of her creators and leaders, but she realized that this coefficient might well be spurious, owing to the embarrassing discovery that both IQ and eminence were themselves positively associated with data reliability. Consequently, Cox computed the partial correlation between IQ and eminence, with data reliability in the place of the third variable, and still found a significant association (Cox 1926, 55). To exemplify her analysis, eminence and intelligence correlate .23, while these two variables correlate .14 and .37, respectively, with data reliability (Simonton 1976a). Plugging these three correlations into equation 7.1 we arrive at the modest though significant coefficient of .19. The Galtonian hypothesis that intelligence affects achievement apparently may have a grain of truth.

This instance concerns the outcome when introducing correction for a third variable weakens if not obliterates a correlation between two variables. Nevertheless, the extraneous variable, as suggested earlier, can obscure a relation much stronger than is apparent in the zero-order correlation in which context the calculation of the first-order partial can allow the third variable to function as a *suppressor*. Partialling, then, suppresses the variance, obstructing a clear view of what is happening between two variables. For example, the correlation between a president's greatness rating and whether or not he had been assassinated is .22, a nonsignificant r given that we have only thirty-six cases. Yet greatness correlates

.59 with the number of years served in office (the top predictor), and the latter variable correlates $-.20$ with assassination. Not surprisingly, assassinated chief executives, on average, have a shorter residence in the White House. So what would we predict when given two former presidents who served an equal number of years but only one tragically cut down by an assassin's bullet? By applying equation 7.1, the correlation almost doubles to .43 (compare Simonton 1987d, chap 5).

At times the investigator demands that more than one "third" variable be statistically controlled, a situation calling for higher-order partials. Even though the formulae for partials above the first order are cumbersome and are best present-ed in matrix algebraic form, the principle is the same. Essentially a kth-order partial is a Pearsonian correlation between two sets of residuals, obtained by regressing each of the two variables on the k potential contaminants.

To illustrate, let us turn to a cross-sectional time-series analysis of the careers of ten top classical composers (Simonton 1977a). The hypothesis tested was the "constant-probability-of-success" model, which claims that quality (or creativity) is a linear function of quantity (or productivity), a probabilistic associa-tion that should hold both across and within careers (Simonton 1984d, 1988e). To verify the longitudinal version of this model, the total thematic output of each composer was tabulated into consecutive five-year age periods, after first splitting the themes according to whether they originated in successful or unsuccessful compositions. A successful theme was one frequently performed, whereas an unsuccessful theme was rarely if ever heard. The zero-order correlation between the production of major and minor works as a career unfolds was found to be .56. To check for the potential intrusion of other factors in this correlation, five distinct controls were defined, including linear and quadratic functions of age in order to ensure that the co-occurrence of great and small was not solely a result the overall age function seen in figure 5.4. The resulting fifth-order partial correlation was .45. Those periods in a composer's life with the most masterpieces are still the same periods, by and large, that witnessed the greater number of musical ideas less than memorable (see also Simonton 1985b).

Although a simple technique, partial correlation analysis is underused. Be-cause investigators are often content with bivariate analyses, spurious correlations proliferate in the literature. Most misleading coefficients do not survive implemen-tation of this most basic of all statistical controls. In the research on presidential leadership, for example, greatness ratings have exhibited zero-order correlations with physical height, eye color, family size, social class, power motivation, charisma, quantity of legislation passed, the number of Supreme Court appoint-ments, party system aging, and so on (for example, J. Holmes and Elder 1989; Kenney and Rice 1988; Nice 1984; Winter 1987b). Yet *not one* of these variables displays a respectable partial that takes into consideration plausible contaminating factors (Simonton 1990d).

Multiple Regression Analysis.

The technique described is essentially a bivariate procedure that has been converted into a multivariate manipulation by a kind of cheating. The focus is on the association between a pair of variables, all other variables interfering. This emphasis may be acceptable when a hypothesis dictates a single link between a cause and an effect variable, yet more often an effect has multiple causes. Psychohistorical phenomena are extremely complex, each event having a myriad antecedents. A more comprehensive treatment that deals with all potential determinants simultaneously is needed to estimate the impact of all causal factors while controlling for all possible contaminating influences. In other words, we must assign mathematical meaning to the classic qualification *ceteris paribus,* or "all other things held constant."

Let us begin with the simplest case, an effect with two causes. Let z_1 be the dependent variable and z_2 and z_3 be the two independent variables, again using standardized scores. We propose that z_1 can be predicted by a linear additive function of both z_2 and z_3, namely

$$\hat{z}_1 = \beta_{12.3}z_2 + \beta_{13.2}z_3 \tag{7.2}$$

where the two betas (β's) are slopes in the multiple regression equation. These are interpretable in much the same way as the correlation coefficient in a bivariate regression (for example, $\hat{z}_1 = r_{12}z_2$). For each unit increase in z_2, $\hat{z}_1$ goes up by $\beta_{12.3}$ units, with the stipulation that z_3 remains constant. A parallel predictive statement can be composed for $\beta_{13.2}$. (The dot notation is in the subscripts because each standardized regression coefficient is actually a partial, though not a partial correlation). These two critical parameters can be estimated by applying the principle of least squares. That is, the two coefficients are adjusted so that the errors of prediction—the residuals obtained by subtracting predicted ($\hat{z}_1$) from observed scores (z_1) across all cases—have the smallest possible variance. This requirement is formally equivalent to demanding that the correlation between predicted and actual scores on the dependent variable be as high as possible given the data. If that correlation is perfect, the variance of the residuals is zero, whereas if it is zero, the variance of the residuals equals the variance of the original scores, with nothing gained from the regression analysis.

Partial regression coefficients. Using calculus, we can derive two formulae for estimating the βs from the initial r's:

$$\beta_{12.3} = \frac{r_{12} - r_{13}r_{23}}{1 - r_{23}{}^2} \qquad \beta_{13.2} = \frac{r_{13} - r_{12}r_{23}}{1 - r_{23}{}^2} \tag{7.3}$$

A quick comparison of the first formula with equation 7.1 reveals that the numerators are identical. Because the denominators in both formulae merely rescale this difference, $\beta_{12.3} = r_{12.3} = 0$ whenever the association ($r_{12} \neq 0$) between z_1 and z_2 is completely attributable to z_3. By the same line of reasoning, $\beta_{13.2} = r_{13.2} = 0$ when the bivariate association between z_1 and z_3 can be totally ascribed to z_2. The formulae for the beta coefficients are intrinsically symmetric, no independent variable assuming special privileges. Each causal effect is calculated after controlling for all rival effects, thereby conducting all tests for spuriousness at once and equitably. This procedure is far more efficient than calculating as many partial correlations as we have independent variables. With this gain in efficiency, we obtain a prediction equation that optimally predicts the dependent variable according to the rugged criterion of least squares. Moreover, the β's can still be interpreted in much the same way as correlation coefficients, given that they also tend to range between -1 and $+1$ (although βs can occasionally overstep those lower and upper bounds). Hence, the standardized partial regression coefficients provide direct clues regarding the comparative importance of the predictors.

So long as the number of predictors is kept comfortably smaller than the number of cases, equation 7.2 can be extended to as many independent variables as desired. The sole consequence is that the standardized partial regression coefficients are no more such simple functions of the zero-order correlations. As in the case of higher-order partials, we have no recourse than to express betas in terms of matrix algebraic manipulations. This mathematical elaboration is best left to standard textbooks. On the other hand, equation 7.2 and its extensions suffer from the limitation that the multivariate regression slopes all apply to standardized variables on both sides of the equation. Even if this feature is useful in comparing the relative impact of each predictor, predictions using the original variables is a more concrete task, particularly when some of the variables are in natural units, including ratio scales, or when dichotomous (zero-one dummy) variables are included in the set of predictors.

Fortunately, standardized regression coefficients can be directly rescaled to unstandardized coefficients by multiplying and dividing by the appropriate standard deviations. For instance, the partial regression coefficient $b_{12.3}$ is derived from $\beta_{12.3}$ when the latter is multiplied by σ_1 and divided by σ_2, representing the standard deviations of the raw scores. With unstandardized variables, however, a constant (or intercept) term must be inserted in the regression equation (by subtracting from the mean of the dependent variable the sum of the products of the b's times the respective means of the raw-score independent variables). Most computer statistical packages will provide both standardized and unstandardized coefficients automatically.

In table 7.1 we see a multiple regression equation specifying presidential greatness as a linear function of six variables—years in office, years of war, assassination, scandal, being a war hero, and intellectual brilliance (Simonton 1986g). Both standardized (β's) and unstandardized (b's) partial regression coefficients are shown, in the second case a constant term being added. The standardized

Table 7.1 *Regression Equation for Predicting Rated Presidential Performance according to Murray-Blessing Survey*

Predictor	β	b	p
Years in office	.36	0.15	.0008
Years of war	.35	0.21	.0015
Assassination	.20	0.73	.0190
Scandal	−.40	−1.44	.0000
War hero	.33	0.87	.0011
Intellectual brilliance	.26	0.26	.0084
Constant term	—	−1.10	.0000

Note. Simonton (1986g, table 3). Copyright 1986 by American Psychological Association. Used by permission.
$R^2 = .82$; adjusted $R^2 = .79$, $F(6, 29) = 22.84$, $p < .0001$.

coefficients tell us about the relative impact of the six predictors, scandal carrying the most weight and assassination the least. However, because virtually all variables are either ratio scaled (years in office and years of war) or dichotomous (assassination, scandal, and being a war hero), the unstandardized coefficients provide more information about exactly how each variable contributes to the prediction of presidential greatness. In the absence of any other knowledge, each president begins with a score of −1.10. Given that greatness is a z score, each chief executive starts more than one standard unit below the mean (see table 4.2). Each year served adds 0.15 points, and each year of war 0.21 points, but even more credit accrues from having been a war hero or assassinated, 0.87 and 0.73 points, respectively. In contrast, these painfully acquired assets may dissipate should scandal tarnish an administration, which mandates the subtraction of 1.44 points. Notice that both β and b are identical for intellectual brilliance, since this predictor, like the criterion variable of greatness, is already standardized (see table 3.10). Each unit change in this personality variable compels about a one-quarter standard unit change in greatness, and in the same direction.

The crucial point is that the effect of each predictor is estimated while simultaneously controlling for the effects of all five remaining predictors, thus helping to promise a linear function that describes a direct covariance. Thus, the number of years that a president scores as wartime commander-in-chief has relevance in anticipating the historians' assessments apart from any correlation the predictor has with years in office; and the beneficial (if tragic) repercussion of assassination for a chief executive's reputation can show up after statistically adjusting for the contaminating influence of the same variable. However, this feature weeds out many other candidates for inclusion in the equation. For example, even though charisma (from table 6.5) correlates .49 with greatness, it cannot enter into the equation with the others (Simonton 1988d). Its effect is evidently either indirect or spurious, owing to charisma's association with intellectual brilliance and other predictors.

Multiple regression is primarily designed to handle situations where the dependent variable is measured on at least an interval scale, although the technique can be applied to the prediction of ordinal data under the assumption that the ranked scores capture the key features of an underlying interval measurement (for example, Simonton 1976a). More problematic is the circumstance where the criterion variable is merely nominal. If the categorical variable is a dichotomy represented by a zero-one dummy variable, a regression analysis can still proceed, although it may better be handled using a *discriminant analysis*. Applied to 326 land battles, this method isolated those individual and situational factors that best predict tactical victory, obviously a dichotomous outcome (Simonton 1980a). When the nominal scale to be predicted is multilevel, we must employ a discriminant analysis. For instance, biographical characteristics were used to predict the domain of individual achievement (Simonton 1986b). Because there were twenty categories (politicians, military figures, explorers, athletes, performers, scientists, and so forth) a multiple discriminant analysis was required. But despite the greater complexity of this method, the basic principle of causal inference remains unaltered.

Multiple correlation. Because selecting beta weights to minimize the variance of the residuals (the least-squares rule) is equivalent to maximizing the correlation between predicted and observed scores, the correlation serves as a straightforward index of how well our supposed causes determine their shared effect. Thus, if we were to plug real values into the equation given in table 7.1 and correlate the result with the actual greatness scores of Murray and Blessing (1983), we would get the number .905 (Simonton 1986h). This *multiple correlation coefficient* is represented by R, the capitalization setting this off from the bivariate r. Nevertheless, R is truly a Pearsonian product-moment correlation and as such has much the same implications for interpreting results. Specifically, the squared multiple correlation, or R^2, indicates the proportion of variance in the criterion that is explained by the predictors as optimally combined. Hence, the six-variable equation in table 7.1 accounts for 82 percent ($R^2 = .82$) of the individual differences in greatness, an excellent level of predictive success. Needless to say, R can never be negative and always falls instead in the interval from 0 to 1, inclusively.

Multiple regression analysis thus becomes the most valuable inferential approach for the historiometrician. The method is handy in controlling for a host of possible methodological artifacts, the investigator introducing variables to adjust for ethnocentric and epochcentric slants, dating biases, and other confounding factors (for example, Simonton 1975f, 1977a, 1980b, 1984g). At the same time, the overall predictability of the dependent variable can be determined by the multiple correlation. When both substantive and methodological factors are combined as independent variables, the determination means that we can partition the total explained variation in the dependent variable into two portions, one concerning fact, the other artifact. As an example, to test the hypothesis that war inhibits scientific and technological creativity, log-transformed annual counts of discoveries and inventions were regressed on measures of military conflict along with several variables controlling for potential biases in the tabulations (Simonton 1980b). Although about 56 percent of the transhistorical variation could be ascribed to possible sources of artifact, 5 percent of the time-series counts could be safely attributed to war.

Multicollinearity. One snag can block an uncomplicated application of multiple regression analysis; it is (somewhat misleadingly) called "multicollinearity." To weigh the impact of one variable while holding other variables constant, what happens when two variables are basically equivalent? It is most difficult, if not impossible, to partial out from the effect of one variable the common variance it shares with its near or exact twin. This difficulty is evident in equation 7.3, for it is patent that $r_{23}^2 \neq 1.0$ or we must divide by zero. In other words, when z_2 is perfectly correlated with z_3, no way exists to separate out the relative importance of each variable. But, of course, this impossibility should be logical; if z_2 is truly identical to z_3, then to look for the impact of z_2 on z_1 controlling for z_3 (or the companion comparison) is to engage in an absurd search. It is then likely that each variable actually measures the same thing, or even that one variable is a simple linear transformation of the other.

Multicollinearity cannot be avoided merely by scanning a zero-order correlation matrix for unity values between two independent variables, for whenever we have a large number of independent variables, multicollinearity can occur if one predictor can be perfectly predicted by some linear combination of the other predictors. This *linear dependency* emerges under various circumstances. For example, one variable might be defined as a linear combination of the other variables in the first place. More irksome is a more subtle condition: From the basic principles of linear algebra we know that the number of linearly independent variables cannot exceed the number of cases on which those variables are measured. If there are N individuals in the study, and k variables are measured on those individuals, a subset of those k variables must necessarily be multicollinear if $k <$ N. In less abstract terms, one cannot gather an unlimited amount of independent information on a restricted set of cases. Sooner or later, the measurements must begin duplicating one another exactly if secretly.

This limitation imposes a severe constraint on how well we can test a causal relation for direct covariance. To ensure that the connection between z_1 and z_2 is not spurious, it is necessary to introduce into the multiple regression equation all other variables that might actually underlie the observed correspondence. The number of potential candidates for this third-variable function may in some applications be quite large. The bigger the inventory of possible contaminants, the larger the number of cases that are required before all pertinent controls can be measured. Yet in some inquiries, there is an upper bound on N that cannot be surpassed. For such problems, N will so limit k that the investigator cannot possibly introduce all the necessary variables into the regression equation. As a case in point, Shakespeare wrote at most thirty-eight plays, so that any regression equation predicting some aesthetic facet of his works cannot contain more than three dozen variables, no matter how many may actually be mandated by the needs of causal inference.

Path Analysis

Partial correlation analysis was criticized for its inability to advance beyond the consideration of bivariate relations. Despite efforts to adapt higher-order partials to more intricate causal hypotheses—the so-called Simon-Blalock strategy (Blalock 1972; Simon 1954b)—these suggestions have made little headway in published research. Multiple regression allows some progress to made toward more elaborate models, by permitting more than one cause for a given effect, including methodological factors that introduce artifacts. Even so, multiple regression is dedicated to discerning the separate and combined contributions of many causes behind *one* effect. Occasions often arise when our causal hypotheses are far more complicated, for what is an effect in one regression equation might be a cause in another. The causal chain sketched in figure 5.6, exemplifies this possibility (Simonton 1984g). A monarch's prominence in history is a function of a concatenation of cause-effect relations, the main sequence running life span $\rightarrow$ reign span $\rightarrow$ historical activity $\rightarrow$ monarchal eminence. Furthermore, impinging on this principal series of causal associations are numerous other variables, both individual and situational.

How can the psychologist decipher cause-effect functions that are so elaborately intertwined? An answer is path analysis. Originally proposed by Sewall Wright (1934), the distinguished population geneticist, this biometric method was later proved to be formally equivalent to the structural equation modeling that had undergone a parallel evolution in econometrics. Once the two traditions were integrated into a more uniform methodology, this technique could be introduced into sociology (Duncan 1975; Heise 1975) and psychology (Kenny 1979). Path analysis is best illustrated by a specific study of 696 composers in the Western music tradition (Simonton 1977c).

Seven variables were defined as potential antecedents of a composer's ultimate standing with posterity: creative longevity, or the length of a composer's career; life span; creative productivity, or the total number of memorable themes generated by the composer; creative precociousness, or the age at which the composer began creative productivity (calculated as the negative age in order to give its association with other key variables the proper sign); geographic marginality, or how far away the composer was born from the center of music activity in his or her generation (defined by the application of a pseudo-Euclidean distance measure); role-model availability, or the number of active composers in the previous generation (logarithmically transformed to linearize the exponential trend); and birth year, which serves as the only true exogenous variable (that is, a variable uncaused by any other variable in the system). The ultimate endogenous variable—the one variable that is only an effect and never a cause in the network—was eminence, which was a reliable composite of multiple indicators. The basic descriptive statistics for all eight variables are offered below the diagonal in table 7.2.

Skipping the raw statistics for eminence, geographic marginality, and role-model availability, which are not in natural units, the means tell us that the average composer in the sample was born in 1796, began creative production at age thirty-three, produced twenty-four notable themes by age forty-three, and lived to be sixty-three years. The Pearsonian correlations among all eight variables indicate the possible causal determinants of creative eminence. It correlates most highly with creative productivity, that is, the most prominent composers are responsible for the largest numbers of significant melodies in the classical repertoire. Besides creative productivity, fame positively correlates with career length and productive precociousness, and negatively relates to birth year, role-model availability, and geographic marginality, though these last three are less conspicuous. Of the seven potential predictors, only life span bears no linear relation to eminence. But to clarify the causal interconnections among the eight variables, we must go beyond the correlations.

After proposing a causal network specifying how the variables might affect each other, the theory was tested using the standard techniques of path analysis, yielding the graph that is figure 7.1. The arrows indicate the presumed direction of causal influence; if there is no arrow, no direct causal relation exists. Thus life span

Table 7.2   *Correlations, Descriptive Statistics, and Deviations from Model-Predicted Correlations for 696 Classical Composers*

Variable	1	2	3	4	5	6	7	8
1. Birth year		.00	.00	.02	.03	.00	.04	.03
2. Role-model availability	.85		.00	.00	.00	.00	.00	.00
3. Geographic marginality	.45	.48		−.03	−.06	.01	−.04	−.03
4. Creative precociousness	.23	.24	.08		.00	.01	.00	.02
5. Creative productivity	.02	−.02	−.07	.32		.01	.00	.00
6. Life span	−.06	−.18	−.14	−.24	−.05		.01	−.03
7. Creative longevity	.09	.03	−.04	.40	.51	.15		−.01
8. Eminence	−.19	−.19	−.14	.26	.71	−.01	.56	
M	1796	4.14	2.38	−33	24	63	10	10
SD	112	.57	1.08	9	74	14	12	22

Note. Taken from Simonton (1977c, table 1). Copyright 1977 by American Psychological Association. Used by permission.
Zero-order correlations are given below the blank diagonal. Differences between these correlations and those predicted by the model in figure 7.1 are shown above the blank diagonal. Correlations must be at least .062 to be significant at the .05 level for a one-tailed test.

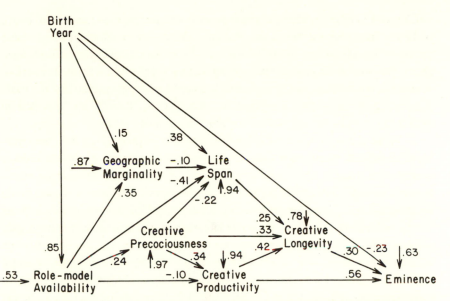

Figure 7.1 Structural equation model of the determinants of eminence for 696 classical composers. Path coefficients show degree and direction of causal influence. (Taken from Simonton 1977c, figure 1. Copyright 1977 by American Psychological Association. Used by permission.)

exerts no direct effect upon eminence; any effect it might have must take place through creative longevity. The decimal fractions beside each arrow are the path coefficients or structural parameters that register the relative contribution of each cause to a particular effect. These coefficients are actually standardized multiple regression coefficients, or betas, and therefore gauge the impact of one independent variable holding the other direct effects constant. Accordingly, the path coefficient of .56 between productivity and eminence shows us the strength of the influence of productivity after controlling for birth year and creative longevity.

Some of the causal coefficients that strike a given effect variable come out of nowhere, parameters that record the influence of all unmeasured causes in the network. These omitted causes have the nasty disposition of boasting the biggest influence on any variable under scrutiny. If the square of this coefficient is subtracted from one, the difference represents the proportion of variance in that dependent variable that is explained by all the explicit dependent variables put together. In the case of eminence, for example, 60 percent of the differential fame of the 696 composers ($1 - .63^2 = .60$) can be explained in terms of productivity, longevity, and birth year. These peculiar causal coefficients are actually derived from the squared multiple correlations for each endogenous variable; these residual paths equal $\sqrt{1 - R^2}$.

The parameters for the observed variables have the most predictive value, for they tell us how many standard deviations above or below the mean a composer will be on the effect variable if that composer is so many standard deviations above or below the mean on the causal variable. Hence, the coefficient of .42 from productivity to longevity signifies that a composer who is one standard deviation above the mean in the production of melodies (24 + 74 = 98), will be .42 standard deviations above the mean in the length of career, or fifteen rather than ten years (10 + .42 × 12 = 15). For negative paths the calculations are executed no differently, except that the minus sign must be included in all calculations.

What about the effect of precociousness on longevity? At first we might simply conclude that for every standard deviation that a career begins earlier than average, the overall career is about one-third longer than the mean. If the career began at twenty-four rather than thirty-three, we might expect that the career would be about fourteen years long (10 + .33 × 12 = 14). Yet this prediction is wrong insofar as it incorporates only the direct effect of precociousness on longevity, thus overlooking two indirect influences, one through life span and the other through creative productivity. Precocious creators tend to be more prolific, but they also tend to die young, a fact as true of scientists as of musicians (Zhao and Jiang 1986). Consequently, we must add to the direct effect these two indirect effects by taking the products of the corresponding path coefficients. The indirect effect of precociousness on longevity through the intervening variable of productivity is equal to .14 (= .34 × .42), while the indirect effect through life span is − .06 (= − .22 × .30). The total effect of precociousness on longevity is equal to the sum of the direct and indirect effects or .41, that is, making allowance for the complexity of the causal relation between precociousness and longevity, for every year of delay in the onset of a composer's life work, the career will be shortened by about two hundred days.

It is no accident that this summary effect coefficient of .41 is remarkably close to the correlation coefficient of .40. We have *decomposed* the bivariate correlation between two variables, in this case precociousness and longevity, into the sum of separate causal paths, one direct and two indirect. The only thing omitted from this decomposition are relatively minor sources of spuriousness from the ultimate dependence of both variables on birth year. The capacity to decompose a relation into distinct causal components is one of the impressive features of path analysis, particularly when it allows us to avoid erroneous conclusions. From table 7.2 it might seem that the availability of role models early in life has little to do with creative productivity later. As seen in figure 7.1, this inference is entirely fallacious, for role-model availability exerts both a direct and an indirect influence upon productivity, the latter effect occurring through precociousness. The more role models during creative development, the earlier a creator will begin to compose memorable melodies. Yet having many models may inhibit the total productive output of original melodies, perhaps because it may encourage excessive imitativeness. The positive indirect effect just about cancels the negative direct effect; adding them yields the virtually nonexistent correlation of − .02. Obviously, the absence of a correlation does not necessarily mean that two variables are not causally related. A zero correlation must always be interpreted in terms of an entire causal network, given that a zero correlation might be partitioned into a sum of nonzero direct and indirect causal paths.

To estimate how much of the correlation between two variables may be the spurious intrusion of common causes, we take the sum of direct and indirect effects and subtract the result from the overall bivariate correlation. Hence, part of the association between longevity and eminence is due to their mutual dependence upon productivity and birth year. If we take the direct effect of longevity on eminence (no indirect effect exists here) and subtract it from the correlation, the result is .26 (= .56 − .30). This spurious effect can be ascribed chiefly to productivity (.56 × .42 = .24), the remainder to the complex direct and indirect consequences of a composer's birth year. The device of decomposing correlations reveals the rich causal intricacy behind the correlation matrix.

Once we know how to decompose a correlation on the basis of a given structural model, and given the estimated causal parameters, we can compare the correlations predicted by the model with those we actually observe. Expressed differently, rather than examine the predicted and observed scores (as with multiple regression), it is more interesting in path analysis to examine how well the causal network allows us to reconstruct the raw matrix of Pearsonian coefficients. This embodies a test of a model's precision in reproducing the causal structure implicit in the correlation matrix. In the current case, the difference between predicted and observed coefficients gives the results seen above the diagonal in table 7.2. Clearly the errors of prediction are negligible, the only appreciable discrepancy being that between geographic marginality and creative productivity. There is some residual tendency, not incorporated in figure 7.1, for those composers born far from the musical center to be less prolific, but this disposition is not potent enough to require another arrow in the structural model.

Path analysis is not as simple as this example would make it appear, nor does the causal model represent a finished product. The model is nothing more than a first approximation, but it does illustrate the general approach to determining direct covariance. Such a method can better capture the complexities of causal networks in real-world settings and makes predictions of superior accuracy and understanding possible.

Covariance Structure Models

Path analysis involves many methodological issues important to any competent application, such as the choice between standardized and nonstandardized coefficients and the best way to accommodate nominal and ordinal measures. Yet these problems are minor compared to what must be assumed for obtaining path coefficients by multiple regression which requires a simplified causal model: (a) all causes are unidirectional, with no two-way causal influences or feedback loops;

(b) the disturbance terms that feed into the endogenous variables do not correlate; and (c) all pertinent variables are perfectly measured and incorporated. Whenever one or more of these assumptions cannot be satisfied, ordinary least-squares regression cannot provide the structural parameters. Instead, the investigator must resort to more advanced techniques that synthesize biometric path analysis, psychometric factor analysis, and econometric simultaneous equation systems. This recent synthesis has several names, including covariance structure modeling (Carmines 1986), LISREL for linear structural relations (Jöreskog and Sörbom 1986), and latent variable modeling (Bentler 1980). Although quite technical introductory texts have been published (Loehlin 1987; Long 1983a, 1983b), more "user-friendly" computer software is emerging (Bentler 1985), and artificial intelligence techniques are being developed to aid the discovery of the best causal model (Glymour, Scheines, Spirtes, and Kelly 1987).

To demonstrate the potential utility of this new approach, let us return to our earlier discussion of the validity of eminence measures. We argued that scores on multiple indicators of fame gauge underlying qualities of genius, creativity, or leadership. The high correlations among separate measures, as indicated by the reliabilities, result from an unmeasurable factor, or latent variable, that we may style "Galton's G." Besides acknowledging Galton's emphatic belief that "the men who achieve eminence, and those who are naturally capable, are, to a large extent, identical," (1869, 34) this term parallels Spearman's g, the construct that hypothetically dwells behind performance on various intelligence tests. Therefore, if we have five alternative reputational measures, for example, m_1 through m_5, we get model a in figure 7.2, a simple single-factor model where the structural coefficients a_1 through a_5 represent factor loadings. Because these loadings are not expected to be unity—owing to the fallibility of any one measure—the path diagram includes the error terms e_1 through e_5.

Three rival causal structures are also graphed. Model b permits two complications: The errors between two measures (e_1 and e_2) might have an independent correlation representing a common influence extraneous to G, such as shared ethnocentric or ideological biases; and scores on one measure might directly affect scores on another (that is, $m_4 \rightarrow m_5$), as when one rater borrows opinions from a predecessor. Although model b elaborates model a without compromising the Galtonian thesis, the other two models pose a serious challenge to the belief that one stable factor lies beneath all reputational measures. Model c specifies a first-order autoregressive scheme where eminence assessments form a causal chain, each measure being determined by the immediately preceding measure plus a random shock. The path coefficients p_{21} through p_{54} indicate the extent to which judgment is carried over from the immediate past. Model d makes the consecutive measures of fame contingent on an underlying consensus that transforms over time by a first-order autoregressive process, obtaining a sequence of five unmeasurable variables F_1 through F_5, disturbance terms d_2 through d_5, plus *both* factor loadings

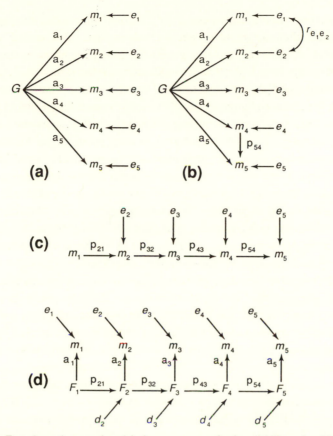

Figure 7.2 Four alternative causal models that may account for the reliability and stability of reputational measures. Source: Simonton 1990b.

and path coefficients. Five factors of transient fashion replace one factor of stable genius.

Although all four models can account for the respectable reliabilities found for eminence measures, they yield predictions sufficiently distinct that they can be tested against the observed correlations among multiple measures of reputation. For instance, it is implied in models c and d that the coefficients become systematically smaller as we look away from the diagonal of the correlation matrix; eminence can display no traitlike stability over time, for eventually any test-retest reliability will become zero. More subtle are mathematical constraints (overidentifying restrictions) placed on the relations among the several correlations. For example, model a yields the *tetrad* equation $r_{13}r_{45} - r_{14}r_{35} = 0$, whereas model c yields the *partial* equation $r_{13} - r_{12}r_{23} = 0$ (see Kenny 1979). If constraints fail to fit the observed correlations, the causal models that imply them are rejected. After a causal model survives these checks, the structural coefficients can be estimated by special algorithms (ML or GLS).

These tests have already been conducted on a wide variety of reputational measures, including the greatness ratings of twenty-nine presidents and the multiple indicators of eminence for 342 monarchs, 2,012 scientists, 2,026 philosophers, 696 composers, and 772 artists (Simonton 1990c), the results uniformly disconfirming models c and d. The only causal structure that generates valid constraints on the correlations is one that incorporates a single stable factor, or Galton's G. This is true even for the three Farnsworth (1969) assessments shown in figure 4.3, despite the fact that these span seventy years; no matter whether we examine music histories, music encyclopedias, or general encyclopedias, model a suffices to explain the observed correlations, with factor loadings ranging from .790 to .999. Even though correlated errors must sometimes be allowed to complicate the structure, as in model b, these involve neither ethnocentric biases nor interindicator influences but rather mundane and trivial method artifacts (for example, difficulty factors owing to distinctive univariate distributions). Indeed, an index of parsimonious fit that, like the adjusted-R^2, penalizes a model for enhancing predictive precision by introducing extraneous parameters, without exception favors model a over any version of model b. These results are critical to any historiometric inquiry that includes eminence as an individual variable, for only the first two models endorse the notion that fame is dominated by a stable traitlike component. Differential distinction otherwise would have no psychological meaning.

This example does not include reciprocal causation, nor does it illustrate latent variable models with complex causal networks like that seen in figure 7.1. But it should suffice to suggest the power of these novel methods of causal inference.

Temporal Priority

Analytical power notwithstanding, direct covariance is a necessary but not sufficient criterion. No matter how elaborate our multivariate perspectives, the association between two variables is causally symmetrical unless some other information can be brought to bear on either side of the relation. Although we can regress z_1 on z_2 and obtain a significant partial regression coefficient after introducing dozens—even hundreds—of third variables, the direction of a one-way arrow cannot be affirmed.

Occasionally a strong theory or logical principle allows us to take sides in causal dilemmas. For instance, for variables at two contrary levels of analysis, the larger system is more likely to be a cause than an effect of the smaller system. The greater the discrepancy between the two systematic levels, the more secure our inference of a single direction. For example, changes in the integrative complexity in the private correspondence of British novelists probably cannot be held responsible for unrest in Ireland (Porter and Suedfeld 1981). Nevertheless, we must be careful in calling up this systemic principle, for circumstances may arise where the causal direction might be opposite to expectation. A primary tenet of the cult of genius is that a lone personality can change the course of a nation. Successful generals may be prone to boast lower casualty rates than their opponents because they have larger armies (Simonton 1980a), yet effective commanders may attract larger forces owing to the confidence they inspire in their soldiers. Over a decade after Wellington defeated Napoleon at Waterloo, the duke could still compliment his erstwhile opponent by saying that Napoleon's "presence on the field made the difference of forty thousand men"—an asset not likely to be ignored by an infantry not fanatically dedicated to becoming cannon fodder!

Besides the criterion of direct covariance, the decision rule with the most universal applicability is temporal priority: Causes cannot follow their effects. In historiometry, the primary means is time-series data. Only when we know how a variable fluctuates over time can we reliably infer the events that anticipate change. Causal inference may be based on two rather different kinds of time series, one interrupted, the other continuous.

Interrupted Time Series

Say that we possess a regular sequence of measurements on a construct extending over a considerable period of time. At some point in the middle of this time series some major event occurs. Will the values taken by the variable be deflected from their anticipated course after some noticeable delay? If the answer is yes, we may speak of the external event as representing a cause of the effect variable registered by the time series. This model of causal inference is part of a larger inventory of *quasi-experimental designs,* a collection closely linked with the name Donald Campbell and his associates (Campbell and Stanley 1966). For instance, in Campbell's 1969 paper "Reforms as Experiments," it was determined whether a deliberate intervention has a specific consequence for the movement of some time series. This approach is useful in applied psychology, such as program evaluation, and a considerable methodological literature has developed (see, for example, Lewis-Beck 1986).

Interrupted time-series analysis has not, however, proved as serviceable in historiometry. If the central aspiration is to confirm or reject nomothetic hypotheses, the intrusion of a single causal event may simply be too particular, too idiosyncratic. As a case in point, generational time series that register the number of European creators will often plunge sharply after the mid-fourteenth century (Simonton 1974)—a setback sometimes attributed to the Black Plague, which struck the continent around 1347. Devastating epidemics may generally depress creative activity in a civilization, yet a great many examples are needed to represent a pervasive law, and it is difficult to provide a substantive interpretation. Perhaps it is simply that the population is lower while the per capita output of creators remains undaunted. Or that the omnipresent prospect of death (as much as one-third of the population succumbed to the disease) thwarts the individual initiative expected in creative thought.

A more disabling liability on inference is that if one event changes the course of a series of events, often more than one discrete event may occur with the studied event. One of those other events, not the one under examination, may be the true cause. Perhaps the only secondary effect of the Black Plague was to provide a setting for Boccaccio's *Decammeron,* final generations of the fourteenth century being so preoccupied with reading these tales that nothing else got done. This confounding of causal effects might be escaped if time-series data are combined with nonsynchronous cross-sectional data (Simonton 1977b). To offer a scientometric illustration, one study strove to detect whether earning academic tenure appreciably depressed the publication rates of psychologists (Bridgwater, Walsh, and Walkenbach 1982). While the tenure decision for any one faculty member would probably coincide with many other discrete events—marriage, a new child, an unusually mild winter, a stock market crash, and so forth—the promotion of almost three hundred associate professors would have few if any extraneous events in common, and those that did would not be likely to affect scholarly output. The larger the number of cross-sectional units and the more variable the dates of the intervention, the more secure the causal inference.

Although this particular mixed design has not yet been gainfully employed in historiometric research proper, another version can be found in Cerulo's inquiry (1984) into how living in a war zone, with bombs and artillery shells exploding all around, affects a musician's compositional style. Not only was a cross-section of composers examined—individuals located in different parts of the globe during World War II—but it was possible to set apart some of the composers in a control group owing to their having been safely tucked away from areas of active combat. The dramatic change in musical creativity was observed only for those in the midst of it all—like Ralph Vaughan Williams, Dmitri Shostakovich, Richard Strauss, Oliver Messiaen, and Béla Bartók.

Hence, for interrupted time-series analyses to make a sound addition, cross-sectional time-series designs should be emphasized, preferably with a control group attached (see Campbell and Stanley 1966; Simonton 1977b).

Continuous Time Series

Another route around the limitations of interrupted time series is to accumulate time series that are sufficiently long that the hypothesized causal event occurs not once but many times. The more often the event is repeated across historical time, the more it would take a rare coincidence for that event to be simultaneous with other events that might support rival causal interpretations. Or better, the supposed causal variable may be assessed on a continuous scale—unlike the nominal scale that characterizes most interrupted time series. We could then compare the magnitude of change in the cause with the size of the shift in the effect after a time lag. This comparison facilitates the rejection of rival explanations insofar as alternative causes would have to display a comparable statistical correspondence. What we would do is convert the analysis of a discrete change in a univariate time series into an analysis of a bivariate time series, the goal being to find that the covariance between the two series eventually maximizes. This test for temporal priority will not work if the causal event studied occurs so rapidly that there is not enough time to show a delay, even with the time-series units of minute dimensions. Historical generalizations are nonetheless plentiful that warrant this type of causal analysis. Typical is the proposition that "as the growth of population accelerated, family tensions increased. So did the incidence of political violence" with a quarter-century lag (Matossian and Schafer 1977, 139).

A specific study will likely clarify the suggested strategy. The focus was on the possibility that the philosophical positions of a given generation may be partly responsive to the political milieu (Simonton 1976g). Because political events presumably affect the early intellectual development of future thinkers, the hypothesis suggests a one-generation lag. According to generational time-series analysis, philosophers who are in their developmental phase in generation g will be in their productive phase in generation $g + 1$, if the unit of analysis is a twenty-year period. Sorokin had a team of experts rate over two thousand thinkers from Western civilization on sixteen ideological positions, tabulating the prominence of each belief in twenty-year intervals, with each representative weighted according to his or her influence on intellectual history. What was necessary was to assess the same generational units on the appearance of various political conditions. The results of correlating two such series, one for civil disturbances (popular revolutions, revolts, and rebellions weighted by length in years, battles or other engagements involved, and whether a government or regime was overthrown) the other for the "ethics of happiness" (a category that includes hedonism, eudemonism, and utilitarianism) are shown in figure 7.3.

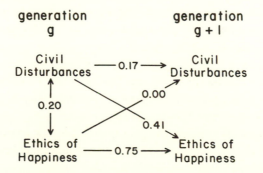

Figure 7.3 Cross-lagged correlation analysis for generational data on the causal relation between civil disturbances and the appearance of philosophers who advocate hedonistic or utilitarian moral systems. The numbers within the arrows are third-order partial correlation coefficients (controlling for third-order time trends). (Taken from Simonton 1984d, figure A.3.)

To guard against a possible source of spuriousness, this analysis was conducted on time-series data first rendered stationary by removing a third-order polynomial time trend. That is, because the data extended 122 generations from 540 B.C. to A.D. 1900, the time-series tended to exhibit an early crest in classical times, a trough in the Dark Ages, and an accelerated surge in recent periods that had yet to peak at the close of the period (Simonton 1976c). All coefficients depicted are therefore third-order partial correlations, yet they represent three distinguishable forms of association. First there is the *synchronous* correlation between the political and the philosophical series across all generations without a lag. Apparently civil disturbances and the ethics of happiness exhibit a slight positive association over intellectual history. Second come the two autocorrelations, which gauge the degree of transhistorical continuity in the two measures. Civil disturbances display only a slight tendency to cluster into contiguous generations, whereas the ethics of happiness exhibits considerable philosophical inertia. Evidently the intellectual zeitgeist does not change overnight, a fact that holds for other philosophical positions (Simonton 1978b).

The most revealing coefficients, nevertheless, are the two *cross-lagged correlations,* one going from civil disturbances at g to the ethics of happiness at $g + 1$, and the other going in the opposite temporal direction. Because the latter is exactly zero, and because the former is over twice the size of the synchronous correlation, it seems that twenty years after a rash of riot, revolt, rebellion, and revolution, a new generation of intellectuals emerges that advocates the pleasure principle as the foundation of moral judgment. In contrast, it would be precarious to argue, according to these results, that an influx of hedonistic or utilitarian philosophers creates an unruly populace after a one-generation incubation period. Our confidence in this inference is reinforced only when we observe that the same pattern appears for other intellectual stances, whether ethical, epistemological, ontological, or sociological (Simonton 1976g). Ideas are more influenced by politics than the other way around. Marx claimed in the preface to the second edition of *Capitol* that he had turned Hegel on his head by making material conditions, not thoughts, the agents of history. The cited investigation carried Marx's acrobatic trick one degree farther.

The comparison of cross-lagged and synchronous correlations between continuous time series can be valuable in treating many other substantive problems. The strategy has been applied to comprehend the causal link between economic investment and technological invention (Schmookler 1966, 127); the need for achievement in children's readers and per capita patent production (deCharms and Mueller 1962); empiricism and skepticism in intellectual history (Simonton 1978c); political fragmentation and ideological diversity (Simonton 1976d); war and scientific productivity (Simonton 1976b, 1976e); discursive and presentational modes of creativity (Simonton 1975c); and major and minor figures in the history of civilization (Simonton 1988c). At the same time, because this inspection of correlations represents a primitive procedure, it can be considered only an initial step. One possible refinement is *Granger causality,* which specifies that "a variable *X* 'causes' another variable *Y,* if by incorporating the past history of *X* one can improve the prediction of *Y* over a prediction based solely on the history of *Y* alone" (Freeman 1983, 327–28). Two methodologies consistent with the spirit of Granger causality have proved applicable in historiometric work, namely dynamic models and transfer functions.

Dynamic models. In considering univariate time-series analysis, we noted how it may be considered a stochastic rendition of difference equations, the discrete analogue of differential equations. Given that there is no requirement that difference equations be univariate, it seems reasonable to ask whether a stochastic parallel exists here as well. In fact, econometricians often take advantage of such multivariate "dynamic" models. In a dynamic equation, a dependent variable is expressed as a function of one or more autoregressive terms (lagged endogenous variables) side by side with contemporaneous and lagged exogenous variables. A specific case is given in table 7.3 where the dependent variable is a log-transformed count of the number of scientists, philosophers, authors, and composers, weighted by differential eminence, tabulated into 127 consecutive twenty-year periods from 700 B.C. to A.D. 1839 (Simonton 1975e). Evidently, creativity at generation *g* is a function of creativity in the two previous generations, *g* − 1 and *g* − 2, and political fragmentation, imperial instability, and political instability all in

Table 7.3 *Time-Series Analysis: Weighted Discursive Creativity at Generation* g

Independent variables	*b*	*SE*	*t*	*p*
Discursive creativity (*g* − 1)	.36335	.0852	4.266	.00004
Discursive creativity (*g* − 2)	.36533	.0834	4.379	.00003
Political fragmentation (*g* − 1)	.01370	.0056	2.423	.01701
Imperial instability (*g* − 1)	.34403	.1192	2.887	.00467
Political instability (*g* − 1)	−.02247	.0109	−2.067	.04104
War (*g*)	.00068	.0034	.205	.83790
Persecution (*g*)	.05524	.0327	1.688	.09418
Time	.00226	.0019	1.167	.24576
Second generation	−.20855	.1773	−1.176	.24193
Third generation	.00581	.1780	.033	.97401
Fourth generation	.05711	.1767	.323	.74716
Fifth generation	−.19033	.1757	−1.083	.28114
Intercept (first generation)	.6164	.226	2.729	

Note. Adapted from study of Western civilization in Simonton (1975e, table 1). Copyright 1975 by American Psychological Association. Used by permission.

The analysis is based on generations 4 to 127 because two observations were lost in creating the lagged functions and another was lost in executing the generalized least-squares data transformation. Therefore there are 111 *df* for the significance tests. Durbin-Watson statistic is 2.09 and the squared multiple correlation R^2 = .72.

generation $g - 1$, plus several insignificant effects, namely war and persecution in the contemporaneous generation g, and the control variables of time and dating-bias intercepts.

This complex equation is essentially a multiple-regression analysis of time-series data. The introduction of variables at $g - 1$ and $g - 2$ to predict changes at g is an explicit recognition of the temporal priority of these variables. Not only are these lagged terms consistent with hypotheses specifying developmental period influences in the acquisition of personal creative potential, but previous scrutiny of the cross-lagged and synchronous correlations verified that the lagged effects were justified empirically. Creative development in childhood and adolescence is indeed influenced by the availability of role models as well as by certain political conditions, some conducive, others inhibitory. Because each of these lagged effects is estimated while controlling for all other variables in the equation—including those methodological—tests for direct covariance can be part of the whole process, yielding causal influences of improved elegance.

The incorporation of lagged variables is by no means confined to continuous time series. The acknowledgement of temporal priority may be accomplished in the multiple-regression analysis of cross-sectional data operating under an individual-generational design. In the study of 2,012 philosophers mentioned in chapter 2 (Simonton 1976f), the unit of analysis is the individual thinker, and the dependent variable is the comparative illustriousness of those thinkers. Some of the independent variables are also defined totally at the individual level, namely the breadth, extremism, and consistency of their respective philosophical systems, as well as the year of birth (as a control variable). Another set of predictors entails those variables that require that the philosophers' beliefs be contrasted with the intellectual zeitgeist: Representativeness gauges how well the thinkers' ideas represented the dominating views of their day, modernity concerns how well those ideas comply with twentieth-century notions, and precursiveness regards whether the philosophers' ideas were more compatible with the preceding $(g - 1)$ or succeeding $(g + 1)$ generation. Finally, purely aggregate indicators recorded the conditions that prevailed when the individual was in his or her developmental period—role-model availability, ideological diversity, political fragmentation, imperial instability, political instability, and war intensity. Because the thinker is assigned to generation g, temporal priority was achieved by placing the generational time-series one unit back to generation $g - 1$. Individual, generational, and individual-generational variables were then placed in a single multiple-regression equation.

Individual-generational analysis with lagged aggregate variables has immense potential, especially in deciphering how the zeitgeist shapes the development of historical personalities (see also Simonton 1977c, 1984a).

Transfer functions. The second approach is to employ methods largely associated with Box and Jenkins (1976). The procedure begins by rendering all time series stationary through skilled differencing and then running the series through stochastic filters that leave only "white-noise" data behind; the cross-correlation of two time series is not attempted until the data exhibit no trends and no serial dependencies (whether from autoregressive or moving-average processes). By comparing the cross-correlations much as discussed previously, a *transfer function* may be built that specifies one variable as a function of one or more predictor variables (Norpoth 1986). Considerable debate persists about the best way to implement the various procedures (for example, Feige and Pearce 1979; Nelson and Schwert 1982). In the process of prewhitening the data, relations between two series may vanish, even when an association was artificially inserted using Monte Carlo simulation.

Nevertheless, with or without modification, this approach to fixing temporal priority has found application in several historiometric inquiries. Martindale and Uemura (1983) have shown how stylistic changes in German music were a contemporaneous and lagged function of changes in the British, Italian, and French traditions (see also Martindale 1984b). Tetlock (1985) examined how the integrative complexity of foreign policy rhetoric for the Soviet Union and the United States was a function of both internal and external conditions, including the rhetoric of the "big-power" rival. Hepworth and West (1988) exploited this strategy to confirm a prediction of the frustration-aggression hypothesis that the lynching of blacks in the American South was a response to downturns in the rural economy.

All tests for temporal priority using continuous time series require long sequences of observations. Without exception, short series mean unstable hypothesis tests and undependable parameter estimates—no matter what analytical strategy is adopted. When the historical record fails to support the reliable and valid quantification of variables, one can turn to the cross-sectional dimension. The fewer units we can collate through time, the more we may gather across separate analytical units. In the extreme case, we may have observations at only two points in time on a multitude of cross-sectional units. Then we could apply the techniques devised for two-wave panel data (Kenney 1975). For instance, in the Cox data (1926), the cross-lagged correlation between IQ from age 0 to 16 and data reliability from 17 to 26 is significantly larger than the reverse cross-lagged correlation from data reliability for 0–16 and IQ for 17–26 (Simonton 1976a). The implication is that if a genius is very precocious in the early years, the biographical information about the later years becomes more accurate. Other examples of this sort of analysis may be found in the work on the relation between achievement motivation and economic prosperity (for example, Frey 1984). Because this analytical tool may prove to be more useful in the future, researchers should be forewarned that the proper methodology is far more complex than first meets the eye (for example, Mayer and Carroll 1987) and should not be applied without sound, substantive ideas and adequate controls for contaminating variables.

The two principles of direct covariance and temporal priority are the sine qua non of causal inference. To draw the safest possible conclusions, the decision rules should operate in concert, for neither can secure a causal relation alone. If two variables remain correlated no matter how much we control for supposed contaminating influences, we can infer only a lack of causal spuriousness. The direction of cause and effect must come from the second criterion. Likewise, temporal priority in the absence of an adequate consideration of potential sources of spuriousness suggests only causal direction and is noncommittal as to actual causality. For example, fluctuations in X might indeed precede changes in Y only because a third variable Z affects both of these variables with differing degrees of causal delay (Kenny and Campbell 1984). Such complications seem to endorse Winthrop Mackworth Praed's ([1825] 1953, 280) precaution that

Events are writ by History's pen:
  Though causes are too much to care for:—
Fame talks about the where and when,
  While folly asks the why and wherefore.

No wonder, then, that so many behavioral scientists prefer the laboratory experiment over correlational analyses. By exerting the human will into the causal sequence, in the form of an active manipulation of the independent variables, judgments of cause and effect seem more assured. Yet this inference is not as secure as it first appears. Too often in the experimental literature one-way causality is surmised from one-way manipulations. If the experimenter manipulates X and measures a corresponding change in Y, all that observation ensures is that the independent variable *can* cause the dependent variable but does not indicate whether Y can also cause X. Perhaps the latter circumstance is more crucial in reality, but because Y is less easily manipulated than X in the artificial setting of the laboratory, a one-way causal inference is mistakenly introduced into the empirical literature. For example, it is much more easy to manipulate the perceived similarity of another person and then assess how that affects prospective liking than to manipulate how much two people like each other and then assess how that affects how similar they perceive each other to be. In everyday living "love is blind" may be far more causally crucial than "birds of a feather flock together," but laboratory experiments are not adept at weighing the comparative causal impact of the contrary arrows.

Whatever the assets of experimental inquiries, historiometricians must deal with what they have—correlational data. The researcher must consequently fall back on the best devices currently available for assessing causality under less than optimal circumstances. Owing to the insufficiency of techniques, these ventures must always be pursued with modesty and restraint.

8 **Refinements**

In the last two chapters we have surveyed the standard means to test nomothetic hypotheses in historiometry. The awesome inventory of analytical devices represents only the basics. In this last methodological chapter, we must spend time on three broad dilemmas that would perplex a sensitive researcher: First, whether reliance on linear and additive models is overly restrictive; second, whether a confirmatory, hypothesis-testing modus operandi should be standard; and third, how to weigh properly the comparative importance of descriptive and inferential statistics. These questions reside somewhere in the shadows of every project. They also raise subsidiary issues, including the consequences of quasi-interval scales, missing values, multicollinearity, and violations of statistical assumptions.

Simple versus Complex Functions

With no notable exceptions, the methods treated in the preceding two chapters presume *linear* relations, that is, we must suppose that the scatterplot describing how two variables are related is best fit by a straight line. A further restriction is that not only are all independent variables linearly related to the dependent variable, but their combined contributions are *additive*. Each variable is simply multiplied by a constant and then all the products summed. In no case are two variables multiplied or taken to a higher power than unity; with the minor exception of the trend analysis mentioned in chapter 6.

Anyone with introductory training in the natural sciences realizes how rare linear and additive relations can be. In Newton's famous law of gravitation, $F = gm_1m_2/d^2$, where m_1 and m_2 are the masses of the two bodies (for example, earth and sun), d is the distance between them and g is the universal gravitational constant. That the two masses must be multiplied means that the function is certainly not additive; this assertion is rendered more emphatic by the need to divide by the distance between two bodies (that is, between their centers of gravity). Furthermore, distance enters the equation in quadratic rather than linear form. If the gravitational force between two bodies of constant mass is plotted as a function of the distance between them, we cannot possibly obtain a straight line, both because we are dealing with a reciprocal and because the denominator of that quotient has an exponent unequal to one. So Newton's formula, though far simpler than what graces the pages of contemporary physics journals, is already more complex than what we have handled up to now. Assuming that behavioral phenomena are at least as complex as natural phenomena, we must go beyond simplistic, linear, and additive functions.

Curvilinear Relations

The notion of moderation in all things goes back at least as far as Aristotle's *Nicomachean Ethics,* where it is argued that the golden mean must be sought between two extremes, that virtue is the midpoint between two opposing vices. A modern variation is the potential encounter with the law of diminishing returns, whereby at some point ever more investment brings proportionately less advantage, the costs gaining faster than the rewards. These articles of wisdom share the belief that two phenomena may not be linearly, nor even monotonically related. Additionally, it is not rare for modern scholars to propound theories that imply curvilinear relations between variables of central interest. Toynbee (1946) argued that the reason why some cultures thrived to become glorious civilizations while others had their development arrested was that it takes a "moderate challenge" to stimulate the human species to innovative action. Davies (1962), a sociologist, put forward a J-curve theory of revolution whereby a populace is more likely to revolt *not* when conditions are horrid but when there is a setback in a long-term trend toward enhanced well-being. Psychologists are fond of unearthing curvilinear relations, especially U-shaped curves, for a diversity of phenomena. The presence of curvilinear relations may, in fact, represent a cross-cultural universal of human nature (Sheils 1975).

When such a possibility arises, investigators must first ask whether they can specify the exact form of the nonlinear function. This specification is best achieved by explicitly transforming an underlying process into differential equations that, when solved, produce the appropriate function. This is what was done to obtain the curve in figure 5.4, which gives the predicted annual productivity over a career according to an information-processing model of the creative process (Simonton 1984b). Nonlinear estimation programs then yield the parameters of the model, bypassing altogether measures of linear association. From time to time, nonetheless, the differential equations will generate a curve that remains open to treatment by linear statistics, with only modest adjustments. An example was provided earlier in the form of the exponential function, a nonlinear function that includes the solution to a simple differential equation that states that the amount of change in a variable at any instant (that is, dy/dt) is proportional to the variable's magnitude at that instant ($cy,$ where c is a positive or negative constant). Not only can exponential functions be made linear by applying the logarithmic transformation, but inversely, a logarithmic curve can be rendered linear by taking the exponential. Other data transformations are at times recommended (for example, arcsine, square root, reciprocal, probit, and logit) that also serve to make curvilinear but monotonic functions linear. Although these manipulations will not always have a theoretical basis, it may be a small price to pay to keep statistics linear.

The foregoing responses, while workable, are far from ubiquitous. Often the differential equations are not sufficiently tractable to yield an explicit function. The solution may be acquired by numerical methods only, which do not lend themselves to such facile curve fitting. More common still is the circumstance where theory does not suffice to derive a precise curve, no matter how calculated. All the behavioral scientist is willing to assert is that the relation is described by a U-curve, an inverted-U curve, a J-curve, or some other roughly hewn proclamation—a state of vague prediction that actually makes analysis simpler. When treating a trend analysis of univariate time series, we observed how trends of whatever complexity can be approximated to any desired criterion of accuracy by polynomial time functions. The curve for creative productivity shown in figure 5.4 can be closely rendered by the quadratic function $p(t) = b_0 + b_1 t + b_2 t^2$; the addition of a cubic term (t^3) offers a better correspondence still (Simonton 1988b)—a specific case of equation 6.1.

The remarkable thing about these polynomial functions is that they are dispatched without incident by mere least-squares multiple regression. A bivariate curvilinear function has been converted into a linear and additive multivariate function. The coefficient of each term is linear, and the contribution of all terms are added together in an unadorned manner. The forbidding curvilinear relation between just two variables has been translated into a multiple-regression equation where one variable is an additive linear function of several variables, all of which were generated from a single variable by squaring, cubing, and so forth. When regression weights are selected to maximize the fit between predicted and observed scores, the algorithm cannot know that one variable is present more than once and in more than one form. However, the complexity has only been shifted to a more tractable position, not obliterated. Calculating partial regression coefficients *is* more complicated than computing correlation coefficients.

Earlier we mentioned findings based on this solution, which are founded mostly on quadratic functions of the form

$$y(x) = b_0 + b_1 x + b_2 x^2 \qquad (8.1)$$

where y is the dependent variable and x the independent variable. Actually, functions like equation 8.1 are usually estimated with many more variables included, such as methodological controls, but this does not alter the mode of analysis. Once the independent variable has been entered as separate linear and squared terms, the regression coefficients can describe an impressive diversity of curves, such as the inverted backward-J curve shown in figure 5.2 (Simonton 1980d), the U-shaped curves between monarchal eminence and morality (Simonton 1984g), and between presidential greatness and dogmatism (Simonton 1986g) (chapter 5). Strictly inverted-U shaped curves have been found between certain compositional characteristics and the differential success of 105 works by Beethoven (Simonton 1987b), while yet another type of function, the J-curve proper, is graphed in figure 8.1 (Simonton 1983c). This shows how presidential dogmatism, or idealistic inflexibility, varies as a function of the level of formal education achieved by each chief executive.

No matter what the concrete application of equation 8.1, the crest or trough of the curve will appear at $x = -b_1/2b_2$. Whether this represents a maximum or minimum depends on the sign of b_2, the regression coefficient for the quadratic term: if positive we have a low point, and if negative we have a high point. When x is in mean-deviation form (that is, it was centered on its mean before generating the quadratic term), the precise shape of the curve can be read directly from the coefficients of equation 8.1. For example, if $b_1 = 0$, so that the linear term can be totally ignored, we have either a U-shaped curve (if $b_2 > 0$) or an inverted-U (if $b_2 < 0$), that intercepts the y-axis at b_0. When $b_1 \neq 0$, then one arm or the other of the U must be lengthened to capture the linear relation. Thus with both coefficients positive a J curve results like that in figure 8.1.

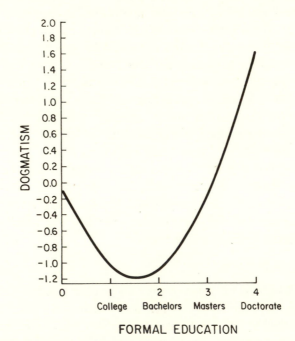

Figure 8.1 The relation between dogmatism and level of formal education for thirty-three U.S. presidents. (Taken from Simonton 1983c, figure 2)

Obviously, if theory and mathematics permit specification of the exact functional relation, reliance on these rudimentary polynomials leaves much to be desired. Nevertheless, these functions should not be denigrated. Scientific advance begins with overly simplistic functions, after which more elaborate descriptions emerge. Given the primitive nature of current psychology, we must start by learning when linear relations do well and when we must go beyond them for a precise account of phenomena. Once the correct curves have been agreed upon, the theoretician has a secure base from which to construct a mathematical model. Thus, it was 150 years after Quetelet ([1835] 1968) first demonstrated the curvilinear relation between age and creative achievement—a curve replicated dozens of times in the intervening years—that someone could risk setting up a formal model (Simonton 1984b, 1989a). Similarly, the conceptually rich and empirically precise mathematics that honors the exact sciences emerged only after physical phenomena were accurately described by empirical formulae. While chemistry is now a discipline of theory-driven equations, at the time that Mendeléev wrote the first volume of his classic text *The Principles of Chemistry*, utterly empirical polynomials cropped up dozens of times (Mellor [1912] 1955, 276).

On the other hand, the dire need for a precise description of historical regularities must not be taken as carte blanche to increase polynomials, introducing independent variables automatically in power functions of any order. Two complications usually spring from promiscuous usage. First, polynomials beyond the second order often implant severe multicollinear problems given that all odd-power terms highly correlate, as do all even-power terms. Although various tactics exist for alleviating the damage done by these strongly associated predictors, such as the use of orthogonal polynomials or mean-deviation scores, these responses may not completely obliterate the difficulties in real data (compare Smith and Sasaki 1979). Second, it is easy to overfit polynomials to data, and frequently the terms beyond the quadratic can become slaves to noise in the measurements. Indeed, the quadratic polynomial of equation 8.1 illustrates itself: If one were to plot the likelihood of finding something scientifically valuable as a function of the order of the polynomial, there would probably emerge a single-peaked curve with the optimum at the second-order function. Quadratic equations may represent the golden mean between linear functions that understate the genuine intricacy of the phenomena and higher-order polynomials that are intellectually indulgent.

Interaction Effects

Whenever promulgators of historical generalizations wish to hedge their bets, they can resort to the qualifier "depending on the circumstances." It is possible to argue that a positive link between two events under one set of conditions might change to a negative link in another context. This may seem exasperating to psychologists searching for simplicity in the formulation of behavioral laws, yet there is nothing inherently unscientific about the practice. For example, the association between temperature and the rate of chemical reaction may change according to whether a particular catalyst is present. So long as the proposition is couched in formal, even mathematical terms, it can earn the status of a universal pattern. In Newton's equation for gravitational force, the two masses operate in a *multiplicative* rather than an additive manner; if either m_1 or m_2 equals zero, the product is zero, and so gravitational attraction vanishes no matter how ponderous the remaining mass may be.

Such complications can be handled in a multiple regression framework by inserting product terms. If y is a function of x_1 and x_2, but besides their additive contributions x_1 and x_2 also interact to produce effects on y that cannot be explained in terms of either acting alone while the other is constant, then we can create the product terms x_1x_2 by multiplying the two independent variables, which is introduced into the equation as a *third* independent variable. Ordinary least-squares estimation may then be applied to the equation

$$y = b_0 + b_1x_1 + b_2x_2 + b_3x_1x_2 \tag{8.2}$$

Here the unstandardized partial regression coefficients b_1 and b_2 assess the additive impacts of x_1 and x_2 separately, whereas b_3 gauges their joint effect. If $b_3 =$ 0, the additive model is vindicated, and there is no reason to confound the causal account. But if b_3 is significantly nonzero, then a full description of how x_1 and x_2 affect y must include a discussion of their joint contribution. Because the combined effect of the two variables in equation 8.2 is perfectly symmetric, we can express the multiplicative function two ways: Either we can say that the effect of x_1 on y varies according to the value of x_2, or we can say that the effect of x_2 on y varies according to x_1. Which expression we favor depends more on substantive considerations than on mathematics. For example, if y is a behavior, such as an act of creativity or leadership, x_1 is a personality trait or biographical attribute, such as intelligence or birth order, and x_2 is a situational characteristic, such as the sociocultural milieu or political zeitgeist, it may be better to assert that the consequence of x_1 for y depends on x_2. We would thus be maintaining that the contextual variable x_2 serves as a *moderator*—that it moderates the relation between y and x_1. Alternatively, it may happen that x_1 is a variable of appreciable theoretical interest, whereas x_2 is merely a control variable inserted to guard against possible artifacts, in which case we can talk about how the causal impact of the substantive variable hinges on the status of the methological variable.

We have once more overcome the obstacle of linear and additive multiple regression. As for curvilinear relations, we defined a new variable that is no more than a transformation of variables in the equation at the start. Complexity of causal effects is translated into a multiplicity of causal terms. Equation 8.1 has two independent variables for only one measured, just as equation 8.2 has three independent variables for only two measured. In fact, curvilinear relations can be constructively viewed as special cases of interaction effects, representing the occurrence where a variable interacts with itself in the prediction of the criterion. A quadratic polynomial like that in equation 8.1 may be read as follows: The impact of x on y is moderated by x, signifying that the slope is not constant but rather itself varies according to the magnitude of the independent variable.

Nevertheless, interaction effects are far more general than curvilinear effects in the measurement scales that can participate in the generation of product terms. Tests for curvilinear functions demand that all variables be assessed on a continuous scale, preferably interval or ratio, though ordinal measurement will do. It is illogical to look for curvilinear relations in a variable nominally scaled, for the numbers themselves have no substantive meaning and usually assume zero-one values incapable of nonlinear functions. The multiplicative terms, in contrast, are much more catholic and invite nominal scales. In equation 8.2, for instance, either x_1 or x_3, or even both, could be dichotomous variables with complete impunity. Hence, we enjoy the freedom to examine three varieties of interaction effects: Categorical-by-categorical, which involve solely nominal scales; categorical-by-continuous, which multiply dummy variables by ordinal, interval, or ratio variables; and continuous-by-continuous, the kind that includes curvilinear relations as a particular example. Furthermore, just as in polynomial regression nothing prevents us from inserting cubic and higher-order powers into the equation, there is no formal reason why the product terms must contain only a pair of variables. Nothing stops us from defining triple (or three-way) and even higher-order interaction effects if given sufficient reason.

Categorical-by-categorical interactions. In our culture, there is a common perception that in literary creativity, poetry is primarily a preoccupation of youth, whereas prose writing demands more maturity in competence and interest. It is this life-span developmental slant that means some poets can die young without sacrificing a durable reputation—Byron at 36, Shelley at 30, Keats at 26, and Chatterton at 18. Even poets who live to old age will usually produce their most widely appreciated poems in the first decade or so of their career. Wordsworth lived to become an octogenarian, but his *Lyrical Ballads* came out in his twenty-eighth year (in collaboration with twenty-six-year-old Coleridge), and his career as a poet was essentially over by his forty-fourth year when *The Excursion* was published. In contrast, novelists, essayists, critics, and historians are seldom allowed to die so young. Fielding wrote *Tom Jones* at forty-two, Bacon his essays between the ages of thirty-six and sixty-four, Johnson the *Lives of the Poets* in his seventies, and Gibbon his *Decline and Fall* between the ages of thirty-nine and fifty-one. It might well be that these examples are exceptional, or at least that these differences are limited to English literature. There might also be something intrinsic to the cognitive and motivational processes that underlie the construction of poetry that gives it a more youthful fascination than the framing of prose (Simonton 1988b). If so, the difference would count as a cross-cultural and transhistorical universal.

In a test of this possibility, a sample of 420 creators was drawn who represented the leading figures of the world's principal literatures (Simonton 1975a). After determining the age at which these individuals had produced their most acclaimed work, which served as the dependent variable, dummy variables were created that registered whether the masterwork was poetry or prose. In addition, categorical variables were defined that recorded whether the literary luminary came from the Western, Near Eastern, or Far Eastern traditions, inclusive categories that suffice to test for cross-cultural invariance. Product terms were then generated by multiplying the two sets of variables by each other, these multiplicative terms checking for the interaction whereby the age difference between poetry and prose varies according to literary tradition. Because numerous control variables were also introduced (including life span), the equation had a total of twenty-three variables. The result confirmed expectation. The average age for producing a poetic masterpiece is thirty-nine, that for a prose masterwork forty-three, a contrast that transcends contrasts in the Western, Near Eastern, and Far Eastern civilizations. None of the product terms gauging two-way interactions had statistically significant regression coefficients. A peak-age gap of four years may not seem great, but it does qualify as a universal. The difference also helps to explain another curious fact demonstrated using the same interaction terms: Poets do die younger than prose authors, by a half-dozen years.

Categorical-by-continuous interactions. Categorical-by-categorical variable interaction effects are not frequent in historiometrics, however prominent those effects may be in experimental psychology. Nominal scales are themselves relatively infrequent, and when two such scales appear in the same equation, there is rarely a theoretical justification for producing multiplicative terms. Categorical-by-continuous variable interactions are slightly more common. The predominant usage of this form is for testing whether a nominal scale has transhistorical relevance. In the study just mentioned, the age difference was shown to be constant not only across three civilization areas but equally through historical time (Simonton 1975a). To show this invariance, the dummy variable noting the type of creative product was multiplied by the date that the literary figure flourished. The personal age at which the best composition emerged did not change across two millennia, and the developmental hiatus between poetic and prose productions did not significantly change either—providing added strength to the position that the contrast is rooted in something fundamental about the human mind (see also Lehman 1962).

Another application of mixed-scale interactions occurs when both variables constituting the multiplicative term are methodological, as part of a search for artifacts. For instance, in studying how the production of melodic material changed over the careers of ten classical composers, there was concern over invasion by dating biases (Simonton 1977a). We mentioned before how for yearly data, historians may prefer assigning dates that end in 0 (Simonton 1980b), a dating bias that becomes insubstantial only when the time-series units are twenty years long (Simonton 1975e, 1988c; Ting 1986). However, the thematic output of the composers was tabulated in five-year age periods, an interval that may be too close to yearly series. Consequently, a dummy variable was defined that equaled 1 if the age period contained a year ending in zero and equaled 0 if otherwise. Even if this dummy control variable turned out to be unnecessary, given that the dating bias was nil, it could be that the bias is substantial only for the earlier composers for whom the dating of compositions, especially the earlier works, is often as speculative as the dating assigned to Shakespeare's plays. Accordingly, a term was introduced by multiplying the dummy variable by the date of the onset of the five-year age period, yielding a date-×-dating-bias interaction. Luckily, despite some tendency for the dating bias to become more prominent for earlier historical periods, this trend was neither statistically significant nor substantial enough for concern. By the criterion of final-integer preferences, the compositions of Bach and Handel can be assigned to half-decade age intervals with only slightly less precision than those of Brahms and Debussy.

Continuous-by-continuous interactions. Tests for transhistorical invariance, whether the effects be theoretically or methodologically derived, can be conducted on ordinal, interval, and ratio measures besides nominal scales. This demands only the definition of continuous-by-continuous variable interaction terms. For example, the multiple-regression equation that predicts presidential greatness on the basis of six variables was shown to display no change in validity from Washington through Carter. This demonstration required multiplicative terms for the three continuous variables (years in office, years of war, and intellectual brilliance) as well as the three categorical variables (assassination, scandal, and being war hero). Historical time was gauged by the year of first inauguration, although the same results occurred when birth year or presidential order was substituted. Given that the regression coefficients for the six two-way interaction terms were, for all practical purposes, zero, the transhistorical invariance of the equation was proved. Being a wartime president was no less important in Lincoln's day than it was in FDR's time, just as having a scandalous administration harmed Grant's reputation no less than Harding's (Simonton 1986h, 1988d).

A second illustration shows how statistically significant interactions can obtain for a theoretically important phenomenon. The study concerns an individual-×-situational interaction effect, namely how the relation between a president's veto behavior and his inflexibility is moderated by the political circumstance in which he must legislate (Simonton 1987c). The unit of analysis was the Congress rather than the administration in order to capture better shifts in the political conditions. One of the veto criteria was how often a chief executive suffered the ignominy of having his vetoes overturned by Congress, an event strongly associated (negatively) with the percentage of the congressional membership that represents the president's own party. Party control, however, also interacts with the president's inflexibility, using the scores given in table 3.10. This multiplicative relation has been christened the "Johnson-Wilson effect" after the two chief executives, Andrew Johnson and Woodrow Wilson, who best exemplify its operation. When the president is extremely flexible, the connection between party control and veto overrides essentially vanishes. A flexible executive can bargain, negotiate, and compromise so that he need not enter into a confrontation with opponents on Capitol Hill. By comparison, when a president scores very high on inflexibility, he lacks this maneuver, thereby becoming vulnerable to how much support he can command in Congress.

The Johnson-Wilson effect should establish that interaction effects are well worth searching for. The inventory of historical generalizations contains many other multiplicative relations as well (see, for example, Derks 1989; Simonton 1990d; L. H. Stewart 1977; Suedfeld and Piedrahita 1984; Tetlock, Hannum, and Micheletti 1984; Winter 1987b). Even so, as in the case of curvilinear functions, the psychologist must show restraint. For an equation of any size, the number of product terms can become intimidating. Care is especially advisable when curvilinear functions and interaction effects are combined in the same analysis.

Both Combined

If both curvilinear and interaction effects can each be addressed by generating new variables as products of old variables, nothing prevents us from multiplying the polynomials of one variable with the linear form of another variable to yield still higher-order terms that gauge nonlinear and nonadditive effects simultaneously. In fact, this further analytical aspect can prove quite useful. For example, suppose that the relation between two variables is thought to be curvilinear, with a single maximum or minimum, but the precise shape of the curve is believed to differ for two distinct subpopulations. Each term in the quadratic polynomial could then be multiplied by the zero-one dummy variable that codes group membership. One of those product terms would involve a linear continuous variable and a categorical variable. The other term, in contrast, would entail multiplying the categorical variable by the squared continuous variable. This second product again tests for a difference between the two groups, only this time the emphasis is on the quadratic component. The analysis has become more complicated, yet the basic interpretive principle is unchanged.

Thus, in a re-analysis of the Cox (1926) data, the question asked was whether ranked eminence is a curvilinear function of formal education (Simonton 1976a). Besides defining a quadratic polynomial, a dichotomous variable recorded whether the genius was a creator or a leader given that academic training might have rather different ramifications for creativity than for leadership. In figure 8.2 the results (after controlling for other factors) are graphed. For the 109

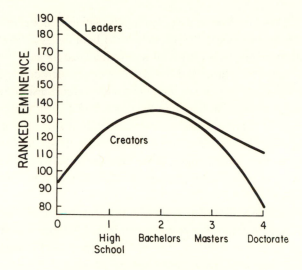

FORMAL EDUCATION

Figure 8.2 The relation between ranked eminence and level of formal education for the 192 creators and 109 leaders in the Cox sample. Source: Simonton 1983c, figure 1.

leaders, the function is nearly linear and strongly negative, whereas for the 192 creators a curvilinear inverted-J function holds, with a peak somewhere in the latter portion of undergraduate education. This crest is almost exactly in the same place as the trough for the curve relating presidential dogmatism and formal education, as depicted in figure 8.1. Indeed, the two curves are mirror images, as reflected off a horizontal line. This inversion is consistent with the negative association between creativity and dogmatism (Simonton 1983c).

The near-perfect horizontal reflection might seem amazing when we consider that the independent variable in these two examples, formal education, has been assessed on a crude rank-category scale, one far more ordinal than interval in nature. The demarcations for the abscissa in figures 8.1 and 8.2 are only ordinally, not intervally, equivalent. Nevertheless, if a nonmonotonic function exists between two variables, that curvilinear relation will hold should the variables degrade into such rank-category scales. In short, owing to fundamental topological constraints, tests for nonmonotonic curvilinearity are robust under distortions of the variables' measurements (Simonton 1984d, appendix B). In the present situation, the squeezings and stretchings are too minimal to obscure the basic shape of the nonlinear function.

If the comparisons get too complicated, the investigator might simplify the analysis by estimating the functions separately for all groups of interest, dispensing with the dummies and recording group assignment along with the corresponding interaction terms. Rather than calculate one multiple-regression equation for the 301 geniuses in the Cox data, the sample may be split into two subsamples, creators and leaders, and then fit the polynomials in the absence of any interaction terms. Despite the simplicity, this concession is both inelegant and inefficient: Parameters are more precisely estimated when calculated for an $N = 301$ than for the two subsamples two-thirds and one-third as large; such divide-and-conquer tactics are unwieldy insofar as they do not provide a direct test of the functional contrasts between groups. Further, investigators would do well to accustom themselves to combining curvilinear and interaction effects in a single multiple-regression equation, since often no choice exists but to confront the equation as a whole. This necessity appears when changes in the curvilinear functions are examined as the moderator variable itself changes *continuously,* as is evident in the next study (Simonton 1984a).

The curves shown in figures 8.1 and 8.2 suggest that formal education may be a mixed blessing in creative development; minimal training is clearly mandatory to have the prerequisite knowledge and expertise, yet too much academic inculcation may induce excessive conformity to established disciplinary perspectives (Simonton 1988e, chap. 5). An analogous trade-off may complicate the use of predecessors as models of achievement in one's chosen field. A balance must be struck between refusing to stand on the shoulders of these giants and succumbing to blind imitation. To confirm this possibility, the 772 Western painters and sculptors who have made artistic history since the Renaissance were assessed on how many predecessors they took as paragons C as well as the (mean) age difference G between each artist and his or her paragon(s). The differential eminence A of these artists was predicted by the formula

$$A = 16 + 12C + 0.15G + 0.23CG + 0.001G^2 - 0.001CG^2 \qquad (8.3)$$

This is a regular multiple-regression equation (with extraneous control variables omitted), and so all the coefficients are unstandardized partial coefficients. The count of paragons and the age gap are both entered as main-effect (linear) variables, but the age gap variable is also squared to produce a second-order polynomial in G. This quadratic function was introduced to test whether there was an optimal historical distance between two artists that maximized the positive influence of the older master upon his or her successor. More critically, linear and quadratic forms of G were each multiplied by the paragon count to discern whether the supposed nonmonotonic function varies according to the number of predecessors emulated. Consistent with expectation, equation 8.3 shows that artistic eminence is a curvilinear, concave downward function of the artist-paragon age gap. A typical situation where the artist admires three models (that is, the average number of paragons is 2.6) (see figure 8.3).

The precise placement of the high point of this single-peaked function was contingent on the number of paragons, as evidenced by the fact that all interaction terms in equation 8.3 (namely, CG and CG^2) were statistically significant, like the rest of the coefficients shown. A proper appreciation of how this maximum point

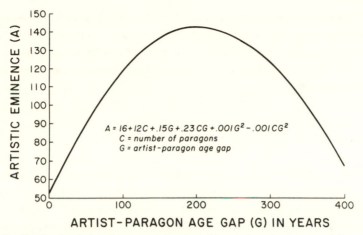

$$A = 16 + 12C + .15G + .23CG + .001G^2 - .001CG^2$$
$$C = number\ of\ paragons$$
$$G = artist\text{-}paragon\ age\ gap$$

Figure 8.3 Predicted artistic eminence as a function of the number of paragons and the mean artist-paragon age gap for the typical case of three paragons. Curve based on equation 8.3 and holds for 772 Western painters and sculptors. (Taken from Simonton 1984a, figure 1. Copyright 1984 by American Psychological Association. Used by permission.)

shifts across paragon count demands that we take the partial derivative of A with respect to G for equation 8.3, set the result equal to zero, and solve for G.

$$G = \frac{75 + 115c}{C - 1} \tag{8.4}$$

This equation indicates the optimal age gap between artist and paragons, given a certain number of paragons. For example, starting with the average situation where an artist has three emulated predecessors, substituting $C = 3$ into equation 8.4 yields $G = 210$ years, the peak shown in figure 8.3. Among those artists who modeled themselves after three past masters, the most famous were those whose models had been born over two centuries earlier. In line with the notion of a trade-off, when C increases, G decreases. Hence, the most paragons or standards of excellence claimed for any artist was seventeen, which when put into equation 5.2, produces an optimum at 127 years. If an artist has fewer sources of inspiration, they must be historically more distant to avoid the temptation of imitation. In fact, in the extreme situation, when a painter or sculptor relies on only one paragon from the past, Equation 8.3 degenerates into the linear equation $A = 28 + 0.38G$, and consequently, equation 8.4 becomes undefined. The more extensive the age gap is, the better it will be for the corresponding artist.

Combining curvilinear and interaction effects into a unified equation can clearly support historiometric inferences of considerable power. The analyses can become involved, given the mathematical possibility of generating both polynomials and interactions of any order whatsoever. In addition, abundant higher-order product terms can again lead to complicated multicollinearity. Consequently, such subtleties should not be entered into without some theoretical expectation. In other words, the methodology works best in a confirmatory mode, when the goal is to test hypotheses. Exploratory inquiries in which sundry polynomials are merged with haphazard interactions are not likely to make many contributions to behavioral science.

Exploratory versus Confirmatory Analyses

In defining historiometry, the notion of "testing hypotheses" deserves considerable emphasis. Behavioral science may work best when it concentrates on verifying or rejecting propositions of either strong theory or past empirical work. Thus the inquiries that led to the curve in figure 5.2, which specifies how aesthetic success varies as an inverted backward-J function of melodic originality, were in part inspired by the optimal-arousal model of artistic appreciation whose origins go back to Wilhelm Wundt, the founder of experimental psychology (Berlyne 1971). Likewise, the discovery of the Johnson-Wilson effect was not by happenstance, for this investigation was informed by basic suppositions about how inflexible people respond to inauspicious circumstances (Sales 1972, 1973). Curvilinear functions and interaction effects are mentioned because it is in the search for complex relations that a researcher most needs guidance. Polynomials and multiplicative terms can be abused, transforming an analysis into "data dredging" where umpteenth-order polynomials, many-way interactions, and their multiple combinations are put into multiple-regression equations in the hope that "something interesting will turn up."

One method in particular, *stepwise multiple regression,* frequently becomes a vehicle for analytical abuse. Here an a posteriori computer algorithm picks the best predictors from a list of potential independent variables. Each predictor is added according to its incremental improvement in the multiple correlation between predicted and observed scores on the criterion variable—an entirely post hoc procedure. While it is guaranteed to yield the largest R^2 (and with each partial coefficient statistically significant by fiat), much of that predictive power may be specious, owing to the exploitation of chance, whether measurement noise or sampling fluctuations. Especially when the sample size is small and the number of candidate predictors large, stepwise regression often results in an equation that cannot be replicated on new samples of individuals. Finally, stepwise regression should never be employed when searching for complex functions, curvilinear or interactive. Because multiplicative terms cannot be interpreted apart from the linear terms, all variables must be either inserted simultaneously or entered hierarchically from lower-order to higher-order terms—*not* helter-skelter.

There still exists, however, a niche for exploratory analyses. For one thing, confirmatory analyses frequently transmogrify into exploratory analyses because the researchers' pet notions are forthrightly contradicted; dumbfounded investigators must then ask what went wrong—compelling them to search the data for answers. Hence in causal modeling it is quite normal for the hypothesized network to be rejected on the first pass, obliging the researcher to look at diagnostics that indicate what changes in the causal structure will narrow the gap between model and data (Kaplan 1988). This business of "theory trimming" (McPherson 1976) and "specification searches" (MacCallum 1986) ceases to be a confirmatory enterprise but rather becomes exploratory moonlighting (Cliff 1983). Consequently, the new causal model that emerges may exploit random features of the specific covariance matrix under view. As such, the revised model can serve only as a hypothesized causal structure for another test on a newly collected data set. Although the revision will probably outperform the original version in the second round, there is no assurance that this revived confirmatory analysis will converge on the right structure. The naively expected confirmation of an initial model has become cyclical procedure, confirmatory and exploratory analyses alternating as the investigator gathers sample after sample. Given that even a strongly confirmatory procedure often converts surreptitiously into an exploratory procedure after its first confrontation with data, we should exhibit more tolerance for those methods quite honestly exploratory in nature. Such tools may prove handy in the preliminary spadework that must so often be done before scientific foundations can be established. Little by little, the conceptual sophistication of the analyses should expand until the merely empirical but inexplicable is absolved by the purely theoretical and predictable.

An example of this evolution from exploration to confirmation is a series of inquiries regarding leader performance in the White House (Simonton 1981b, 1985c, 1986c, 1986g, 1986h, 1987d, 1988d, 1990f). These investigations helped resolve the issue of why some presidents are praised as great while others are condemned as failures. A subset of these studies scrutinized the basis for the vice-presidential succession effect, a phenomenon germane to the actual objective performance of "accidental" presidents. The discovery process began with an initial reconnoiter that sorted hundreds of correlations between leadership criteria and their potential predictors (Simonton 1981b). Even if this search was partially informed by prior empirical studies (for example, Wendt and Light 1976; Winter 1973; Winter and Stewart 1977), the main thrust clearly depended on the unabashed exploitation of exploratory procedures.

Subsequent investigations attempted to tie down more central findings, in part by using the newest presidential ratings (Murray and Blessing 1983) that had superseded those employed earlier (Maranell 1970) and by expanding the inventory of potential predictors more than twofold (Simonton 1986g). Two follow-up studies delved into the character traits most pertinent to predicting presidential leadership, including the fourteen personality factors in table 3.10 (Simonton 1986h) and five dimensions of presidential style (Simonton 1988d). Once certain results looked sufficiently robust—and survived tests for transhistorical invariance—it became desirable to transform the research program into a more confirmatory mode. One line of pursuit zeroed in on the vice-presidential succession effect from several angles to show how this curious phenomenon ensued from situationally swayed attributions rather than personality or experience or competence (Simonton 1985c, 1986g, 1986h, 1988a). This attributional interpretation was extended to the predictors of presidential greatness and then tested in a laboratory experiment on how persons observe political leaders (Simonton 1986c).

That the nomothetic hypotheses were confirmed did not end matters, for all the while other investigators were offering alternative correlates of presidential performance (Baltzell and Schneiderman 1988; Holmes and Elder 1989; Kenney and Rice 1988; Nice 1984, 1986; Winter 1987b). Accordingly, more confirmatory analyses were required to prove that the original equation indeed survived the challenges (Simonton 1987d, 1990f). Although new data on future presidents may require additional amendments in the explanatory model, further endeavors must henceforth operate from a hypothesis-testing framework. This secure position was consolidated by concurrent investigations that demonstrated substantial parallels between the greatness ratings of American presidents and the eminence of European monarchs (Simonton 1983d, 1984g).

The lesson from this program of research is that if one is willing to pursue all serendipitous findings to the end, intellectually satisfying results may be attained. Exploratory analyses are not encouraged where ample nomothetic hypotheses await confirmation. Even so, in some domains of inquiry our concepts are so primitive and our intuitions so crude that everything is wide open. Scientific theorizing is impossible without some rough sketch of how the phenomena actually take place.

Descriptive versus Inferential Statistics

Debates about the comparative value of exploratory and confirmatory approaches frequently must introduce another dilemma—whether the goal is to describe what is happening in a particular sample or to make inferences about the more extensive population from which the sample was supposedly drawn. If the aim is to engage in population inferences, exploratory statistics are risky. To maximize the amount of variance explained in a sample is by no means tantamount to deriving an equation that accurately depicts what may be going on in the larger world. This disparity of purpose is reflected in a statistic known as the *adjusted* or *shrunken* R^2. Because the least-squares criterion selects the partial regression coefficients to optimize the correlation between predicted and observed scores, opportunity exists for taking advantage of random sampling fluctuations. The multiple correlation in the sample will be inflated in comparison to what would have obtained had they been estimated for all cases in the population. The formula for computing this adjustment is

$$\hat{R}^2 = 1 - (1 - R^2) \frac{N - 1}{N - k - 1} \tag{8.4}$$

Here N continues to represent the number of cases and k the number of independent cases in the sample (and $N > k$). If k is held constant, as N becomes ever larger the correction mandated by this equation becomes puny, for then one is working with a "sample" that is practically equivalent to the entire population. For instance, a thirty-five-variable regression equation could account for 44 percent of the variance in the differential aesthetic success of 15,618 themes in the classical repertoire (that is, $R^2 = .436$, $N = 15,618$ and $k = 35$). Substituting the necessary values in equation 8.4 yields a corrected squared multiple correlation of .435, signifying that even in a more comprehensive population 44 percent of the variance would still be explained. Yet for a small and constant N, increasing k compels a growing discrepancy between the original R^2 and its toned-down restatement $\hat{R}^2$. Equation 8.4 does not by itself exclude the possibility that the squared multiple correlation might shrink to zero. When the sample size is respectable relative to the supply of predictors, the reduction may be tolerable rather than devastating. For example, the equation for predicting presidential greatness has an $R^2 = .82$, with $N = 36$ and $k = 6$ (see table 7.1). Unlike the preceding case where the number of cases was hundreds of times bigger than the number of variables, the number of cases is merely six times the number of variables. Substituting the needed values in equation 8.4, we obtain $\hat{R}^2 = .78$, a figure only modestly adjusted.

To be sure, this equation came from exploratory procedures that scanned through far more than a half-dozen variables before stopping at the restricted subset—which must inflate the variance explained much more. But should we then substitute into equation 8.4 the value $k = 300$? Given that this would yield a meaningless outcome, we might mistakenly conclude that we know absolutely *nothing* about the antecedents of presidential greatness. Obviously we are dealing here with *the* population, despite the small N. Except for the deletion of the first Harrison and the only Garfield, whose terms in office were too short to warrant evaluation, *all* occupants of that office from Washington through Carter have had their say in the estimation of the regression weights. Therefore, we can assert without hesitation that the six-variable equation accounts for 82 percent of the variance in greatness in the *population* of rated presidents. The distinction between diminutive sample and inaccessible population breaks down in the process, rendering irrelevant the division between descriptive and inferential statistics. What describes the sample can be safely inferred as descriptive of the population, owing to this equivalence.

The contrast between descriptive and inferential statistics is thus substantially ambiguous. We first examine what it means to state that a given finding is "statistically significant," taking us to the question of probability levels. Next we discuss what is meant by saying that a finding is "substantively significant," obliging a consideration of effect sizes.

Probability Levels

Scientific articles that use biometrics, psychometrics, or econometrics normally contain statements about the odds of results emerging by the operation of chance alone. In some disciplines, such as political science, this is most often accomplished by setting confidence intervals around the descriptive statistics, a practice reflected in table 7.3, which gives regression coefficients for predicting generational time series of creativity in Western civilization (Simonton 1975e). For each parameter b there is a corresponding *standard error* SE_b that indicates the "plus or minus" of the estimate. As a rule of thumb, investigators look at the interval fixed by plus or minus *twice* the standard error, which approximates the 95 percent confidence interval in samples of moderate size. That is, we can be reasonably sure that the population value of the parameter will fall within the interval $b \pm 2SE_b$, the odds being only one in twenty that we are wrong. If the confidence interval contains zero, we are in deep trouble, for this implies that we cannot reject the *null hypothesis* that the parameter is actually zero, no matter what its value may be in the sample. Thus, the partial coefficient for discursive creativity at generation $g - 1$ is around .36, whereas the standard error is about .08, meaning that there is but a 5 percent chance that the coefficient's value in the population lies outside the interval $.36 \pm .08$, or .28 to .44. The null hypothesis is easily denied in this instance, given that zero is a safe distance from this band of possibilities. In contrast, the comparable confidence interval for war at generation g easily includes zero, a not surprising fact given that the coefficient in the sample nears zero.

In the psychological literature it is considered more desirable to report t or F tests and then specify the probability levels for these statistics. This practice is the same wine in a different bottle. For regression coefficients, $t = b/SE_b$, and $F = t^2$. Before convenient computer programs, the test statistic would then be looked up in a published table under the appropriate degrees of freedom ($N - k - 1$ for t, 1 and $N - k - 1$ for F). Hence, the guide that the absolute distance between a parameter and zero must be at least equal to two times the parameter's standard error is equivalent to requiring that $t = 2.0$ or $F = 4.0$, which are approximately the cut-off points for rejecting the null hypothesis at the .05 level. As long as the degrees of freedom equal 60 or more, when the ratio of the regressed coefficient to its standard error exceeds two, we can say that the odds are less than five in a hundred (or one in twenty) that we could have garnered a coefficient of this absolute magnitude in a sample drawn from a population in which the true value is exactly zero. Hence, in table 7.3 we see that for discursive creativity at $g - 1$, $t = 4.266 = b/SE_b = .36335/.0852$, a statistic expected only four times out of one hundred thousand samples. By comparison, the *t* for war is so minimal that such an effect could appear 84 percent of the time even if the population parameter is precisely zero.

When two columns are placed side by side, one labeled "*b*" and the other "*SE*$_b$," it is easy to slip into the false illusion that the two sets of numbers possess the same epistemological status. Assuming that the partial regression slopes, the *b*'s, have emerged from a least-squares criterion (rather than maximum likelihood), these coefficients are descriptive statistics pure and simple. They summarize the observed associations in the cases actually under view, making no assumptions whatsoever about where the data come from. In stark contrast, the standard errors, or *SE*$_b$s, represent statements about a hypothetical population from which the present sample was putatively derived. As such, this column of numbers embodies inferential statistics. That is, the standard errors, in conjunction with the sample coefficients, are used to infer the probable magnitude of the parameters in a population far remote from the sample in our midst. In Kantian terms, we are passing from mere phenomena, the appearances that impinge on our senses, to the noumena, the true reality that underlies what we directly experience.

One cannot go from sample characteristics to population attributes without paying a price. To *calculate* the regression slopes by least squares, we need not make many assumptions other than that our variables have been correctly scaled and accurately measured. But to *estimate* the standard errors of those slopes, or to *derive* a *t* or *F* ratio from which we can affirm the probability that the null hypothesis is justified, we must make additional and far more stringent assumptions. Three postulates are especially pertinent to judging the meaningfulness of inferential statistics in historiometric data (compare Floud 1973, 182–86).

First, the sample must entail unrelated cases so that each constitutes an independent test of the nomothetic hypothesis. In regression analysis, this prerequisite takes the form of assuming that the true residuals are free from autocorrelation or autoregression. Yet many powerful designs violate this assumption. In time-series analyses, for example, consecutive observations normally exhibit a positive autocorrelation, a temporal continuity amply displayed in table 6.3, where first- and even second-order autoregressive processes reign with scant challenge (Simonton 1988c). Nor are time series the sole culprits; not all cross-sectional data can be trusted either. One of the oldest obstacles to cross-cultural studies is "Galton's problem" (Naroll 1970; Simonton 1975b). Because contiguous societies may borrow freely from each other (cultural diffusion) or have shared historical roots (common decent), each culture of the globe cannot possibly count as a completely independent test of some hypothesized relation.

One might think that this issue would not arise were the units of analysis confined to individuals, yet safety is not assured here either. In any study of revolutionaries, several of the individuals invariably come from the same revolution (for example, Rejai and Phillips 1979; Suedfeld and Rank 1976). Likewise in the study of painters and sculptors, some artists were related by master-apprentice and even parent-child relations (Simonton 1984a). And any examination of U.S. presidents would show that some executives have hand-picked their successors, whether by choice (Jackson and Van Buren) or by happenstance (Lincoln and Johnson). Given how often the statistical independence of the cases does not hold in real data, we must then wonder what the consequence will be for the inferential statistics.

The implications are potentially devastating: In the usual circumstance of positive (temporal or spatial) autocorrelation, the degrees of freedom for significance tests will be biased upward, which seems reasonable given that N is not as large as it superficially appears, considering how many cases are a chip off the old (preceding or contiguous) block (Orcutt and James 1948). For regression analysis this translates into the warning that the standard errors of the slopes are *too small*. Because the t (or F) ratios are derived from these standard errors, these statistics will be *too large*, perhaps leading us to think that the coefficient is nonzero when the null hypothesis should be properly rejected. That is, given that the probability levels are biased downward, we may be misled into thinking that a relation might be significant at the .05 level when the genuine likelihood of the null hypothesis is .09, or some still larger and insignificant number. Nevertheless, these biases confound only the population inferences, not the sample description. Specifically, the slope b still describes the connection between two variables in the sample and offers the best point estimate of the population parameter. Only when we wish to set confidence intervals around b to offer an interval estimate of b in the population, should nonindependence of observations provoke alarm.

Second, derivations of the t and F distributions, which are needed to determine the probability levels, are founded on the assumption of normality. Not only should each continuous variable exhibit a normal distribution, but the joint distribution should also be multivariate normal. The last requirement is not the easiest to demonstrate given that all the variables may be univariate normal without their joint distribution being multivariate normal. However, univariate normality is a necessary even if not sufficient condition, and hence it should be obvious that historiometric data will often not satisfy this postulate. As we have repeatedly observed, historical phenomena typically yield skewed distributions. Whenever this happens, the t and F tests become only approximate, and the probability levels must be taken with a grain of salt. Fortunately, the significance tests are robust under even extreme departures from normality, and multivariate normality is *not* assumed by the descriptive statistics most frequently employed. For instance, ordinary least-squares regression estimators make *no* distributional assumptions in calculating the coefficients, or slopes, whether in bivariate or multivariate analyses.

Third and last, inferential statistics presume that the sample has been randomly drawn from an indefinitely large population of potential cases. The entities that define the sample must be the winners in a scientific lottery in which all units have had an equal probability of receiving the prize, curiously, a requisite seldom met in practical research. Much behavioral science research depends not on random but on convenience samples, especially college sophomores. Reality is appreciably less obliging in historiometry: Historiometricians study quite an elite in capacities and opportunities. As noted before, a key strategy is eminence sampling whereby the most illustrious figures in a field enter the sample first, after which the less distinguished are added, descending to obscurity until a workable N obtains. With this rule, those who qualify for inclusion cannot possibly be taken as representative of those who do not. Moreover, the sample is sometimes so inclusive that it *is* the population, no matter what the N—like *all* U.S. chief executives, Canadian prime ministers, Nobel Prize recipients, or Roman Catholic popes.

Even when lesser figures are denied admission into the honored group, those who have been glorified suffice to confirm or reject the hypothesis being considered. This security of inference certainly holds when we examine 2,026 scientists, 2,012 philosophers, or even "just" 772 artists, 696 classical composers, and 342 European monarchs. With samples of this magnitude, it does not matter whether the findings can be generalized to those who did not make the grade. Hence, the postulate of random sampling from an infinite population is not so much violated as incapacitated by the very nature of historiometric data. The requisite can be made relevant only in hypothetical fashion: *If* the presidents, monarchs, revolutionaries, philosophers, scientists, artists, or composers under investigation *were* randomly selected from an indefinitely large population of leaders or creators, could we reasonably expect to obtain descriptive statistics of the magnitude witnessed in the sample of historical notables notwithstanding that the true parameters are zero? The answer to this question may or may not enhance our confidence in the findings, yet the problem itself has only peripheral interest, given how incredibly hypothetical is its phrasing. What the central concern should be is whether the hypothesis successfully endures a test against those cases that best exemplify the phenomenon.

Simply expressed, tests of statistical significance lose significance whenever we are inspecting significant samples. The historical generalizations of most intense concern to the psychologist apply to a select sample of individuals who have left their mark on history. Even when attention turns to collective behavior, such as riot or revolution, suicide or crime, the focus remains on characteristic events. Because the data harbor such a priori importance, it is almost impertinent to inquire whether the results may be extended to a hypothetical population. As a consequence, inferential statistics, and the assumptions that they require—whether independence, normality, or random sampling—must take a back seat to descriptive statistics. This is not to say that the investigator can ignore the question of generality, but only that this issue takes on an altogether different aspect. Transhistorical and cross-cultural invariance is a far more urgent matter than is population inference. For example, one may seriously wonder whether what holds for the 2,012 philosophers applies equally to the numerous thinkers who graced the civilizations of Islam, India, or China, yet whether the findings are valid for Western civilization is really not a question for inferential statistics to decide (Simonton 1976f). Nor do statistically significant results guarantee that what works for Aristotle, Descartes, and Kant functions just as well for al-Ghazālī, Shankara, and Zhu Xi. To ascertain that the effects of specific variables on ultimate distinction are significant at certain probability levels is not to augment appreciably the persuasiveness of the analysis.

Effect Sizes

Many readers trained in behavioral sciences will have some familiarity with the "significance test controversy" (Morrison and Henkel 1970). Scientists of many persuasions have voiced suspicions about the value of setting a priori alpha levels, testing null hypotheses, and using the other paraphernalia of inferential statistics. It has been argued from the logically pure perspective of the philosophy of science that the emphasis on probability levels has led the behavioral sciences, especially psychology, down the primrose path to doom (Meehl 1978). Conducting significance tests too often becomes numerological game that corresponds minimally to the reality being investigated. Gardner Murphey (1968, 19), the historian of psychology, once inquired whether this misguided emphasis on magical numbers had reached Pythagorean proportions: "psychology is, of course, shot through with preference for specific numbers. A p value (probability value), for example, at a level of .05 is significant, but at .06 is not significant, I suppose because few of us have six fingers. Here we have misplaced the discontinuity, that is, where there is a real continuity we have made a gulf between .05 and .06, or indeed for certain problems, .01 rather than .02." Today the standard format of the leading psychology journals requires that the significance levels of statistical tests in tables be assigned one, two, or three asterisks, indicating whether the corresponding effect satisfies, respectively, the .05, .01, or .001 criterion (American Psychological Association 1983). The infinitely divisible continuity of the descriptive statistics has undergone a strange metamorphosis into the artificial world of inferential statistics with quantum steps. One descriptive statistic, no matter how large, may be conceptually reset to exactly zero should the finding fail the a priori litmus test; another statistic, no matter how small, may be accepted as definitely nonzero, and correspondingly deemed theoretically potent, just because its probability level passed the discrete threshold.

Furthermore, the danger is ever present that investigators will become so infatuated with the asterisks, inequality signs, and decimals that they will lose sight of where the chief responsibility lies. Too often the significance tests become the raison d'être: It is not uncommon for a researcher to believe it suffices to state p values without having descriptive statistics. Even when the sample coefficients or mean differences are hidden in the body of a paper, the stress of discussion is often on probability levels. Because even rather worthless relations can qualify for one or more asterisks merely by arising from a huge N, some other criterion must provide the foundation for interpretation. Should the investigator analyze cases that embody the truest exemplars of a phenomenon, the source of judgments must center on statistics describing what is taking place within the data set. No special advantages are granted the scholar who insists on Platonic speculations about what may be happening in a hypothetical population that cannot ever exist. In short, the probability statements of inferential statistics must always have a subordinate position vis-à-vis discussion of effect sizes.

In the two sections that follow, we will review the statistics that provide the best clues regarding the strength of an effect and offer caveats about the interpretation of these statistics.

Clues. When dealing with bivariate relations, the Pearsonian r provides a direct guide to the magnitude of effect. If the emphasis is on prediction, we can treat r as a standardized coefficient in a regression equation: As the independent variable changes by one standard deviation, the dependent variable changes by r standard deviations, where the sign of r is retained to register direct or inverse proportionality. For instance, when we learn that intelligence and eminence correlate .23 across Cox's geniuses, we can say that increasing IQ by one standard unit (or by 13.9 points) means an increase in ranked eminence of .26 units (or by .26 × 87 = 23 notches up the scale). Alternatively, we may focus on the proportion of variance shared between the two variables, in which case we can speak of r^2. So from the correlation of .36 between secondary process imagery in English poetry and treatment of the ethics of principles in Western philosophy, we can affirm that generational fluctuations between the two time series have about 13 percent of their variance in common (Martindale 1975). Similarly, the square of a partial correlation of whatever order is interpretable as the proportion of variance shared between two variables after extirpating any variance these may share with one or more extraneous variables. Consequently, the twenty-eighth-order partial correlation of −.27 between a monarch's chronological age and the number of military victories in battles under the ruler's personal command shows that a little more than 7 percent of the variance between individual attribute and national condition overlaps even after controlling for twenty-eight extraneous variables (Simonton 1984f).

In evaluating predictive prowess within a multivariate design, the partial-regression coefficient can often be recruited into service. If the scores are in natural units, it is often most instructive to scrutinize the unstandardized weights (the b's). Hence, when a general's edge in battle casualties can be predicted from his relative advantage in the size of his army, with an unstandardized partial coefficient of 0.4281, we can say that for each additional thousand soldiers above the number his opponent has, he can inflict 428 more casualties on his enemy than must be suffered by his own forces (Simonton 1980a). A special case of this situation occurs when a dummy variable serves as the predictor, for then the unstandardized coefficient gives the difference in the average level of the dependent variable between the group for which the dummy is zero and that for which the dummy is one (controlling for all other variables in the equation). In the study testing whether poetry is produced at younger ages than literary prose, the b for the corresponding dummy variable ($= 1$ if poetry and $= 0$ if prose) was -3.910, showing that for 420 figures drawn from the world's major literary traditions the best poems were written at ages about four years younger than the best prose compositions (Simonton 1975a).

More frequently, one or more measures are devoid of direct interpretability, making standardized coefficients (βs) more informative. Neither the aesthetic success of Shakespeare's sonnets nor the amount of primary process imagery they contain can be assessed on a natural scale, leading us to look at the $\beta = .24$ in order to infer that for every unit increase in the z score on primary process the z score on sonnet popularity should climb by about one-quarter of a unit, assuming that the other variables in the equation have been held constant (Simonton 1989b). As stated before, standardized weights are valuable even when using natural units so long as the task is to compare the relative predictive power of independent variables measured on incommensurate scales. In predicting the veto use by American presidents, we find that the incumbent's electoral mandate has a standardized coefficient of $.12$, an effect that can be said to be about the same magnitude as that for an economic slump, $\beta = .10$, despite the lack of direct comparability between the two predictors, which cannot possibly be measured on the same scale (Copeland 1983).

Last but not least, we have the squared multiple correlation, or R^2, with its tremendous usefulness as a gauge of effect size. Because R^2 represents the proportion of variance in the dependent variable that can be handled by an optimal linear combination of the independent variables, we can now explain 72 percent of the generational fluctuations in European creativity (Simonton 1975e), 68 percent of the yearly shifts in presidential veto behavior (Copeland 1983), 22 percent of the differential eminence of Western thinkers (Simonton 1976f), and 50 percent of the differential repertoire popularity of classical compositions (Simonton 1986a). Besides such global statements, the investigator often wants to determine the R^2 change that results from inserting a variable (or set of variables) into an equation when the other predictors are already there. This increment assessment provides a vehicle for addressing the question: Does the variable (or set of variables) enhance our knowledge about the phenomenon? For instance, in predicting career changes in the contribution rate in mathematics, the linear age function accounts for 12 percent of the variance, the quadratic component adds another 72 percent, whereas a cubic term accommodates only 7 percent more and a fourth-power term adds only a 3 percent increment, implying that productivity is mostly explicated by a second-order polynomial (Simonton 1984b).

Caveats. In inspecting descriptive statistics, several precautions are in order, some concerning distortions in the estimated effects, others concerning the proper appreciation of the observed effect sizes.

In the first group is the irritating problem of *missing values* (compare Floud 1973, 186–93). Sometimes it is not practical to obtain scores for all cases on all variables, because of gaps in the historical record. This difficulty can be dealt with by six common means, each having some consequence for the effect sizes that result (compare Hertel 1976). First, we can simply delete all cases that lack observations on all measures, assuming that a substantial number of cases have no missing values. This listwise deletion is recommended only when the analytical units that remain can still be considered representative of the phenomenon. If otherwise, then the effect sizes obtained may not be extrapolated to those not in the calculations. Second, we might drop all those offending variables, retaining solely those without missing values, a procedure that obviously does not try to gauge the effect of the measures omitted. Third, we can substitute sample means, which would produce effect sizes that are biased downward, or fourth, substitute group means (when the cases can be so classified), which tends to yield effect sizes biased upward. Fifth and most usefully, we can have a preliminary regression analysis predict each variable on the basis of other measured variables, and then insert the predicted value in each empty spot on the data sheet.

The sixth and final response to missing values is a delicate one—the pairwise deletion of cases. Here the correlations among variables are estimated a pair at a time, using all those cases with complete scores on both variables. While pairwise deletion may seem to save much data that would be otherwise thrown out, the practice also complicates the comparison of different bivariate associations, for the statistics do not describe the same sample of cases. It is perfectly possible for two correlations to be based on totally different cases even when they share a variable in common. Hence, if the aim is to compare magnitudes of statistical association, the investigator should either employ listwise deletion or reconstruct the missing values.

If the comparison of bivariate effects is risky under pairwise deletion, it is sometimes fatal to look at multivariate effects when this solution to missing values is employed. Because each bivariate correlation originates in a distinct and perhaps nonoverlapping set of cases, it may happen that the correlation matrix that summarizes the relations among all variables is mathematically impossible. The correlation between two variables, for example, might be too low given how highly each correlates with other variables in the matrix. Should the investigator naively subject such an impossible matrix to further multivariate manipulations, bizarre results could emerge. It is no accident that most computer software programs impose listwise deletions as the default for all multivariate analyses. Nevertheless, under special circumstances both pairwise and listwise deletion will yield much the same outcomes anyway. This was witnessed in chapter 4 (see table 4.5) when we factor analyzed the assessments of the American presidents and got the same two dimensions, with nearly identical loadings, for both solutions to the missing values problem (Simonton 1986g). Yet such a convergence can be expected only when the number of missing values is small and the bivariate associations stable across various subsamples of cases.

Another distortion of the effect sizes stems from the consequences of *near* multicollinearity. The separate effects of two independent variables cannot be dissociated if the two variables are perfectly correlated. Even should the bivariate association be strong without attaining a 1.0 figure, using the analytical procedure to separate out the supposedly independent effects will be difficult. It may even happen that by putting two highly correlated predictors into the same equation, neither will exhibit a substantively or statistically significant effect despite the fact that their total incremental addition to the R^2 is undeniable. Such repercussions make advisable the possible omission of evidently redundant predictors.

Beyond these matters of descriptive distortions, some principles of interpretation should make us better appreciate observed effects. One might think that investigators are inclined to exaggerate the substantive import of a discovered link, yet the bias often goes in the opposite direction. A case in point is Hull, Tessner, and Diamond's test (1978) of Planck's principle that "a new scientific truth does not triumph by convincing its opponents and making them see the light, but rather because its opponents eventually die, and a new generation grows up that is familiar with it" (Planck 1949, 33–34). They concluded that a person's age had little to say about why some British biologists were disinclined to accept Darwin's theory of evolution by natural selection—because age explained "only" 6 percent of the variance in an individual's willingness to adopt the theory. Diamond (1980) drew the same inference after finding that age once more accounted for "only" 6 percent of the variation in an economic historian's acceptance of cliometrics.

Negative interpretations notwithstanding, these effect sizes are actually striking. To see why, we must carefully consider what kinds of effect sizes we can reasonably expect, according to theory and intuition. Surely whether a scientist accepts a new theory or a historian adopts a new methodology is governed by dozens of factors besides age, including professional affiliations, personal friendships, patriotic loyalties, power of argument and expression, ideology, religion, and personality. Let us postulate that there exist twenty independent considerations that might lead someone to love or detest an innovation and that all twenty influences have about equal weight. Any one of these determinant criteria can account for only 5 percent of the variance in the final decision to assent or dissent. Given how complex the phenomena are that the behavioral scientist strives to comprehend, any effect above 1 percent deserves celebration, not resignation.

With suitable changes, this same argument applies to multiple effects, as registered by R^2 in a regression analysis or the proportion of correct classification in a discriminant analysis. To be sure, given the participation of more predictors, we would expect the overall proportion of variance to climb in multiple-variable equations. Yet myriad potential antecedents could be omitted from our formula, requiring us to have modest expectations. A four-variable regression equation can dispatch only 18 percent of the variance in battle casualty edge enjoyed by a particular general on the battlefield—not surprising given how many variables were not included in the original pool of a dozen potential predictors (Simonton 1980a). Especially problematic is the exclusion of certain intangibles—like irrational panic, esprit de corps, discipline, sleep, physical illness, terrain, weather, and gunsmoke—that certainly have a part when two armies meet. By the same token, another four-variable discriminant function can identify the victor on the battlefield only 71 percent of the time, when the winner could be picked half the time by flipping a coin (Simonton 1980a). Yet again, many potential discriminators are not to be found among the dozen inspected. For both predictions, one continuous and the other discrete, any investigator's claim that 100 percent of the variation could be successfully anticipated by such a diminutive batch of variables should be dismissed as either fraudulent or incompetent. A psychologist with a sound intuition about how historical figures and events behave should expect that scientific explanations will require numerous factors, not a skeleton crew.

Even if investigators should always have their expectations properly lowered, interpretations of even small effect sizes should not be hesitant. Small effects can have large consequences, and accordingly such effects should not be taken lightly. In "A Note on Percent of Variance Explained as a Measure of the Importance of Effects," Rosenthal and Rubin (1979) offer an illustration. Suppose that we are evaluating a new medical treatment for an often fatal disease. Given one hundred patients diagnosed as having the illness, half were assigned to the novel treatment, the other half to the standard treatment, the assignment made by tossing a coin. For example, of the fifty who received the traditional procedure, only fifteen were alive a year later, whereas of the fifty who had the experimental procedure, thirty-five survived after a one-year observation period. That means that under the old procedure 30 percent survived in comparison to the 70 percent under the new procedure, decidedly a substantial effect. Yet when we calculate the Pearsonian correlation for this hypothetical example, we find that only 16 percent of the variance in the occurrence of death can be explained by the treatment (that is $\phi^2 = .16$). In a similar vein, variables that determine victory on the battlefield may not explain great variance, yet they do account for numerous *single* deaths.

In a paper "A Variance Explanation Paradox: When a Little Means a Lot," Abelson (1985) deals with another means by which seemingly small effects have consequences far beyond the standard gauges of impact. His example is taken from the baseball field and concerns the problem of predicting a player's performance at bat according to that player's batting average. Aficionados believe that some major league players are clearly superior to others, a differential manifested in each player's statistics. If the batting averages could range from 1.0 (a hit every time) to

0.0 (never a hit), there would be no doubt that these numbers would predict performance each time a player comes to the plate. But the realities of the sport preclude this variation: Excellent pitchers make sure that even the best batters will not earn hits more than one-third of the time, while intelligent managers ensure that batters cannot earn hits less than one-fifth of the time and still get dressed for the game. Given this restricted range, Abelson calculated that "the percentage of variance in any single batting performance explained by batting skill is about one-third of 1 percent" (p. 131). Does this mean that batting average can be ignored as a predictor variable?

Abelson wisely points out that baseball games are not decided by a single time at bat, but rather by the accumulation of hits that results in runs scored. Therefore, given two teams with distinctively different mean batting averages, that team with the better players will have a definite edge. The tiny influence of the batting average for any one batter waiting for a pitch accumulates each inning until by the bottom of the ninth, one team should have hit at least one more run than the other; by the end of the season, such small increments may add up to a pennant. Using the same logic, given two nations otherwise equal, the nation that loses more pitched battles and suffers more killed and wounded on each encounter will, in the long run, forfeit more strategic locations and suffer a more severe rate of attrition in personnel and morale. The outcome will be a lost war.

The lesson is that we must take care not to discount effects just because they appear small. This advice must be coupled with the earlier admonition that one not overlook an effect simply because it may not satisfy some formal criterion of statistical significance. Whenever one studies significant samples that have inherent interest apart from how well those samples represent a larger and often totally hypothetical population, one should first address whether the effects under scrutiny really matter in the sample, population inferences aside. To illustrate, Gieryn and Hirsh (1983) wished to determine whether the greatest innovators in a scientific discipline are those individuals who are marginal to the field, as expressed in Kuhn's (1970, 90) historical generalization that "almost always the men who achieve these fundamental inventions of a new paradigm have been either very young or very new to the field whose paradigm they change." This nomothetic hypothesis was tested on nearly a hundred American scientists who contributed at least seven papers to X-ray astronomy between 1960 and 1975, assessing these on seven distinct indicators of marginality besides counting the number of innovations made by each. Unluckily, there were many missing values scattered throughout the data, meaning that almost half of the individuals had to be dropped when estimating a seven-variable multiple-regression equation. Because the multiple correlation for the equation was not significant at an acceptable probability level, Gieryn and Hirsch concluded that marginality is an irrelevant factor in predicting a scientist's propensity to innovate. Perhaps the unremarkable probability level resulted from a drastic reduction in sample size. When we estimate the probability level had all ninety-eight X-ray astronomers been included in the analysis, we get a comfortable $p < .01$ (Simonton 1984e).

Let us move beyond this inferential question to the issue of how to describe best what actually took place in this particular sample, a significant sample that certainly has interest in its own right. The seven-variable regression equation claims an $R^2 = .205$, meaning that over 20 percent of the variance in the number of innovations made by each scientist could be predicted on the basis of factors indicative of their disciplinary marginality. Should this effect hold for other scientific fields and across diverse historical periods, the cumulative impact of professionally marginal scientists would be immense. Hence, it would be hasty to promulgate the inference that "'marginal' scientists are no more likely than others to contribute innovations" (Gieryn and Hirsh 1983, 87). That statement does not accurately describe what occurred in X-ray astronomy in its formative years, nor can one safely assume that the null effect exists in the world beyond this significant sample. Indeed, the marginality effect has been independently documented as a factor governing the reaction of earth scientists to the upstart theory of plate tectonics (J. A. Stewart 1986).

9 Evaluation

This treatise on historiometry has traversed a long and tortuous path of conceptual issues and has occasionally dipped into technical topics that may have confused readers lacking expertise in psychometric, econometric, or biometric methods. Fortunately, an easier task is now before us, to offer a final appraisal of the discipline from a more panoramic perspective, ending with observations about historiometry's prospects as a serious and coherent endeavor.

Perspectives

As was depicted in figure 1.1, historiometrics dwells in the interface of psychology, science, and history. At this juncture are historical generalizations of sufficient breadth that they can be taken to represent nomothetic propositions about human nature—inductions cast in terms so general that they cannot be ignored by any science of human behavior that searches for laws, patterns, regularities, or statistical associations. Granting this tripartite status of historiometry, it is natural that a complete evaluation proceed from three angles—the psychological, the scientific, and the historical.

Historiometry as Psychology

The discipline so enthusiastically advocated has its center of gravity in psychology owing to the historiometrician's main fascination with individual thought, feeling, and behavior. Even when historiometric work has been conducted by nonpsychologists, the implications of those inquiries should be of interest to those engaged in the scientific study of personal behavior. It is by this inclusive conception of psychological science that we should evaluate the attainments of historiometric inquiries. That in mind, the approach has contributed to psychology both substantively and methodologically.

Substantive contributions. Since historiometry has been around for well over a century, it is possible to summarize here only the signal topics that have attracted successful historiometric treatment. *Genius, Creativity, and Leadership: Historiometric Inquiries* (Simonton 1984d) presents the highlights of findings bearing on several core substantive questions. Subsequent monographs, book chapters, journal articles, and encyclopedia entries have reviewed key empirical conclusions on more specific issues in the behavioral sciences (for example, Simonton 1987a, 1987d, 1988e, 1990e). Three comprehensive groupings, corresponding to the subdisciplines of psychology in which historiometry has proved most constructive, contain those topics that have seen illuminating results.

1. Personality and differential psychologists study how human beings consistently vary on stable cognitive, affective, and behavioral attributes. Given that the first true differential psychologist of any note was Francis Galton, it is not surprising that this quest for individual differences became an integral part of historiometry early on. Besides Galton's (1869) effort, and the classic inquiries of Woods (1906, 1913), Terman (1917), Cox (1926), and Thorndike (1936, 1950), there has been a long parade of investigators who have assessed the intellectual capacity of historical individuals to show how intellectual variation correlates with other personality traits and with significant behaviors (Knapp 1962; Simonton 1976a, 1983d, 1984g, 1986h, 1988d; Sorokin 1925; Walberg, Rasher, and Parkerson 1980; R. K. White 1931). Affiliated with this tradition is more recent work relating integrative complexity to leader performance (Ballard 1983; Raphael 1982; Suedfeld, Corteen, and McCormick 1986; Suedfeld and Rank 1976); decision making (Suedfeld and Bluck 1988; Suedfeld and Tetlock 1977; Suedfeld, Tetlock, and Ramirez 1977; Tetlock, Bernzweig, and Gallant 1985; Wallace and Suedfeld 1988); political ideology (Tetlock 1983, 1984; Tetlock and Boettger 1989; Tetlock, Hannum, and Micheletti 1984); and other practical human realities (Porter and Suedfeld 1981; Suedfeld 1980, 1985; Suedfeld and Piedrahita 1984).

Still, many researchers have recognized the role that motivation plays in human life, including Cox (1926) and Thorndike (1950), who directly assessed that role. Among the motives that have received the most attention are the drives toward achievement (Bradburn and Berlew 1961; Cortés 1960; deCharms and Moeller 1962; Finison 1976; Frey 1984; Mazur and Rosa 1977; McClelland 1961; Winter and Carlson 1988); power and dominance (Etheredge 1978; McClelland 1975; Winter 1973; Winter 1987a); and affiliation and extroversion (R. B. Cattell 1963; Etheredge 1978; Frey, Piernot, and Elhardt 1981) (see also Walker and Falkowski 1984; Wendt and Light 1976; Winter 1987b; Winter and Steward 1977). In addition, numerous attempts have been made to extend the range of personality traits assessed in historical figures, beginning with the Cox (1926) measurements on sixty-seven attributes, to more recent assessments on as many as three hundred descriptors (HFAC 1977; Simonton 1986g, 1988d). Among the individual-difference variables quantified are psychopathology (Martindale 1972; Raskin 1936; R. K. White 1931); flexibility and dogmatism (Ballard and Suedfeld 1988; Hoffer 1978; G. Schubert 1983; Simonton 1983c, 1986g, 1987c); virtue and morality

(Ballard and Suedfeld 1988; Simonton 1983d, 1984g; Thorndike 1936; Woods 1906); familiarity (Miller and Stiles 1986); future orientation (Evered 1983); cognitive impairment (Gottschalk, Uliana, and Gilbert 1988); pessimistic rumination (Zullow, Oettingen, Peterson, and Seligman 1988); and values (Mahoney, Coogle, and Banks 1984; Rokeach, Homant, and Penner 1970; Smith, Stone, and Glenn 1966; R. K. White 1947).

Finally, there are those investigations that concentrate on individual differences in prominent acts of creativity or leadership, embracing inquiries into variation in lifetime creative output (Dennis 1954a, 1954c, 1955; Price 1963; Simonton 1977c, 1990a); the link between quantity and quality of productivity (R. A. Davis 1987; Dennis 1954a); and participation in multiple discoveries and inventions (Simonton 1979a), as well as legislative accomplishments (Copeland 1983; Edwards 1985; Hammond and Fraser 1984 Lee 1975; Ringelstein 1985; Rivers and Rose 1985; Rohde and Simon 1985; Zeidenstein 1985); the use of military force (Winter 1973, 1987b); foreign policy preferences (M. G. Hermann 1977, 1980b; Tetlock 1981a); and judicial influence (Gates and Cohen 1988; King 1987; Ulmer 1982).

2. Historiometry has made substantial contributions to life-span developmental psychology. Galton's (1869) and Cox's (1926) concerns about the impact of genetic endowment on personality development continues in more current work (for example, Bramwell 1948; Simonton 1983d). Similarly, Galton (1874) and Ellis (1904) introduced birth order as a central developmental event, a factor that remains prominent in recent research on general achievement (Albert 1980; Goertzel, Goertzel, and Goertzel 1978); creativity (Bliss 1970; Clark and Rice 1982; Schubert, Wagner and Schubert 1977); and political leadership (Barry 1979; Holmes and Elder 1989; L. H. Stewart 1977; Simonton 1986g, 1988d; Weber 1984). Other important early developmental experiences are orphanhood (Albert 1971; Eisenstadt 1978; Illingworth and Illingworth 1969; Martindale 1972; Silverman 1974; Woodward 1974); family background (Baltzell and Schneiderman 1988; Berry 1981; Lehman and Witty 1931; McCurdy 1960; Moulin 1955; Raskin 1936; Simonton 1986b; Walberg, Rasher, and Parkerson 1980); role models (Sheldon 1979, 1980; Simonton 1975e, 1976f, 1977c, 1978b, 1983d, 1984a, 1988c); formal education and expertise acquisition (Gieryn and Hirsh 1983; Goertzel, Goertzel, and Goertzel 1978; Hayes 1981, 209–14; Holmes and Elder 1989; Hudson 1958; Pressey and Combs 1943; Simonton 1983c; Walberg, Rasher, and Parkerson 1980); and the pervasive sociocultural and political milieu (Kroeber 1944; Naroll et al. 1971; Simonton 1975e, 1976f, 1976g, 1984a; Sorokin 1937–41; Ting 1986).

Nor does historiometric inquiry cease once an individual attains majority, given that the earliest historiometric study on record may be Quetelet's ([1835] 1968) examination of how the production of successful dramas changes as a playwright ages (see also Beard 1874). Since then, the connection between individual age and outstanding achievement has the largest literature of any topic in historiometric psychology (Simonton 1988b), especially the notable efforts summarized by Harvey C. Lehman (1953; see also Lehman 1958, 1960, 1962, 1963, 1966a, 1966b). Researchers have studied how creative output, leader influence, receptiveness to innovation, financial success, athletic prowess, and criminal aggression longitudinally vary (for example, Abt 1983; C. W. Adams 1946; Bullough, Bullough, and Mauro 1978; Dennis 1956b, 1966; Diamond 1980; Diemer 1974; D. B. Hermann 1988; Hull, Tessner, and Diamond 1978; Manniche and Falk 1957; Messerli 1988; A. B. Murphy 1984; Oleszek 1969; Raskin 1936; G. Schubert 1983; Schulz and Curnow 1988; Zhao 1984; Zhao and Jiang 1985, 1986). In addition, investigators have scrutinized such specialized questions as the relation between quantity and quality of production (Lehman 1953; Oromaner 1977; Quetelet [1835] 1968; Simonton 1977a, 1985b) and the interconnection between precocity, longevity, and mean annual output rate (Dennis 1954a, 1954b; Raskin 1936; Simonton 1977c; Zhao and Jiang 1986), these two substantive issues tying in with the literature on individual differences (Albert 1975; Simonton 1988b, 1990a). Noteworthy, too, are various endeavors to examine how personality is represented over the course of an individual life (McCurdy 1940a, 1940b, 1953; Rosenberg 1989; Sears, Lapidus, and Cozzens 1978). Showing that historiometrics can be truly life-span developmental in perspective, not only can inspection begin at the moment of birth, but additionally the study can endure to the very instant of death. A clear example is an inquiry into the swan-song phenomenon or last-works effects wherein a historical figure undergoes a sudden qualitative change in output just before death (Simonton 1989c), a shift that parallels the "terminal drop" observed in integrative complexity across diverse samples of creators and leaders (Porter and Suedfeld 1981; Suedfeld 1985; Suedfeld and Piedrahita 1984). Linked with this subject are studies on the life span of historical figures (Barry 1983–84; Cox 1926; Harrison and Kroll 1985–86, 1989–90; Lehman 1943; Mills 1942; Simonton 1975a, 1977c; Sorokin 1925, 1926; Zhao and Jiang 1986).

3. Because a central topic in social psychology concerns attitudes and beliefs relating to the social world, historiometry has greatly enhanced our understanding of how the notorious authoritarian personality is encouraged by particular economic and political conditions (Jorgenson 1975; McCann and Stewin 1984, 1987; Padgett and Jorgenson 1982; Sales 1972, 1973), as well as how attitudes toward politics and politicians are influenced by specific persuasion techniques (R. Erikson 1976; Goggin 1984; Lewis-Beck and Rice 1983; Page and Shapiro 1984; Shyles 1984; Stiles, Au, Martello, and Perlmutter 1983; Tetlock 1981b). Political scientists are particularly fond of showing how certain events and situations determine the behavior of individual voters (Abramowitz 1985; Atkin 1969; Bloom and Price 1975; Brody and Page 1975; J. E. Campbell 1985; Feldman and Jondrow 1984; Lewis-Beck and Rice 1984; Poole and Rosenthal 1984; Sigelman 1979;

Stoll 1984). Others have concentrated on the often parallel determinants of a politician's popularity with the people (Hibbs, Rivers, and Vasilatos 1982; Kenski 1977; Kernell 1978; Lanoue 1987; Miller and Wattenberg 1985; Mueller 1973; Norpoth 1986; Sigelman and Knight 1983; Stimson 1976).

Likewise, aggression and violence, whether individual or collective, have inspired the exploitation of historical data to fathom the etiology of homicide, rape, and other violent crimes (C. A. Anderson 1987, 1989; Anderson and Anderson 1984; W. C. Bailey 1980; Bell and Fusco 1986; Cotton 1986; Harries and Stadler 1983, 1988; Phillips 1980; Rotton and Frey 1985); suicide (Boor 1980; Boor and Fleming 1984; Stack 1987; Wasserman 1983, 1984); lynchings (Hepworth and West 1988; Hovland and Sears 1940; Mintz 1946); riot (Baron and Ransberger 1978; Carlsmith and Anderson 1979); revolution (Matossian and Schafer 1977; Zuk and Thompson 1982); and war (Suedfeld and Bluck 1988; Suedfeld, Corteen, and McCormick 1986; Suedfeld and Rank 1976; Suedfeld and Tetlock 1977; Suedfeld, Tetlock, and Ramirez 1977). On the last subject we should acknowledge the prodigious efforts of political scientists (Russett 1972; Singer 1981). Despite favoring analyses that operate at the institutional rather than individual level, problems are sometimes addressed with psychological relevance, such as the "war weariness hypothesis" (Levy and Morgan 1984, 1986) and the conjecture that failures to avoid war during international crises result from information overload in participants (Midlarsky 1984).

In a different vein are studies devoted to group dynamics, such as groupthink (Tetlock 1979) and social loafing (Jackson and Padgett 1982; Smart and Bayer 1986). But the most popular subject here is leadership, whether political (Ballard and Suedfeld 1988; Cell 1974; Simonton 1985c; Tetlock 1985; Winter 1980; Woods 1913); military (Simonton 1979b, 1980a; Suedfeld and Bluck 1988; Suedfeld, Corteen, and McCormick 1986); revolutionary (Ramirez and Suedfeld 1988; Rejai and Philips 1979; Suedfeld and Rank 1976); or judicial (G. Schubert 1983; Tetlock, Bernzweig, and Gallant 1985; Weber 1984). Given how many researchers are Americans, U.S. chief executives have received more attention than other leaders (for example, Hart 1984; Holmes and Elder 1989; Kenney and Rice 1988; Nice, 1984, 1986). Aesthetics represents an important form of symbolic communication, and there is hefty literature on music (Cerulo 1984, 1988, 1989; Jackson and Padgett 1982; Martindale and Uemura 1983; Paisley 1964; Peterson and Berger 1975; Simonton 1980c, 1980d, 1984h, 1986a, 1987b, 1989c); literature (Adamopoulos 1982; Derks 1989; Martindale 1975, 1984a, 1984b; Rosenberg 1989; Rosenberg and Jones 1972; Rosengren 1985; Simonton 1975a, 1983a, 1986f, 1988a, 1989b, 1990d); the visual arts (Dressler and Robbins 1975; Martindale 1986b; Simonton 1984a); and popular fashions (Lowe and Lowe 1982; J. Richardson and Kroeber 1940; D. E. Robinson 1975, 1976; Simonton 1977d). Other social psychological subjects subjected to historiometric scrutiny include social comparison (Suls and Fletcher 1983); person perception (Benjafield and

Carson 1985; Benjafield and Muckenheim 1989; Harrison, Struthers, and Moore 1988); social and political cognition (Granberg and Brent 1983; Grush 1980; Grush, McKeough, and Ahlering 1978; Simonton 1986c; Swede and Tetlock 1986); racial discrimination (Beck 1980a, 1980b); and the role of zeitgeist in the appearance of genius, creativity, or leadership (Brannigan and Wanner 1983a, 1983b; Gray 1958, 1961, 1966; Kenney and Rice 1988; Price 1978; Rainoff 1929; Schmookler 1966; Simonton 1976c, 1979a; Taagepera and Colby 1979; Yuasa 1974).

These are the more noteworthy substantive contributions of historiometry to psychology, even if progress has been made in other domains as well, such as the history of psychology (for example, Over 1982; Suedfeld 1985; Zusne 1976, 1987). The three subdisciplines of personality, developmental, and social psychology, however, command our greatest attention owing to the singular technical virtues of the historiometric approach.

Methodological assets.   Historiometricians possess several appealing features, including advantages not claimed by any other technique, at least not entirely. One critical benefit has to do with the inescapable reality that many concepts of undeniable psychological interest cannot be effectively examined except by drawing upon the historical record. If the goal is to understand, for example, whether capital punishment provides an efficacious deterrent to murder, the logical choice is to inspect the appropriate historical time series (for example, W. C. Bailey 1980; Phillips 1980). Even when technically feasible to obtain passable indicators of some construct in a more standard research setting, historiometric measures often claim far superior validity—frequently leading psychologists trained in conventional methods to draw upon history and biography. Many of these pioneers were curious about such phenomena as genius, creativity, or leadership, and they could conceive no better operational definition than that which requires the systematic observation of universally recognized geniuses, creators, or leaders.

Even if a real-world phenomenon can be reasonably transported to a laboratory cubicle for controlled experimental study, reactivity induced by the artificial situation often undermines the validity of findings. For example, a little controversy has brewed over whether the relation between individual aggressiveness and ambient temperature is a nonmonotonic function. While laboratory experiments seem to favor a curvilinear association, the archival data on the genuine incidence of collective and personal violence lean more toward a positive linear function. Which are we to believe, the historical record of real riots and homicides or the behavior of college students in a laboratory cubicle? The most current and comprehensive review of this massive literature, although conceived by a psychologist with solid training in experimental research, chose history over the laboratory (C. A. Anderson 1989). Experiments are obtrusive—with their "aggression machines" and turned up thermostats—that they may introduce insurmountable artifacts. In general, when experimenters strive to duplicate the variation exhibited in the actual world, subjects are bound to react to the contrivances. By comparison, historiometric measures are inherently unobtrusive, obviating worries that the subjects may feel like guinea pigs and thereby acquire a mental set that destroys the naturalness of the observations (Webb, Campbell, Schwartz, Sechrest, and Grove 1981).

Reliance on a subject pool of college students considerably restricts the scientific generalizability of much research (D. A. Sears 1986). As much as 80 percent of all published work in the most prestigious psychological journals may be carried out on college undergraduates. This can result in numerous disadvantages in comparison with historiometric research. College students form a highly homogeneous population, especially since most of the published research is executed at elite state and private universities. In contrast, historiometric inquiries often inspect the full range of individual-difference variables. Studies of intellectual ability, for example, by taking full advantage of one sad disadvantage of hereditary monarchies, have managed to examine leaders with intellects ranging from imbeciles to geniuses. Even in a sample of historical personalities, a criterion variable like creativity or leadership can exhibit a phenomenal variance: from Peter III of Russia to Louis XIV of France for hereditary monarchs, Harding to Lincoln for U.S. presidents, Burnside to Napoleon for generals, William Higgins to Newton for scientists, Henri de Roy to Aristotle for philosophers, Hendrick Bloemaert to Michelangelo for artists, and Louis Beydts to Beethoven for composers. Likewise in the case of predictor variables, we can investigate the complete range of such variables as war, political fragmentation, assassination, ambient temperature, role-model availability, intellectual ferment, cultural persecution, and so forth. This enhanced variability is not just cross-sectional, but also longitudinal. The age range of college undergraduates, even with the recent influx of older students, is rather limiting for serious life-span developmental work. In comparison, the historiometrician can easily study individuals over their entire life span.

Beyond maximizing validity and variance, other assets ensue from the investigation of historical individuals. In chapter 2 we mentioned the advantage of unit replicability whereby researchers can replicate prior work *exactly* by the simple expedient of subjecting identical cases to further scrutiny. Of more general utility is the common capacity to work with large sample sizes, in the hundreds or even thousands, a magnitude often logistically impossible in conventional methods. Besides augmented generalizability, big Ns allow the use of more sophisticated analytical tools. Moreover, whatever the size of the sample, it is often possible to study telling exemplars of the phenomenon, as in the examination of 2,026 scientists or 15,618 classical melodies, and even to exhaust the potential subject pool, as in studies of presidential leadership.

Because the historical record extends far back in the past and covers vast distances on the globe, it is also conceivable to have a sample of sufficient breadth that any discovered relations will transcend the idiosyncrasies of a separate time and place. Critics of psychology frequently point to its spatio-temporal enslavement (for example, Gergen 1973). As Collingwood ([1946] 1972, 224) expressed the objection in his *Idea of History*, "To regard such a positive mental science as rising above the sphere of history, and establishing the permanent and unchanging laws of human nature, is therefore possible only to a person who mistakes the transient conditions of a certain historical age for the permanent conditions of human life." Such objections can be broken only by adopting a sample broad enough in space and time to guarantee that central results are cross-culturally and transhistorically invariant.

Many conservative psychologists may still feel that somehow historical figures are not the proper subjects of psychological inquiry. Napoleon, Lincoln, Copernicus, Aristotle, Cervantes, Beethoven, and Michelangelo are seen as out of place in psychological journals whose articles are normally populated by college sophomores. Yet this conception of appropriate subject pools seems misplaced; psychologists should be driven by the phenomena, not by the method. Psychology can be enriched only when it encourages its practitioners to explore thought, feeling, and behavior in its varied manifestations, with all the scientific rigor the circumstances allow. Thus some psychologists study children, senior citizens, or schizophrenics, while others employ computers and animals—all without worrying about whether they are "doing psychology." Historiometric samples are selected for the same scientific purposes. A historical figure, no matter how illustrious, remains an individual human being and as such is no less an exemplar of humanity than is an undergraduate, a patient in a mental hospital, or an infant, and is definitely more representative than a computer, a rat, or a cockroach.

A psychologist may still challenge historiometrics on such scientific issues as the reliability and validity of data and the logical power of causal inferences. These difficulties can, however, often be overcome and historiometric work can stand on a par with alternative approaches. Any residual problems are compensated by historiometry's prominent advantages, such as the data's superior real-world validity. A fanatically resistant opponent may respond that all phenomena that can be best investigated using historical data are not the province of psychology anyway. Substantive contributions may accordingly be placed under some other head, whether sociology, political science, anthropology, history, or philosophy. Nonetheless, adopting this stance signifies that numerous phenomena of great importance in human affairs are not pertinent to psychological science.

In the last analysis, the crucial issue is *not* whether a historiometrician is engaged in psychological research, but rather whether what is being done justly qualifies as doing science.

Historiometry as Science

If psychology counts as a legitimate scientific discipline, and if historiometry represents a bona fide subdiscipline of psychology, then historiometry is a science. Nevertheless, should any doubts linger, a separate defense is in order. Given that in figure 1.1 much of psychology was deliberately kept from overlapping with science proper—marking the distinction often voiced between "human" and "natural" science—we are obliged to prove that historiometry does not join in that intersecting set where psychology merges with history to the exclusion of science proper, meeting psychohistory and psychobiography. The demonstration requires that we touch upon two obvious discrepancies between historiometry and those more accepted sciences. One discrepancy concerns the formal status of the theories, the other the empirical precision of the data by which those theories are tested.

Deterministic versus statistical models.   The first successes in the physical sciences came when a handful of variables were interconnected by relatively complex functions. In Galileo's ballistics, the movement of a free-moving projectile was described by a quadratic polynomial in time. In Kepler's third law of planetary movement, the square of the period of revolution for any planet is proportional to the cube of the planet's mean distance from the sun. We examined earlier how Newton's gravitational formula expresses the attractive force as a complex multiplicative and nonlinear function. Advances in the physical sciences often mean applying ever more sophisticated mathematics to describe the intricacies of the relations among the central variables that define the behavior of physical phenomena. These formal treatments, moreover, were deterministic in that they specified exactly what the value of a dependent variable should be given pertinent information about the independent variable(s). Discrepancies between observed and predicted scores were normally ascribed to measurement errors rather than dispense with deterministic forecasts. When departures from expectation could not be successfully dismissed as observational error—as in the definite empirical inadequacy of the nineteenth century models of blackbody radiation—these mistakes were attributed most frequently to temporary simplifications in the mathematical model. As a matter of faith, some elaboration in the functional form would accommodate the appearances far better, leaving once and for all a residual well within the confines of measurement precision.

Last, these intricate predictive equations almost invariably had a sound theoretical foundation. The typical situation in setting up a deterministic model is to state differential equations (ordinary or partial) that specify how some variables change with respect to other variables. Under ideal conditions, these equations obtain a solution in the form of an explicit mathematical function. Should equations not originate in such a hypothetico-deductive display but rather emerge by induction from the raw data, the expectation remains that a theoretician will subsume the empirical generalization under an abstract and logical scheme that accurately describes an elementary physical process. Thus were the conclusions of both Galileo and Kepler shown by Newton to be derivable from the universal law of gravitation plus his laws of motion. And the utterly empirical Balmer formula for the hydrogen spectrum was reduced to an implication of Bohr's atomic model.

When historiometry is compared to the standards implied by the norms established in the master sciences, it is evident that whenever historiometricians achieve success, it is more modest. Rather than complex functions that almost perfectly relate the dependent variable to its independent variables, the common practice is to accept linear and additive functions that accommodate too little variance to warrant celebration that a deterministic function has been isolated. The predictive inferiority can prove frustrating given that the investigator may have considered many potential causes for a given effect and still comes out with a handful of tidbits. Further, the variation left unexplained is typically much too large to be discounted as a measurement error, even when the reliability of the instruments may make this excuse far more plausible than in the physical sciences. At best, historiometric equations are statistical rather than deterministic; a stochastic "disturbance" term is always inserted so that the prediction and observation columns can match perfectly. Finally, the statistical models are seldom deduced from a unifying theory, but rather they represent empirical summaries of the data. In lieu of a rigorous derivation from first principles, statistical models are vigorously built up empirically and accordingly always have a more tentative flavor. Inductive information can never be as secure as deductive inference, at least not when the latter comes from logically self-evident or empirically incontrovertible axioms.

This said, however, the foregoing comparison has been deliberately made to accentuate contrasts; the reality is much less cleanly drawn. Those sciences that are unchallenged do not always deal with deterministic equations. Treatments of Brownian motion have no choice but to formulate stochastic models, and, ever since Max Planck's solution to the blackbody problem, classical determinism has yielded ground to the probabilistic equations of quantum mechanics, a shattering change in perspective captured so well in the notorious Heisenberg uncertainty principle. With the advent of mathematical theories of chaos, purely deterministic predictions are becoming increasingly outmoded for many natural phenomena. Historiometry, on the other hand, does not always rely exclusively on empirically based statistical models that specify simple functions. Lewis Richardson (1960a) made a heroic effort to apply the technique of deterministic differential equations to arms races and war, and this author has exploited the same methodology to advance a theoretical model of how creative productivity changes over a life span (Simonton 1984b, 1990a). Yet these and other imitations of the physical sciences have not been nearly as successful (see also Rashevsky 1968). Perhaps the inadequacies stem from a dearth of behavioral scientists with the mathematical training needed, so that first approximations are seldom the basis for further analytical improvements.

More fundamental, human thoughts, feelings, and actions, especially on the stage of history, may well be extremely complex in their causal determination. This complexity has two sources. First, many relations, perhaps the majority, are best described in the real world by nonadditive and nonlinear functions, comparable to the processes that permeate the physical world. This complication, by itself, would be no more problematic than in the natural sciences were it not for the second source of complexity, namely the likelihood that human activities are determined by hundreds, even thousands of variables. Though experimentation might permit the behavioral scientist to trace some causal connections, too many crucial variables are unavailable owing to practical and ethical considerations. So an appreciable portion of the intricate manifold of cause-effect links can never be completely unveiled in the laboratory. Accordingly, we cannot expect the psychologist to adopt the same strategies as the physical scientist and boast the same triumph. Unless the investigator can somehow accurately measure and properly incorporate *all* determinants of a given phenomenon, parameter estimates will be insecure, and there will inevitably remain a substantial residual error of prediction. Models will have to be statistical rather than deterministic.

Moreover, it is unlikely that the models can ever be imbued with an impressive theoretical derivation. The number of causes involved and the convolutions in their effects, prohibit complete analytical treatment. An appreciable segment of any statistical model may have the status of a mere factual inventory, for the mathematical analyses needed to render these findings a priori exceed by far what is humanly possible. As anyone knows who has experience with differential-equation models, it is easy to posit a system of equations that have no closed-form solution. The more complex the process being modeled, the more intractable the differential equations become. Although simplifying assumptions can often be introduced to make equations tractable, they may undermine the theoretical plausibility of the model, putting theorists in a genuine quandary: Does one opt for solvable equations or realistic postulates?

Even in the modeling of elementary physical phenomena, the mathematical requirements can quickly outstrip the best intellects. At the time that Newton wanted to show his laws of motion and gravitation could predict as well as explain the orbit of a planet around the sun, he derived a differential equation that could not be solved explicitly except by performing twelve successive integrations. Yet when Newton turned to the "three-body problem," such as the sun-earth-moon system, the resulting differential equation demanded eighteen integrations, a task beyond Newton's prodigious powers. Indeed, for the next two centuries this puzzle stumped an elite club of skilled astronomers, physicists, and mathematicians. Only near the end of the nineteenth century was Henri Poincaré able to advise the intellectual community not to waste any more time: The three-body problem has no exact solution, and therefore it can be treated only by conceptually inelegant numerical approximations (Olinick 1978, 381). It is certainly an understatement to say that *no* phenomenon in historiometry is so accessible as this to analytical solution.

Therefore, it may make no sense to take the physical sciences as the touchstone for assaying the scientific merit of historiometric research. Individual genius, creativity, leadership, collective violence, economic prosperity, and cultural change, or any other activity by which persons impress themselves on their world, are not to be neatly bundled up using a handful of variables, and the causal interconnections are too intertwined to be separated analytically or experimentally. The historiometrician seems to be eternally confronted by the choice of hypothesizing complex relations among a few variables or specifying simple relations among hundreds of variables. To formulate elaborate multivariate models that include the required nonlinear and nonadditive functions may not be feasible, not because no techniques are possible but because the human mind is physically incapable of conceiving analytical strategies of sufficient sophistication (Faust 1984).

Historiometry's restrictions in this respect are probably comparable to those of other sciences that must cope with events governed by a myriad uneasy determinants. Kindred disciplines include population genetics, ecology, meteorology, oceanography, economics, and political science. If any of these are considered true sciences, then historiometry deserves the same name. Yet the chief accomplishments of such disciplines are seldom cast in the Newtonian style. Statistical models abound, deterministic models are few, and of these few most are implausible. None of these disciplines in the biological, earth, and social sciences contends with phenomena as straightforward as the three-body problem. Imagine how far Newton would have progressed had he tried to tackle the million-body problem, the attractive forces between the bodies decided by hundreds of factors entering curvilinear functions and interaction terms, the movements deflected by randomly scattered obstacles and perverse winds, and the velocities dictated by internal means of acceleration and deceleration!

Hard versus soft data. Anytime a scientist struggles to treat human phenomena by the classic approaches of the physical sciences, one difficulty emerges over and over—the absence of information of sufficient power to support genuine tests of theoretical models. A solution to a differential equation contains parameters that must be estimated from the data before predictions can be generated. Even in the hardest and most exacting disciplines within the behavioral sciences, that empirical base is often inadequate. For example, in cognitive psychology— certainly one of the most scientifically respectable behavioral disciplines today— it is commonplace to infer mental processes according to reaction times, a practice that has been going on ever since the 1868 work of F. C. Donders (see Luce 1986). Mathematically proficient theorists have devised sophisticated models to explicate the data. Although most of the models are probabilistic rather than deterministic, they still stumble over the embarrassing variability of the response times—such as a standard deviation of 100 milliseconds for a mean around 400 milliseconds. It was this disconcerting plus or minus in human reaction times that dissuaded Helmholtz from extending his preliminary inquiries on the subject over a century ago. With data this rough, parameter estimation can only be crude under the most optimal conditions. Moreover, with noise so obscuring the signal transmitted from the things-in-themselves, it is possible to conceive several alternative models that dispatch the data with equal precision. This renders unlikely a "critical test" that can distinguish between models that make even totally contrary assumptions about the underlying cognitive processes. This lack of discriminatory power cannot but cause the theoretician considerable chagrin. The data offer too much latitude for the proliferation of conceptually incompatible yet empirically equivalent theories.

If model building is so problematic in the response-time research, what can we reasonably anticipate from historiometric inquiries? Woods (1911) may have identified historiometry as an "exact science," yet it would be difficult to make this generic label encompass historiometrics. Reliabilities for most variables are seldom near unity. Further, many variables of critical theoretical importance can often be tapped only indirectly, by mere "indicators" or "proxy variables," whose associations with the true constructs are tenuous at best. When Richardson (1960a, 1960b) endeavored to supply an empirical demonstration for his deterministic model of arms races, he was obliged to define measures that had only a tangential link with the variables in his equations. Likewise, attempts to devise stochastic models that explain multiple discovery and invention are confounded by the unavailability of precise estimates of how frequently singletons and nulltons appear (Simonton 1986d, 1986e). Without reliable figures, alternative models treat the data with comparable aplomb. Hence, often the historiometric data are not hard enough to support strong theories.

Before deciding from this discussion that historiometry is unfit to be called a science, we must note that matters are hardly any better in many other respectable sciences. The paleontological record, for example, does not suffice to make a decisive discrimination between gradualist and punctuated-equilibrium models of biological evolution. In meteorology, controversy still rages about something so basic as whether the sunspot cycle has any real consequence for weather patterns. In economics, opposing theories can be generated spontaneously with minimal limitations imposed by the econometric data. Indeed, when one looks at the frontiers of the most exact sciences, the empirical indeterminacy of theories prevails. In high-energy physics, one theoretician after another has offered approximations to a grand Theory of Everything, introducing concepts as strange as superstrings and ubiquitous black holes, without the slightest impediment from whatever facts can be distilled from the biggest particle colliders. In fact, the data in many domains of physics can be no less soft than those in psychology, a shocking possibility shown in a delightful article entitled "How Hard is Hard Science, How Soft is Soft Science? The Empirical Cumulativeness of Research" (Hedges 1987). Homogeneity statistics from reviews in high-energy physics (relating to the lifetime or mass of various elementary particles) were contrasted with those in social science reviews (concerning such difficult constructs as spatial perception, verbal ability, self-concept, teacher expectancy, and so forth), and the latter was not found wanting! Quite soft is any science's leading edge.

Historiometry as History

To the extent that we worry about historiometry's status as a science, we must be proportionately less obsessed with the contributions that historiometry may make to history. This follows from historiometry's fundamental dedication to the discovery of nomothetic principles, the goal of any true science, whereas history's devotions are eternally idiographic. In the historiometric enterprise, history provides only the data, while science inspires the analyses. Considering how little tolerance historians often have for either generalization or quantification, the legitimate historian might find such efforts not merely irrelevant, but irreverent besides. Instead of the historians' proper nouns and specific dates insightfully interlinked with qualitative narrative, historiometricians offer superficially bland technical articles, with names, dates, and places almost absent and with the delicate interweaving of unique and striking events rudely replaced by tables of integers and decimals—parameters and coefficients that bind abstract variables that aggregate across particulars. History is always a better read than science.

Yet even the best historians lapse from the expressed views of their discipline and venture into speculative activities that may be far better assigned to historiometricians. Here historians should repress any distrust of scientific analysis in order to appreciate what historiometricians have to offer. Two circumstances encourage this. The first occurs when historians engage in explanation, the second when they risk prediction.

Historical explanation. At first it would seem that the historiometrician has little to offer the historian bent on analyzing some event. While the historiometrician is preoccupied with testing nomothetic hypotheses through quantitative analyses on many cases, the historian is concerned with an idiographic interpretation of qualitative information about a distinct case. Nevertheless, the disparity of purpose is not essential. To realize this, we must ask what it means to explain a historical happening successfully (see Murphey 1973, chap. 3). A minimal definition should suffice, namely a simple paraphrase of the Hempelian "covering law" model (Hempel 1965). A particular event is said to be explicated if it can be logically subsumed under a general principle that is applicable to a diversity of specific circumstances. If we wish to know why person A performed behavior B, we may show, on the whole, (1) that persons of the type X tend to execute the act Y and (2) that A is a specific case of X just as action B exemplifies Y. Why did Julius Caesar cross the Rubicon? As a person both ambitious and at the same time vulnerable to the machinations of enemies should he relinquish his command before returning to Rome, he engaged in a preemptive strike that anyone with the same personality profile in the same situation would have attempted.

This interpretation illustrates adequately what can qualify for an explanation in history (Popper 1963, 265; Wilkins 1978, chap. 2). Given the complexity of human behavior, these covering laws will actually constitute statistical regularities more than deterministic rules. But that limitation does not preclude deduction of the explanation from the generalization, as long as qualifiers are added with caution. People in state X have a "tendency to," "disposition for," or "likelihood of" emitting behavior Y, and thus it is not irrational to think that A may have done B after the same probabilistic pattern. In other words, a reasonably sound generalization permits a historian to comprehend the underlying causes of an observed succession of events. Indeed, the common impetus for historians hinting at an abstract proposition is to explain a single event or personality. The appeal is to a general principle of behavior that the specific case concretely exemplifies. Because the generalizations are postulated rather than demonstrated, however, the explanatory deduction may be shaky.

This insecurity helps us to appreciate why some historians have become so allied with standard psychobiography and psychohistory (Gay 1985; Langer 1952). Given a comprehensive theory of human motivation, such as that proffered by psychoanalysis, the details should fall nicely into place within a nomothetic framework. The landmark psychobiographies of Freud, Erikson, and others establish a paradigm to be followed by historians who want to understand the careers of other creators and leaders. Likewise, Freud's exploratory treatment of entire cultures, such as found in his *Group Psychology and the Analysis of the Ego* and *Totum and Taboo,* became a harbinger of the "group fantasy analysis," which purports to offer the means to interpret mass movements, collective events, and popular culture within the confines of a powerful theory (deMause 1981). The difficulty in all this, of course, is that psychoanalytic theory may be no more secure than the commonsense psychology usually relied upon in traditional historiography. We need not repeat all the arguments to be found in Stannard's (1980) controversial (and sometimes intemperate) critique to justify the recommendation that historians searching for scientific generalizations to subsume historical particulars might be advised to look outside the psychoanalytic tradition.

This is where the historiometrician steps in. Because historiometry strives to establish scientific principles, it might provide a far more solid base for explanation than either the intuitive conjectures of the historian or the theoretical speculations of the psychoanalyst. Moreover, unlike psychoanalytic psychohistory and psychobiography, which fall back on a stretched extrapolation from clinical impressions to historical phenomena, historiometry may not require an extrapolation whatsoever. A special case under consideration may already have part of the larger sample on which a historiometric analysis was conducted.

Do you want to know why Napoleon was defeated at Waterloo, Louis XIV could be called "The Great," Andrew Johnson had such poor relations with Congress, Aristotle was so influential, Mozart so prolific, Shakespeare's 116th sonnet so profound, or the Golden Age of Greece so creative? Scientific journals contain articles in which these very cases were examined on the relevant criteria, as part of a more exhaustive multiple-case and multivariate inquiry. Whatever holds for the entire sample of commanders, monarchs, presidents, philosophers, composers, sonnets, or generations must prove (measurably) germane to each entity within the sample. Even when a specific case is not privileged to have been a member of the elite group on which the nomothetic principles were established, the extrapolation will usually enjoy an inferential security that cannot be boasted by alternative explanatory approaches. A clinical population cannot offer laws nearly as pertinent as what can be surmised from actual historical creators and leaders, real achievements and disasters. The power of historiometric interpretation is especially potent when every effort has been made to demonstrate the transhistorical and cross-cultural invariance of the propositions, thereby strengthening their nomothetic position.

Historiometric accounts feature two additional assets not always claimed by rival interpretative strategies. First, because from the start historiometric inquiries calculate the proportion of variance of each explanatory variable, we obtain some measure of the comparative adequacy of an interpretation. Second, because historiometric problems are almost always stated in a multivariate framework, historiometric explanations have a built-in resistance to simple-minded, single-cause statements. Together these two assets mean that the historiometrician favors multiple-cause explanations with a specification of the relative influence of each explicit cause. This twofold advantage may be illustrated by the specific example of Napoleon. To what can we attribute his tactical success in warfare? According to Carlyle (1841), Napoleon was an unadulterated genius, a man whose mental powers were so far beyond the norm that his will swept all before him. Tolstoy ([1865–69] 1952) objected, relegating much of the epilogues of *War and Peace* to destroying not just the genius theory, but the chance theory besides.

> Why did it happen in this and not in some other way?
>
> Because it happened so! "*Chance* created the situation; *genius* utilized it," says history.
>
> The words *chance* and *genius* do not denote any really existing thing and therefore cannot be defined. Those words only denote a certain state of understanding of phenomena. (646)

Behind each event, Tolstoy claims, was neither genius nor chance, nor genius exploiting chance, but the zeitgeist.

Yet need we express this debate in such either/or terms? Might not events be multiply caused? Perhaps Napoleon's prowess was exceptional relative to his contemporaries, even though the politico-military machine of revolutionary France had its part, coupled with many examples of plain luck. In one pilot inquiry, both Carlyle and Tolstoy were shown to have captured a particle of truth (Simonton 1979b). On the one hand, Napoleon's tactical success rate was safely higher than that of his fellow French generals, by a contrast of 85–47 percent. On the other hand, a biographical time-series analysis revealed that Napoleon's rate of victory was strongly associated with the success rate of his colleagues fighting at the same time, suggesting a shared strategic dependence on the comparative power of the French army vis-à-vis its chief enemies. While about 9 percent of the variation in battlefield victory may be attributed to Napoleon's apparent genius, around 25 percent may be ascribed instead to military zeitgeist.

Do these percentages inform us that the remaining 66 percent can be credited to chance? Not necessarily, for as Tolstoy warned, chance is often no more than a euphemism for ignorance. To dismiss an event as a result of luck is to conflate random influx with the state of our knowledge. Perhaps once we define more predictors or measure the predictors that we have with superior precision, we might reduce the portion of the phenomenon that cannot be clearly explained. Nevertheless, it may also be that no matter how complex our models, an irreducible residual persists. For example, notwithstanding a coordinated search through hundreds of variables, 18 percent of the variation in presidential greatness remains unaccounted for. Considering the supreme reliability of the dependent and independent variables, this residual cannot be discounted as measurement error. Given the exhaustiveness of the quest, perhaps no factor hides that, when added to the regression equation, can remove the last bit of uncertainty. Instead, corresponding to each president there may be some unique influence that cannot be shared with any other chief executive—a distinctive intrusion that may count as luck, whether good or bad.

The observed greatness assessments and the predicted scores according to the six-variable equation given in are shown in table 9.1. Notice that Washington's standing with posterity is somewhat higher than the model can accommodate, yielding a discrepancy of nearly a standard deviation. We may speculate that a fragment of this difference may owe its existence to his unparalleled place as the precedent-setting first president, a status that adds further luster to those assets already incorporated in the model, such as his having been a war hero. Since only one president can be lucky enough to have been the first president, the extra points so accumulated cannot be allotted to any other chief executive for the rest of history. Despite this advantage, this factor need not be considered idiographic. Further analyses may reveal that the first in any line of succession usually gets a special boost in reputation—and evidence can be found for just such a "founders effect" in the dynasties of European hereditary monarchies (Simonton 1984g).

Table 9.1   *Observed, Predicted, and Residual Scores*
for Presidential Greatness

President	Observed	Predicted	Residual
1. Washington	1.87	1.03	0.84
2. J. Adams	0.59	0.29	0.30
3. Jefferson	1.52	1.73	−0.21
4. Madison	0.23	0.90	−0.67
5. Monroe	0.19	−0.24	0.42
6. J. Q. Adams	0.13	−0.17	0.30
7. Jackson	1.02	0.82	0.20
8. Van Buren	−0.32	−0.57	0.25
9. W. Harrison	—	−0.24	—
10. Tyler	−0.83	−0.44	−0.39
11. Polk	0.42	−0.04	0.46
12. Taylor	−0.70	−0.33	−0.37
13. Fillmore	−0.86	−0.86	0.01
14. Pierce	−1.11	−0.56	−0.55
15. Buchanan	−1.27	−0.69	−0.58
16. Lincoln	1.99	1.30	0.68
17. A. Johnson	−1.23	−0.80	−0.43
18. Grant	−1.35	−0.81	−0.54
19. Hayes	−0.38	−0.53	−0.15
20. Garfield	—	−0.05	—
21. Arthur	−0.53	−0.33	−0.20
22. Cleveland	0.12	−0.02	0.14
23. B. Harrison	−0.66	−0.66	0.00
24. McKinley	−0.16	0.37	−0.53
25. T. Roosevelt	1.34	1.14	0.20
26. Taft	−0.23	−0.43	0.25
27. Wilson	1.22	0.86	0.36
28. Harding	−1.60	−2.68	1.08
29. Coolidge	−0.87	−0.63	−0.24
30. Hoover	−0.36	−0.35	−0.01
31. F. Roosevelt	1.91	1.78	0.13
32. Truman	0.92	0.96	−0.04
33. Eisenhower	0.48	0.81	−0.33
34. Kennedy	0.36	0.52	−0.15
35. L. Johnson	0.58	0.68	−0.11
36. Nixon	−1.30	−0.76	−0.54
37. Ford	−0.60	−0.86	0.26
38. Carter	−0.63	−0.50	−0.13
39. Reagan	—	0.22	—

Note. Adapted from Simonton (1986c, table 5). Copyright 1986 by
American Psychological Association. Used by permission.

Admittedly, even if we were to subtract the segment of the residual that might be attributed to this nomothetic effect, a discrepancy may remain that cannot be chipped away by anything else. This final and true residual may indeed represent something profoundly unsurpassed about Washington, something incommensurate with any other historical figure, some genuinely chance element in his life.

But we cannot speculate on this matter until we first make a convincing case that no nomothetic factor has been inadvertently omitted from the historiometric explanation.

This last point deserves expansion. Historians often explain what seem to be the genuinely peculiar occasions and people in the annals of civilization. It is not what appears normal that so frequently attracts the scholar's pen, but what looks blatantly abnormal (M. White 1965, chap. 4). We cited evidence on behalf of this abnormalism when we discussed eponymic theory; if one aspires to make a big splash in the history books, one should stand out from the crowd. Given the historian's preoccupation with the unusual, historiometricians have one crucial item of advice to offer: Do not waste time trying to explain that which requires no elucidation. What is abnormal must be dictated by a nomothetic baseline that specifies which historical entities exhibit the grandest departures from scientific expectation. This task of specification marks one of the main contributions of historiometry, not just to history but also to psychohistory and psychobiography. Only after scholars have a list of the typical and the singular can they freely proceed with interpretative endeavors.

For example, if we examine more closely table 9.1, we learn that it is Harding rather than Washington who shows the most impressive residual error, the difference between scientific prediction and historical fact exceeding a standard deviation. In particular, Harding is not as bad as the equation makes him out to be, suggesting that he may have some redeeming qualities that enhance his attractiveness to those experts who are asked to rate the presidents. Of all the chief executives he was certainly among those who *looked* most "presidential," an appearance that may partly compensate for his failure to have *acted* presidential. Whatever the proper interpretation, an American historian is probably better off tackling the question of why Harding is more highly regarded than the theoretical issue of why Harding was one of the worst presidents in U.S. history. Speculations on the second subject have been incorrect when weighed against objective data (Simonton 1987d). Qualitative and intuitive judgments are ill-equipped for the job of deciphering multivariate statistical associations (Dawes, Faust, and Meehl 1989; Faust 1984; Meehl 1954).

This is a good place to make a point that is implicit in this discussion: Historiometric explanations are not at all confounded by the existence of exceptions to the rule. The laws of genius, creativity, leadership, aesthetic success, collective aggression, or any other historical phenomenon are most unlikely to be deterministic in form. For reasons outlined earlier, the best we can likely expect for most phenomena is a reasonably accurate statistical model. Historiometric principles, however nomothetic, will therefore prove valid only on the average or in the long run. But because investigators never forget to insert (overtly or covertly) a disturbance term or "random shock" into an explanatory formula, discrepancies from prediction cause no uneasiness. By acknowledging these infractions by unspecified events, generalizations can be confidently promulgated notwithstanding their imperfections.

That a rule may be valid despite discrepancies in its application may be difficult to accept, yet it is nothing more than common sense. For example, in Mediterranean climates one meteorological regularity endures above all others—winter rains, summer shines. That sometimes January may come and go without a sprinkle, while July is hit with a thunder shower does not weaken the rule. The same robustness in the face of contradiction saves the historiometrian from being considered either a charlatan or an equivocator. When expectations are violated, it is a spur to search for new causal effects hitherto ignored. Nothing prevents the investigator from examining the residuals for clues as to what variables should be inserted next into an equation to enlarge explanatory precision. To restless historiometricians, an exception is a challenge.

Historians may still object that historiometric generalizations may not elucidate historical particulars. Sympathetic historians may vainly seek in the literature established principles with clear-cut applicability to a given enigma. In fact, some historians may continue to feel that the putative covering laws to be found in reading Freud or Erikson are more valuable, especially when the aim is to comprehend the unconscious motives of historical figures. Historiometric findings may not seem relevant despite historiometry's long history; its full-time practitioners have always been few, indicating that the collection of regularities may be too small to support historical explanation. Thus, it may seem advisable to lean on a suitable psychoanalytic theory (the questionable scientific utility be what it may) rather than rely on historiometric results, however secure.

Yet historians—even psychobiographers and psychohistorians—should actually consider becoming historiometricians from time to time. Historiometry can often deal with an $N = 1$ problem if the unit of analysis is defined properly. Hence, idiographically oriented scholars have an opportunity to test an explanatory hypothesis against a perplexing case. By thus engaging in historiometric work, the historian or psychohistorian can circumvent gaps in current knowledge.

In an interesting paper, "Progress in Psychobiography," Runyan (1988a) supported an affirmative claim with a specific case history, namely work on why King George III of England suffered from five different bouts with an illness that ultimately destroyed his sanity. Runyan reviewed the diverse interpretations of the tragic events, including both medical and psychodynamic accounts. The favorite explanations, such as that concerning the disease porphyria, depend on the prevailing assumption that "George III's attacks did not come at times which appear to be of greatest personal and political stress" (Runyan 1988a, 317). This conclusion implicitly specifies a zero correlation between two variables, illness and stress. Yet the inference was drawn from a qualitative inspection of the raw biographical data, despite ample evidence from both experimental investigations (Dawes, Faust, and Meehl 1989) and historiometric inquiries (Simonton 1984d, 1987d,

1988e) that neither naive nor professional judges can accurately intuit the absence, presence, magnitude, direction, or form of bivariate relations. When the data are at all rich, inductions of covariances tend to be contaminated excessively by impertinent influences like cognitive availability, representativeness, salience, ignored baseline information, and confirmatory bias (Faust 1984). Indeed, another knowledgeable historian could easily offer the contrary claim that "the stresses endured by this hard-working man seemed sufficient to account for his violent breakdown" (Watson 1974, 1127). As a case in point, before his 1788 illness, George III began experiencing deep conflicts with his male offspring, not excluding his heir the Prince of Wales, and just before his last and permanently debilitating breakdown he was struck by the death of his youngest child, the Princess Amelia, who had provided him with stable emotional support during his unpleasant dealings with her brothers.

Which subjective insight is justified by the facts? We could try to pose one qualitative impression against its opposite, but it is doubtful that a consensus either way would have any validity. The subjectivities of many do not amount to the objectivity of one reality, no more than universally experienced optical illusions prove the existence of a strange perceptual world. Instead, this particular problem could be translated into a hypothesis for single-case historiometry. Specifically, we can inspect the cross-correlations between two sets of biographical time series, one assessing the length and influence of the breakdowns, the other gauging the appearance and magnitude of stressful events both political and personal. Facilitating this reformulation are the efforts of previous investigators who have developed techniques for quantifying the requisite time series from biographical and historical sources (Porter and Suedfeld 1981; Simonton 1977a, 1986a, 1987b). Indeed, a prototype may be found in an examination of Beethoven in which the Pearsonian correlation between biographical stress and physical illness in a yearly time series is .53, a coefficient that suggests a confirmatory outcome should the same analysis be performed on the composer's older contemporary, George III (Simonton 1989c). Even if the results of an inquiry using these tools would not settle the debate, quantitative findings should substantially advance the qualitative controversy. It certainly must matter in any historical explanation of these particulars whether the correlation is really zero rather than reliably and sizably positive.

Historical prediction. In establishing the place of historiometry in historical explanation, historians presumably sought a scientific style of interpretation like that of the Hempelian covering-law model. Yet many historians argue emphatically that this approach is ill-suited to the needs of historical inquiry. One forthright rival to Carl Hempel is William Dray (1957), who propounds a view that has antecedents at least as far back as Giambattista Vico and Wilhelm Dilthey. As Dray sees it, history departs from science in its empathic understanding of the actions and motives of historical personalities. The historian tries to climb into the skin of the subject, exploiting this unique perspective to convert basic data into meaningful narrative. Causation per se has little relevance in comparison to unifying concepts that put flesh and blood on a historical event or figure. Another route to describing this critical contrast is to draw a comparison with the two alternative modes of doing psychology, namely the natural science versus human science models. In German terminology, the former is committed to developing an *erklärende Psychologie* that explains key phenomena "from the outside" (objectively), whereas the latter propounds a *verstehende Psychologie* that depicts subjective experience underlying a phenomenon, "from the inside."

It is the historian's prerogative to decide what explanatory ethos is most compatible with the discipline. Still, those historians resistant to scientific interpretation must persist with a rigorous consistency. To avoid being hounded by historiometricians with their nomothetic principles, the historian must eschew any reliance on the general. Once an interpretation leans on some abstraction—about how leaders lead, why creators create, who emerges victorious, when people revolt, where genius begins, what makes a masterpiece, or the like—the Dray paradigm becomes instantaneously inapplicable and must be replaced by Hempel's alternative. If the particular is to be explicated through the general, the historian must ensure that the statements so exploited are the best that a natural science has to offer. Because idiographic analysis cannot then serve as an excuse for a studied ignorance, the historian must become a social scientist.

Even if the historian succeeds at totally idiographic narrative, with no dependence on a nomothetic principle, he or she may still need historiometric techniques. One advantage that Hempel's paradigm has over Dray's is that Hempel's more strongly supports historical prediction. Given an appropriate covering law, the historian can anticipate currently unknown facts, especially events in the future or in a past in which information is lacking. Hempel (1965), in fact, has defended the notion that explanation and prediction are closely connected. An event can be said to have been explained when that same event could have been predicted were it unknown to have taken place. Despite certain inadequacies in this formulation, it does imply another worthy asset of historiometry, given how intimately related explanation and prediction are in quantitative and nomothetic analyses—where prediction encompasses postdiction. The links among these concepts can again be seen in table 9.1.

For those thirty-six presidents rated by the 846 historians polled by Murray and Blessing (1983), the six-variable equation provides an explanation, the comparison of predicted and observed scores indicating the adequacy of that substantive interpretation. Nonetheless, three presidents received no greatness rating—William Harrison, Garfield, and Reagan. Harrison and Garfield were ignored owing to their short terms of office and Reagan owing to his being the incumbent at the time of the poll. The equation nonetheless leads to two postdictions and one prediction regarding these unrated chief executives. For Harrison and Garfield we merely have planted in the equation the appropriate values on the six predictors. It is evident that neither man would be expected to come out well had the historians rated the two anyway. Harrison gains a little from his war hero status, just as Garfield acquires a few points from his tragic assassination, but otherwise both are nondescript by the standards applied to their assessed predecessors and successors. As for Reagan, he was completing his second term at the time that table 9.1 was originally devised (before 1986). Consequently, the forecast had to be predicated on several assumptions, namely that he would finish out his term and avoid both assassination and scandal. Because the last variable required the commission of a felony by members of the president's cabinet, Reagan then squeaked by on this score. At any rate, on the basis of the information available, plus conjecture, Reagan received a predicted rating only a little above the mediocre. This prediction holds under the assumption that historians will not drastically alter their criteria in a subsequent round of questionnaires. When we consider that the predictors originated by looking at ratings that spanned thirty-five years, from Schlesinger (1948) to Murray and Blessing (1983)—and when we recall that the formula is transhistorically and perhaps cross-culturally invariant—this forecast seems firm.

Another reason why we can be fairly confident about how Reagan will appear to posterity (or at least to later experts who define posterity's opinions) is that historiometry has previously been exploited in this very manner with success. In the preliminary search for an explanation of presidential greatness based on the Maranell poll (1970), it was discovered that the predicted score for Kennedy was not nearly as good as his genuine rating (Simonton 1981c). It was then pointed out that this result may have been the outcome of the specific period in which Maranell conducted his survey: The respondents received their questionnaires not too long after Kennedy's assassination, when memories and emotions were still fresh. Awareness of this political tragedy was probably refreshed by two more recent assassinations, one of JFK's brother Robert and the other of Martin Luther King, both with public associations with the deceased president. Further, Sokolsky (1964) had recently published a book entitled *Our Seven Greatest Presidents,* which can be viewed as something of an apotheosis of Kennedy, given how this chief executive was so confidently included among the elite seven. But it was forecast at the time of the historiometric analysis that once passions had cooled and perspective obtained, Kennedy would settle down to a rating only slightly above average. If one compares Kennedy's earlier ratings with those he received thirteen years later, according to Murray and Blessing (1983), this descent is exactly what is seen (see table 4.2). The earlier equation had predicted that Kennedy would earn about the same reputation as Cleveland, and that placement eventually came to pass.

Naturally, real prediction and postdiction can get far more complicated than the above illustration implies. For one thing, we have concentrated solely on point estimates, when a genuine prediction strategy would probably demand interval estimates for predicted values (Cohen and Cohen 1983, 111–13). In addition, nothing has been said about the most effective procedures for deducing forecasts and backcasts from time-series data (Hay and McCleary 1980, chap. 4). These methodologies advise us that we cannot overlook certain inherent difficulties that must be faced by any scholar seeking a second career as a prophet. For example, a prediction equation is most effective when the phenomenon to be anticipated has scores on the predictors that fall within the range of those cases on which the equation was originally constructed. Otherwise we would have no assurance that the functional relations do not take on an altogether different form. Thus, just because intellectual brilliance seems linearly linked with greatness for thirty-six presidents does not mean that if by some quirky electoral process we had a superbright chief executive in the statistical hopper we would anticipate still higher greatness ratings. On theoretical grounds, a president with an IQ clearing two hundred might very well be a disaster as national leader (Simonton 1985a).

Hence, prediction, like explanation, is safest when we are engaged in interpolation, not extrapolation. This becomes especially severe when historical time is included among the predictor variables, whether in linear or curvilinear form. We cannot know whether a trend will persist. A linear function, for example, may in reality be but a segment of an exponential growth or decay curve that will not disclose its secret self for many years. Particularly hazardous are predictions of cyclical behaviors. Can we expect that the oscillations found for melodic originality (in figure 5.1) will continue their upward spiral unabated? That expectation may not be justified if serious composers have already reached the upper limits of auditory complexity that an audience can understand and withstand. In the same manner, cyclical trends, should they exist, may either dampen or intensify over time, just as exponential growth may eventually decelerate into a logistic curve once external constraints are confronted. All in all, extrapolations from past trends may be among the most foolish of intellectual games.

Another consideration that necessitates caution is the empirical precision of the predictive model. If the multiple correlation for a equation is respectable, we can risk predictions, at least in the short term. Hence, the multiple correlation for the six-variable equation used in table 9.1 is .91, signifying that the postdictions for Harrison and Garfield as well as the prediction for Reagan should be secure. Yet seldom is the accuracy so impressive. With multiple correlations in the more middling but common ranges, the plus or minus on a point prediction can rival the framing of the Colorado River by the rim of the Grand Canyon. Such sweeping confidence intervals render all predictions suspect.

To get a better perspective on this complication we can do a figure-ground reversal, focusing on the unexplained variance. With a multiple correlation of around .70—which is still an honorable figure—a bit over half of the variation in the phenomenon is accounted for by factors not explicitly in the statistical expectation. Not only does this allow much mischief on the part of unspecified forces, but additionally even trivial effects might accumulate over time to vitiate the value of long-term forecasts. We previously discussed the "variance explanation paradox," when a "little means a lot" (Abelson 1985), an analysis that can just as adequately rule against the power of prediction. Of course, in the historiometrician's fantasy life there is the dream of eventually incorporating enough predictors to minimize these contaminations. But we have already confessed that it is unlikely that most historical phenomena will ever be granted exhaustive explication. Invariably there will survive a residual impervious to nomothetic onslaughts. Yet only when historiometric regularities account for the phenomena with near perfection will historical prediction ever progress beyond the chimerical.

If prediction is so precarious, why even mention the possibility in an evaluation of historiometry as history? The answer lies in the recognition that historians frequently indulge a sweet tooth for predictions in some guise, and that when they do so these endeavors may be enhanced by an awareness of historiometric findings and methods, notwithstanding the pitfalls. Certainly one of the main arguments for knowing the past is that the past is a guide not only to the present, but to the future as well. It is for this cause that some historians find it so difficult to resist the temptation to become the prophets of their times, forecasting the direction to be taken by contemporary trends. Toynbee's (1946) thought typifies well enough the conversion of narration to prediction. This transformation of past facts into forecasts first required the formulation of historical generalizations that transcend the particulars narrated. Taken *as a whole,* the ascent, acme, and aftermath of world civilizations follow the same organic pattern. Granting this regularity writ large, all that must be done is to determine where the present moment sits in the current cycle of birth, life, and death.

This method of concocting prophecy out of history is popular and universal, especially in the speculative philosophy of history. Even should modern professional historians look askance at grandiose prophetic schemes, their suspicions do not prevent respectable members of the discipline from pursuing more modest forms of the same enterprise. For example, in the best-selling book *The Rise and Fall of the Great Powers* (1987), Paul Kennedy delineates how political empires ultimately decline by an inevitable logic, and thereby he leads us to some expectations about the probable future of the American and Soviet empires. Notwithstanding the wealth of detail about the histories of specific imperial systems, Kennedy's thesis itself rises and falls according to the validity of a nomothetic proposition: The "history of the rise and later fall of the leading countries in the Great Power system . . . shows a very significant correlation *over the longer term* between productive and revenue-raising capacities on the one hand and military strength on the other" (xvi). Once we notice the essential contribution of this supposed relation to the entire argument, we realize that Kennedy is working within the tradition of the Hempelian covering law to derive both explanatory and predictive remarks. Hence, the same criteria behind any critique of historiometric explanation and prediction apply in this case too. Is an association actually present between the two variables? If so, how much variance is explained? Are values on the predictor variables stable enough to support reasonably accurate forecasts years in advance? Or is there a diversity of factors extraneous to the Kennedy model that make such extrapolations too risky for sober analysis? Can his model be extrapolated into postdictions regarding the explosive emergence of the Arabian and Mongolian peoples in medieval times?

Apropos of the last query, a second sort of prediction occupies a more curious position in historiography—those speculative postdictions concerning the great what ifs of history. This discussion of alternative histories or "pasts that might have been" might be considered a favorite intellectual pastime (Hacker and Chamberlain 1981). Thus, Gibbon ([1776–88] 1952, 492), after observing how an Ottoman conquest was thwarted by an episode of gout that struck the Sultan Bajazet, concluded that "an acrimonious humour falling on a single fibre of one man may prevent or suspend the misery of nations." More dramatic still is Pascal's ([1670] 1952, 202) famous claim that "Cleopatra's nose: had it been shorter, the whole aspect of the world would have been altered." Remarks such as these cannot be evaluated without a strong nomothetic theory. For instance, among the notable attainments of cliometrics is the application of economic theory to fix the plausibility of such alternative histories, whether the matter regards how slavery could have disappeared in the South without the Civil War (Fogel and Engerman 1974) or how the American West would have developed without the railroads (Fogel 1964).

Analogously, historiometricians may apply their accumulated knowledge to speculate on relevant issues. After establishing a highly accurate equation that could predict the victor in U.S. presidential elections, Rosenstone (1983) examined what would have happened under different circumstances, thereby generating alternative histories. For example, Hubert H. Humphrey had no chance to become president, for he would have lost to Nixon in 1972 and to Ford in 1976. Similarly, Lyndon Johnson's smashing victory over Goldwater in 1964 cannot be blamed on the Republican extremists having their say at the nominating convention, given that the more moderate Rockefeller would have lost by nearly as much. Finally, if racial issues had been as prominent in 1960 as they were to become in 1968, or if the disposable income at the end of Eisenhower's administration had been only 1 percent higher, Nixon would have been inaugurated as the thirty-fifth rather than the thirty-seventh chief executive.

Postdictions like these are feasible in many other substantive domains as well. If Einstein had died in the crib, how long would physics have had to wait for a theory of relativity? Was it inevitable that Trotsky had to lose out to Stalin in the struggle for power after Lenin's death? What would have happened to Beethoven's reputation had Mozart lived past thirty-five and Schubert past thirty-one? Answers to enigmas like these can be presented only in probabilistic language, naturally, but historiometric findings already suffice to support competent responses. This feature has yet to be exploited in history, but the application may earn more attention in the future as nomothetic results accumulate and disseminate.

Prospects

As surveyed from the three perspectives of psychology, science, and history, historiometry has much to offer the curious and systematic intellect. Its unparalled virtues might even encourage enough workers to join the ranks that we will see an actual growth in the enterprise. Three facts elicit this optimistic forecast. First, considerable progress has been seen in quantitative techniques, an advance coupled with the tremendous growth in computing power that has amazed the world in recent years. An investigator can perform sophisticated analyses on a home computer that could not have been imagined a few decades ago. Second, psychology and affiliated sciences are attaining a level of theoretical sophistication that permits the generation of hypotheses far more deserving than ever of empirical scrutiny. Some of these propositions can be scientifically assessed only by historiometric methods. Third and last, the historical data on which these tests must be conducted are dramatically improving in both quantity and quality. Each day mounds of new data are added to a truly global historical record, all as a by-product of the awesome explosion of population and information. We may even witness the time when these facts are routinely compiled into computer data bases for convenient distribution to investigators. In this respect, historiometry looks like certain earth sciences, such as meteorology and geology, in which the data points are becoming sufficiently numerous and accurate that scientists can begin to answer questions that were subjects of speculation a few generations ago.

This upbeat projection must be tempered by a lamentable truth. As C. P. Snow (1960) observed in his essay *The Two Cultures,* two separate species have evolved in the intellectual world, creating a division that threatens the vitality of historiometry. A sizable proportion of scientists acquire not even a passable acquaintance with art, literature, philosophy, and music, an ignorance nurtured by the advent and proliferation of the bachelor of science degree. Those scholars who are knowledgeable in these cultural areas reciprocate by acquiring virtually no competence in mathematical and scientific reasoning. The intellectual universe thus seems bifurcated into those who appreciate quantity, abstraction, and precision, on the one hand, and those who relish quality, detail, and insight, on the other. This bifurcation is seen almost everywhere, even in endeavors that would seem to have close affinities; witness the evidently unleapable chasm that divides literary criticism from literary computing (Potter 1988).

No doubt scientists do exist who exhibit a profound understanding of the humanistic disciplines—and it is said that any first-rate graduate program in theoretical physics can strike up a string quartet on a moment's notice—yet unless these scientists happen to be psychologists too, it is unlikely that they will feel a pull toward doing historiometry. For historians and other humanistic scholars, a few may comprehend the utility of the scientific orientation, and a subset of these may even acquire a certain proficiency in quantitative methods and nomothetic theory, yet this select group may not feel the need to combine the two domains into an integrated exercise. Indeed, it may be cliometrics and psychohistory, not historiometry, that offer an outlook more sympathetic to professional commitments. Occasionally, behavioral scientists will emerge who can successfully unify these separate conceptual domains and thus follow in the widely spaced footsteps that began with Quetelet and Galton over a century ago, but this will probably be something of a rarity. Only when our educational system is reconstructed so that all scientists receive an excellent liberal arts education, and all humanists obtain a rigorous but encouraging grounding in the modes of scientific thought, can we rationally expect historiometry to be anything more than an occasional occupation.

May I end this prognostication, and this treatise, on a more personal note? It was over a score years ago, in 1966, when I first speculated on how science and history might be integrated, and a dozen years and more have passed since those speculations began to assume specific form as a concrete and directed program of psychological research (Simonton 1990b). By the time I submitted my doctoral dissertation in 1974, I naively thought that this little methodological specialty of psychology was on the threshold of attracting the continuous and serious efforts of numerous colleagues. But now, in retrospect, I realize that the prospects for a popular historiometry are not nearly so rhapsodic. Historiometry will always be with us, as each generation produces a collection of scholars with the requisite cluster of curiosities and capacities. Yet the club of practitioners may always be exclusive, not out of an arrogant elitism on the part of the membership, but owing to the paucity of applicants for admission. Nevertheless, the clubhouse provides a cozy retreat for those who seek the convergence of psychology, science, and history.

Abelson, R. P. 1985. A variance explanation paradox: When a little is a lot. *Psychological Bulletin 97,* 129–33.

Abramowitz, A. I. 1985. Economic conditions, presidential popularity, and voting behavior in midterm congressional elections. *Journal of Politics 47,* 31–43.

Abt, H. A. 1983. At what ages do outstanding American astronomers publish their most cited papers? *Publications of the Astronomical Society of the Pacific 95,* 13–16.

Achenbaum, W. A. 1978. *Old age in the new land.* Baltimore: Johns Hopkins University Press.

Adamopoulos, J. 1982. Analysis of interpersonal structures in literary works of three historical periods. *Journal of Cross-Cultural Psychology 13,* 157–68.

Adams, C. W. 1946. The age at which scientists do their best work. *Isis 36,* 166–69.

Albert, R. S. 1971. Cognitive development and parental loss among the gifted, the exceptionally gifted and the creative. *Psychological Reports 29,* 19–26.

———. 1975. Toward a behavioral definition of genius. *American Psychologist 30,* 140–51.

———. 1980. Family positions and the attainment of eminence: A study of special family positions and special family experiences. *Gifted Child Quarterly 24,* 87–95.

Aldenderfer, M. S., and Blashfield, R. K. 1984. *Cluster Analysis.* Beverly Hills, Calif.: Sage.

Allison, P. D. 1977. The reliability of variables measured as the number of events in an interval of time. In *Sociological methodology 1978,* ed. K. F. Schuessler, pp. 238–53. San Francisco: Jossey-Bass.

Allport, G. W. 1937. *Personality: A psychological interpretation.* New York: Holt.

American Psychological Association. 1983. *Publication manual,* 3d ed. Washington, D.C.

Anderson, C. A. 1987. Temperature and aggression: Effects on quarterly, yearly, and city rates of violent and nonviolent crime. *Journal of Personality and Social Psychology 52,* 1161–73.

Anderson, C. A. 1989. Temperature and aggression: Ubiquitous effects of heat on occurrence of human violence. *Psychological Bulletin 106,* 74–96.

Anderson, C. A., and Anderson, D. C. 1984. Ambient temperature and violent crime: Tests of the linear and curvilinear hypotheses. *Journal of Personality and Social Psychology 46,* 91–97.

Anderson, J. W. 1981. The methodology of psychological biography. *Journal of Interdisciplinary History 11,* 455–74.

Armanjani, Y. 1970. *Middle East past and present.* Englewood Cliffs, N.J.: Prentice-Hall.

Armbruster, M. E. 1982. *The presidents of the United States and their administrations from Washington to Reagan.* 7th ed., rev. New York: Horizon Press.

Aronson, E. 1958. The need for achievement as measured by graphic expression. In *Motives in fantasy, action, and society,* ed. J. W. Atkinson, pp. 249–65. Princeton, N.J.: Van Nostrand.

Ashton, S. V., and Oppenheim, C. 1978. A method of predicting Nobel prizewinners in chemistry. *Social Studies of Science 8,* 341–48.

Atkin, C. K. 1969. The impact of political poll reports on candidate and issue preference. *Journalism Quarterly 46,* 515–21.

Aydelotte, W. O. 1971. *Quantification in history.* Reading, Mass.: Addison-Wesley.

Aydelotte, W. O.; Bogue, A. G.; and Fogel, R. W., eds. 1972. *The dimensions of quantitative research in history.* Princeton, N.J.: Princeton University Press.

Bailey, R. W., ed. 1982. *Computing in the humanities.* Amsterdam: North-Holland Publishing.

Bailey, T. A. 1966. *Presidential greatness.* New York: Wiley.

Bailey, W. C. 1980. A multivariate cross-sectional analysis of the deterrent effect of the death penalty. *Sociology and Social Research 64,* 183–207.

Ballard, E. J. 1983. Canadian prime ministers: Complexity in political crises. *Canadian Psychology 24,* 125–29.

Ballard, E. J., and Suedfeld, P. 1988. Performance ratings of Canadian prime ministers: Individual and situational factors. *Political Psychology 9,* 291–302.

Baltzell, E. D., and Schneiderman, H. G. 1988. Social class in the Oval Office. *Society 25,* 42–49.

Barber, R. J. 1981. Comments on the quantitative study of creativity in Western civilization. *American Anthropologist 83,* 143–44.

Barnett, H. G. 1953. *Innovation.* New York: McGraw-Hill.

Baron, R. A., and Ransberger, V. M. 1978. Ambient temperature and the occurrence of collective violence: The "long, hot summer" revisited. *Journal of Personality and Social Psychology 36,* 351–60.

Barry, H., III. 1957. Relationships between child training and the pictorial arts. *Journal of Abnormal and Social Psychology 54,* 380–83.

———. 1979. Birth order and paternal namesake as predictors of affiliation with predecessor by presidents of the United States. *Political Psychology 1,* 61–66.

———. 1983–84. Predictors of longevity of United States presidents. *Omega 14,* 315–21.

Barzun, J. 1974. *Clio and the doctors: Psycho-history, quanto-history, and history.* Chicago: University of Chicago Press.

Baumol, W. J. 1970. *Economic dynamics,* 3d ed. New York: Macmillan.

Beard, G. M. 1874. *Legal responsibility in old age.* New York: Russell.

Beck, E. M. 1980a. Discrimination and white economic loss: A time series examination of the radical model. *Social Forces 59,* 148–68.

———. 1980b. Labor unionism and racial income inequality: A time-series analysis of the post–World War II period. *American Journal of Sociology 85,* 791–814.

Bell, P. A., and Fusco, M. E. 1986. Linear and curvilinear relationships between temperature, affect, and violence: Reply to Cotton. *Journal of Applied Social Psychology,* 802–7.

Benjafield, J., and Carson, E. 1985. An historicodevelopmental analysis of the circumplex model of trait descriptive terms. *Canadian Journal of Behavioural Science 17,* 340–45.

Benjafield, J., and Muckenheim, R. 1989. A further historicodevelopmental study of the interpersonal circumplex. *Canadian Journal of Behavioural Science 21,* 83–93.

Bennett, W. 1980. Providing for posterity. *Harvard Magazine 82* (3), 13–16.

Benson, L. 1967. An approach to the scientific study of past public opinion. *Public Opinion Quarterly 31,* 522–67.

———. 1972. *Toward the scientific study of history.* Philadelphia: Lippincott.

Bentler, P. M. 1980. Multivariate analysis with latent variables: Causal modeling. *Annual Review of Psychology 31,* 419–56.

———. 1985. *The theory and implementation of EQS.* Los Angeles: BMDP Statistical Software.

Ben-Yehuda, N. 1983. History, selection and randomness—Towards an analysis of social historical explanations. *Quality and Quantity 17,* 347–67.

Berk, R. A.; Hennessy, M.; and McCleary, R. 1976. Descriptive distortions in covariance based statistics. *Social Science Research 5,* 107–26.

Berlyne, D. 1971. *Aesthetics and psychobiology.* New York: Appleton-Century-Crofts.

Berry, C. 1981. The Nobel scientists and the origins of scientific achievement. *British Journal of Sociology 32,* 381–91.

Blalock, H. M. 1968. The measurement problem: A gap between the languages of theory and research. In *Methodology in social research,* ed. H. M. Blalock and A. B. Blalock, pp. 5–28. New York: McGraw-Hill.

———. 1972. *Causal inferences in nonexperimental research.* New York: Norton.

Bliss, W. D. 1970. Birth order of creative writers. *Journal of Individual Psychology 26,* 200–202.

Blondel, J. 1980. *World leaders.* Beverly Hills, Calif.: Sage.

Bloom, H. S., and Price, H. Douglas. 1975. Voter response to short-run economic conditions: The asymmetric effect of prosperity and recession. *American Political Science Review 69,* 1240–54.

Bogue, A. G. 1968. United States: The "new" political history. *Journal of Contemporary History 3,* 5–27.

Bond, J. R., and Fleisher, R. 1984. Presidential popularity and congressional voting: A reexamination of public opinion as a source of influence in congress. *Western Political Quarterly 37,* 291–306.

Boor, M. 1980. Effects of United States presidential elections on suicide and other causes of death. *American Sociological Review 46,* 616–18.

Boor, M., and Fleming, J. A. 1984. Presidential election effects on suicide and mortality levels are independent of unemployment rates. *American Sociological Review 49,* 706–7.

Boswell, J. [1791] 1952. *Life of Johnson.* In *Great books of the Western world,* vol. 44, ed. R. M. Hutchins. Chicago: Encyclopaedia Britannica.

Box, G. E. P., and Jenkins, G. M. 1976. *Time series analysis: Forecasting and control,* rev. ed. San Francisco: Holden-Day.

Bradburn, N. M., and Berlew, D. E. 1961. Need for achievement and English economic growth. *Economic Development and Cultural Change 10,* 8–20.

Brainerd, B. 1980. The chronology of Shakespeare's plays: A statistical study. *Computers and the Humanities 14,* 221–30.

Bramwell, B. S. 1948. Galton's "Hereditary Genius" and the three following generations since 1869. *Eugenics Review 39,* 146–53.

Brannigan, A., and Wanner, R. A. 1983a. Historical distributions of multiple discoveries and theories of scientific change. *Social Studies of Science 13,* 417–35.

———. 1983b. Multiple discoveries in science: A test of the communication theory. *Canadian Journal of Sociology 8,* 135–51.

Bridgwater, C. A.; Walsh, J. A.; and Walkenbach, J. 1982. Pre- and post-tenure productivity trends of academic psychologists. *American Psychologist 37,* 236–38.

Brodetsky, S. 1942. Newton: Scientist and man. *Nature 150,* 698–99.

Brody, R. A., and Page, B. I. 1975. The impact of events on presidential popularity: The Johnson and Nixon administrations. In *Perspectives on the presidency,* ed. A. Wildavsky. Boston: Little, Brown.

Brody, R., and Sigelman, L. 1983. Presidential popularity and presidential elections: An update and extension. *Public Opinion Quarterly 47,* 325–28.

Brook, B. S. 1969. Style and content analysis in music: The simplified "Plaine and Easie Code." In *The analysis of communication content,* ed. G. Gerbner, O. R. Holsti, K. Krippendorff, W. J. Paisley, and P. J. Stone, pp. 287–96. New York: Wiley.

Brown, S. R. 1986. Q technique and method: Principles and procedures. In *New tools for social scientists,* ed. W. D. Berry and M. S. Lewis-Beck, pp. 57–76. Beverly Hills, Calif.: Sage.

Bullough, V., Bullough, B., and Mauro, M. 1978. Age and achievement. A dissenting view. *Gerontologist 18,* 584–87.

Butterfield, H. 1931. *The Whig interpretation of history.* London: Bell and Sons.

Byron, Lord. [1812–18] 1898. *Childe Harold,* 3d ed., ed. H. F. Tozer, Oxford: Clarendon.

———. [1818–21] 1949. *Don Juan.* London: Lehmann.

Campbell, D. T. 1969. Reforms as experiments. *American Psychologist 24,* 409–42.

Campbell, D. T., and Fiske, D. W. 1959. Convergent and discriminant validation by the multitrait-multimethod matrix. *Psychological Bulletin 56,* 81–105.

Campbell, D. T., and Stanley, J. C. 1966. *Experimental and quasi-experimental designs for research.* Chicago: Rand McNally.

Campbell, D. T., and Tauscher, H. 1966. Schopenhauer (?), Séguin, Lubinoff, and Zehender as anticipators of Emmert's Law: With comments on the uses of eponymy. *Journal of the History of the Behavioral Sciences 2,* 58–63.

Campbell, J. E. 1985. Explaining presidential losses in midterm congressional elections. *Journal of Politics 47,* 1140–57.

Carlsmith, J. M., and Anderson, C. A. 1979. Ambient temperature and the occurrence of collective violence: A new analysis. *Journal of Personality and Social Psychology 37,* 337–44.

Carlyle, T. 1841. *On heroes, hero-worship, and the heroic.* London: Fraser.

Carmines, E. G. 1986. The analysis of covariance structure models. In *New tools for social scientists,* ed. W. D. Berry and M. S. Lewis-Beck, pp. 23–55. Beverly Hills, Calif.: Sage.

Carneiro, R. L. 1970. Scale analysis, evolutionary sequences, and the rating of cultures. In *A Handbook of Method in Cultural Anthropology,* ed. R. Naroll and R. Cohen, pp. 834–71. New York: Natural History Press.

Carruth, G., ed. 1979. *The encyclopedia of American facts and dates,* 7th ed. New York: Crowell.

Cattell, J. M. 1903. A statistical study of eminent men. *Popular Science Monthly 62,* 359–77.

———. 1910. A further statistical study of American men of science. *Science 32,* 633–48.

Cattell, R. B. 1953. A quantitative analysis of the changes in culture patterns of Great Britain, 1837–1937, by p-technique. *Acta Psychologica 9,* 99–121.

———. 1963. The personality and motivation of the researcher from measurements of contemporaries and from biography. In *Scientific Creativity,* ed. C. W. Taylor and F. Barron, pp. 119–31. New York: Wiley.

Cattell, R. B., and Adelson, M. 1951. The dimensions of social change in the U.S.A. as determined by p-technique. *Social Forces 30*, 190–201.

Cell, C. P. 1974. Charismatic heads of state: The social context. *Behavior Science Research 9*, 255–305.

Cerulo, K. 1984. Social disruption and its effects on music: An empirical analysis. *Social Forces 62*, 885–904.

————. 1988. Analyzing cultural products: A new method of measurement. *Social Science Research 17*, 317–52.

————. 1989. Variations in musical syntax: Patterns of measurement. *Communication Research 16*, 204–35.

Christie, R., and Geis, F. *Studies in Machiavellianism.* New York: Academic Press.

Clark, R. D., and Rice, G. A. 1982. Family constellations and eminence: The birth orders of Nobel Prize winners. *Journal of Psychology 110*, 281–87.

Cliff, N. 1983. Some cautions concerning the application of causal modeling methods. *Multivariate Behavioral Research 18*, 115–26.

Cocks, G. 1986. Contributions of psychohistory to understanding politics. In *Political psychology,* ed. M. G. Hermann, pp. 139–66. San Francisco: Jossey-Bass.

Cocks, G., and Crosby, T. L., eds. 1987. *Psycho/history.* New Haven, Conn.: Yale University Press.

Cohen, J., and Cohen, P. 1983. *Applied multiple regression/correlation analysis for the behavioral sciences,* 2d ed. Hillsdale, N.J.: Erlbaum.

Cole, J. R., and Cole, S. 1972. The Ortega hypothesis. *Science 178*, 368–75.

Collingwood, R. G. 1946. *The idea of history.* Oxford: Clarendon.

Conrad, A. H., and Meyer, J. R. 1964. *The economics of slavery.* Chicago: Aldine.

Copeland, G. W. 1983. When Congress and the President collide: Why presidents veto legislation. *Journal of Politics 45*, 696–710.

Cortés, J. B. 1960. The achievement motive in the Spanish economy between the thirteenth and eighteenth centuries. *Economic Development and Cultural Change 9*, 144–63.

Cotton, J. L. 1986. Ambient temperature and violent crime. *Journal of Applied Social Psychology 16*, 786–801.

Cox, C. 1926. *The early mental traits of three hundred geniuses.* Stanford, Calif.: Stanford University Press.

Dante Alighieri. [c. 1307] 1952. *Divine comedy,* tr. C. E. Norton. In *Great books of the Western world,* vol. 21, ed. R. M. Hutchins. Chicago: Encyclopaedia Britannica.

Danto, A. C. 1965. *Analytical philosophy of history.* Cambridge: Cambridge University Press.

Darmstaedter, L. 1908. *Handbuch zur Geschichte der Naturwissenschaften und der Technik.* Berlin: Springer.

Davies, J. C. 1962. Toward a theory of revolution. *American Sociological Review 27*, 5–19.

Davis, H. T. 1941. *The analysis of economic time series.* Bloomington, Ind.: Principia Press.

Davis, R. A. 1987. Creativity in neurological publications. *Neurosurgery 20*, 652–63.

Dawes, R. M.; Faust, D.; and Meehl, P. E. 1989. Clinical versus actuarial judgment. *Science 243*, 1668–74.

Debus, A. G., ed. 1968. *World who's who in science.* Chicago: Marquis-Who's Who.

deCandolle, A. 1873. *Histoire des sciences et des savants depuis deux siecles.* Genève: Georg.

deCharms, R., and Moeller, G. H. 1962. Values expressed in American children's readers: 1800–1950. *Journal of Abnormal and Social Psychology 64*, 136–42.

deMause, L. 1981. What is psychohistory? *Journal of Psychohistory 9*, 179–84.

Dennis, W. 1954a. Bibliographies of eminent scientists. *Scientific Monthly 79*, 180–83.

———. 1954b. Predicting scientific productivity in later maturity from records of earlier decades. *Journal of Gerontology 9*, 465–67.

———. 1954c. Productivity among American psychologists. *American Psychologist 9*, 191–94.

———. 1955. Variations in productivity among creative workers. *Scientific Monthly 80*, 277–78.

———. 1956a. Age and achievement: A critique. *Journal of Gerontology 11*, 331–33.

———. 1956b. Age and productivity among scientists. *Science 123*, 724–25.

———. 1958. The age decrement in outstanding scientific contributions: Fact or artifact? *American Psychologist 13*, 457–60.

———. 1966. Creative productivity between the ages of twenty and eighty years. *Journal of Gerontology 21*, 1–8.

Derks, P. L. 1989. Pun frequency and popularity of Shakespeare's plays. *Empirical Studies of the Arts 7*, 23–31.

Derry, V. 1985. Charles IV (Emperor). In *One hundred great kings, queens and rulers of the world*, ed. J. Channing, pp. 393–99. New York: Bonanza Books.

Dewey, E. R. 1970. *Cycles: Selected writings*. Pittsburgh, Penn.: Foundation for the Study of Cycles.

Diamond, A. M., Jr. 1980. Age and acceptance of cliometrics. *Journal of Economic History 40*, 838–41.

Diehl, P. F. 1985. Contiguity and military escalation in major power rivalries, 1816–1980. *Journal of Politics 47*, 1203–11.

Diemer, G. 1974. Creativity versus age. *Physics Today 27*, 9.

Donley, R. E., and Winter, D. G. 1970. Measuring the motives of public officials at a distance: An exploratory study of American presidents. *Behavioral Science 15*, 227–36.

Dray, W. 1957. *Laws and explanation in history*. London: Oxford University Press.

Dressler, W. W., and Robbins, M. C. 1975. Art styles, social stratification, and cognition: An analysis of Greek vase painting. *American Ethnologist 2*, 427–34.

Duncan, O. D. *Introduction to structural equation models*. New York: Academic Press.

Dupuy, R. N., and Dupuy, T. N. 1970. *The encyclopedia of military history*. New York: Harper and Row.

Durant, W., and Durant, A. 1935–67. *The story of civilization*, 10 vols. New York: Simon and Schuster.

———. 1968. *The lessons of history*. New York: Simon and Schuster.

Edwards, A. L. 1957. *Techniques of attitude scale construction*. New York: Appleton-Century-Crofts.

Edwards, G. C., III. 1985. Measuring presidential success in Congress: Alternative approaches. *Journal of Politics 47*, 667–85.

Eggenberger, D. 1967. *A dictionary of battles*. New York: Crowell.

Eisenstadt, J. M. 1978. Parental loss and genius. *American Psychologist 33*, 211–23.

Ellis, H. 1904. *A study of British genius*. London: Hurst and Blackett.

Elms, A. 1975. The crisis of confidence in social psychology. *American Psychologist 30*, 967–76.

———. 1988. Freud as Leonardo: Why the first psychobiography went wrong. *Journal of Personality 56*, 19–40.

Erikson, C. 1975. Quantitative history. *American Historical Review 80*, 351–65.

Erikson, E. H. 1958. *Young man Luther: A study in psychoanalysis and history*. New York: Norton.

———. 1969. *Gandhi's truth*. New York: Norton.

Erikson, R. 1976. The influence of newspaper endorsements in presidential elections. *American Journal of Political Science 20*, 207–33.

Etheredge, L. S. 1978. Personality effects on American foreign policy, 1898–1968: A test of interpersonal generalization theory. *American Political Science Review 78*, 434–51.

Evered, R. 1983. Who's talking about the future? An analysis of the U.S. presidents. *Technological Forecasting and Social Change 24*, 61–77.

Farnsworth, P. R. 1969. *The Social Psychology of Music*, 2d ed. Ames: Iowa State University Press.

Faust, D. 1984. *Limits of scientific reasoning*. Minneapolis: University of Minnesota Press.

Feierabend, I. K., and Feierabend, R. L. 1966. Aggressive behavior within polities, 1948–1962: A cross-national study. *Journal of Conflict Resolution 10*, 249–71.

Feige, E. L., and Pearce, D. K. 1979. The causal relationship between money and income: Some caveats for time series analysis. *Review of Economics and Statistics 76*, 521–33.

Feldhaus, F. 1904. *Lexicon der Erfindungen und Entdeckungen auf den Gelieten der Naturwissenschaften und Technik*. Heidelberg: Winter.

Feldman, P., and Jondrow, J. 1984. Congressional elections and local federal spending. *American Journal of Political Science 28*, 147–64.

Finison, L. J. 1976. The application of McClelland's national development model to recent data. *Journal of Social Psychology 98*, 55–59.

Fischer, D. H. 1970. *Historian's fallacies*. New York: Harper and Row.

Floud, R. 1973. *An introduction to quantitative methods for historians*. London: Methuen.

———. 1984. Quantitative history and people's history: Two methods in conflict? *Social Science History 8*, 151–68.

Fogel, R. W. 1964. *Railroads and American economic growth*. Baltimore: Johns Hopkins Press.

———. 1975. The limits of quantitative methods in history. *American Historical Review 80*, 329–50.

Fogel, R. W., and Engerman, S. L. 1974. *Time on the cross*. Boston: Little, Brown.

Freeman, J. R. 1983. Granger causality and the time series analysis of political relationships. *American Journal of Political Science 27*, 327–58.

Freud, S. [1910] 1964. *Leonardo da Vinci and a memory of his childhood*, tr. A. Tyson. New York: Norton.

Freud, S., and Bullitt, W. C. 1967. *Thomas Woodrow Wilson: A psychological study*. Boston: Houghton Mifflin.

Frey, R. S. 1984. Does n-achievement cause economic development? A cross-lagged panel analysis of the McClelland thesis. *Journal of Social Psychology 122*, 67–70.

Frey, R. S.; Piernot, C. A.; and Elhardt, D. G. 1981. An analysis of Riesman's historical thesis through American film titles. *Journal of Social Psychology 113*, 57–64.

Frost, W. H. 1940. The age selection of mortality from tuberculosis in successive decades. *Milbank Memorial Fund Quarterly 18*, 61–66.

Galton, F. 1869. *Hereditary genius*. London: Macmillan.

———. 1874. *English men of science*. London: Macmillan.

———. 1883. *Inquiries into human faculty and its development*. London: Macmillan.

Gardiner, P., ed. 1974. *The philosophy of history*. London: Oxford University Press.

Garfield, E. 1979. *Citation indexing*. New York: Wiley.

Gates, J. B., and Cohen, J. E. 1988. Presidents, Supreme Court justices, and racial equality cases: 1954–1984. *Political Behavior 10*, 22–36.

Gay, P. 1985. *Freud for historians*. New York: Oxford University Press.

George, A. L., and George, J. L. 1956. *Woodrow Wilson and Colonel House*. New York: Day.

Gergen, K. J. 1973. Social psychology as history. *Journal of Personality and Social Psychology 21*, 309–20.

Geyl, P. 1958. *Debates with historians*, rev. ed. New York: Meridian.

Gibbon, E. [1776–88] 1952. *Decline and fall of the Roman Empire*. In *Great books of the Western world*, vols. 40–41, ed. R. M. Hutchins. Chicago: Encyclopaedia Britannica.

Gieryn, T. F., and Hirsh, R. F. 1983. Marginality and innovation in science. *Social Studies of Science 13*, 87–106.

Glymour, C.; Scheines, R.; Spirtes, P.; and Kelly, K. 1987. *Discovering causal structure*. New York: Academic Press.

Godechot, J. 1974. Napoleon. In *Encyclopaedia Britannica: Macropaedia*, 15th ed., vol. 12, pp. 831–39. Chicago.

Goertzel, V., and Goertzel, M. G. 1962. *Cradles of Eminence*. Boston: Little, Brown.

Goertzel, M. G.; Goertzel, V.; and Goertzel, T. G. 1978. *Three hundred eminent personalities*. San Francisco: Jossey-Bass.

Goethe, W. [1808–32] 1952. *Faust*, tr. G. M. Priest. In *Great books of the Western world*, vol. 47, ed. R. M. Hutchins. Chicago: Encyclopaedia Britannica.

Goggin, M. L. 1984. The ideological content of presidential communications: The message-tailoring hypothesis revisited. *American Politics Quarterly 12*, 361–84.

Gorsuch, R. L. 1983. *Factor analysis*, 2d ed. Hillsdale, N.J.: Erlbaum.

Gottschalk, L., ed. 1963. *Generalization in the writing of history*. Chicago: University of Chicago Press.

Gottschalk, L. A.; Uliana, R.; and Gilbert, R. 1988. Presidential candidates and cognitive impairment measured from behavior in campaign debates. *Public Administration Review 48*, 613–19.

Gough, H. G., and Heilbrun, A. B., Jr. 1965. *The adjective check list manual*. Palo Alto, Calif.: Consulting Psychologists Press.

Graber, R. B. 1985. A foolproof method of disposing of multiple discoveries: Comment on Patinkin. *American Journal of Sociology 90*, 902–3.

Granberg, D., and Brent, E. 1983. When prophecy bends: The preference-expectation link in U.S. presidential elections, 1952–1980. *Journal of Personality and Social Psychology 45*, 477–91.

Gray, C. E. 1958. An analysis of Graeco-Roman development: The epicyclical evolution of Graeco-Roman civilization. *American Anthropologist 60*, 13–31.

———. 1961. An epicyclical model for Western civilization. *American Anthropologist 63*, 1014–37.

———. 1966. A measurement of creativity in Western civilization. *American Anthropologist 68*, 1384–1417.

Greenstein, F. I. 1982. *The hidden-hand presidency*. New York: Basic Books.

Grun, B. 1975. *The timetables of history*. New York: Simon and Schuster.

Grush, J. E. 1980. Impact of candidate expenditures, regionality, and prior outcomes on the 1976 Democratic presidential primaries. *Journal of Personality and Social Psychology 38*, 337–47.

Grush, J. E.; McKeough, K. L.; and Ahlering, R. F. 1978. Extrapolating laboratory exposure research to actual political elections. *Journal of Personality and Social Psychology 36*, 257–70.

Hackler, B. C., and Chamberlain, G. B. 1981. Pasts that might have been: An annotated bibliography of alternative history. *Extrapolation 22*, 334–78.

Halsey, R. S. 1976. *Classical music recordings for home and library*. Chicago: American Library Association.

Hammond, T. H., and Fraser, J. M. 1984. Judging presidential performance on House and Senate roll calls. *Polity 16*, 624–46.

Hannan, M. T. 1971. Problems of aggregation. In *Causal models in the social sciences*, ed. H. M. Blalock, pp. 473–508. Chicago: Aldine-Atherton.

Harbottle, T. B. 1971. *Dictionary of battles*, rev. and updated by G. Bruce. London: Rupert Hart-Davis.

Harries, K. D., and Stadler, S. J. 1983. Determinism revisited: Assault and heat stress in Dallas, 1980. *Environment and Behavior 15*, 235–56.

_____. 1988. Heat and violence: New findings from Dallas field data, 1980–1981. *Journal of Applied Social Psychology 18*, 129–38.

Harrison, A. A., and Kroll, N. E. A. 1985–86. Variations in death rates in the proximity of Christmas: An opponent process interpretation. *Omega 16*, 181–92.

_____. 1989–90. Birth dates and death dates: An examination of two baseline procedures and age at time of death. *Omega 20*, 127–37.

Harrison, A. A.; Struthers, N. J.; and Moore, M. 1988. On the conjunction of national holidays and reported birthdates: One more path to reflected glory? *Social Psychology Quarterly 51*, 365–70.

Hart, R. P. 1984. *Verbal style and the presidency: A computer-based analysis*. New York: Academic Press.

Hasenfus, N.; Martindale, C.; and Birnbaum, D. 1983. Psychological reality of cross-media artistic styles. *Journal of Experimental Psychology: Human Perception and Performance 9*, 841–63.

Havlicek, L. L., and Peterson, N. L. 1977. Effect of the violation of assumptions upon significance levels of the Pearson *r*. *Psychological Bulletin 84*, 373–77.

Hayes, J. R. 1981. *The complete problem solver*. Philadelphia: Franklin Institute Press.

Hedges, L. V. 1987. How hard is hard science, how soft is soft science? *American Psychologist 42*, 443–55.

Hegel, [1821] 1952. *Philosophy of right*, trans. T. M. Knox. In *Great books of the Western world*, vol. 46, ed. R. M. Hutchins, pp. 1–150. Chicago: Encyclopaedia Britannica.

Heise, D. R. 1975. *Causal analysis*. New York: Wiley.

Hempel, C. G. 1965. *Aspects of scientific explanation, and other essays in the philosophy of science*. New York: Free Press.

Henry, F. 1982. Multivariate analysis and ordinal data. *American Sociological Review 47*, 299–307.

Hepworth, J. T., and West, S. G. 1988. Lynchings and the economy: A Time-series reanalysis of Hovland and Sears (1940). *Journal of Personality and Social Psychology 55*, 239–47.

Hermann, D. B. 1988. How old were the authors of significant research in twentieth century astronomy at the time of their greatest contribution? *Scientometrics 13*, 135–38.

Hermann, M. G. 1977. Some personal characteristics related to foreign aid voting of congressmen. In *The psychological examination of political leaders*, ed. M. G. Hermann, pp. 313–34. New York: Free Press.

_____. 1980a. Assessing the personalities of Soviet Politburo members. *Personality and Social Psychology 6*, 332–52.

_____. 1980b. Explaining foreign policy behavior using the personal characteristics of political leaders. *International Studies Quarterly 24*, 7–46.

Hertel, B. R. 1976. Minimizing error variance introduced by missing data routines in survey analysis. *Sociological Methods and Research 4*, 459–74.

Hibbs, D. A., Jr.; Rivers, R. D.; and Vasilatos, N. 1982. The dynamics of political support for American presidents among occupational and partisan groups. *American Journal of Political Science 26*, 312–32.

Historical Figures Assessment Collaborative (HFAC). 1977. Assessing historical figures: The use of observer-based personality descriptions. *Historical Methods Newsletter 10*, 66–76.

Hockey, S. 1980. *A guide to computer applications in the humanities.* Baltimore: Johns Hopkins University Press.

Hoffer, P. C. 1978. Psychohistory and empirical group affiliation: Extraction of personality traits from historical manuscripts. *Journal of Interdisciplinary History 9*, 131–45.

Holmes, J. E., and Elder, R. E. 1989. Our best and worst presidents: Some possible reasons for perceived performance. *Presidential Studies Quarterly 19*, 529–57.

Holmes, T. S., and Rahe, R. H. 1967. The social readjustment rating scale. *Journal of Psychosomatic Research 11*, 213–18.

Holsti, O. R. 1969. *Content analysis for the social sciences and humanities.* Reading, Mass.: Addison-Wesley.

Houweling, H. W., and Siccama, J. G. 1985. The epidemiology of war, 1816–1980. *Journal of Conflict Resolution 29*, 641–63.

Houweling, H. W., and Kune, J. B. 1984. Do outbreaks of war follow a Poisson-process? *Journal of Conflict Resolution 28*, 51–62.

Hovland, C. J., and Sears, R. R. 1940. Minor studies in aggression: 6. Correlation of lynchings with economic indices. *Journal of Psychology 9*, 301–10.

Hudson, L. 1958. Undergraduate academic record of Fellows of the Royal Society. *Nature 182*, 1326.

Hull, D. L.; Tessner, P. D.; and Diamond, A. M. 1978. Planck's principle: Do younger scientists accept new scientific ideas with greater alacrity than older scientists? *Science 202*, 717–23.

Hutchins, R. M., ed. 1952. *Great books of the Western world,* 54 vols. Chicago: Encyclopaedia Britannica.

Illing, R. 1963. *Pergamon dictionary of musicians and music,* vol. 1. Oxford: Pergamon Press.

Illingworth, R. S., and Illingworth, C. M. 1969. *Lessons from childhood.* Edinburgh: Livingston.

Jackson, J. M., and Padgett, V. R. 1982. With a little help from my friend: Social loafing and the Lennon-McCartney songs. *Personality and Social Psychology Bulletin 8*, 672–77.

Jöreskog, K. G., and Sörbom, D. 1986. *LISREL VI: Analysis of linear structural relationships by maximum likelihood, instrumental variables, and least squares methods,* 4th ed. Mooresville, Ind.: Scientific Software.

Jorgenson, D. O. 1975. Economic threat and authoritarianism in television programs: 1950–1974. *Psychological Reports 37*, 1153–54.

Judd, C. M., and Kenny, D. A. 1981. *Estimating the effects of social interventions.* Cambridge: Cambridge University Press.

Kane, J. N. 1974. *Facts about the presidents,* 3d ed. New York: Wilson.

Kaplan, D. 1988. The impact of specification error on the estimation, testing, and improvement of structural equation models. *Multivariate Behavioral Research 23*, 69–86.

Kennedy, P. 1987. *The rise and fall of the great powers.* New York: Random House.

Kenney, P. J., and Rice, T. 1988. The contextual determinants of presidential greatness. *Presidential Studies Quarterly 18*, 161–69.

Kenny, D. A., 1975. Cross-lagged panel correlation: A test for spuriousness. *Psychological Bulletin 82*, 887–903.

———. 1979. *Correlation and causality*. New York: Wiley.

Kenny, D. A., and Campbell, D. T. 1984. Methodological considerations in the analysis of temporal data. In *Historical social psychology*, ed. K. Gergen and M. Gergen, pp. 125–38. Hillsdale, N.J.: Erlbaum.

Kenski, H. C. 1977. The impact of economic conditions on presidential popularity. *Journal of Politics 39*, 764–73.

Kernell, S. 1978. Explaining presidential popularity: How ad hoc theorizing, misplaced emphasis, and insufficient care in measuring one's variables refuted common sense and led conventional wisdom down the path of anomalies. *American Political Science Review 72*, 506–22.

King, G. 1987. Presidential appointments to the Supreme Court: Adding systemic explanation to probabilistic description. *American Politics Quarterly 15*, 373–86.

Klingemann, H.-D.; Mohler, P. P.; and Weber, R. P. 1982. Cultural indicators based on content analysis: A secondary analysis of Sorokin's data on fluctuations of systems of truth. *Quality and Quantity 16*, 1–18.

Knapp, R. H. 1962. A factor analysis of Thorndike's ratings of eminent men. *Journal of Social Psychology 56*, 67–71.

Knight, F. 1973. *Beethoven and the age of revolution*. New York: International.

Kohut, T. A. 1986. Psychohistory as history. *American Historical Review 91*, 336–54.

Kousser, J. M. 1984. The revivalism of narrative: A response to recent criticisms of quantitative history. *Social Science History 8*, 133–49.

Kroeber, A. 1917. The superorganic. *American Anthropologist 19*, 163–214.

———. 1944. *Configurations of culture growth*. Berkeley: University of California Press.

———. 1958. Gray's epicyclical evolution. *American Anthropologist 60*, 31–38.

Kuhn, T. S. 1970. *The structure of scientific revolutions*, 2d ed. Chicago: University of Chicago Press.

Kull, I. S., and Kull, N. M. 1952. *A short chronology of American history 1492–1950*. New Brunswick, N.J.: Rutgers University Press.

Kynerd, T. 1971. An analysis of presidential greatness and "president rating." *Southern Quarterly 9*, 309–29.

Lamb, D., and Easton, S. M. 1984. *Multiple discovery*. England: Avebury.

Langer, W. L. 1958. The next assignment. *American Historical Review 63*, 283–304.

———, ed. 1972. *An encyclopedia of world history*, 5th ed. Boston: Houghton-Mifflin.

Lanoue, D. J. 1987. Economic prosperity and presidential popularity: Sorting out the effects. *Western Political Quarterly 40*, 237–45.

Lee, J. R. 1975. Presidential vetoes from Washington to Nixon. *Journal of Politics 37*, 522–46.

Lehman, H. C. 1943. The longevity of the eminent. *Science 98*, 270–73.

———. 1947. The exponential increase of man's cultural output. *Social Forces 25*, 281–90.

———. 1953. *Age and achievement*. Princeton, N.J.: Princeton University Press.

———. 1956. Reply to Dennis' critique of Age and Achievement. *Journal of Gerontology 11*, 333–37.

———. 1958. The chemist's most creative years. *Science 127*, 1213–22.

————. 1960. The age decrement in outstanding scientific creativity. *American Psychologist 15*, 128–34.

————. 1962. More about age and achievement. *Gerontologist 2*, 141–48.

————. 1963. Chronological age versus present-day contributions to medical progress. *Gerontologist 3*, 71–75.

————. 1966a. The most creative years of engineers and other technologists. *Journal of Genetic Psychology 108*, 263–77.

————. 1966b. The psychologist's most creative years. *American Psychologist 21*, 363–69.

Lehman, H. C., and Witty, P. A. 1931. Scientific eminence and church membership. *Scientific Monthly 33*, 544–49.

Lenard, P. 1933. *Great men of science*, trans. H. S. Hatfield. New York: Macmillan.

Levinson, D. 1977. What have we learned from cross-cultural surveys? *American Behavioral Scientist 20*, 757–92.

Levy, J. S., and Morgan, T. C. 1984. The frequency and seriousness of war: An inverse relationship? *Journal of Conflict Resolution 28*, 731–49.

————. 1986. The war-weariness hypothesis: An empirical test. *American Journal of Political Science 30*, 26–49.

Lewis-Beck, M. S. 1986. Interrupted time series. in *New tools for social scientists*, ed. W. D. Berry and M. S. Lewis-Beck, pp. 209–40. Beverly Hills, Calif.: Sage.

Lewis-Beck, M. S., and Rice, T. W. 1983. Localism in presidential elections: The home state advantage. *American Journal of Political Science 27*, 548–56.

————. 1984. Forecasting presidential elections: A comparison of naive models. *Political Behavior 6*, 9–21.

Lindsey, D. 1988. Assessing precision in the manuscript review process: A little better than a dice roll. *Scientometrics 14*, 75–82.

Loehlin, J. C. 1987. *Latent variable models*. Hillsdale, N.J.: Erlbaum.

Lomax, A. 1968. *Folk song style and culture*. Washington, D.C.: American Association for the Advancement of Science.

Lombroso, C. 1891. *The man of genius*. London: Scott.

Long, J. S. 1983a. *Confirmatory factor analysis: A preface to LISREL*. Beverly Hills, Calif.: Sage.

————. 1983b. *Covariance structure models: An introduction to LISREL*. Beverly Hills, Calif.: Sage.

Lorwin, V. R., and Price, J. M., eds. 1972. *The dimensions of the past: Materials, problems, and opportunities for quantitative work in history*. New Haven, Conn.: Yale University Press.

Lotka, A. J. 1926. The frequency distribution of scientific productivity. *Journal of the Washington Academy of Sciences 16*, 317–23.

Lowe, J. W. G., and Lowe, E. D. 1982. Cultural pattern and process: A study of stylistic change in women's dress. *American Anthropologist 84*, 521–44.

Luce, R. D. 1986. *Response times: Their role in inferring elementary mental organization*. New York: Oxford University Press.

MacCallum, R. 1986. Specification searches in covariance structure modeling. *Psychological Bulletin 100*, 107–20.

Machiavelli, N. [1516] 1952. *The prince*, tr W. K. Marriott. In *Great books of the Western world*, vol. 23, ed. R. M. Hutchins, pp. 1–37. Chicago: Encyclopaedia Britannica.

Mahoney, J.; Coogle, C.; and Banks, P. D. 1984. Values in presidential inaugural addresses: A test of Rokeach's two-factor theory of political ideology. *Psychological Reports 55*, 683–86.

Mannheim, K. 1952. The problem of generations. In *Essays on the sociology of knowledge,* ed. P. Kecskemati, pp. 276–322. London: Routledge and Kegan Paul.

Manniche, E., and Falk, G. 1957. Age and the Nobel Prize. *Behavioral Science 2,* 301–7.

Mansfield, E. 1961. Technical change and the rate of imitation. *Econometrica 29,* 741–66.

Maranell, G. M. 1970. The evaluation of presidents: An extension of the Schlesinger polls. *Journal of American History 57,* 104–13.

Maranell, G., and Dodder, R. 1970. Political orientation and the evaluation of presidential prestige: A study of American historians. *Social Science Quarterly 51,* 415–21.

Marchetti, C. 1980. Society as a learning system: Discovery, invention, and innovation cycles revisited. *Technological Forecasting and Social Change 18,* 267–82.

Martindale, C. 1972. Father absence, psychopathology, and poetic eminence. *Psychological Reports 31,* 843–47.

———. 1975. *Romantic progression: The psychology of literary history.* Washington, D.C.: Hemisphere Publishing.

———. 1976. Primitive mentality and the relationship between art and society. *Scientific Aesthetics 1,* 5–18.

———. 1984a. Evolutionary trends in poetic style: The case of English metaphysical poetry. *Computers and the Humanities 18,* 3–21.

———. 1984b. The evolution of aesthetic taste. In *Historical social psychology,* ed. K. J. Gergen and M. M. Gergen, pp. 347–70. Hillsdale, N.J.: Erlbaum.

———. 1986a. Aesthetic evolution. *Poetics 15,* 439–73.

———. 1986b. The evolution of Italian painting: A quantitative investigation of trends in style and content from the late Gothic to the rococo period. *Leonardo 19,* 217–22.

———, ed. 1988. *Psychological approaches to the study of literary narratives.* Hamburg: Buske.

Martindale, C., and Uemura, A. 1983. Stylistic evolution in European music. *Leonardo 16,* 225–28.

Matossian, M. K., and Schafer, W. D. 1977. Family, fertility, and political violence, 1700–1900. *Journal of Social History 11,* 137–78.

Mayer, A. 1949. *Annals of European civilization 1501–1900.* London: Cassell.

Mayer, L. S., and Carroll, S. S. 1987. Testing for lagged, cotemporal, and total dependence in cross-lagged panel analysis. *Sociological Methods and Research 16,* 187–217.

Mayer, T. F., and Arney, W. R. 1974. Spectral analysis and the study of social change. In *Sociological methodology 1973–1974,* ed. H. L. Costner, pp. 309–55. San Francisco: Jossey-Bass.

Mazur, A., and Rosa, E. 1977. An empirical test of McClelland's "Achieving Society" theory. *Social Forces 55,* 769–74.

McAdams, D. P., and Ochberg, R. L., eds. 1988. *Psychobiography and life narratives.* Durham, N.C.: Duke University Press.

McCann, S. J. H., and Stewin, L. L. 1984. Environmental threat and parapsychological contributions to the psychological literature. *Journal of Social Psychology 122,* 227–35.

McCann, S. J. H., and Stewin, L. L. 1987. Threat, authoritarianism, and the power of U.S. presidents. *Journal of Psychology 121,* 149–57.

McCleary, R., and Hay, R. A., Jr. 1980. *Applied time series analysis for the social sciences.* Beverly Hills, Calif.: Sage.

McClelland, D. C. 1961. *The achieving society.* New York: Van Nostrand.

———. 1975. *Power: The inner experience.* New York: Irvington.

McCurdy, H. G. 1939. Literature and personality. *Character and Personality 7,* 300–308.

———. 1940a. Literature and personality: Analysis of the novels of D. H. Lawrence, part 1. *Character and Personality 8,* 181–203.

———. 1940b. Literature and personality: Analysis of the novels of D. H. Lawrence, part 2. *Character and Personality 8*, 311–22.

———. 1947. A study of the novels of Charlotte and Emily Brontë as an expression of their personalities. *Journal of Personality 16*, 109–52.

———. 1953. *The personality of Shakespeare*. New Haven, Conn.: Yale University Press.

———. 1960. The childhood pattern of genius. *Horizon* (May) *2*, 33–38.

McGuire, W. J. 1973. The yin and yang of progress in social psychology: Seven koan. *Journal of Personality and Social Psychology 26*, 446–56.

———. 1976. Historical comparisons: Testing psychological hypotheses with cross-era data. *International Journal of Psychology 11*, 161–83.

McPherson, J. M. 1976. Theory trimming. *Social Science Research 5*, 95–105.

Meehl, P. 1954. *Clinical vs. statistical prediction*. Minneapolis: University of Minnesota Press.

———. 1978. Theoretical risks and tabular asterisks: Sir Karl, Sir Ronald, and the slow progress of soft psychology. *Journal of Consulting and Clinical Psychology 46*, 806–34.

Mellor, J. W. [1912] 1955. *Higher mathematics for students of chemistry and physics*, 4th ed. New York: Dover.

Merton, R. K. 1961. Singletons and multiples in scientific discovery: A chapter in the sociology of science. *Proceedings of the American Philosophical Society 105*, 470–86.

Messerli, P. 1988. Age differences in the reception of new scientific theories: The case of plate tectonics theory. *Social Studies of Science 18*, 91–112.

Midlarsky, M. I. 1984. Preventing systemic war: Crisis decision-making amidst a structure of conflict relationships. *Journal of Conflict Resolution 28*, 563–84.

Miller, A. H., and Wattenberg, M. P. 1985. Throwing the rascals out: Policy and performance evaluations of presidential candidates, 1952–1980. *American Political Science Review 79*, 359–72.

Miller, N. L., and Stiles, W. B. 1986. Verbal familiarity in American presidential nomination acceptance speeches and inaugural addresses (1920–1981). *Social Psychology Quarterly 49*, 72–81.

Mills, C. A. 1942. What price glory? *Science 96*, 380–87.

Mintz, A. 1946. A re-examination of correlations between lynchings and economic indices. *Journal of Abnormal and Social Psychology 41*, 154–60.

Mohler, P. P., and Zuell, C. 1986. *TEXTPACK V*. Mannheim: ZUMA.

Moles, A. [1958] 1968. *Information theory and esthetic perception*, tr. J. E. Cohen. Urbana: University of Illinois Press.

Monroe, K. R. 1984. *Presidential popularity and the economy*. New York: Praeger.

Morris, R. B., ed. 1976. *Encyclopedia of American history*, bicentennial ed. New York: Harper and Row.

Morrison, D. E., and Henkel, R. E., eds. 1970. *The significance test controversy*. Chicago: Aldine.

Moulin, L. 1955. The Nobel Prizes for the sciences from 1901–1950: An essay in sociological analysis. *British Journal of Sociology 6*, 246–63.

Mueller, J. E. 1973. *War, presidents and public opinion*. New York: Wiley.

Murphey, M. G. 1973. *Our knowledge of the historical past*. Indianapolis: Bobbs-Merrill.

Murphy, A. B. 1984. Evaluating the presidents of the United States. *Presidential Studies Quarterly 14*, 117–26.

Murphy, G. 1968. *Psychological thought from Pythagoras to Freud*. New York: Harcourt, Brace, and World.

Murray, H. A. 1938. *Explorations in personality*. New York: Oxford University Press.

———. 1951. In nomine diaboli. *New England Quarterly 24*, 435–52.

Murray, R. K., and Blessing, T. H. 1983. The presidential performance study: A progress report. *Journal of American History 70*, 535–55.

Naroll, R. 1968. Some thoughts on comparative method in cultural anthropology. In *Methodology in social research*, ed. H. M. Blalock and A. B. Blalock, pp. 236–77. New York: McGraw-Hill.

———. 1970. Galton's problem. In *A handbook of method in cultural anthropology*, ed. R. Naroll and R. Cohen, pp. 974–89. New York: Natural History Press.

Naroll, R.; Benjamin, E. C.; Fohl, F. K.; Fried, M. J.; Hildreth, R. E.; and Schaefer, J. M. 1971. Creativity: A cross-historical pilot survey. *Journal of Cross-Cultural Psychology 2*, 181–88.

Naroll, R.; Bullough, V. L.; and Naroll, F. 1974. *Military deterence in history: A pilot cross-historical survey*. Albany: State University of New York Press.

Naroll, R., and Michik, G. L. 1975. HRAFLIB: A computer program library for hologeistic research. *Behavioral Science Research 10*, 283–96.

Nelson, C. R., and Schwert, G. W. 1982. Tests for predictive relationships between time series variables: A Monte Carlo investigation. *Journal of the American Statistical Association 77*, 11–17.

Nice, D. C. 1984. The influence of war and party system aging on the ranking of presidents. *Western Political Quarterly 37*, 443–55.

———. 1986. In retreat from excellence: The single six-year presidential term. *Congress and the Presidency 13*, 209–20.

Nisbet, R. A. 1969. *Social change and history*. New York: Oxford University Press.

Norling, B. 1970. *Timeless problems in history*. Notre Dame, Ind.: University of Notre Dame Press.

Norpoth, H. 1984. Economics, politics, and the cycle of presidential popularity. *Political Behavior 6*, 253–73.

———. 1986. Transfer function analysis. In *New tools for social scientists*, ed. W. D. Berry and M. S. Lewis-Beck, pp. 241–73. Beverly Hills, Calif.: Sage.

Nunnally, J. 1978. *Psychometric theory*, 2d ed. New York: McGraw-Hill.

Ogburn, W. K., and Thomas, D. 1922. Are inventions inevitable? A note on social evolution. *Political Science Quarterly 37*, 83–93.

Oleszek, W. 1969. Age and political careers. *Public Opinion Quarterly 33* 100–103.

Olinick, M. 1978. *An introduction to mathematical models in the social and life sciences*. Reading, Mass.: Addison-Wesley.

Orcutt, G. H., and James, S. F. 1948. Testing the significance of correlation between time series. *Biometrica 35*, 397–413.

Oromaner, M. 1977. Professional age and the reception of sociological publications: A test of the Zuckerman-Merton hypothesis. *Social Studies of Science 7*, 381–88.

Ortega y Gasset, J. [1932] 1957. *The Revolt of the Masses*, tr. M. Adams. New York: Norton.

———. [1933] 1962. *Man and crisis*, tr. M. Adams. New York: Norton.

Over, R. 1982. The durability of scientific reputation. *Journal of the History of the Behavioral Sciences 18*, 53–61.

Padgett, V., and Jorgenson, D. O. 1982. Superstition and economic threat: Germany 1918–1940. *Personality and Social Psychology Bulletin 8*, 736–41.

Page, B. I., and Shapiro, R. 1984. Presidents as opinion leaders: Some new evidence. *Policy Studies Journal 12*, 649–61.

Paisley, W. J. 1964. Identifying the unknown communicator in painting, literature and music: The significance of minor encoding habits. *Journal of Communication 14*, 219–37.

Parkinson, C. L. 1985. *Breakthroughs: A chronology of great achievements in science and mathematics.* Boston: Hall.

Pascal, B. [1670] 1952. *Pensées,* trans. W. F. Trotter. In *Great books of the Western world,* vol. 33, ed. R. M. Hutchins, pp. 171–352. Chicago: Encyclopaedia Britannica.

Patinkin, D. 1983. Multiple discoveries and the central message. *American Journal of Sociology 89,* 306–23.

————. 1985. Reply to Graber. *American Journal of Sociology 90,* 904.

Peterson, R. A., and Berger, D. G. 1975. Cycles in symbol production: The case of popular music. *American Sociological Review 40,* 158–73.

Phillips, D. P. 1980. The deterrent effect of capital punishment: New evidence on an old controversy. *American Journal of Sociology 86,* 139–48.

Planck, M. 1949. *Scientific autobiography and other papers,* trans. F. Gaynor. New York: Philosophical Library.

Poole, K. T., and Rosenthal, H. 1984. U.S. presidential elections 1960–80: A spatial analysis. *American Journal of Political Science 28,* 282–312.

Popper, K. R. 1959. *The logic of discovery.* New York: Basic Books.

————. 1963. *The open society and its enemies,* vol. 2. Princeton, N.J.: Princeton University Press.

Porter, C. A., and Suedfeld, P. 1981. Integrative complexity in the correspondence of literary figures: Effects of personal and societal stress. *Journal of Personality and Social Psychology 40,* 321–30.

Potter, R. G. 1980. Toward a stylistic differentiation of period style in modern drama: Significant between-play variability in twenty-one English language plays. *Computers and the Humanities 14,* 187–96.

————. 1988. Literary criticism and literary computing: The difficulties of a synthesis. *Computers and the Humanities 22,* 91–97.

Praed, W. M. [1825] 1953. Epitaph on the late King of the Sandwich Islands. In *Selected poems,* ed. K. Allott, pp. 279–82. London: Routeledge and Kegan Paul.

Prentky, R. A. 1980. *Creativity and psychopathology.* New York: Praeger.

Pressey, S. L., and Combs, A. 1943. Acceleration and age of productivity. *Educational Research Bulletin 22,* 191–96.

Price, D. 1963. *Little science, big science.* New York: Columbia University Press.

————. 1976. A general theory of bibliometric and other cumulative advantage processes. *Journal of the American Society for Information Science 27,* 292–306.

————. 1978. Ups and downs in the pulse of science and technology. In *The Sociology of Science,* ed. J. Gaston, pp. 162–71. San Francisco: Jossey-Bass.

Przeworski, A., and Teune, H. 1970. *The logic of comparative social inquiry.* New York: Wiley.

Quetelet, A. [1835] 1968. *A treatise on man and the development of his faculties,* 1842 Edinburgh translation. New York: Franklin.

Rainoff, T. J. 1929. Wave-like fluctuations of creative productivity in the development of West-European physics in the eighteenth and nineteenth centuries. *Isis 12,* 287–319.

Ramirez, C. E., and Suedfeld, P. 1988. Nonimmediacy scoring of archival materials: The relationship between Fidel Castro and "Che" Guevara. *Political Psychology 9,* 155–64.

Raphael, T. D. 1982. Integrative complexity theory and forecasting international crises. *Journal of Conflict Resolution 26,* 423–50.

Rashevsky, N. 1968. *Looking at history through mathematics.* Cambridge, Mass.: MIT Press.

Raskin, E. A. 1936. Comparison of scientific and literary ability: A biographical study of eminent scientists and men of letters in the nineteenth century. *Journal of Abnormal and Social Psychology 31,* 20–35.

Redman, R. R., ed. 1968. *The portable Voltaire.* New York: Viking Press.

Rejai, M., and Phillips, K. 1979. *Leaders of revolution.* Beverly Hills, Calif.: Sage.

Richardson, J., and Kroeber, A. L. 1940. Three centuries of women's dress fashions: A quantitative analysis. *Anthropological Records 5,* 111–50.

Richardson, L. F. 1922. *Weather prediction by numerical process.* Cambridge: Cambridge University Press.

———. 1939. Generalized foreign policy. *British Journal of Psychology: Monograph Supplement 23.*

———. 1960a. *Arms and insecurity: A mathematical study of the causes and origins of war.* Pittsburgh: Boxwood Press.

———. 1960b. *Statistics of deadly quarrels,* ed. Q. Wright and C. C. Lienau. Chicago: Quadrangle Books.

Ringelstein, A. C. 1985. Presidential vetoes: Motivations and classification. *Congress and the Presidency 12,* 43–55.

Rivers, D., and Rose, N. L. 1985. Passing the president's program: Public opinion and presidential influence in congress. *American Journal of Political Science 29,* 183–96.

Robinson, D. E. 1975. Style changes: Cyclical, inexorable, and foreseeable. *Harvard Business Review 53,* 121–31.

———. 1976. Fashions in shaving and trimming of the beard: The men of the *Illustrated London News,* 1842–1972. *American Journal of Sociology 81,* 1133–41.

Robinson, D. N. 1986. *An intellectual history of psychology.* Madison: University of Wisconsin.

Robinson, W. S. 1950. Ecological correlations and the behavior of individuals. *American Sociological Review 15,* 351–57.

Rohde, D. W., and Simon, D. M. 1985. Presidential vetoes and congressional response: A study of institutional conflict. *American Journal of Political Science 29,* 397–427.

Rohner, R. P. 1977. Advantages of the comparative method of anthropology. *Behavior Science Research 12,* 117–44.

Rokeach, M.; Homant, R.; and Penner, L. 1970. A value analysis of the disputed Federalist papers. *Journal of Personality and Social Psychology 16,* 245–50.

Rosenberg, S. 1989. A study of personality in literary autobiography: An analysis of Thomas Wolfe's *Look Homeward, Angel. Journal of Personality and Social Psychology 56,* 416–30.

Rosenberg, S., and Jones, R. A. 1972. A method for investigating and representing a person's implicit personality theory: Theodore Dreiser's view of people. *Journal of Personality and Social Psychology 22,* 372–86.

Rosengren, K. E. 1985. Time and literary fame. *Poetics 14,* 157–72.

Rosenstone, S. J. 1983. *Forecasting presidential elections.* New Haven, Conn.: Yale University Press.

Rosenthal, R., and Rubin, D. B., 1979. A note on percent variance explained as a measure of the importance of effects. *Journal of Applied Social Psychology 9,* 395–96.

Rossiter, C. 1956. *The American presidency.* New York: Harcourt, Brace.

Rotberg, R. I., and Rabb, T. K., eds. 1981. *Climate and history: Studies in interdisciplinary history.* Princeton, N.J.: Princeton University Press.

Rotton, J., and Frey, J. 1985. Air pollution, weather, and violent crime: Concomitant time-series analysis of archival data. *Journal of Personality and Social Psychology 49,* 1207–20.

Rowney, D. K., and Graham, J. Q., Jr., eds. 1969. *Quantitative history: Selected readings in the quantitative analysis of historical data.* Homewood, Ill.: Dorsey Press.

Runyan, W. M. 1982. *Life histories and psychobiography.* New York: Oxford University Press.

———. 1988a. Progress in psychobiography. *Journal of Personality 56,* 295–326.

———, ed. 1988b. *Psychology and historical interpretation.* New York: Oxford University Press.

Russett, B. M., ed. 1972. *Peace, war, and numbers.* Beverly Hills, Calif.: Sage.

Ryder, N. B. 1965. The cohort as a concept in the study of social change. *American Sociological Review 30,* 843–61.

Sales, S. [M.] 1972. Economic threat as a determinant of conversion rates in authoritarian and non-authoritarian churches. *Journal of Personality and Social Psychology 23,* 420–28.

———. 1973. Threat as a factor in authoritarianism: An analysis of archival data. *Journal of Personality and Social Psychology 28,* 44–57.

Samuelson, F. 1974. History, origin myth and ideology: "Discovery" of social psychology. *Journal for the Theory of Social Behavior 4,* 217–31.

Sarup, G. 1978. Historical antecedents of psychology: The recurrent issue of old wine in new bottles. *American Psychologist 33,* 478–85.

Schaefer, J. M.; Babu, M. C.; and Rao, N. S. 1977. Sociopolitical causes of creativity in India 500 B.C. – 1800 A.D.: A regional time-lagged study. Paper presented at the meeting of the International Studies Association, St. Louis.

Schlesinger, Jr., A. M. 1948. Historians rate the U.S. presidents. *Life 25* (1 November), 65–66, 73–74.

———. 1962a. The humanist looks at empirical social research. *American Sociological Review 27,* 768–71.

———. 1962b. Our presidents: A rating by seventy-five historians. *New York Times Magazine,* 29 July, 12–13, 40–41, 43.

———, ed. 1983. *The almanac of American history.* New York: Putnam.

Schmookler, J. 1966. *Invention and economic growth.* Cambridge: Harvard University Press.

Schneider, J. 1937. The cultural situation as a condition for the achievement of fame. *American Sociological Review 2,* 480–91.

Schroder, H. M.; Driver, M. J.; and Suedfeld, P. 1967. *Human information processing.* New York: Holt, Rinehart and Winston.

Schubert, D. S. P.; Wagner, M. E.; and Schubert, H. J. P. 1977. Family constellation and creativity: Firstborn predominance among classical music composers. *Journal of Psychology 95,* 147–49.

Schubert, G. 1983. Aging, conservatism, and judicial behavior. *Micropolitics 3,* 135–79.

Schulz, R., and Curnow, C. 1988. Peak performance and age among super athletes: Track and field, swimming, baseball, tennis, and golf. *Journal of Gerontology 43,* 113–20.

Sears, D. O. 1986. College sophomores in the laboratory: Influences of a narrow data base on social psychology's view of human nature. *Journal of Personality and Social Psychology 51,* 515–30.

Sears, R. R.; Lapidus, D.; and Cozzens, C. 1978. Content analysis of Mark Twain's novels and letters as a biographical method. *Poetics 7,* 155–75.

Sheils, D. 1975. Statistical explanation in cross-cultural research: A comparison of the utility of linear and curvilinear correlation. *Sociological Quarterly 16,* 115–23.

Sheldon, J. C. 1979. Hierarchical cybernets: A model for the dynamics of high level learning and cultural change. *Cybernetica 22,* 179–202.

———. 1980. A cybernetic theory of physical science professions: The causes of periodic normal and revolutionary science between 1000 and 1870 A.D. *Scientometrics 2*, 147–67.

Shockley, W. 1957. On the statistics of individual variations of productivity in research laboratories. *Proceedings of the Institute of Radio Engineers 45*, 279–90.

Shyles, L. 1984. The relationships of images, issues and presentational methods in televised spot advertisements for 1980's American presidential primaries. *Journal of Broadcasting 28*, 405–21.

Sigelman, L. 1979. Presidential popularity and presidential elections. *Public Opinion Quarterly 43*, 532–34.

Sigelman, L., and Knight, K. 1983. Why does presidential popularity decline? A test of the expectation/disillusion theory. *Public Opinion Quarterly 47*, 310–24.

Silverman, S. M. 1974. Parental loss and scientists. *Science Studies 4*, 259–64.

Simon, H. A. 1954a. Productivity among American psychologists: An explanation. *American Psychologist 9*, 804–5.

———. 1954b. Spurious correlation: A causal interpretation. *Journal of the American Statistical Association 49*, 467–79.

———. 1955. On a class of skew distribution functions. *Biometrika 42*, 425–40.

Publications by D. K. Simonton

1974. *The social psychology of creativity: An archival data analysis.* Ph.D. diss., Harvard University.

1975a. Age and literary creativity: A cross-cultural and transhistorical survey. *Journal of Cross-Cultural Psychology 6*, 259–277.

1975b. Galton's problem, autocorrelation, and diffusion coefficients. *Behavior Science Research 10*, 239–48.

1975c. Interdisciplinary creativity over historical time: A correlational analysis of generational fluctuations. *Social Behavior and Personality 3*, 181–88.

1975d. Invention and discovery among the sciences: A p-technique factor analysis. *Journal of Vocational Behavior 7*, 275–81.

1975e. Sociocultural context of individual creativity: A transhistorical time-series analysis. *Journal of Personality and Social Psychology 32* 1119–33.

1976a. Biographical determinants of achieved eminence: A multivariate approach to the Cox data. *Journal of Personality and Social Psychology 33* 218–26.

1976b. The causal relation between war and scientific discovery: An exploratory cross-national analysis. *Journal of Cross-Cultural Psychology 7*, 133–44.

1976c. Do Sorokin's data support his theory? A study of generational fluctuations in philosophical beliefs. *Journal for the Scientific Study of Religion 15*, 187–98.

1976d. Ideological diversity and creativity: A re-evaluation of a hypothesis. *Social Behavior and Personality 4*, 203–7.

1976e. Interdisciplinary and military determinants of scientific productivity: A cross-lagged correlation analysis. *Journal of Vocational Behavior 9*, 53–62.

1976f. Philosophical eminence, beliefs, and zeitgeist: An individual-generational analysis. *Journal of Personality and Social Psychology 34*, 630–40.

1976g. The sociopolitical context of philosophical beliefs: A transhistorical causal analysis. *Social Forces 54*, 513–23.

1977a. Creative productivity, age, and stress: A biographical time-series analysis of ten classical composers. *Journal of Personality and Social Psychology 35*, 791–804.

1977b. Cross-sectional time-series experiments: Some suggested statistical analyses. *Psychological Bulletin 84*, 489–502.

1977c. Eminence, creativity, and geographic marginality: A recursive structural equation model. *Journal of Personality and Social Psychology 35*, 805–16.

1977d. Women's fashions and war: A quantitative comment. *Social Behavior and Personality 5*, 285–88.

1978a. Independent discovery in science and technology: A closer look at the Poisson distribution. *Social Studies of Science 8*, 521–32.

1978b. Intergenerational stimulation, reaction, and polarization: A causal analysis of intellectual history. *Social Behavior and Personality 6*, 247–51.

1978c. Time-series analysis of literary creativity: A potential paradigm. *Poetics 7*, 249–59.

1979a. Multiple discovery and invention: Zeitgeist, genius, or chance? *Journal of Personality and Social Psychology 37*, 1603–16.

1979b. Was Napoleon a military genius? Score: Carlyle 1, Tolstoy 1. *Psychological Reports 44*, 21–22.

1980a. Land battles, generals, and armies: Individual and situational determinants of victory and casualties. *Journal of Personality and Social Psychology 38*, 110–19.

1980b. Techno-scientific activity and war: A yearly time-series analysis, 1500–1903 A.D. *Scientometrics 2*, 251–55.

1980c. Thematic fame and melodic originality: A multivariate computer-content analysis. *Journal of Personality 48*, 206–19.

1980d. Thematic fame, melodic originality, and musical zeitgeist: A biographical and transhistorical content analysis. *Journal of Personality and Social Psychology 39*, 972–83.

1981a. Creativity in Western civilization: Intrinsic and extrinsic causes. *American Anthropologist 83*, 628–30.

1981b. Presidential greatness and performance: Can we predict leadership in the White House? *Journal of Personality 49*, 306–23.

1983a. Dramatic greatness and content: A quantitative study of eighty-one Athenian and Shakespearean plays. *Empirical Studies of the Arts 1*, 109–23.

1983b. Esthetics, biography, and history in musical creativity. In *Documentary report on the Ann Arbor Symposium on the Application of Psychology to the Teaching and Learning of Music: Session III. Motivation and Creativity*, pp. 41–48. Reston, Va.: Music Educators National Conference.

1983c. Formal education, eminence, and dogmatism. *Journal of Creative Behavior 17*, 149–62.

1983d. Intergenerational transfer of individual differences in hereditary monarchs: Genes, role-modeling, cohort, or sociocultural effects? *Journal of Personality and Social Psychology 44*, 354–64.

1983e. Psychohistory. In *Encyclopedic Dictionary of Psychology*, ed. R. Harré and R. Lamb, pp. 499–500. Oxford: Blackwell.

1984a. Artistic creativity and interpersonal relationships across and within generations. *Journal of Personality and Social Psychology 46*, 1273–86.

1984b. Creative productivity and age: A mathematical model based on a two-step cognitive process. *Developmental Review 4*, 77–111.

1984c. Generational time-series analysis: A paradigm for studying sociocultural influences. In *Historical social psychology*, ed. K. Gergen and M. Gergen, pp. 139–55. Hillsdale, N.J.: Erlbaum.

1984d. *Genius, creativity, and leadership: Historiometric inquiries.* Cambridge: Harvard University Press.

1984e. Is the marginality effect all that marginal? *Social Studies of Science 14,* 621–22.

1984f. Leader age and national condition: A longitudinal analysis of twenty-five European monarchs. *Social Behavior and Personality 12,* 111–14.

1984g. Leaders as eponyms: Individual and situational determinants of monarchal eminence. *Journal of Personality 52,* 1–21.

1984h. Melodic structure and note transition probabilities: A content analysis of 15,618 classical themes. *Psychology of Music 12,* 3–16.

1984i. Scientific eminence historical and contemporary: A measurement assessment. *Scientometrics 6,* 169–82.

1985a. Intelligence and personal influence in groups: Four nonlinear models. *Psychological Review 92,* 532–47.

1985b. Quality, quantity, and age: The careers of ten distinguished psychologists. *International Journal of Aging and Human Development 21,* 241–54.

1985c. The vice-presidential succession effect: Individual or situational determinants? *Political Behavior 7,* 79–99.

1986a. Aesthetic success in classical music: A computer analysis of 1935 compositions. *Empirical Studies of the Arts 4,* 1–17.

1986b. Biographical typicality, eminence, and achievement style. *Journal of Creative Behavior 20,* 14–22.

1986c. Dispositional attributions of (presidential) leadership: An experimental simulation of historiometric results. *Journal of Experimental Social Psychology 22,* 389–418.

1986d. Multiple discovery: Some Monte Carlo simulations and Gedanken experiments. *Scientometrics 9,* 269–80.

1986e. Multiples, Poisson distributions, and chance: An analysis of the Brannigan-Wanner model. *Scientometrics 9,* 129–39.

1986f. Popularity, content, and context in thirty-seven Shakespeare plays. *Poetics 15,* 493–510.

1986g. Presidential greatness: The historical consensus and its psychological significance. *Political Psychology 7,* 259–83.

1986h. Presidential personality: Biographical use of the Gough Adjective Check List. *Journal of Personality and Social Psychology 51,* 1–12.

1986i. Stochastic models of multiple discovery. *Czechoslovak Journal of Physics B 36,* 52–54.

1987a. Developmental antecedents of achieved eminence. *Annals of Child Development 5,* 131–69.

1987b. Musical aesthetics and creativity in Beethoven: A computer analysis of 105 compositions. *Empirical Studies of the Arts 5,* 87–104.

1987c. Presidential inflexibility and veto behavior: Two individual-situational interactions. *Journal of Personality 55,* 1–18.

1987d. *Why presidents succeed: A political psychology of leadership.* New Haven, Conn.: Yale University Press.

1988a. Aesthetic success in thirty-six Hungarian and American short stories. In *Psychological Approaches to the Study of Literary Narratives,* ed. C. Martindale. Hamburg: Buske.

1988b. Age and outstanding achievement: What do we know after a century of research? *Psychological Bulletin 104,* 251–67.

1988c. Galtonian genius, Kroeberian configurations, and emulation: A generational time-series analysis of Chinese civilization. *Journal of Personality and Social Psychology 55,* 230–38.

1988d. Presidential style: Personality, biography, and performance. *Journal of Personality and Social Psychology 55*, 928–36.

1988e. *Scientific genius: A psychology of science.* Cambridge: Cambridge University Press.

1989a. Age and creative productivity: Nonlinear estimation of an information-processing model. *International Journal of Aging and Human Development 29*, 23–37.

1989b. Shakespeare's sonnets: A case of and for single-case historiometry. *Journal of Personality 57*, 695–721.

1989c. The swan-song phenomenon: Last-works effects for 172 classical composers. *Psychology and Aging 4*, 42–47.

1990a. Career landmarks in science: Individual differences and interdisciplinary contrasts. *Developmental Psychology.*

1990b. History, chemistry, psychology, and genius: An intellectual autobiography of historiometry. In *Theories of creativity*, ed. M. Runco and R. Albert. Beverly Hills, Calif.: Sage.

1990c. Latent variable models of posthumous reputation: A quest for Galton's *G.* University of California, Davis.

1990d. Lexical choices and aesthetic success: A computer analysis of 154 Shakespeare sonnets. *Computers and the Humanities.*

1990e. Personality and politics. In *Handbook of personality theory and research*, ed. L. A. Pervin. New York: Guilford.

1990f. Predicting presidential greatness: An alternative to the Kenney and Rice Contextual Index. *Presidential Studies Quarterly.*

Singer, J. D. 1981. Accounting for international war: The state of the discipline. *Journal of Peace Research 18*, 1–18.

Smart, J. C., and Bayer, A. E. 1986. Author collaboration and impact: A note on citation rates of single and multiple authored articles. *Scientometrics 10*, 297–305.

Smith, K. W., and Sasaki, M. S. 1979. Decreasing multicollinearity: A method for models with multiplicative functions. *Sociological Methods and Research 8*, 35–56.

Smith, M. S.; Stone, P. J.; and Glenn, E. N. 1966. A content analysis of twenty presidential nomination acceptance speeches. In *The General Inquirer: A computer approach to content analysis*, ed. P. J. Stone, D. C. Dunphy, M. S. Smith, and D. M. Ogilvie, pp. 359–400. Cambridge, Mass.: MIT Press.

Snow, C. P. 1960. *The two cultures and the scientific revolution.* New York: Cambridge University Press.

Sokal, R., and Sneath, P. 1963. *Principles of numerical taxonomy.* San Francisco: Freeman.

Sokolsky, E. 1964. *Our seven greatest presidents.* New York: Exposition Press.

Sorokin, P. A. 1925. Monarchs and rulers: A comparative statistical study. I. *Social Forces 4*, 22–35.

———. 1926. Monarchs and rulers: A comparative statistical study. II. *Social Forces 4*, 523–33.

———. 1927. A survey of the cyclical conceptions of social and historical processes. *Social Forces 6*, 28–40.

———. 1937–41. *Social and cultural dynamics*, 4 vols. New York: American Book.

———. [1947] 1969. *Society, culture, and personality.* New York: Cooper Square.

Sorokin, P. A., and Merton, R. K. 1935. The course of Arabian intellectual development, 700–1300 A.D. *Isis 22*, 516–24.

Spengler, O. [1926–28] 1945. *The decline of the west*, tr. C. F. Atkinson. New York: Knopf.

Spiller, G. 1929. The dynamics of greatness. *Sociological Review 21*, 218–32.

Spitzer, R. C., Gibbon, M., and Endicott, J. 1975. *Global assessment scale*. New York: New York State Psychiatric Institute.

Sprecht, D. A. 1975. On the evaluation of causal models. *Social Science Research 4*, 113–33.

Stack, S. 1987. Celebrities and suicide: A taxonomy and analysis, 1948–1983. *American Sociological Review 52*, 401–12.

Stannard, D. E. 1980. *Shrinking history: On Freud and the failure of psychohistory*. New York: Oxford University Press.

Steinberg, S. H. 1964. *Historical tables 58 B.C.–A.D. 1963*, 7th ed. London: Macmillan.

Stewart, J. A. 1986. Drifting continents and colliding interests: A quantitative application of the interests perspective. *Social Studies of Science 16*, 261–79.

Stewart, L. H. 1977. Birth order and political leadership. In *The psychological examination of political leaders*, ed. M. G. Hermann, pp. 205–36. New York: Free Press.

Stigler, S. M. 1986. *The history of statistics*. Cambridge: Harvard University Press.

Stiles, W. B.; Au, M. L.; Martello, M. A.; and Permutter, J. A. 1983. American campaign oratory: Verbal response mode use by candidates in the 1980 American presidential primaries. *Social Behavior and Personality 11*, 39–43.

Stimson, J. A. 1976. Public support for American presidents: A cyclical model. *Public Opinion Quarterly 40*, 1–21.

Stocking, G. W., Jr. 1965. On the limits of "presentism" and "historicism" in the historiography of the behavioral sciences. *Journal of the History of the Behavioral Sciences 1*, 211–18.

Stoll, R. J. 1984. The guns of November: Presidential reelections and the use of force, 1947–1982. *Journal of Conflict Resolution 28*, 231–46.

Stone, P. J.; Dunphy, D. C.; Smith, M. S.; and Ogilvie, D. M., eds. 1966. *The General Inquirer*. Cambridge: MIT Press.

Suedfeld, P. 1980. Indices of world tension in the Bulletin of the Atomic Scientists. *Political Psychology 2*, 114–23.

———. 1985. APA presidential addresses: the relation of integrative complexity to historical, professional, and personal factors. *Journal of Personality and Social Psychology 49*, 1643–51.

Suedfeld, P., and Bluck, S. 1988. Changes in integrative complexity prior to surprise attacks. *Journal of Conflict Resolution 32*, 626–35.

Suedfeld, P.; Corteen, R. S.; and McCormick, C. 1986. The role of integrative complexity in military leadership: Robert E. Lee and his opponents. *Journal of Applied Social Psychology 16*, 498–507.

Suedfeld, P., and Piedrahita, L. E. 1984. Intimations of mortality: Integrative simplification as a precursor of death. *Journal of Personality and Social Psychology 47*, 848–52.

Suedfeld, P., and Rank, A. D. 1976. Revolutionary leaders: Long-term success as a function of changes in conceptual complexity. *Journal of Personality and Social Psychology 34*, 169–78.

Suedfeld, P., and Tetlock, P. 1977. Integrative complexity of communications in international crises. *Journal of Conflict Resolution 21* 169–84.

Suedfeld, P.; Tetlock, P. E.; and Ramirez, C. 1977. War, peace, and integrative complexity. *Journal of Conflict Resolution 21*, 427–42.

Suls, J., and Fletcher, B. 1983. Social comparison in the social and physical sciences: An archival study. *Journal of Personality and Social Psychology 44*, 575–80.

Swede, S. W., and Tetlock, P. E. 1986. Henry Kissinger's implicit theory of personality: A quantitative case study. *Journal of Personality 54*, 617–46.

Taagepera, R. 1978. Size and duration of empires: Systematics of size. *Social Science Research 7*, 108–27.

———. 1979. Size and duration of empires: Growth-decline curves, 600 B.C. to 600 A.D. *Social Science History 3*, 115–38.

Taagepera, R., and Colby, B. N. 1979. Growth of Western civilization: Epicyclical or exponential? *American Anthropologist 81*, 907–12.

Taylor, T. 1972. *The book of presidents*. New York: Arno Press.

Terman, L. M. 1917. The intelligence quotient of Francis Galton in childhood. *American Journal of Psychology 28*, 209–15.

———. 1925. *Mental and physical traits of a thousand gifted children*. Stanford, Calif.: Stanford University Press.

Terman, L. M., and Oden, M. H. 1959. *The gifted group at mid-life*. Stanford, Calif.: Stanford University Press.

Tetlock, P. E. 1979. Identifying victims of groupthink from public statements of decision makers. *Journal of Personality and Social Psychology 37*, 1314–24.

———. 1981a. Personality and isolationism: Content analysis of senatorial speeches. *Journal of Personality and Social Psychology 41*, 737–43.

———. 1981b. Pre- to postelection shifts in presidential rhetoric: Impression management or cognitive adjustment. *Journal of Personality and Social Psychology 41*, 207–12.

———. 1983. Cognitive style and political ideology. *Journal of Personality and Social Psychology 45*, 118–26.

———. 1984. Cognitive style and political belief systems in the British House of Commons. *Journal of Personality and Social Psychology 46*, 365–75.

———. 1985. Integrative complexity of American and Soviet foreign policy rhetoric: A time-series analysis. *Journal of Personality and Social Psychology 49*, 1565–85.

Tetlock, P. E.; Bernzweig, J.; and Gallant, J. L. 1985. Supreme Court decision making: Cognitive style as a predictor of ideological consistency of voting. *Journal of Personality and Social Psychology 48*, 1227–39.

Tetlock, P. E., and Boettger, R. 1989. Cognitive and rhetorical styles of traditionalist and reformist Soviet politicians: A content analysis study. *Political Psychology 10*, 209–32.

Tetlock, P. E.; Crosby, F.; and Crosby, T. L. 1981. Political psychobiography. *Micropolitics 1*, 191–213.

Tetlock, P. E.; Hannum, K. A.; and Micheletti, P. M. 1984. Stability and change in the complexity of senatorial debate: Testing the cognitive versus rhetorical style hypothesis. *Journal of Personality and Social Psychology 46*, 979–90.

Textor, R. B., comp. 1967. *A cross-cultural summary*. New Haven, Conn.: Human Relations Area Files.

Thorndike, E. L. 1936. The relation between intellect and morality in rulers. *American Journal of Sociology 42*, 321–34.

———. 1950. Traits of personality and their intercorrelations as shown in biography. *Journal of Educational Psychology 41*, 193–216.

Ting, S.-S. 1986. *The social psychology of Chinese literary creativity: An archival data analysis*. Ph.D. diss., University of California, Davis.

Tolstoy, L. [1865–69] 1952. *War and peace*, tr. L. Maude and A. Maude. In *Great books of the Western world*, vol. 51, ed. R. M. Hutchins. Chicago: Encyclopaedia Britannica.

Toynbee, A. J. 1946. *A study of history,* 2 vols., abridged by D. C. Somervell. New York: Oxford University Press.

Tyndall, J. 1897. *Fragments of science,* vol. 2. New York: Appleton.

Ulmer, S. S. 1982. Supreme Court appointments as a Poisson distribution. *American Journal of Political Science 26,* 113–16.

Urdang, L., ed. 1981. *The timetables of American history.* New York: Simon and Schuster.

Walberg, H. J., Rasher, S. P., and Parkerson, J. 1980. Childhood and eminence. *Journal of Creative Behavior 13,* 225–31.

Walker, S. G., and Falkowski, L. S. 1984. The operational codes of U.S. presidents and secretaries of state: Motivational foundations and behavioral consequences. *Political Psychology 5,* 237–66.

Wallace, M. D., and Suedfeld, P. 1988. Leadership performance in crisis: The longevity-complexity link. *International Studies Quarterly 32,* 439–51.

Wasserman, I. 1983. Political business cycles, presidential elections, and suicide and mortality patterns. *American Sociological Review 48,* 711–20.

———. 1984. Imitation and suicide: A reexamination of the Werther Effect. *American Sociological Review 49,* 427–36.

Watson, J. S. 1974. George III of Great Britain. In *Encyclopaedia Britannica: Macropaedia,* 15th ed., vol. 7, pp. 1125–27. Chicago.

Webb, E. J., Campbell, D. T., Schwartz, R. D., Sechrest, L., and Grove, J. B. 1981. *Nonreactive measures in the social sciences,* 2d ed. Boston: Houghton Mifflin.

———. 1984. The birth order oddity in Supreme Court appointments. *Presidential Studies Quarterly 14,* 561–68.

Weber, R. P. 1985. *Basic content analysis.* Beverly Hills, Calif.: Sage.

Weitman, S.; Shapiro, G.; and Markoff, J. 1976. Statistical recycling of documentary information: Estimating regional variations in a pre-censal population. *Social Forces 55,* 338–66.

Wendt, H. W., and Light, P. C. 1976. Measuring "greatness" in American presidents: Model case for international research on political leadership? *European Journal of Social Psychology 6,* 105–9.

Wendt, H. W., and Muncy, C. A. 1979. Studies of political character: Factor patterns of twenty-four U.S. vice-presidents. *Journal of Psychology 102,* 125–31.

White, M. 1965. *Foundations of historical knowledge.* New York: Harper and Row.

White, R. K. 1931. The versatility of genius. *Journal of Social Psychology 2,* 460–89.

———. 1947. Black Boy: A value-analysis. *Journal of Abnormal and Social Psychology 42,* 440–61.

Whiting, J. W. M. 1968. Methods and problems in cross-cultural research. In *Handbook of social psychology,* 2d ed., ed. G. Lindzey and E. Aronson, pp. 693–728. Reading, Mass.: Addison-Wesley.

Wilkins, B. T. 1978. *Has history any meaning?* Ithaca, N.Y.: Cornell University Press.

Williams, N. 1968. *Chronology of the modern world: 1763 to the present time,* rev. ed. New York: McKay.

———. 1969. *Chronology of the expanding world: 1492 to 1762.* New York: McKay.

Williams, T. I., ed. 1974. *A biographical dictionary of scientists,* 2d ed. New York: Wiley.

Wills, G. 1981. *The Kennedy imprisonment.* Boston: Little, Brown.

Winter, D. G. 1973. *The power motive.* New York: Free Press.

———. 1980. Measuring the motives of southern African political leaders at a distance. *Political Psychology 2,* 75–85.

———. 1987a. Enhancement of an enemy's power motivation as a dynamic of conflict escalation. *Journal of Personality and Social Psychology 52,* 41–46.

————. 1987b. Leader appeal, leader performance, and the motive profiles of leaders and followers: A study of American presidents and elections. *Journal of Personality and Social Psychology, 52,* 196–202.

————. 1988. What makes Jesse run? *Psychology Today 22* (July/August), 20, 22, 24.

Winter, D. G., and Carlson, D. G. 1988. Using motive scores in the psychobiographical study of an individual: The case of Richard Nixon. *Journal of Personality 56,* 75–103.

Winter, D. G., and Stewart, A. J. 1977. Content analysis as a technique for assessing political leaders. In *The psychological examination of political leaders,* ed. M. G. Hermann, pp. 27–61. New York: Free Press.

Woods, F. A. 1906. *Mental and moral heredity in royalty: A statistical study in history and psychology.* New York: Holt.

————. 1909. A new name for a new science. *Science 30,* 703–4.

————. 1911. Historiometry as an exact science. *Science 33,* 568–74.

————. 1913. *The influence of monarchs.* New York: Macmillan.

Woodward, W. R. 1974. Scientific genius and loss of a parent. *Science Studies 4,* 265–77.

Wright, Q. 1965. *A study of war,* 2d ed. Chicago: University of Chicago Press.

Wright, S. 1934. The method of path coefficients. *Annals of Mathematical Statistics 5,* 161–215.

Yuasa, M. 1974. The shifting center of scientific activity in the West: From the sixteenth to the twentieth century. In *Science and Society in Modern Japan,* ed. N. Shigeru, D. L. Swain, and Y. Eri, pp. 81–103. Tokyo: University of Tokyo Press.

Zeidenstein, H. G. 1985. President's popularity and their wins and losses on major issues in Congress: Does one have greater influence over the other? *Presidential Studies Quarterly 15,* 287–300.

Zhao, H.-Z. 1984. An intelligence constant of scientific work. *Scientometrics 6,* 9–17.

Zhao, H.-Z., and Jiang, G. 1985. Shifting of world's scientific center and scientist's social ages. *Scientometrics 8,* 59–80.

————. 1986. Life-span and precocity of scientists. *Scientometrics 9,* 27–36.

Zuckerman, H. 1977. *Scientific elite.* New York: Free Press.

Zuk, G., and Thompson, W. R. 1982. The post-coup military spending question: A pooled cross-sectional time series analysis. *American Political Science Review 76,* 60–74.

Zullow, H. M.; Oettingen, G.; Peterson, C.; and Seligman, M. E. P. 1988. Pessimistic explanatory style in the historical record: CAVing LBJ, presidential candidates, and East versus West Berlin. *American Psychologist 43,* 673–82.

Zusne, L. 1976. Age and achievement in psychology: The harmonic mean as a model. *American Psychologist 31,* 805–7.

————. 1987. Contributions to the history of psychology: XLIV. Coverage of contributors in history of psychology. *Psychological Reports 61,* 343–50.

Zwick, W. R., and Velicer, W. F. 1986. Comparison of five rules for determining the number of components to retain. *Psychological Bulletin 99,* 432–42.

Index